## OTHER A TO Z GUIDES FROM
## THE SCARECROW PRESS, INC.

1. *The A to Z of Buddhism* by Charles S. Prebish, 2001.
2. *The A to Z of Catholicism* by William J. Collinge, 2001.
3. *The A to Z of Hinduism* by Bruce M. Sullivan, 2001.
4. *The A to Z of Islam* by Ludwig W. Adamec, 2002.
5. *The A to Z of Slavery & Abolition* by Martin A. Klein, 2002.
6. *Terrorism: Assassins to Zealots* by Sean Kendall Anderson and Stephen Sloan, 2003.
7. *The A to Z of the Korean War* by Paul M. Edwards, 2005.
8. *The A to Z of the Cold War* by Joseph Smith and Simon Davis, 2005.
9. *The A to Z of the Vietnam War* by Edwin E. Moise, 2005.
10. *The A to Z of Science Fiction Literature* by Brian Stableford, 2005.
11. *The A to Z of the Holocaust* by Jack R. Fischel, 2005.
12. *The A to Z of Washington, D.C.* by Robert Benedetto, Jane Donovan, and Kathleen DuVall, 2005.
13. *The A to Z of Taoism* by Julian F. Pas, 2006.
14. *The A to Z of the Renaissance* by Charles G. Nauert, 2006.
15. *The A to Z of Shinto* by Stuart D. B. Picken, 2006.
16. *The A to Z of Byzantium* by John H. Rosser, 2006.
17. *The A to Z of the Civil War* by Terry L. Jones, 2006.
18. *The A to Z of the Friends (Quakers)* by Margery Post Abbott, Mary Ellen Chijioke, Pink Dandelion, and John William Oliver Jr., 2006
19. *The A to Z of Feminism* by Janet K. Boles and Diane Long Hoeveler, 2006.
20. *The A to Z of New Religious Movements* by George D. Chryssides, 2006.
21. *The A to Z of Multinational Peacekeeping* by Terry M. Mays, 2006.
22. *The A to Z of Lutheranism* by Günther Gassmann with Duane H. Larson and Mark W. Oldenburg, 2007.
23. *The A to Z of the French Revolution* by Paul R. Hanson, 2007.
24. *The A to Z of the Persian Gulf War 1990–1991* by Clayton R. Newell, 2007.
25. *The A to Z of Revolutionary America* by Terry M. Mays, 2007.
26. *The A to Z of the Olympic Movement* by Bill Mallon with Ian Buchanan, 2007.

# The A to Z of the Northern Ireland Conflict

Gordon Gillespie

*The A to Z Guide Series, No. 95*

The Scarecrow Press, Inc.
Lanham • Toronto • Plymouth, UK
2009

Published by Scarecrow Press, Inc.
A wholly owned subsidary of
The Rowman & Littlefield Publishing Group, Inc.
4501 Forbes Boulevard, Suite 200, Lanham, Maryland 20706
http://www.scarecrowpress.com

Estover Road, Plymouth PL6 7PY, United Kingdom

British Library Cataloguing in Publication Information Available

**Library of Congress Cataloging-in-Publication Data**

The hardback version of this book was cataloged by the Library of Congress as
follows:

Gillespie, Gordon.
   Historical dictionary of the Northern Ireland conflict / Gordon Gillespie.
     p. cm. — (Historical dictionaries of war, revolution, and civil unrest ;
   No. 35)
   Includes bibliographical references.
   1. Northern Ireland–History–1969–1994. 2. Northern Ireland–History–1994–
   3. Northern Ireland–History–Dictionaries. 4. Political violence–Northern
   Ireland–History–Dictionaries. 5. Social conflict–Northern Ireland–History–
   Dictionaries. I. Title.
   DA990.U46G545  2008
   941.60824–dc22                                                    2007027190

ISBN 978-0-8108-6882-3 (pbk. : alk. paper)
ISBN 978-0-8108-7045-1 (ebook)

To my mother, Margaret Jane (Rita) Gillespie

# Contents

# Editor's Foreword

The Northern Ireland conflict—more familiarly called "the Troubles"—is one of the longest and most entangled confrontations in recent history. For nearly four decades now, it has embittered relations between and within the communities living there and spoiled relations between the Republic of Ireland and Great Britain, while also causing severe strains within the latter. For three decades it escalated, punctuated by periodic bloody clashes followed by somewhat calmer periods of tension, during which violence of all sorts, robberies, kidnappings, serious injuries, and deaths were all too common. During the past decade, fortunately, all sides have realized that armed solutions were unlikely to solve anyone's problems and that peace should be given a chance. The signing of the Good Friday Agreement in 1998 seemed to bring the conflict to an end, but it took nine more years before a stable Northern Ireland executive would finally be established. By mid-2007, Northern Ireland at last appeared to have put the conflict behind it and has moved on to important but more mundane issues of governance, such as rates and water charges.

*The A to Z of the Northern Ireland Conflict* helps clarify what is a terribly complicated situation, but it does not do so by simplifying this into a standoff between the Catholics and the Protestants or even the Republicans and the Unionists. This sort of dichotomy is more likely to confuse than to enlighten because the two—or actually four sides, once you include Great Britain and Ireland—were and still are so divided internally. The chronology charts the many milestones, initially negative and then gradually more positive, while the introduction sketches the overall context. But it is the dictionary section, with several hundred entries, that provides the vital details, with information on important figures on all sides; major organizations, parties, and paramilitary groups; the legal institutions and more informal ones; and the major events and crucial issues. The bibliography then offers access to the substantial and constantly growing related literature.

This volume was written by Gordon Gillespie, who was born in Belfast and lived in Northern Ireland during the Troubles and the peace process. This topic has become his main interest as an academic, first at the School of Economics and Politics of the University of Ulster and now as a research associate at the Institute of Irish Studies of Queen's University, Belfast. He also worked as a political researcher in the Northern Ireland Assembly. Dr. Gillespie has written extensively on the Northern Ireland conflict including *Northern Ireland: A Chronology of the Troubles*, coauthored with Paul Bew. This historical dictionary builds on his earlier work but also goes considerably further and provides an impressively fair and balanced guide to a conflict that more often elicits passion and bias.

Jon Woronoff
Series Editor

# Acknowledgments

I thank my colleagues at the Institute of Irish Studies, Queen's University, Belfast: Dominic Bryan, Catherine Boone, Eamonn Hughes, Gillian McIntosh, Valerie Miller, and Joan Watson for their support during the preparation of this work. I also thank the staff of the Northern Ireland Political Collection of the Linen Hall Library, Belfast: Yvonne Murphy, Alistair Gordon, and Ross Moore for their assistance. In addition to those mentioned above, Professors Richard English and Rick Wilford of the School of Politics, International Studies, and Philosophy at Queen's University, Belfast, provided invaluable comments on some of the material.

Several reference sources have been invaluable in the writing of this dictionary: the CAIN website, *Northern Ireland: A Political Directory 1968–1999*, *Lost Lives*, *Interpreting Northern Ireland*, the Northern Ireland Elections website, and *Northern Ireland: A Chronology of the Troubles 1968–1999*. I particularly thank the authors of these works: Martin Melaugh, Brendan Lynn, Fionnuala McKenna, Sydney Elliott, the late W. D. Flackes, David McKittrick, Seamus Kelters, Brian Feeney, Chris Thornton, David McVea, Nicholas Whyte, and my colleague Paul Bew for creating the essential works of reference mentioned above. Any serious researcher of the Northern Ireland conflict and peace process should refer to these sources for more detailed information on the Northern Ireland Troubles and peace process. Finally, thanks are also due to my editor, Jon Woronoff, for his help and patience in seeing this work through to completion.

# Acronyms and Abbreviations

| | |
|---|---|
| ABD | Apprentice Boys of Derry |
| AIA | Anglo–Irish Agreement |
| AIIC | Anglo–Irish Intergovernmental Council |
| AOH | Ancient Order of Hibernians |
| APNI | Alliance Party of Northern Ireland |
| BA | Bachelor of Arts |
| BBC | British Broadcasting Corporation |
| BIC | British–Irish Council |
| BIIPB | British–Irish Inter-Parliamentary Body |
| CAJ | Committee on the Administration of Justice |
| CCDC | Central Citizens' Defence Committee |
| CDU | Campaign for Democracy in Ulster |
| CEC | Campaign for Equal Citizenship |
| CIRA | Continuity IRA |
| CLMC | Combined Loyalist Military Command |
| Co. | County |
| CRC | Community Relations Council |
| CRF | Catholic Reaction Force |
| CSJ | Campaign for Social Justice |
| DAAD | Direct Action Against Drugs |
| DCAC | Derry Citizens' Action Committee |
| DED | Department of Economic Development |
| DFM | Deputy First Minister |
| DHAC | Derry Housing Action Committee |
| DL | Democratic Left |
| DoE | Department of the Environment |
| DUP | Democratic Unionist Party (also Ulster Democratic Unionist Party) |
| ECHR | European Commission of Human Rights |

| ECNI | Equality Commission for Northern Ireland |
|------|------|
| EEC | European Economic Community |
| EPA | Emergency Provisions Act |
| EU | European Union |
| FEA | Fair Employment Agency |
| FEC | Fair Employment Commission |
| FF | Fianna Fail |
| FG | Fine Gael |
| FM | First Minister |
| GAA | Gaelic Athletic Association |
| GB | Great Britain |
| GFA | Good Friday Agreement |
| GOC | General Officer Commanding |
| HET | Historical Enquiries Team |
| ICTU | Irish Congress of Trade Unions |
| IDB | Industrial Development Board |
| IFI | International Fund for Ireland |
| IGC | Intergovernmental Conference |
| IICD | International Independent Commission on Decommissioning |
| IIP | Irish Independence Party |
| IMC | Independent Monitoring Commission |
| INC | Irish National Caucus |
| INLA | Irish National Liberation Army |
| IPLO | Irish People's Liberation Organisation |
| IRA | Irish Republican Army |
| IRSP | Irish Republican Socialist Party |
| ITN | Independent Television News |
| JORT | Journey of Reconciliation Trust |
| LAW | Loyalist Association of Workers |
| Lb | Pound |
| LOL | Loyal Orange Lodge |
| LVF | Loyalist Volunteer Force |
| MA | Master of Arts |
| MBE | Member of the British Empire |
| MEP | Member of the European Parliament |
| MLA | Member of the Legislative Assembly (NI Assembly, 1998– ) |
| MoD | Ministry of Defence |
| MP | Member of Parliament (Westminster) |

| | |
|---|---|
| MPA | Member of the Parliamentary Assembly (NI Assembly, 1982–86) |
| NDP | National Democratic Party |
| NI | Northern Ireland |
| NICRA | Northern Ireland Civil Rights Association |
| NICVA | Northern Ireland Council for Voluntary Action |
| NIHE | Northern Ireland Housing Executive |
| NIHRC | Northern Ireland Human Rights Commission |
| NIHT | Northern Ireland Housing Trust |
| NILP | Northern Ireland Labour Party |
| NIO | Northern Ireland Office |
| NIUP | Northern Ireland Unionist Party |
| NIWC | Northern Ireland Women's Coalition |
| NORAID | Irish Northern Aid Committee |
| NP | Nationalist Party |
| NSMC | North–South Ministerial Council |
| NUM | New Ulster Movement |
| NUPRG | New Ulster Political Research Group |
| OBE | Order of the British Empire |
| OIRA | Official IRA |
| OUP | Official Unionist Party (also UUP) |
| PAF | Protestant Action Force |
| PD | People's Democracy |
| PD | Progressive Democrats |
| PIRA | Provisional IRA |
| POW | Prisoner of War |
| PR | Proportional Representation |
| PSF | Provisional Sinn Fein |
| PSNI | Police Service of Northern Ireland |
| PTA | Prevention of Terrorism Act |
| PUP | Progressive Unionist Party |
| QC | Queen's Counsel |
| QUB | Queen's University, Belfast |
| RAF | Royal Air Force |
| RC | Roman Catholic |
| RHC | Red Hand Commando |
| RHD | Red Hand Defenders |
| RIR | Royal Irish Regiment |

| | |
|---|---|
| RIRA | Real IRA |
| RSF | Republican Sinn Fein |
| RTE | Radio Telefis Eireann |
| RUC | Royal Ulster Constabulary |
| SACHR | Standing Advisory Commission on Human Rights |
| SAS | Special Air Service |
| SDA | Shankill Defence Association |
| SDLP | Social Democratic and Labour Party |
| SDP | Social Democratic Party |
| SF | Sinn Fein |
| STV | single transferable vote |
| TD | teachta dala (member of the Irish Parliament) |
| TOM | Troops Out Movement |
| TUC | Trades Union Congress |
| UAC | Ulster Army Council |
| UCD | University College Dublin |
| UCDC | Ulster Constitution Defence Committee |
| UDA | Ulster Defence Association |
| UDI | Unilateral Declaration of Independence |
| UDP | Ulster Democratic Party |
| UDR | Ulster Defence Regiment |
| UFF | Ulster Freedom Fighters |
| UIP | Ulster Independence Party |
| U.K. | United Kingdom |
| UKUP | U.K. Unionist Party |
| ULA | Ulster Loyalist Association |
| ULCCC | Ulster Loyalist Central Coordinating Committee |
| ULDP | Ulster Loyalist Democratic Party |
| UN | United Nations |
| UPNI | Unionist Party of Northern Ireland |
| UPUP | Ulster Popular Unionist Party |
| UPV | Ulster Protestant Volunteers |
| USC | Ulster Special Constabulary (B Specials) |
| UTV | Ulster Television |
| UU | University of Ulster |
| UUAC | United Unionist Action Council |
| UUC | Ulster Unionist Council |
| UUP | Ulster Unionist Party |

| | |
|---|---|
| UUUC | United Ulster Unionist Council |
| UUUM | United Ulster Unionist Movement |
| UUUP | United Ulster Unionist Party |
| UVF | Ulster Volunteer Force |
| UWC | Ulster Workers' Council |
| VSC | Vanguard Service Corps |
| VULC | Vanguard Unionist Loyalist Coalition |
| VUPP | Vanguard Unionist Progressive Party |
| WP | Workers' Party |
| WPRC | Workers' Party–Republican Clubs |

# Chronology

**1967** **1 February** The Northern Ireland Civil Rights Association (NICRA) is formed. **11 December** Northern Ireland prime minister Terence O'Neill meets the taoiseach (Irish prime minister), Jack Lynch, at Stormont, seat of the Northern Ireland Parliament.

**1968** **20 June** Squatters protesting against the allocation of council houses in Caledon, Co. Tyrone, are evicted by the Royal Ulster Constabulary (RUC). **24 August** An NICRA protest march from Coalisland to Dungannon, Co. Tyrone, is curtailed by a loyalist counterdemonstration. **5 October** Rioting breaks out after a confrontation between the RUC and civil rights marchers in Derry. **22 November** The Northern Ireland government introduces a reform package addressing some, but not all, of the issues raised by NICRA. **9 December** As intercommunal tension continues, Terence O'Neill makes a television address appealing for calm and states that "Ulster stands at the crossroads."

**1969** **4 January** A People's Democracy (PD) march is attacked by loyalists at Burntollet Bridge near Derry and is followed by rioting in Derry itself. **3 February** O'Neill responds to internal party and external criticism by calling a general election for the Northern Ireland Parliament. **24 February** The Northern Ireland parliamentary election proves indecisive and highlights unionist division over reform. **21 April** Fifteen hundred troops take responsibility for guarding public buildings and utilities following a series of terrorist attacks later revealed to be the work of the loyalist Ulster Volunteer Force (UVF). **28 April** O'Neill resigns as Ulster Unionist Party (UUP) leader and prime minister of Northern Ireland and is replaced by James Chichester-Clark. **12 July** On the traditional date of Orange Order celebrations, sectarian rioting occurs across Northern Ireland. **14 July** Francis McCloskey from Dungiven dies after being struck by a police baton. He is usually considered the first victim of the Troubles. **12 August** An Apprentice Boys of Derry (ABD) parade sparks riots in the Bogside area of the city. The "Battle of the Bogside" leads to sectarian rioting in Belfast. **14 August** Soldiers are deployed on the streets of Derry and in Belfast on the following day. **27 August** British home secretary James Callaghan visits Northern Ireland and puts pressure on the Northern Ireland government to introduce further reforms. **10 October** The announcement that the wholly Protestant B Special police reserve is to be disbanded leads to rioting by loyalists and the death of Constable Victor Arbuckle on the Shankill Road, Belfast. **28 December** A statement from the "Provisional Army Council" signals a split in the Irish Republican Army (IRA) between what will become the Official and Provisional wings of the IRA.

**1970   11 January** The Sinn Fein (SF) ard fheis (conference) in Dublin witnesses a split between Provisional and Official SF and consequently also a split in the IRA. **1 April** The Ulster Defence Regiment (UDR) replaces the B Specials. Ballymurphy, Belfast, sees the first major clash between nationalists and the British Army. **21 April** The cross-community Alliance Party of Northern Ireland (APNI) is formed. **18 June** A Westminster general election returns the Conservative Party to power with Edward Heath as prime minister. **22 June** Bernadette Devlin, Member of Parliament (MP), loses an appeal against a six-month jail sentence for her part in disturbances in Derry in August 1969. **27 June** The first sustained military action by the Provisional IRA (PIRA) takes place in the Short Strand area of Belfast during sectarian rioting. **2 July** In Dublin former Irish agriculture minister Neil Blaney is cleared of plotting to smuggle guns to the IRA. In October former finance minister Charles Haughey is also cleared. **3 July** A curfew lasting 36 hours begins in the Catholic Lower Falls area of Belfast. The curfew further sours relations with the British Army. **16 July** Thirty people are injured when a bomb explodes in a bank in Belfast. The explosion is part of an IRA bombing campaign throughout the summer. **21 August** The Social Democratic and Labour Party (SDLP) is formed with Gerry Fitt as leader.

**1971   6 February** Gunner Robert Curtis, shot by the PIRA, is the first soldier to die on duty in the Troubles. **25 February** The building and allocation of public authority housing becomes the responsibility of the Northern Ireland Housing Executive (NIHE). **March** The PIRA begins a campaign of attacks on RUC stations and police officers and their families. **9 March** Three off-duty soldiers are murdered by the PIRA in Belfast. **20 March** Chichester-Clark resigns as prime minister of Northern Ireland after the Conservative British Government fails to support his demand for a tougher security policy. He is succeeded by Brian Faulkner. **22 June** Faulkner announces a plan to include all parties in a parliamentary committee system at Stormont. **July** The PIRA steps up its bombing campaign, increasing sectarian tensions. **16 July** The SDLP withdraws from Stormont after the Northern Ireland government refuses to hold an inquiry into the deaths of two men in Derry a week earlier. They establish an "Assembly of the Northern Irish People" and call for a campaign of civil disobedience. **9 August** Internment without trial is introduced. Three hundred forty-two men, mainly associated with the Official IRA (OIRA), are arrested. There is a massive increase in the level of violence. **September** The loyalist Ulster Defence Association (UDA) is formed by the merging of local Protestant vigilante groups. **5 September** The PIRA makes constitutional proposals based on the idea of a nine-county Ulster regional assembly. **30 October** Rev. Ian Paisley and Desmond Boal launch the Democratic Unionist Party (DUP). **16 November** The Compton report concludes that detainees had suffered ill treatment but not brutality. Detainees had endured "in-depth" interrogation but not torture. **25 November** Labour leader Harold Wilson announces a 15-point plan, including a move toward a united Ireland over a 15-year period. **4 December** Fifteen people are killed by a UVF bomb placed in McGurk's Bar in Belfast. **12 December** Unionist Senator Jack Barnhill is murdered by the OIRA at his home in Strabane, Co. Tyrone.

**1972  30 January** Fourteen men are shot dead by the army after rioting breaks out at the end of a civil rights rally in Derry. The sequence of events of "Bloody Sunday" continue to be highly contested. **9 February** Former Northern Ireland minister of home affairs William Craig launches Ulster Vanguard as a pressure group within the UUP. **22 February** Seven people are killed by an OIRA bomb at Aldershot military barracks. **25 February** Northern Ireland minister for home affairs John Taylor survives an OIRA assassination attempt in Armagh. **24 March** Conservative prime minister Edward Heath suspends the Northern Ireland Parliament for a year after the Northern Ireland government refuses to accept loss of security powers to the national Parliament at

Westminster. **26 March** William Whitelaw is appointed as the first secretary of state for Northern Ireland under the new system of direct rule from Westminster. **22 April** Eleven-year-old Francis Rowntree is the first person to die as a result of injuries caused by a plastic bullet. **25 May** The OIRA kidnap and kill a 19-year-old Derry man serving in the British Army while he is home on leave. Local reaction to the murder is so hostile that the OIRA calls a permanent halt to its military campaign. **15 June** Whitelaw meets SDLP members for political talks. Whitelaw later concedes "special category status" to loyalist and republican prisoners. **30 June** The UDA begins creating loyalist "no-go areas" in Belfast and Portadown in response to continued republican no-go areas. **7 July** Whitelaw meets IRA members for secret talks in London during an IRA ceasefire. The talks are unsuccessful and the ceasefire ends a week later. **21 July** The PIRA detonates 26 bombs in Belfast, killing 9 people and injuring 130. The devastation caused leads to the day being dubbed "Bloody Friday." **31 July** The British military carry out "Operation Motorman," which ends republican "no-go areas" in Belfast and Derry. The UDA helps soldiers dismantle barricades in Protestant areas. Three IRA bombs later kill nine people in Claudy, Co. Londonderry. **25 September** A conference on political options for Northern Ireland is held in Darlington, England. **30 October** The government publishes a discussion paper, *The Future of Northern Ireland*, which proposes a power-sharing administration and a formalized relationship with the Irish Republic.

**1973   1 January** Ireland and the United Kingdom become members of the European Economic Community (EEC). **5 February** Two men arrested on suspicion of murder two days earlier become the first loyalist internees. **7 February** A one-day strike called in protest at the internment of two loyalists is characterized by violence and intimidation. **1 March** After a general election in the Irish Republic, a Fine Gael (FG)–Labour coalition government is formed. **8 March** A "border poll" produces a massive majority in favor of Northern Ireland remaining as part of the United Kingdom. Most nationalists abstained from voting. **20 March** The government issues "Northern Ireland Constitutional Proposals" suggesting a Northern Ireland Assembly elected by proportional representation (PR), an executive enjoying "widespread support" in the community, and an "Irish Dimension" involving a more formalized relationship with the Irish Republic. **27 March** The Ulster Unionist Council (UUC), governing body of the UUP, votes not to reject the government's proposals. Three days later some of those who opposed this decision leave the UUP to form the Vanguard Unionist Progressive Party (VUPP) led by William Craig. **30 May** Elections are held for the newly reformed district councils. PR voting is used in elections in Northern Ireland for the first time since 1929. **12 June** Six pensioners are killed when a bomb explodes in Coleraine, Co. Londonderry. **26 June** Gerry Fitt's election agent is murdered by a new loyalist group, the Ulster Freedom Fighters (UFF), later revealed to be part of the UDA. **28 June** Northern Ireland Assembly elections return an overall majority in favor of government proposals; however, a majority of unionists are opposed. **5 October** UUP, APNI, and SDLP representatives meet at Stormont Castle to discuss the possible formation of an executive. **22 November** The formation of a cross-community executive is announced with Brian Faulkner as chief executive and Gerry Fitt as deputy chief executive. The announcement brings fierce criticism from some unionists and loyalists. **3 December** Francis Pym replaces Whitelaw as secretary of state. **6 December** British, Irish, and Northern Irish politicians meet at Sunningdale Park in England for discussions surrounding the "Irish dimension." The conference concludes on 9 December with the release of an agreed communiqué. **10 December** Loyalist paramilitary groups react to the Sunningdale Agreement by establishing an umbrella organization, the Ulster Army Council.

**1974 1 January** The Northern Ireland executive takes office. **4 January** The UUC rejects the Sunningdale Agreement, and Faulkner resigns as UUP leader three days later. **16 January** The Dublin High Court rules that the Sunningdale communiqué's recognition of Northern Ireland was "no more than a statement of policy." **1 February** Irish Ministers and Northern Ireland executive members meet in Hillsborough, Co. Down, for talks, including the functions of the North–South "Council of Ireland." **4 February** Eleven people are killed by a bomb explosion on a coach carrying soldiers and their families near Bradford. **28 February** A minority Labour government is returned in a Westminster general election. Anti-Sunningdale unionists, under the umbrella name the United Ulster Unionist Council (UUUC), win 11 of the 12 Northern Ireland seats. **14 May** The Ulster Workers' Council (UWC) calls for an indefinite strike after the Northern Ireland Assembly votes not to reject power sharing and the Council of Ireland. **17 May** Thirty-three people die after loyalist bombs explode in Dublin and the town of Monaghan. **21 May** As the UWC strike intensifies, a "back to work" march fails to garner significant support. **22 May** The executive agrees to the Council of Ireland being introduced in stages. By this time the political initiative increasingly lies with loyalist and unionist opponents of the Sunningdale Agreement. **25 May** In a television broadcast, Prime Minister Wilson describes the strikers as "sponging on Westminster and British democracy." The comments bring a hostile reaction from unionists at large and further undermines support for the executive. **28 May** With water and sewerage systems deteriorating, Faulkner calls on Secretary of State Merlyn Rees to negotiate with UWC leaders. Rees refuses, and Faulkner resigns, effectively ending the power-sharing executive. The UWC strike is called off the following day. **30 May** The Northern Ireland Assembly is suspended. **4 July** A government paper, "The Northern Ireland Constitution," proposes a Constitutional Convention to draft an agreed-upon plan for the government of Northern Ireland. **5 October** Five people are killed and 54 injured when IRA bombs explode in two public houses in Guildford, Surrey. **10 October** A U.K. general election returns a Labour government. **21 November** Twenty-one people are killed and 182 injured by IRA bomb explosions in two public houses in Birmingham. Four days later the government introduces the Prevention of Terrorism Act. **8 December** The Irish Republican Socialist Party (IRSP) emerges after a split in Official SF. The paramilitary wing of the organization, the Irish National Liberation Army (INLA), appears the following year. **10 December** Protestant churchmen meet PIRA leaders for talks. **20 December** The PIRA declares a ceasefire over the Christmas and New Year period, later extended to 17 January 1975. **22 December** Government officials begin talks with Provisional Sinn Fein (PSF).

**1975   9 February** The PIRA announces an indefinite ceasefire. "The Truce" is monitored by "incident centers" manned by members of PSF who liaise with British government officials. **20 February** A feud breaks out between the OIRA and the INLA. **15 March** A feud breaks out between rival loyalist organizations, the UDA and UVF. **2 April** The bombing of a travel agency marks the first breach of the PIRA ceasefire in Belfast; however, the truce has already begun to break down in other areas of Northern Ireland. **1 May** Elections to the Constitutional Convention returns a UUUC majority pledged to oppose power sharing and an Irish dimension. **1 September** Four people are killed and seven others injured in an attack by IRA members on an Orange Hall in Newtownhamilton, Co. Armagh. **8 September** A proposal by William Craig for a voluntary coalition government for Northern Ireland is rejected by the UUUC. The outcome leads to the fragmentation of Vanguard. **22 September** A series of PIRA bombs explodes across Northern Ireland, suggesting the effective end of the truce. **4 November** Merlyn Rees announces that special category status will not be accorded to those convicted of terrorist crimes from March 1976. **7 November** The Convention report endorses the UUUC view, which rejects power sharing with nationalists and an Irish dimension. **12 November** The government announces the closure of the incident centers, saying they serve no useful purpose.

**1976** **5 January** Ten Protestants are murdered by the IRA at Kingsmills, Co. Armagh. **3 February** The Constitutional Convention reconvenes for interparty talks but fails to make progress and is dissolved on 5 March. **25 March** Rees announces a policy of "police primacy" in security matters in Northern Ireland. **5 April** James Callaghan replaces Wilson as prime minister. **21 July** The British ambassador to Dublin is killed when a land mine explodes under his car. **10 August** Two children are killed when a gunman's getaway car crashes into them after the driver is shot dead by soldiers. The event leads to a number of rallies in support of peace and the creation of the Women's Peace Movement (later called the Peace People). **2 September** The European Commission of Human Rights (ECHR) rules that interrogation techniques used against internees breach the European Convention on Human Rights. **10 September** Roy Mason becomes secretary of state for Northern Ireland. **15 September** PIRA member Kieran Nugent is refused special category status. On entering the H Blocks at the Maze Prison, he refuses the prison uniform and wears only a blanket in protest. **27 November** Thirty thousand people take part in a march held in London and rally for peace in Northern Ireland. **1 December** The Fair Employment Act comes into effect, making it illegal to discriminate in employment on religious or political grounds.

**1977** **3 May** The United Unionist Action Council (UUAC), led by Ian Paisley and former Vanguard member Ernie Baird, demand improved security and a return to majority rule in Northern Ireland. Their strike is supported by the UDA and UWC. **13 May** The loyalist strike is called off after it fails to win widespread unionist support. A more effective government campaign against the stoppage is also instrumental in defeating the strike. **16 June** Following a general election in the Republic, Fianna Fail (FF) returns to power. **5 October** Seamus Costello, founder and leader of the IRSP, is murdered in Dublin. **10 October** Betty Williams and Mairead Corrigan, founders of the Peace People, are awarded the Nobel Peace Prize.

**1978   17 February** Twelve people are killed and 23 injured by an IRA incendiary bomb at the La Mon House Hotel in Co. Down. **19 April** It is announced that Northern Ireland's representation at Westminster will be increased to between 16 and 18 seats. **14 November** Having regrouped and stockpiled weapons, the PIRA launches a fresh bombing campaign. **26 November** The deputy governor of the Crumlin Road Prison is shot dead by the IRA in Belfast.

**1979   20 February** Eleven members of the UVF-linked loyalist gang known as the Shankill Butchers are convicted of 19 murders. **30 March** The Conservative Party spokesman in Northern Ireland, Airey Neave, dies after an INLA bomb explodes under his car. **3 May** The Conservative Party, led by Margaret Thatcher, wins the U.K. general election. **7 June** The first direct elections to the European Parliament are held. In Northern Ireland Ian Paisley (DUP), John Hume (SDLP), and John Taylor (UUP) are elected. **27 August** The Queen's cousin, 79-year-old Earl Mountbatten, is killed by an IRA bomb on his boat at Mullaghmore, Co. Sligo, in the Republic. Later 18 soldiers are killed by two IRA bombs at Narrow Water in Co. Down. **7 September** James Molyneaux becomes leader of the UUP in succession to Harry West. **30 September** On a visit to the Republic, Pope John Paul II calls for an end to violence. The IRA rejects this appeal on 2 October. **25 October** Secretary of State Humphrey Atkins announces plans for a conference to discuss possible paths to devolution. **20 November** Government proposals for devolution include no discussion of the Irish dimension. Under pressure from the SDLP, Atkins concedes parallel talks on this issue. **22 November** Gerry Fitt, who was prepared to begin talks on devolution without an included Irish dimension, resigns as leader of the SDLP. He is succeeded by John Hume. **11 December** Charles Haughey succeeds Jack Lynch as taoiseach.

**1980** **1 January** John Hermon succeeds Sir Kenneth Newman as chief constable of the RUC. **7 January** The Atkins Talks begin with the DUP, SDLP, and APNI involved but not the UUP, which claims the talks are merely a gimmick. The DUP and SDLP also disagree on whether the Irish dimension should be discussed. **16 February** The IRA shoot dead a British Army colonel in West Germany. **24 March** The Atkins Talks end without any significant progress. **26 March** Atkins announces the end of special category status for all prisoners from 1 April. **19 June** The ECHR rejects a case brought by republican prisoners claiming prison conditions during the "dirty protest" were inhumane on the grounds that the conditions were self-inflicted. **15 October** Two leading IRSP members are killed by the UFF. **27 October** Seven H Block prisoners begin a hunger strike, demanding the right to wear their own clothes. **8 December** Thatcher and Haughey meet for an Anglo–Irish summit meeting in Dublin. The summit demonstrates the beginning of a more formalized relationship in Anglo–Irish affairs. **12 December** Three republican female prisoners in Armagh jail join the hunger strike. Thirty more republican prisoners join the hunger strike in the following days. **18 December** The hunger strike is called off after 53 days following an appeal from the Catholic Primate Cardinal Tomas O Fiaich. Confusion as to whether the government has conceded to any of the prisoners' demands leaves the seeds for further conflict.

**1981** **21 January** The former speaker of the Northern Ireland Parliament, 86-year-old Sir Norman Stronge, and his son are murdered by the IRA at their home. **1 March** The IRA leader in the Maze Prison, Bobby Sands, launches another hunger strike campaign by republican prisoners aimed at regaining special category status. Other IRA and INLA prisoners also join the protest in the following weeks. **5 March** Frank Maguire, MP for the Westminster seat of Fermanagh-South Tyrone, dies. **9 April** Bobby Sands wins the by-election for Fermanagh-South Tyrone. The result boosts support for the prisoners' campaign but also leads to increased violence. **5 May** Bobby Sands dies on the 66th day of his hunger strike. Almost 100,000 people attend Sands's funeral two days later. **12 May** The death of hunger striker Francis Hughes brings a renewed wave of rioting in republican areas. A crowd of 2,000 people attempt to break into the British embassy in Dublin. **20 May** In a highly polarized atmosphere, the DUP out-polls the UUP in district council elections. **2 June** The UDA launches a new political party, the Ulster Loyalist Democratic Party (ULDP), later renamed the Ulster Democratic Party (UDP). **3 June** The Irish Commission for Justice and Peace, a body set up by the Catholic Bishops' Conference, issues proposals aimed at resolving the Maze dispute. The proposals are initially welcomed by both the prisoners and the Northern Ireland Office (NIO), but by the end of the month, the two sides seem to be moving further apart, and by mid-July it appears that the mediation has failed. **11 June** A general election in the Republic leads to the formation of a minority FG–Labour coalition government. Two H Block prisoners are also returned in the election. **4 July** The hunger strikers say they would be happy to see any changes in prison conditions applied to all prisoners. This opens the possibility of the government making concessions without conceding political status to republican prisoners. **16 July** Members of the International Red Cross visit prisoners on hunger strike in the Maze. A week later the leader of the delegation says they can play no role in the dispute because it is completely deadlocked. **20 August** INLA member Michael Devine is the 10th republican prisoner to die during the hunger strike. A second Fermanagh-South Tyrone by-election is won by Bobby Sands's election agent Owen Carron. **23 August** PSF announces that in the future it will contest Northern Ireland elections. **6 September** The INLA says it will not replace prisoners on hunger strike at the same rate as before. **13 September** James Prior replaces Humphrey Atkins as secretary of state. **27 September** Taoiseach Garret FitzGerald announces his ideas for a "constitutional crusade" to liberalize society in the Republic and make it more appealing to Northern Protestants. **29 September** The Labour Party annual conference votes to "campaign actively" for a united Ireland by consent. **3 October** The hunger strike is called off after prisoners' relatives say they will intervene to save their lives. **6 October** Prior concedes to the prisoners' demand for the right to wear their own clothing and makes partial concessions on other demands. **31 October** At the SF ard fheis, Danny Morrison suggests that SF take power in Ireland "with a ballot paper in one hand and the Armalite in the other." **14 November** Methodist minister and UUP MP Rev. Robert Bradford is killed by the IRA in Belfast. **21 December** The U.S. State Department revokes Ian Paisley's visa because of statements he has made in Northern Ireland.

**1982   29 January** Leading loyalist John McKeague is shot dead by the INLA. **18 February** A general election in the Republic leads to a FF minority government. **5 April** A government paper proposes a Northern Ireland Assembly where power could be devolved on a department-by-department basis where cross-community agreement was reached. Only APNI shows any enthusiasm for this plan for "rolling devolution." Events in Northern Ireland and Anglo–Irish relations are also overshadowed by Argentina's invasion of the Falklands in April. **20 July** Eight soldiers are killed by IRA bombs in London. **20 October** Elections are held for the Northern Ireland Assembly. SF takes 10.1 percent of the vote in the first Northern Ireland elections contested by the party. **11 November** Three unarmed IRA men are shot dead by the RUC near Lurgan, Co. Armagh, sparking claims of a "shoot-to-kill" policy. **6 December** Seventeen people, including 11 soldiers, are killed by an INLA bomb at the Droppin' Well disco at Ballykelly, Co. Londonderry. **12 December** Two INLA men are shot dead by police near Armagh city.

**1983   23 February** The European Parliament decides to investigate whether the EEC can help solve Northern Ireland's economic and political problems. The move is opposed by the British government. **11 March** The Irish government announces that it is setting up an all-Ireland forum. The UUP, DUP, and APNI reject invitations to take part in the New Ireland Forum. **11 April** In the first of a number of "supergrass" cases, 14 UVF members are jailed based on evidence given by a former member of the organization. **9 June** The Conservative Party wins the U.K. general election. Gerry Adams wins the West Belfast seat for SF. **25 September** Thirty-eight IRA members break out of the Maze Prison; 19 are soon recaptured, but the others escape. **7 November** Thatcher and FitzGerald hold the first formal meeting between British and Irish prime ministers in two years. **13 November** Gerry Adams is elected president of SF at the party's annual ard fheis. **20 November** Three church elders are killed and seven other people are wounded in an INLA attack on a Pentecostal church in Darkley, Co. Armagh. The UUP withdraws from the Northern Ireland Assembly in a protest against government security policies. **7 December** A UUP Assembly member is murdered by the IRA at Queen's University, Belfast. **12 December** A European Parliamentary report on Northern Ireland calls for power sharing and for an EEC plan to help the economic development of Northern Ireland. The report is formally approved in March 1984.

**1984   6 March** A deputy governor of the Maze Prison is shot dead by the IRA at his Belfast home. **14 March** Gerry Adams and three other SF members are wounded in a UFF gun attack in Belfast. **2 May** The New Ireland Forum report calls for a united Ireland. **11 September** Douglas Hurd becomes secretary of state. **29 September** Irish police seize the trawler *Marita Ann* carrying seven tons of arms and ammunition for the IRA. **12 October** The IRA bombs the Grand Hotel in Brighton, being used by many Conservative members during their party conference, and kills five people. Prime Minister Thatcher narrowly escapes injury. **4 November** The MacBride Principles on fair employment in Northern Ireland are launched. **19 November** Thatcher rejects the proposals of the New Ireland Forum report, leading to a souring in relations with the Irish government. **18 December** The lord chief justice for Northern Ireland rejects the evidence of a supergrass and acquits 35 defendants. Convictions in other supergrass cases are also overturned in the following year.

**1985   28 February** Nine RUC officers are killed and 30 injured in an IRA mortar attack in Newry, Co. Down. **14 June** A 1,000-pound IRA bomb causes widespread damage in Belfast. **21 July** A loyalist organization is formed in Portadown, Co. Armagh, to oppose the rerouting of Orange parades by the RUC. **3 September** Tom King becomes secretary of state for Northern Ireland. **2 November** A campaign is launched by loyalists to establish Ulster Clubs across Northern Ireland to oppose the implementation for the forthcoming Anglo–Irish agreement. **15 November** Margaret Thatcher and Garret FitzGerald sign the Anglo–Irish Agreement, which gives the Republic an official right to be consulted on Northern Ireland matters. **19 November** Eighteen unionist-controlled district councils begin adjourning meetings in protest against the Anglo–Irish Agreement. **23 November** As many as 200,000 unionists attend a demonstration against the Anglo–Irish Agreement at Belfast City Hall. **11 December** The first session of the Anglo–Irish Conference at Stormont sees clashes between the RUC and loyalist protesters. **17 December** Unionist MPs resign their seats in order to fight by-election campaigns on the grounds of opposition to the Anglo–Irish Agreement.

**1986   24 January** By-elections in 15 of the 17 Northern Ireland Westminster seats see almost 420,000 unionists vote against the Anglo–Irish

Agreement; however, the UUP loses a seat to the SDLP. **7 February** The Northern Ireland High Court orders Belfast City Council to resume normal business. **25 February** Belfast City Council refuses to set a household rate; other unionist councils follow their lead. **3 March** A loyalist Day of Action shuts down most commerce and industry but is followed by rioting. **11 March** The U.S. House of Representatives approves a $250 million aid package to Northern Ireland in support of the Anglo–Irish Agreement. **31 March** The banning of an Apprentice Boys of Derry March in Portadown leads to severe rioting in loyalist areas. **23 June** The Northern Ireland Assembly is dissolved by the government. Twenty-two unionist members are forcibly ejected from Stormont by the RUC. **7 August** Peter Robinson (DUP) is arrested in Clontibret, Co. Monaghan, after hundreds of loyalists temporarily take over the village in the Republic and two gardai are assaulted. **18 September** The British and Irish governments establish an international aid fund to promote social and economic development in Northern Ireland and border areas of the Republic. **October** Unemployment reaches 135,000, or 23 percent of those available for work. **15 October** The IRA announces it will support SF members taking their seats in the Dail. **2 November** An SF conference votes to end abstention from the Dail. One hundred members leave the meeting in protest and later form Republican Sinn Fein (RSF). **10 November** Ian Paisley launches Ulster Resistance with the aim of destroying the Anglo–Irish Agreement. **15 November** On the first anniversary of the Anglo–Irish Agreement, approximately 200,000 unionists attend a rally at Belfast City Hall. Rioting breaks out later and continues for two days.

**1987    20 January** A renewed feud erupts between the INLA and a breakaway faction. **29 January** A paper from the UDA's political think-tank calls for a written constitution for Northern Ireland and devolved government based on consensus and shared responsibility. **13 February** The DUP-controlled Castlereagh Council is fined £10,000 for failing to conduct normal council business. **19 February** A general election in the Republic leads to a minority FF government led by Charles Haughey. **23 February** Belfast City Council is fined £25,000. The government later appoints commissioners to set council rates. **17 March** President Ronald Reagan authorizes a $50 million grant to the International Fund for Ireland. **25 April** A senior Northern Ireland judge and his wife are killed by the IRA at Killeen, Co. Armagh. **8 May** Eight IRA men are shot dead in an army ambush after they launch an attack on Loughgall police station in Co. Armagh. **11 June** The Conservative Party wins the U.K. general election. **14 September** UUP leader James Molyneaux and DUP leader Ian Paisley meet Tom King for "talks about talks." **1 November** One hundred fifty tons of Libyan arms and ammunition bound for the IRA are found onboard the *Eksund* off the French coast. Three earlier deliveries had already been smuggled into Ireland. **8 November** An IRA bomb explodes near a Remembrance Day ceremony in Enniskillen, Co. Fermanagh, killing 11 people and injuring 63 others.

**1988   11 January** John Hume begins discussions with Gerry Adams to find common ground on conditions for an all-Ireland settlement. **6 March** Three unarmed IRA members are shot dead by the Special Air Service (SAS) in Gibraltar. **16 March** At Milltown Cemetery in Belfast, three mourners are killed by loyalist Michael Stone at the funerals of the IRA members killed in Gibraltar. **19 March** Two soldiers are killed by the IRA after their car was surrounded by a crowd in the funeral cortege of one of those killed at Milltown Cemetery three days earlier. **15 June** Six soldiers are killed after taking part in a race in Lisburn, Co. Antrim, when a bomb explodes under their van. **20 August** Eight soldiers are killed and 28 injured by an IRA landmine near Ballygawley, Co. Tyrone. **14 October** UUP, DUP, SDLP, and APNI representatives meet for talks in Duisberg, West Germany. **19 October** Home Secretary Douglas Hurd announces a ban on the broadcasting of direct statements by members of SF, RSF, and the UDA. **15 December** The government introduces a new Fair Employment Bill for Northern Ireland, strengthening existing regulations and changing the Fair Employment Agency to the Fair Employment Commission.

**1989   12 February** Solicitor Patrick Finucane is shot dead by loyalists. The murder encourages claims of collusion between loyalists and the security forces. **21 March** Two senior RUC officers are killed by the IRA as they return to Northern Ireland after a meeting with gardai in the Republic. **21 April** Three loyalists are arrested in Paris during an abortive arms deal with a South African embassy official. **15 June** A general election in the Republic leads to an FF–Progressive Democrat (PD) coalition government. **30 August** The UFF hands copies of official documents to the British Broadcasting Corporation (BBC) and claims that the security forces leak information to them. **22 September**

An IRA bomb kills 10 Royal Marines and injures 22 in Deal, Kent. **19 October** Three of the Guildford Four are released after their convictions are overturned. Paul Hill is held in connection with another case but released in April 1994. **3 November** Secretary of State Peter Brooke suggests the government might talk to SF, provided the IRA renounces the use of violence.

**1990  9 January** Peter Brooke attempts to launch a new round of interparty talks aimed at achieving devolution. Ards Borough Council becomes the first unionist-controlled council to end its boycott of NIO ministers. **24 February** The UUP says councilors can meet NIO ministers on matters of specific importance to councils. **1 March** In a test case brought by two UUP members, the Irish Supreme Court rules that the Republic's claim to Northern Ireland is a "constitutional imperative" and not merely a political aspiration. **11 April** Against a background of strained Anglo–Irish relations caused by the failure of a number of extradition cases, Taoiseach Charles Haughey attends a conference held by the Institute of Directors in Belfast. **16 April** There is trouble at Crumlin Road Prison in Belfast over the question of the segregation of loyalist and republican prisoners. **17 May** The Stevens Report says that while collusion between loyalists and security force members had occurred, only a small number of individuals were involved. **20 July** An IRA bomb at the London Stock Exchange causes extensive damage. **30 July** Conservative MP Ian Gow is killed by an IRA bomb in his car. **24 October** Six soldiers and a civilian are killed when the IRA forces civilians to drive car bombs toward security force positions. **9 November** Mary Robinson is elected president of Ireland. **27 November** John Major succeeds Margaret Thatcher as prime minister and Conservative Party leader.

**1991  7 February** An IRA mortar bomb lands in the garden of 10 Downing Street, only yards from where a cabinet meeting is taking place. **4 March** Unionists on Belfast City Council vote to end their ban on meeting NIO ministers. **14 March** The Birmingham Six are freed after 16 years in jail. **17 March** A loyalist paramilitary umbrella organization, the Combined Loyalist Military Command (CLMC), announces a ceasefire to coincide with forthcoming political talks. **28 March** Peter Brooke outlines a "three strand" approach to future political discussions: internal Northern Ireland matters, North–South relations, and relations between Britain and Ireland. **9 April** The Anglo–Irish Intergovernmental Conference announces a 10-week gap in meetings to allow unionists to join political discussions. **17 June** Political talks finally commence after weeks of procedural wrangling but again stop on 3 July as the date for another Intergovernmental Conference meeting approaches. **26 June** The Maguire Seven are cleared by the Court of Appeal. **16 September** Brooke meets local party leaders in an attempt to restart the political talks process. An SF councilor is shot dead by the UVF.

**1992  17 January** Eight Protestant building workers are killed by an IRA bomb at Teebane crossroads near Cookstown, Co. Tyrone. **9 April** The Conservatives win the U.K. general election. Sir Patrick Mayhew later replaces Peter Brooke as secretary of state. **10 April** Two IRA bombs in London kill three people and cause an estimated £800 million damage. **27 April** The Intergovernmental Conference announces a three-month suspension in meetings. Two days later political talks reconvene at Stormont. **1 July** The Royal Irish Regiment comes into existence with the amalgamation of the Ulster Defence Regiment (UDR) and the Royal Irish Rangers. **6 July** Talks involving Northern Ireland parties and the British and Irish governments are held in London on the issue of North–South relations. **10 August** Sir Patrick Mayhew announces the banning of the UDA. **10 November** Despite in-depth discussions of all three strands of political relations, the talks fail to reach agreement. **23 November** Following an upsurge in IRA car-bomb attacks, many towns begin closing security gates for the first time since the 1970s. **24 December** The IRA announces a three-day-long ceasefire.

**1993  24 February** John Major meets President Bill Clinton in Washington. Issues discussed include Clinton's idea for a U.S. "peace envoy" to Northern Ireland. **20 March** The deaths of two boys aged 3 and 12 years in IRA bombs in Warrington, Cheshire, creates a wave of revulsion against terrorism in Britain and Ireland. **10 April** John Hume and Gerry Adams meet for talks in Derry. **24 April** An IRA bomb at the Nat West Tower in London kills 1 person, injures 30, and causes an estimated £1 billion damage. **7 September** An independent American fact-finding visit to Northern Ireland coincides with a weeklong lull in IRA activity. **25 September** Hume and Adams say they have agreed to forward a report on their discussions to the Irish government for consideration. **22 October** John Hume says his talks with Gerry Adams provide the best chance for lasting peace in 20 years. **23 October** An IRA bomb in a shop on the Shankill Road, Belfast kills 10 people and injures 57 others. **27 October** In the Dail, Irish Foreign Minister Dick Spring proposes a list of six "democratic principles" he believes could lead to a sustained peace. **30 October** UFF gunmen kill 7 people and injure 13 in an attack on a bar in Greysteel, Co. Londonderry. Twenty-seven people die due to the Troubles this month, the greatest number in any month since October 1976. **28 November** The *Observer* newspaper reveals that the British government has had a secret channel of communication with SF and the IRA for three years and has been in regular contact since February. The revelation leaves unionists outraged and leads to disputes between the government and SF as to the exact nature of the discussions. **15 December** John Major and Taoiseach Albert Reynolds issue a joint declaration on Northern Ireland. The "Downing Street Declaration" attempts to address conflicting unionist and nationalist objectives and becomes arguably the cornerstone of the developing peace process. In the Dail, Dick Spring says that a permanent end to violence would involve paramilitaries handing over arms.

**1994   29 January** President Clinton authorizes a limited-duration visa to the United States for Gerry Adams. **19 May** responding to SF demands for "clarification" of the Downing Street Declaration, the NIO issues a 21-page "commentary." **2 June** A helicopter carrying senior antiterrorist experts crashes in Scotland, killing all those onboard. **18 June** UVF gunmen murder six people and wound five others in an attack on a bar at Loughinisland, Co. Down. **29 August** Gerry Adams says he has met the IRA Army Council and told it that he believes the conditions exist to move the peace process forward. **31 August** The IRA announces a "complete cessation of military operations" from midnight. **16 September** On a visit to Belfast, John Major says any political agreement will be subject to approval by the people of Northern Ireland in a referendum. **13 October** The CLMC says it has received assurances in relation to Northern Ireland's constitutional position within the United Kingdom and calls a ceasefire from midnight. **28 October** Taoiseach Albert Reynolds opens a Forum for Peace and Reconciliation in Dublin. **10 November** A man is killed by the IRA during the robbery of a post office in Newry, Co. Down.

The IRA says the operation was not sanctioned by its leadership. **19 November** Bertie Ahern replaces Albert Reynolds as leader of FF. **1 December** President Clinton appoints Senator George Mitchell as a special economic advisor on Ireland. **9 December** British civil servants meet SF representatives for the first formal meeting in more than two decades. **15 December** Following the collapse of the Irish coalition government, John Bruton of FG becomes taoiseach.

**1995  22 February** The government publishes "Frameworks for the Future," outlining plans for a Northern Ireland Assembly and North–South relations. The proposals are rejected by unionists as being too pronationalist. **15 March** An American decision to grant Gerry Adams a visa and permission to raise funds leads to a row between Major and Clinton. **28 April** An alleged drugs dealer is shot dead by a group called Direct Action Against Drugs (DAAD), a cover name for the IRA. **10 May** An SF delegation meets an NIO minister for talks at Stormont. **9 July** The RUC and Orange Order members are involved in a confrontation over a march along the Garvaghy Road in Portadown. The standoff is referred to as the "siege of Drumcree," after the name of the local parish church. The confrontation brings a deterioration in relations between nationalists and unionists. **13 August** Gerry Adams is widely criticized after he tells a demonstration in Belfast that the IRA "haven't gone away." **8 September** David Trimble is elected leader of the UUP. **3 November** The NIO publishes a paper suggesting all-party preparatory talks with an independent international body to consider the issue of paramilitary decommissioning of weapons running parallel to talks. **28 November** A joint Anglo–Irish statement launches the "twin track" approach of political talks alongside an independent body, chaired by George Mitchell, to advise on decommissioning. **30 November** President Clinton makes a two-day visit to Northern Ireland.

**1996  24 January** The report of the Independent Body on Decommissioning accepts that there is a commitment by paramilitaries to get rid of weapons but not before all-party talks. The report also sets out a number of principles opposing the use of violence—the Mitchell Principles. John Major announces that elections will be held to an all-party talks forum. This is welcomed by unionists but opposed by nationalists. **9 February** The IRA ends its ceasefire with a bomb at Canary Wharf in London, killing 2 people and injuring 100 others. **28**

**February** The British and Irish governments announce a package aimed at restarting the peace process, but these make little initial headway. **30 May** Elections to all-party negotiations are held. **10 June** Multiparty talks commence at Stormont. SF is barred from taking part because of the ongoing IRA campaign. **7 July** There is a confrontation between police and Orange marchers at Drumcree for a second year. **11 July** A decision to allow the march to proceed leads to rioting in nationalist areas. **13 July** The SDLP announces it is withdrawing from the Northern Ireland Forum. **14 July** A 1,200-pound car bomb at a hotel near Enniskillen is attributed to a group called Continuity IRA (CIRA). **2 August** The UVF says its Portadown unit is to be disbanded. The decision later leads to the formation of the Loyalist Volunteer Force (LVF), led by Billy Wright. **7 October** Two IRA car bombs explode in Lisburn army barracks, killing a soldier and injuring 30 people. The bombing almost leads loyalist paramilitary groups to end their ceasefires. **4 November** Ronnie Flanagan succeeds Sir Hugh Annesley as chief constable of the RUC.

**1997** **13 January** Political talks resume but remain deadlocked and are adjourned on 5 March. **30 January** The report of an independent review committee calls for the creation of a Parades Commission to play the main role in parades disputes. **1 May** The U.K. general election sees a landslide victory for Labour. Tony Blair becomes prime minister, with Majorie (Mo) Mowlam becoming the first female secretary of state for Northern Ireland. **21 May** District council elections see an increase in votes for SF, which receives 16.9 percent of the vote. Martin McGuinness meets senior civil servants for the first time in more than a year. **2 June** Alban Maginness of the SDLP becomes the first nationalist to be elected lord mayor of Belfast. **6 June** A general election in the Republic leads to an FF–PD coalition government led by Bertie Ahern. **25 June** Tony Blair says that an immediate ceasefire by the IRA could lead to SF being invited to talks by the end of July. **6 July** Rioting breaks out in nationalist areas after an Orange march takes place along Garvaghy Road in Portadown. **16 July** The British and Irish governments push through a document downgrading paramilitary decommissioning to a side issue in the talks despite unionist opposition. **19 July** The IRA announces a ceasefire. **21 July** As SF prepares to join the talks process, the DUP and smaller U.K. Unionist Party (UKUP) walk out permanently. The UUP, however, remains in the talks. **26 August** The

British and Irish governments sign an agreement establishing an Independent International Commission on Decommissioning (IICD). **9 September** SF members sign the Mitchell Principles and join the all-party talks, which formally recommence on 15 September. **13 October** Tony Blair visits Belfast and shakes hands privately with Gerry Adams. Later, in a Protestant area of East Belfast, he is visibly shaken after being jeered at by protestors. The failure of Progressive Unionist Party (PUP) representatives to appear at a UDA rally to mark the third anniversary of the loyalist ceasefire highlights deteriorating relations between the loyalist groups. **31 October** Belfast-born academic Mary McAleese is elected president of Ireland. **5 December** In Dublin the Forum for Peace and Reconciliation meets for the first time since February 1996. **7 December** Republicans opposed to the peace process launch the 32-county Sovereignty Committee. A paramilitary organization associated with this group, the Real IRA (RIRA), emerges later. **22 December** Four UUP MPs write to David Trimble and call for the party to withdraw from the talks. **27 December** LVF leader Billy Wright is shot dead by INLA prisoners inside the Maze Prison.

**1998 12 January** Talks resume at Stormont. The British and Irish governments present a "Heads of Agreement" document to the parties suggesting balanced constitutional change, a new Northern Ireland Assembly, a new British–Irish Agreement to replace the Anglo–Irish Agreement, an Intergovernmental Council with representatives from political assemblies throughout Britain and Ireland, and a North–South Ministerial Council (NSMC) with implementation bodies for policies agreed on by this council. **26 January** The UDP is expelled from the talks process because the UFF has committed a series of murders. **29 January** Tony Blair announces a new inquiry into the events of Bloody Sunday. **20 February** SF is temporarily expelled from the talks process because of IRA involvement in two murders earlier in the month. **23 March** SF returns to talks. **10 April** The Belfast Agreement, also referred to as the Good Friday Agreement (GFA), is signed by political parties after days of intense negotiations. The agreement's vague language on the issue of decommissioning of weapons remains one potential future area of dispute. **18 April** The Ulster Unionist Council votes in favor of the Belfast Agreement by 72 percent to 28 percent. **23 April** Three UUP MPs attend an anti-Agreement rally in Belfast. **1 May** The Orange Order says it cannot endorse the Belfast Agreement.

**5 May** "United Unionists" launch a campaign in opposition to the Agreement. **10 May** A special SF ard fheis votes to allow party members to sit in a new Northern Ireland Assembly and to campaign for a yes vote on referendums on the Agreement in the North and South. **22 May** Referendums on the Agreement are passed in Northern Ireland and in the Republic. In Northern Ireland 71 percent vote in favor; 94 percent vote in in the Republic. **25 June** Northern Ireland Assembly elections are held. Unionists are almost evenly split between pro– and anti–Agreement assembly members. **1 July** At the first meeting of the Assembly, David Trimble and Seamus Mallon are jointly elected as first minister and deputy first minister. **5 July** The blocking of an Orange parade along Garvaghy Road in Portadown leads to rioting in Protestant areas of Northern Ireland. **15 August** Twenty-nine people are killed and 360 injured by a RIRA car bomb in Omagh, Co. Tyrone. **22 August** The INLA announces a "complete ceasefire." **3 September** President Clinton pays a one-day visit to Northern Ireland. **8 September** The RIRA announces a "complete cessation of all military activity." **10 September** David Trimble and Gerry Adams meet for discussions. It is the first meeting between UUP and SF leaders in more than 75 years. **12 September** The army ends patrols in the greater Belfast area. **16 October** John Hume and David Trimble are awarded the Nobel Peace Prize. **31 October** The parties fail to meet the deadline for the formation of an executive and the NSMC mainly because of disputes surrounding decommissioning. **18 December** The LVF hands over a small amount of arms and ammunition in the first voluntary act of decommissioning.

**1999    16 February** The Assembly votes to endorse structures of government proposed in a report by Trimble and Mallon. **8 March** The British and Irish governments sign four treaties providing the legal framework for the North–South implementation bodies. **15 March** Solicitor Rosemary Nelson is killed by a loyalist car bomb in Lurgan, leading to rioting by nationalist youths. **1 April** Political parties again fail to meet a deadline for agreement for devolution to begin because of decommissioning of weapons disputes. **30 June** Parties fail to meet another deadline for agreement on devolution. **15 July** An attempt to launch the Northern Ireland executive fails when unionists refuse to nominate members. **17 July** The British and Irish governments approach George Mitchell to help in negotiations once more. **6 September** The Mitchell review begins. **9 September** The Patten report on police reform is published. **11 October** Peter Mandelson replaces Mo Mowlam as secretary of state. **18 November** George Mitchell releases details of the proposals for the establishment of the executive. **27 November** The Ulster Unionist Council votes in favor of the Mitchell proposals opening the way for devolution. **29 November** The Northern Ireland executive is selected using the D'Hondt mechanism. The executive includes members from the UUP, DUP, SDLP, and SF. **1 December** Power is devolved to the Northern Ireland Assembly from midnight. On the following day, the Irish government removes the constitutional claim to Northern Ireland while the Anglo–Irish Agreement is also replaced. **13 December** The first meeting of the NSMC is held. **17 December** The first meeting of the British–Irish Council is held.

**2000** **31 January** General John de Chastelain of the IICD delivers a report on the likelihood of arms decommissioning to the British and Irish governments. **3 February** With David Trimble threatening to resign as first minister over the issue of paramilitary weapons, Peter Mandelson says he will suspend the Assembly if the IRA does not begin decommissioning weapons. **11 February** Negotiations fail to resolve the issue of the decommissioning of weapons and Mandelson suspends the executive. **25 March** UUP MP Rev. Martin Smyth opposes Trimble in a party leadership contest. Trimble wins by 56.8 percent to 43.2 percent, highlighting divisions within the party on the Agreement. **6 May** An IRA statement says it is ready to begin a process that will "completely and verifiably" put its weapons beyond use within the context of devolution. **16 May** A government bill to reform the police is published. **27 May** The Ulster Unionist Council agrees to reenter the executive prior to IRA decommissioning. **29 May** Power is again devolved at midnight. **26 June** Two international arms inspectors say they have inspected IRA arms dumps and that the arms cannot be used without this being detected. There are further inspections on 26 October and on 30 November 2001. **21 September** The DUP wins a by-election in South Antrim. The result indicates increasing unionist disillusionment with the Agreement. **28 October** David Trimble wins a vote in the Ulster Unionist Council but promises to take a stronger line on the decommissioning of weapons and to bar SF members from meetings of the NSMC. **22 November** Legislation on the reform of policing becomes law; however, the name of the new police force has yet to be decided. **5 December** The IRA calls for the full implementation of the Patten Report. **12 De-**

**cember** President Clinton pays a third visit to Northern Ireland, as well as visiting the Republic.

**2001    24 January** John Reid is appointed secretary of state for Northern Ireland. **30 January** Belfast High Court rules against Trimble's ban on SF ministers attending NSMC meetings. **7 June** The U.K. general election sees further gains for SF and the DUP. **19 June** Rioting breaks out in North Belfast after loyalist protests surrounding Holy Cross Primary School. **1 July** Trimble resigns as first minister over the lack of movement on arms decommissioning, triggering a six-week period to resolve the arms dispute. **9 July** Political talks are held in Weston Park, England, but fail to break the political deadlock. The UFF withdraws its support for the Belfast Agreement. **1 August** A package of measures from the British and Irish governments aimed at breaking the political deadlock fails to win the support of most Northern Ireland parties. **10 August** John Reid suspends the Assembly for 24 hours, thus providing 6 more weeks for negotiation. **21 September** A second technical suspension of the Assembly provides six more weeks for negotiation. **8 October** The SDLP rejects a UUP motion to exclude SF from the executive. **12 October** The government withdraws recognition of the UDA's ceasefire because of continuing loyalist violence. **18 October** UUP ministers resign from the executive. **23 October** The IRA says it has begun a process of putting arms beyond use. The IICD confirms it has witnessed the disposal of arms. **24 October** Trimble renominates UUP ministers to the Northern Ireland executive. **2 November** Trimble fails to be reelected as first minister when two members of his own party do not support him. **4 November** The Police Service of Northern Ireland (PSNI) replaces the RUC. **6 November** Trimble is finally reelected with the help of middle-ground parties. **11 November** Mark Durkan succeeds John Hume as leader of the SDLP. **28 November** The UDP is disbanded by the UDA and replaced by the Ulster Political Research Group.

**2002    21 January** SF MPs take offices at Westminster but do not take part in debates or House of Commons committee work. **17 March** There is a break-in at the special branch offices at Castlereagh police station in Belfast. **8 April** The IRA puts a second batch of weapons beyond use. **17 May** FF wins the Irish general election but has no overall majority. **29 May** Hugh Orde is appointed chief constable of the PSNI.

**2 June** Sectarian rioting occurs in East Belfast. **5 June** Alex Maskey becomes the first SF member to be elected lord mayor of Belfast. **17 July** The IRA issues a statement apologizing to "noncombatant" victims of its campaign. **25 September** The UDA expels its West Belfast leader, Johnny Adair, over links with the LVF. **4 October** SF offices at Stormont are raided by police investigating republican intelligence gathering. **8 October** Trimble says the UUP will withdraw from the executive in a week unless the government proposes the expulsion of SF. **14 October** John Reid suspends devolved institutions. **24 October** Paul Murphy becomes secretary of state.

**2003  2 February** A leading UDA member is shot dead during an ongoing loyalist feud. Johnny Adair, his family, and supporters subsequently leave Northern Ireland. **22 February** The UDA announces a 12-month ceasefire. **10 April** A joint British–Irish plan for the complete implementation of the GFA is postponed because the IRA's response is considered insufficient. **1 May** The British government postpones Northern Ireland Assembly elections because the IRA position lacks clarity. **17 June** Trimble wins a narrow majority in the UUC to support government proposals to break the GFA deadlock—this includes an independent monitoring commission on paramilitary ceasefires. Three UUP MPs say they are resigning the party whip. **21 October** Blair announces Assembly elections. A third act of decommissioning of IRA weapons takes place, but there is a dispute surrounding details of the amount of weapons involved. **26 November** Northern Ireland Assembly elections see the DUP and SF become the biggest unionist and nationalist parties. **18 December** UUP MP Jeffrey Donaldson and two other Assembly members resign from the party.

**2004  5 January** Jeffrey Donaldson and the two Assembly members who resigned from the UUP join the DUP. **7 January** The British and Irish governments establish an Independent Monitoring Commission (IMC) to report on activity by paramilitary groups, the normalization of security measures, and claims by Assembly parties that other parties, or ministers in a devolved executive, are not living up to the standards required of them. **3 February** A review of the working of the GFA begins at Stormont. **20 February** The police say the IRA is responsible for kidnapping a republican from a bar in Belfast. **2 March** The UUP withdraws from the review because the government will not exclude SF from talks following the kidnapping of 20 February. **20 April** The IMC recommends financial penalties against SF and the PUP because of ongoing IRA and UVF activity. **11 June** In European Parliamentary elections, Jim Allister retains a seat for the DUP formerly held by Ian Paisley while SF wins a seat instead of the SDLP. The UUP retains the third seat. **18 September** Intensive negotiations between the parties at Leeds Castle, England, fail to achieve a breakthrough. **4 October** Ian Paisley meets Taoiseach Bertie Ahern in Dublin for talks. **12 November** The government accepts a UDA ceasefire declared in February 2003 as valid. **17 November** The British and Irish governments present a set of proposals to the DUP and SF to try to break the political deadlock. **29 November** Gerry Adams meets the chief constable of the PSNI for talks in London. **7 December** Adams says SF should accept the latest proposals. The DUP remains concerned over the issue of decommissioning. **20 December** There is a £26.5 million bank robbery on the Northern Bank in central Belfast.

**2005** **7 January** The PSNI says the IRA carried out the Northern Bank robbery of 20 December 2004. **9 January** Taoiseach Bertie Ahern says SF leaders knew the IRA was planning the Northern Bank robbery. **18 January** The IRA denies any involvement in the Northern Bank robbery. **30 January** A Belfast man, Robert McCartney, is murdered by IRA members following an argument in a bar in central Belfast. **10 February** A report from the IMC says senior SF members authorized the Northern Bank robbery. **25 February** The IRA says it has dismissed three of its members associated with the McCartney murder. **12 March** The Orange Order formally severs its links with the UUP. **30 March** The UDA expels its East Belfast leader, Jim Gray. **5 May** The DUP wins nine seats in the U.K. general election; SF wins five, the SDLP three, while the UUP retains only one seat. **7 May** Peter Hain replaces Paul Murphy as secretary of state. **24 June** Sir Reg Empey becomes leader of the UUP in succession to David Trimble. **28 July** An IRA statement announces an end to their armed campaign. **1 August** The government announces that the number of troops in Northern Ireland will be reduced from more than 10,500 to 5,000 within two years. **20 August** Sectarian rioting breaks out at an interface in East Belfast. **10 September** A wave of loyalist rioting lasting three days breaks out following the blocking of an Orange parade in part of West Belfast. **26 September** The IICD says it believes the IRA has decommissioned all its weapons. **4 October** Jim Gray is shot dead by rival loyalists. **22 November** The government announces proposals for the biggest changes to local government in 30 years. **23 November** The House of Commons introduces legislation exempting those wanted for crimes committed before the GFA from serving jail terms. The bill is dropped in January 2006 due to widespread opposition. **8 December** A political row erupts after charges against three men allegedly involved in the "Stormontgate" affair, which led to the suspension of the Assembly, were dropped. **16 December** It emerges that Denis Donaldson, one of those who had faced charges, had been spying on republicans for the government.

**2006    1 February** An IMC report says that all paramilitary groups are still involved in illegal activity, but the level of violence is decreasing. **8 February** The House of Commons votes to restore Westminster allowances to SF MPs who had been withdrawn following allegations of IRA involvement in the Northern Bank robbery. The move is a response to the IMC report recognizing the scaling-down of IRA activity. **25 February** Forty people are arrested after a republican protest against a proposed unionist rally in Dublin erupts into violence. **9 March** The government announces details of redundancy packages for 3,000 soldiers in the Northern Ireland–based regiments of the Royal Irish Regiment, which are to be phased out in August 2007. **4 April** Denis Donaldson is found shot dead at a cottage in Co. Donegal. **6 April** Blair and Ahern announce that the Northern Ireland Assembly is to be recalled on 15 May to attempt to form an executive. If no agreement is reached then, Assembly members' salaries will be stopped on 24 November. **11 April** Former UUP leader David Trimble is awarded a peerage. Three DUP members also receive peerages and become the party's first members in the House of Lords. **11 May** The Northern Ireland Women's Coalition announces that it is to disband after 10 years in politics. **15 May** Political parties meet at Stormont for talks. **22 May** An attempt to elect a new Northern Ireland executive fails. **19 June** Police arrest 10 people in connection with an RIRA attempt to purchase weapons. **3 August** Following the UDA inner council decision to replace the organization's leadership in North Belfast, a number of people associated with the previous leadership leave Northern Ireland. **9 August** RIRA firebombs destroy four shops in Newry, Co. Down. There are further attacks by the organization in the following days. **13 October** After three days of talks, the British and Irish governments announce the St. Andrews

Agreement. **17 October** In the Assembly, the Preparation for Government Committee begins meeting to work toward agreement on devolution. A meeting of the Programme for Government Committee is postponed following a dispute over the details of the proposed ministerial pledge of office. **31 October** A number of shops in Belfast are damaged by firebombs planted by republican dissidents. **6 November** The SF national executive gives qualified support to the St. Andrews Agreement. **16 November** The government outlines proposals to turn parts of the St. Andrews Agreement into law. **24 November** The Assembly meets at Stormont in an attempt to nominate first and deputy first ministers. **12 December** The UDA says that it rejects the St. Andrews Agreement.

**2007** **8 January** PUP leader David Ervine dies following a heart attack and stroke. **22 January** A police ombudsman's report reveals collusion between RUC special branch members and the UVF. **28 January** SF votes to support the PSNI. **30 January** An IMC report says that the IRA has abandoned violence and terrorism. **7 March** A Northern Ireland Assembly election returns the DUP and SF as the two largest parties. **26 March** The latest deadline for devolution passes. Ian Paisley and Gerry Adams meet for direct talks for the first time. Devolution is agreed for 8 May. **27 March** Jim Allister, Member of European Parliament (MEP), resigns from the DUP. **2 April** Parties indicate their choices of ministerial posts in advance of devolution. **4 April** Paisley and Ahern meet for talks in Dublin. **16 April** An SF delegation meets the Policing Board for the first time. **3 May** The UVF says it is taking a nonmilitary role and has put its weapons beyond reach. **8 May** Power is devolved to the Northern Ireland Assembly. **27 June** Gordon Brown becomes prime minister of the United Kingdom. **28 June** Shaun Woodward becomes secretary of state. **31 July** The British Army operation in support of the police is officially ended.

# Introduction

## THE NORTHERN IRELAND CONFLICT— WHY IS ANYONE INTERESTED?

It has often been noted that in relation to its size, approximately 5,500 square miles and with a population of less than 1.7 million, Northern Ireland is possibly the most researched area in the world. Why should this be the case? The answer lies partly in the fact that the conflict in Northern Ireland, which broke out in 1968, was viewed as an anomaly; it was a "religious" conflict in a world where religious adherence was apparently in decline; it was taking place in western Europe, one of the most politically stable parts of the world; and it was a conflict within the borders of one of the wealthiest nations in the world, the United Kingdom. Another important factor was the interest of the United States, both because of the "historic relationship" with Great Britain and the potential damage to American interests that instability in the United Kingdom might cause. In addition to this, there was the interest of Irish Americans in the outcome of the conflict.

Another reason for the inordinate interest in Northern Ireland, leading to an abundance of material being produced about it, has been that Northern Ireland has been an easily accessible area for researchers. Many of those directly involved have also been willing to express their viewpoints, making the causes of the conflict more transparent. The presence of two universities, libraries, and other centers of research have also provided a base for academics and students of the conflict and peace process, in turn leading to the production of a veritable mountain of material on the Troubles.

## BACKGROUND

Culture, economics, and geography all played a part in the formation of political identity in Britain and Ireland, but as Irish nationalism developed in the 19th century, it was religious affiliation that became the easiest identifier of national identity. The conflicting demands of nationalists in Ireland for greater self-government and of unionists, who feared the political implications of government by a Catholic nationalist Dublin-based Parliament, were never successfully reconciled. The outbreak of World War I and the Easter Rising of 1916 by radical republicans shifted the framework of the debate from one of home rule for Ireland to one of independence from Britain, with unionists, if possible, even more opposed to the latter. The outcome of the subsequent conflict was a somewhat makeshift settlement that effectively made 26 of Ireland's counties self-governing, while the 6 counties in the northeast with the highest proportion of Protestants (and therefore unionists) controlled domestic affairs in the new state of Northern Ireland. Crucially, however, as part of the United Kingdom, the Parliament of Northern Ireland remained subordinate to Parliament in London.

For most of the four decades after the partitioning of Ireland in 1921, relations between Northern Ireland and the Free State (later the Republic of Ireland) remained cold—as indeed did relations between the Republic and Britain. Within Ireland, the general situation was summed up by the Ulster Unionist prime minister of Northern Ireland, Lord Craigavon, who told the Northern Ireland Parliament in April 1934 that "in the south they boasted of a Catholic State. They still boast of Southern Ireland being a Catholic State. All I boast of is that we are a Protestant Parliament and a Protestant state." Thus the rights of minorities on both sides of the border fell far behind the desire of the majorities to promote their own exclusivist national agenda.

While the attitude of "taking care of your own" was widely accepted practice in the period before 1945, in the post–World War II era, different views prevailed. There was greater support for the concepts of human and civil rights and for the rights of specific groups. Within the United Kingdom, reforms in the educational system opened up access to university education, and the greater numbers of students and graduates who were emerging from these institutions were demanding jobs and pay in line with their qualifications. In Northern Ireland this helped produce a radical elite more willing to challenge the social, economic, and political status quo. Developments in communications, not least in radio and television coverage, also opened up coverage of events and government policy to closer inspection. The late 1960s was also a period when the baby boom generation were in their late teens and early twenties, creating a larger number of potentially radical younger people within the population as a whole.

Within Northern Ireland additional factors with the potential to lead to political instability were also at play. Northern Ireland remained the poorest part of the United Kingdom, with the highest rate of unemployment, and its often provincial, if not parochial, attitudes may have made it slower to adapt to the need to change. However, at a time when the Catholic population within Northern Ireland was growing and demanding an increased share of jobs, Northern Ireland's traditional industries were in decline. The location of new industries, for example, factories producing manmade fibers, predominantly in the more accessible (but also more Protestant) east of the province, was, therefore, also a source of grievance among Catholics.

## THE APPROACH OF THE TROUBLES

Although there had been significant sectarian conflict at the time of partition in the early 1920s, Northern Ireland remained relatively peaceful for most of the 50 years that followed. There was a severe but short-lived outbreak of rioting in Belfast in July 1935 and a more prolonged, but low-key, Irish Republican Army (IRA) campaign along the border with the Republic between 1956 and 1962, but these served more to keep Protestant–Catholic mutual suspicions alive rather than to pose a threat to the existence of the state. Throughout this period the Ulster Unionist Party (UUP) continued to provide the government and prime minister in Northern Ireland, but the 1950s and early 1960s saw growing support for the Northern Ireland Labour Party (NILP) in Belfast, where the NILP threatened to displace the UUP as the largest political party. It was partly as a result of this that Terence O'Neill, UUP leader and prime minister of Northern Ireland from 1963, undertook a program of economic reform allied to a policy aimed at improving relations with Catholics within Northern Ireland, as well as with the Republic of Ireland.

Any move toward social and political reform inevitably risked a reaction from the right wing of unionism, both from within the UUP itself and from outside, the latter most prominently represented by firebrand Protestant fundamentalist minister Rev. Ian Paisley, as well as from the loyalist terrorist organization Ulster Volunteer Force (UVF), which emerged in 1966. The hand of history also continued to play a part in the situation in that celebrations of the 50th anniversary of the Easter Rising in 1916 strengthened both nationalist expectations and unionist fears over the prospect of a united Ireland. From this point, pressure continued to grow on O'Neill from those who, on one side, believed reform was going too slowly or, on the other, believed it was either unnecessary or moving too quickly. O'Neill's position was further complicated by the return of a Labour government to power at Westminster in 1964, with the expectation that Labour would be more sympathetic toward nationalist concerns than previous Conservative governments had been. O'Neill was, therefore, caught between the need to continue political and economic reform while retaining party support for the UUP and maintaining political stability.

The Campaign for Social Justice (formed in 1964) had already begun campaigning against discriminatory practices against Catholics in employment, public appointments, housing allocation, electoral boundaries, and electoral practices, but after the formation of the Northern Ireland Civil Rights Association (NICRA) in 1967, this campaign was expanded, leading to a series of protest marches in 1968. The left wing and republican connections of a number of those associated with NICRA inevitably led unionists to question whether the organization's "real" agenda was the reform of Northern Ireland or the destruction of the state.

While the first civil rights protests occurred in Catholic areas, where they received greater support, the security situation began to deteriorate when marches were planned to pass through what were perceived to be Protestant areas. In this arena, as in so many others associated with the Northern Ireland conflict, perception was highly important. Although most Protestants viewed these marches as nationalist and republican protests, most Catholics saw them as protests for civil rights and against discrimination. The use of force by the Royal Ulster Constabulary (RUC) against civil rights marchers in the Waterside area of Derry in October 1968 helped harden attitudes on both sides. For nationalists, the "Orange State" had shown that it was incapable of providing equal treatment to Catholics, while for unionists demands for "civil rights" were merely a front for an attack on Northern Ireland itself. A march by the radical students' group People's Democracy (PD) in January 1969, which was attacked by loyalists near Derry, strengthened these views and was arguably the point of no return from which major sectarian conflict became inevitable.

Under increasing pressure, O'Neill called a general election for the Northern Ireland Parliament in February 1969 but failed to see off the critics of his moderate reformist policies. Instead, the outcome of the election served only to highlight the political divisions within unionism between the more liberal and conservative wings and was followed by O'Neill's resignation.

## THE OUTBREAK OF SECTARIAN CONFLICT

There had been rumblings of discontent and protest during the spring of 1969, but the advent of the Protestant Orange Order's marching season ratcheted up tension even further with rioting breaking out on the main Orange day of the year, 12 July. This outbreak of violence saw the first death of the modern Troubles, Francis McCloskey, who died after being struck by a police baton. Where the RUC had generally been able to contain violence up to this time, the riots that followed an Orange parade in Derry on 12 August (the "Battle of the Bogside") spread to Belfast and other areas and disintegrated into open sectarian conflict. The deployment of soldiers on the streets of Derry and Belfast in support of the RUC in the following days was the beginning of a policy that would continue for more than three decades. The Ulster Unionist government continued to introduce reforms, but in the face of increasing nationalist expectations, unionist opposition, and continuing violence, this proved a more difficult task than before. The situation was further complicated by the emergence and growth of republican and loyalist vigilante "paramilitary" groups in the shape of the IRA and the loyalist Ulster Defence Association (UDA) in addition to the already existing UVF.

In August 1971, the Ulster Unionist government, now led by Brian Faulkner, introduced internment without trial in an attempt to undermine republican paramilitaries. However, the impact was disastrous and led instead to a further escalation in violence and the onset of the worst period of the Troubles. In January 1972, the political situation deteriorated further when 13 protestors were shot dead by the British Army at the end of a civil rights march and rally in Derry in what became known as "Bloody Sunday" (a 14th man died later). The U.K. government, now under Conservative Prime Minister Edward Heath, demanded that the Ulster Unionists give up control of security policy to the Westminster government, and when the Northern Ireland government rejected this demand, the Northern Ireland Parliament was suspended and a system of "direct rule" from London was introduced with a new government department, the Northern Ireland Office (NIO), headed by a secretary of state who was part of the British cabinet, being established to run Northern Ireland affairs.

## THE SEARCH FOR A NEW POLITICAL SETTLEMENT

Having removed one political framework, however, the U.K. government found it impossible to find a workable replacement. The realistic limits of a settlement were clear enough—unionists would not accept a united Ireland, while nationalists would not accept unionist domination, and any agreement would require the acceptance of both the British and Irish governments. In practical terms, however, this still left an enormous gap in what the various political actors wanted or at least would accept. Many republicans and nationalists still wanted a united Ireland immediately, and many unionists wanted majority rule to be restored. Even among those who were prepared to compromise, there were directly opposing objectives—nationalists required a settlement to have a dynamic that would inevitably lead to a united Ireland, while unionists rejected this and would only work with the Republic on issues that it considered to be of practical benefit to Northern Ireland but without posing a threat to Northern Ireland's position within the United Kingdom. In practice, the mutual antipathy of unionists and nationalists, added to each groups' expectations and fears against an ongoing background of violence, made any political settlement almost impossible to achieve.

If a settlement was to be achieved, it had to reflect the political geography of the situation; in effect, this meant that as a minimum nationalists required a direct input into how Northern Ireland was governed (effectively a "power-sharing" administration) and a formal political arrangement between Northern Ireland and the Republic. Many unionists also supported the idea of a devolved administration for Northern Ireland but were suspicious of the potential slippage toward either joint British–Irish authority over Northern Ireland or a united Ireland, and they were suspicious of the political intent behind North–South bodies. As a minimum, unionists required an assurance that they would not be coerced into any political arrangement against their wishes. The success or failure of any structures would also depend on stable and generally amicable relations between Great Britain and the Republic with regard to Northern Ireland matters.

A variety of political initiatives emphasizing one or more aspects of these relationships were tried over the next 25 years: the Sunningdale Agreement, the Constitutional Convention, the Atkins Talks, Rolling Devolution, the Anglo–Irish Agreement, the Brooke and Mayhew Talks, and the Frameworks Documents, but all failed to produce a settlement acceptable to a broad enough audience. Lack of trust between unionists and nationalists was also exacerbated by continuing violence, which, by itself, had the potential to undermine any agreement reached by the political parties.

## THE PEACE PROCESS

It is difficult to put a precise starting date to the peace process in Northern Ireland; the level of violence, though still significant, had generally been in decline after its peak in the early and mid-1970s, but republican and loyalist paramilitary groups still continued to think primarily in terms of the use of violence to achieve their aims.

By the 1990s, the security situation had reached a stalemate. While British security forces had been unable to defeat the IRA, equally the IRA's military campaign showed no sign of achieving their political objective of a united Ireland. Loyalist paramilitaries also continued to attack republicans and often Catholics at large as a way of, as some of them saw it, "terrorizing the terrorist."

The IRA's political wing, Sinn Fein (SF), had entered Northern Irish politics in the wake of the 1981 hunger strike campaign by republican prisoners to regain political status, but the party's level of electoral support appeared to be stuck at approximately 10 percent of the poll. Republican leaders were, however, increasingly coming to believe that political methods, or at least an armed campaign allied with electoral politics, would have a better chance of bringing about a united Ireland than the use of violence alone. A number of misjudged IRA operations, not least the Enniskillen "Poppy Day" bomb of 1987 in which 11 civilians were killed, also encouraged republicans to look for an alternate approach. As a result, throughout the 1990s political activity increasingly took precedence over paramilitary activity leading to the declaration of an IRA ceasefire in August 1994.

Before this position was reached, however, there was a long "feeling out" period between the British government and SF and the IRA, which included a secret "back channel" route of communication between the two sides. Discussions began to pick up pace in February 1993 when the British claimed that they received a statement from the IRA saying, "The conflict is over, but we need your advice on how to bring it to a close." Although republicans have continually denied that they sent this message, the outcome was that a more detailed level of communication between the two sides did develop. Contacts between loyalist paramilitary groups and the British and Irish governments also began to grow at this time.

Arguably the key political document of this period, and perhaps of the previous quarter century, was the Downing Street Declaration of December 1993, signed by British prime minister John Major and Irish taoiseach Albert Reynolds. Unlike its predecessors, the declaration managed to successfully balance the aspirations of many nationalists and unionists without arousing undue fear on either side. The British government stated that it had no selfish interest in Northern Ireland's affairs and that it wanted to see peace, stability, and reconciliation among all the people of Ireland. It added that such an agreement might lead to a united Ireland and that it was for the people of Ireland alone to decide this. This statement was generally in line with proposals that had been submitted to the Irish government by nationalist Social Democratic and Labour Party's (SDLP) leader John Hume and SF president Gerry Adams in September 1993.

Where the Declaration differed fundamentally from the Hume–Adams proposals was in stating that it was for the people of Ireland alone, "by agreement between the two parts, to exercise their right of self-determination on the basis of consent, freely and concurrently given, North and South, to bring about a united Ireland, if that is their wish." This somewhat convoluted sentence was crucial in maintaining a degree of unionist support for the developing peace process. It took the nationalist rhetoric of the Hume–Adams proposals but inserted what republicans would refer to as the "unionist veto" by accepting the need for the consent of Northern unionists to any future settlement. While any future settlement might lead to a united Ireland, equally the "agreed Ireland" reached in the settlement might well be one in which Ireland was politically divided. While republicans did not accept the Declaration, equally they did not reject it out of hand, and with most unionists also prepared to accept the Declaration, the peace process was kept alive.

Although the transition to democratic politics for republicans was not easy or straightforward—the IRA broke its ceasefire in February 1996 before resuming it in July 1997 (and even after this there were high-profile breaches of its ceasefire)—nevertheless a transition did take place. This change was aided by the growing electoral success of SF, a success that was itself partly a result of the party's role in the developing peace process. By mid-2005, SF had become the second largest party in the North and was also a growing political force in the Republic. With the reduction in the level of violence brought about by the IRA ceasefire, added to ceasefires by the major loyalist paramilitary organizations (which were also far from perfectly observed), the prospects of attaining a stable political settlement improved.

Even with the substantial amount of political negotiation that had taken place between the parties (SF excluded) in the Brooke and Mayhew talks, the process of negotiation still took longer than many expected. If the Downing Street Declaration set the broad terms for the political settlement, then the British and Irish governments' Heads of Agreement document of January 1998 narrowed the parameters further. This document proposed balanced constitutional changes to the Republic's claim to Northern Ireland and the United Kingdom's Government of Ireland Act, a new Northern Ireland Assembly with responsibility for local government departments, a new British–Irish Agreement to replace the Anglo–Irish Agreement so loathed by unionists, an intergovernmental council consisting of representatives of political assemblies throughout Britain and Ireland, a North–South Ministerial Council that would be accountable to the Northern Ireland Assembly, and the Irish Parliament with implementation bodies to oversee policies agreed upon by this Council.

After further negotiation, a political package did eventually emerge in the form of the Belfast Agreement on Good Friday 1998. Also known as the Good Friday Agreement (GFA), the Belfast Agreement was a more wide-ranging document than any of its predecessors, but inevitably areas of "constructive ambiguity" were required to ensure that agreement between unionists and nationalists was reached in the first place, and this would become a source of difficulty as the implementation of the Agreement progressed.

Although the package was overwhelmingly endorsed in referendums in Northern Ireland and the Republic of Ireland, it was clear from the outset that Protestants were more tentative about the GFA than Catholics—approximately 55 percent of Protestants voted for the Agreement compared to 95 percent of Catholics. This division within the Protestant community became more apparent in the first elections to the new Northern Ireland Assembly when almost half of the unionists returned were opponents of the GFA.

As the implementation of the Agreement followed, it became evident that there was a distinct difference in how Protestants and Catholics viewed this process. For most Catholics, nationalists and unionists benefited equally from the GFA, but for most Protestants it was nationalists who gained most from the Agreement. Once again, security-related issues were a significant factor in the decline of unionist support for the Agreement—while the government chose to downplay paramilitary criminality, such as internal disputes or attacks on individuals allegedly linked to petty crime in an attempt not to destabilize their ceasefires, at the same time the scaling-down of security force numbers and the reform of the police continued apace. As a result, the Agreement was often accused by its critics of helping to create a "mafia culture." The issue of the decommissioning of paramilitary weapons, and in particular IRA weapons because SF was entitled to two seats in the Northern Ireland executive (loyalist paramilitary-related parties won only two Assembly seats and were not entitled to any executive representation), became the key issue during the Northern Ireland Assembly's first term. The failure to resolve this issue led to intermittent, and eventually a final, suspension of the Assembly in October 2002. Fresh Assembly elections in November 2003 saw Ian Paisley's Democratic Unionist Party (DUP) and SF returned as the two largest parties, confirming the decline in unionist support for the Agreement and SF's rise to become the largest nationalist party.

The main republican movement's progression toward exclusively political means was continuing meanwhile; several caches of IRA weapons had already been put "beyond use" (though not decommissioned in the way the GFA had implied) before the IRA declared in July 2005 that it was ending its "armed campaign." In September, it was announced that almost all of its weapons had been put beyond use.

Despite this, the mutual antipathy of the two main parties, now the DUP and SF, remained, and while both parties supported the return of a devolved administration to Northern Ireland, it was unclear what form this would take. By the end of 2005, it seemed likely that while the general structure of the GFA would remain intact, it would not operate in the way that had originally been intended in 1998. Further political discussions took place in 2006, with DUP objections to entering an executive that included SF now centering on SF's failure to give support to the Police Service of Northern Ireland (PSNI). Following political talks at St. Andrews in Scotland in October 2006, the government introduced new legislation paving the way for fresh Assembly elections in March 2007, which it hoped would then be followed by the creation of an executive.

## THE LEGACY OF THE TROUBLES

Despite the signing of the GFA, the legacy of the Troubles was far from being resolved. More than 3,500 deaths, tens of thousands injured, and hundreds of millions of pounds worth of damage could not simply be forgotten. While the "war" might be over, suspicion and, in some cases hatred, remained. This was clear in the continuing residential segregation of Protestants and Catholics and the continued building of peace lines to prevent sectarian conflicts after 1998. The "zero sum" mentality, where one side believed it had lost if the other gained and vice versa, still had a stronghold on the political psyche of Northern Irish politics, and if Catholics felt less isolated and alienated from the state, this had partly been bought at the cost of greater Protestant alienation, particularly in

Protestant working-class areas that (like their Catholic counterparts) had been on the frontline of the Troubles.

By 2007, Northern Ireland remained something of a paradox. There was increasing prosperity, more people were in employment than ever before, and government statistics claimed that unemployment was at an all-time low at just over 4 percent. At the same time, there was no "feel good" factor. The government was determined to reduce Northern Ireland's heavy reliance on public sector employment, bringing a degree of uncertainty to job security, while the "peace dividend" hyped by Tony Blair and others in an attempt to sell the GFA in 1998 had, as far as the people of Northern Ireland were concerned, singularly failed to appear. Northern Ireland's economy, however, remained heavily reliant on government expenditure, with £8,200 per person being spent in Northern Ireland in 2006 (the area with the next highest level of government spending was Scotland, which received £7,600 per person). With rising local taxes, as well as continuing, if slowly diminishing, paramilitary activity (not least the IRA's record £26.5 million robbery of a Belfast bank in late 2004), it was hardly surprising that there was disillusionment with the GFA, particularly among unionists.

Another underlying issue in many of the disputes that surrounded events in Northern Ireland after 1998 was that of political legitimacy. The Troubles had ended with no clear winner or loser between unionism and nationalism—Northern Ireland remained part of the United Kingdom for as long as the people of Northern Ireland wished it to remain so; however, post-GFA Northern Ireland was not an "Orange state" dominated by unionists, and an Irish dimension had become part of the political framework. Still, one might conjecture that, given the growing Catholic population of Northern Ireland and the increasing cooperation between the United Kingdom and Ireland over the previous three decades, such developments were probably inevitable. If this was the case, it raised the question of why paramilitary organizations, and particularly the IRA, who were by far the largest single agency responsible for deaths, continued their campaigns for such a long time. Although loyalist paramilitaries could at least make the claim (which was open to debate) that they had helped safeguard the union with Britain, republicans had fought for 30 years to achieve a 32-county socialist republic and had failed to achieve it. As a result, it became particularly important for republicans to legitimize the achievements of the "armed struggle." This was done primarily by claiming that their campaign had helped bring about a transitional phase, which, through the mechanisms of the GFA, would lead to a united Ireland. Some republicans also laid claim to the mantel of civil rights campaigners, arguing that their campaign had been for civil and human rights as much as for national rights. Government activity in Northern Ireland also appeared to be somewhat schizophrenic. On one hand, overall government policy in the arena of community relations called for Northern Irish society to have a shared future, yet on the other hand, it also pursued policies, such as the proposals for the restructuring of district councils, which had the potential to create even greater sectarian division. By early 2007 the framework for a political settlement existed, and the level of violence had been dramatically reduced, but continuing political disagreements meant that a Northern Ireland executive could still not be established.

In the wake of the March 2007 Assembly elections, however, another political breakthrough occurred when the DUP and SF, now clearly established as the two largest parties, agreed to participate in a devolved executive. The announcement was accompanied by a historic photograph of Ian Paisley and Gerry Adams sitting at adjacent tables (though not side by side). The following months saw SF signing up to participate in the policing board, the allocation of executive ministries, and the devolution of power on 8 May. Northern Ireland at last appeared to be entering a new era and putting the conflict behind it.

Despite this, after three decades of conflict and another covering a peace process, Northern Ireland is still far from being a society fully at peace with itself. In many ways repairing the physical damage of the Troubles appears to be a less difficult task than repairing the emotional damage of the conflict, and significant reconciliation may well take many more decades.

# The Dictionary

**ADAMS, GERARD (GERRY) (1948– ).** President of **Sinn Fein** (SF), Gerry Adams was born in **Belfast** on 6 October 1948 into a strongly Irish **republican** family. He was educated at St. Mary's Christian Brothers School, Belfast. He left school at the age of 17 and worked as a barman before becoming involved in the events of **the Troubles**. Although he is widely believed to have become a member of the **Irish Republican Army** (IRA), Adams himself has always denied this assertion. In 1971 he was interned on the basis that he was the leader of the Provisional IRA (PIRA) in the Ballymurphy area of West Belfast at that time. Following the announcement of a short-lived ceasefire in late June 1972, he participated in talks between IRA leaders and Secretary of State **William Whitelaw**. He was rearrested in 1973, and subsequent failed attempts to escape from the **Maze Prison** saw him sentenced to a further 18 months of imprisonment. In the following four years, while still in prison, he is reputed to have written a series of articles for *Republican News* under the penname Brownie. Significantly, these articles called for republicans to develop a political program besides continuing an armed campaign to achieve a united Ireland.

In November 1978 Adams was **elected** vice president of SF, demonstrating the shift in power within the republican movement toward the North. This shift was again highlighted during the 1981 **hunger strike** campaign when Adams played a significant, if sometimes cautious, role in encouraging the move toward greater political action by republicans in the wake of the hunger strikes.

In October 1982 SF contested the **Northern Ireland Assembly** elections on an abstentionist policy but won five seats, with Adams topping the poll in the West Belfast constituency. In June 1983 he won the West Belfast seat at **Westminster** when the constitutional **nationalist** vote was split between Joe Hendron of the **Social Democratic and Labour Party** (SDLP) and the sitting Member of Parliament (MP), **Gerry Fitt**. In November of the same year, he was elected president of SF, a position he has retained since then.

In March 1984 he and three other SF members were wounded in an **Ulster Freedom Fighters'** (UFF) gun attack in Belfast. In 1986 he and his supporters overturned the policy of abstention in relation to seats in the **Dail**, prompting the withdrawal of those who formed **Republican Sinn Fein** (RSF). In 1988 he began discussions with SDLP leader **John Hume** to find common ground on the conditions for an all-Ireland settlement. This eventually led to a report on their position being sent to the Irish government in September 1993. In April 1992 he narrowly lost the West Belfast seat in the Westminster general election to the SDLP, with some Protestants choosing to vote for Joe Hendron in order to help defeat Adams. Despite this, the developing republican **peace process** proved popular among Catholic voters and Adams' central role in it gave electoral benefits to him and his party.

In the wake of the IRA ceasefire of August 1994, he became a key figure in political developments, particularly in attempting to maintain the cohesion of the republican movement while meeting the main concerns of other political actors. In practice, however, political developments became stalled on the issue of the **decommissioning** of IRA weapons in advance of SF's participation in political talks. The breakdown of the IRA ceasefire in February 1996 may have damaged Adams and SF's reputation internationally but had no impact on support within republican circles.

In May 1996 he was elected to the **Northern Ireland Forum** and in May 1997 easily won back the West Belfast seat at Westminster, a seat he has retained since that time. With the **Labour Party** in power in Great Britain, the demand for the decommissioning of IRA weapons in advance of all-party talks was dropped, and SF entered negotiations in September 1997 following the reinstatement of an IRA ceasefire in July 1997.

In the wake of the **Good Friday Agreement** (GFA), he was successful in maintaining support for his policies with the bulk of the republican movement, presenting involvement in the institutions of

Northern Ireland as part of a transitional phase toward a united Ireland. However, he was unable to reconcile **unionist** and British demands for IRA decommissioning and an end to continuing IRA activities with the requirements of the republican movement. This created instability in the devolved administration, leading to suspensions, and then the collapse, of the Northern Ireland executive. Despite this, SF continued to make electoral advances under Adams's leadership. In the 2001 Westminster and **district council** elections, SF overtook the SDLP to become the largest nationalist party in Northern Ireland and in 2002 won five seats in the Dail general election. Having been elected to the Northern Ireland Assembly for West Belfast in 1998, he was again returned in 2003 but chose not to be nominated for a ministerial position in the Assembly.

In May 2006 he proposed **Ian Paisley** as first minister and his colleague **Martin McGuinness** as deputy first minister as part of a failed attempt to elect a new Northern Ireland executive. In September 2006, during a visit to the Middle East, he met with members of Hamas in the Palestinian Parliament. In November 2006 he faced renewed death threats from dissident republicans who accused him of selling out republican values as well as from **loyalist paramilitary** Michael Stone. In January 2007, after an SF ard fheis voted to support the **Police Service of Northern Ireland** (PSNI), he called on republicans to join and support the police. In March 2007 he was again returned to the Northern Ireland Assembly in West Belfast. On 26 March 2007, he met Ian Paisley directly for talks for the first time.

**AHERN, BARTHOLOMEW (BERTIE) (1951– ). Fianna Fail** (FF) leader and taoiseach, Bertie Ahern was born in Dublin on 12 September 1951. He was educated at St. Patrick's National School, Drumcondra; St. Aidan's Christian Brothers School, Whitehall; Rathmines College of Commerce; and University College Dublin. Born into a family with strong FF sympathies, he was involved with the party from an early age. After leaving university he initially worked as an accountant but was **elected** to the **Dail** in 1977 from the Dublin central constituency. Under **Charles Haughey** he was an assistant whip (1980–82) and chief whip (March–November 1982). In opposition he held a number of positions, and when FF returned to power in 1987, he was appointed minister for labor. Under **Albert Reynolds**

he was appointed minister of finance in November 1991 and succeeded Reynolds as FF leader in November 1994 but was unable to form a government when the **Irish Labour Party** opted to form a coalition with **Fine Gael** (FG) and the Democratic Left.

After the general election of June 1997, FF returned to power in coalition with the Progressive Democrats (PD), with Ahern becoming taoiseach. His premiership coincided with a new phase in the **peace process**. The advent of a **Labour Party** government in Britain and the reduction of requirements for the **decommissioning** of **paramilitary** weapons were followed by a renewed **Irish Republican Army** (IRA) ceasefire in July 1997 and opened the way for fresh negotiations. Ahern worked closely with British prime minister **Tony Blair** in facilitating the negotiations, which eventually led to the **Good Friday Agreement** (GFA). He received praise from all sides when, in early April 1998, he returned to the negotiations shortly after the death of his mother.

After the signing of the GFA, he campaigned strongly in favor of a *yes* vote in the referendum held on the GFA, and it received an overwhelming endorsement in the Republic. Despite this, difficulties with the implementation of the GFA in Northern Ireland continued to consume a great deal of his time. With Tony Blair he was involved in the **Weston Park**, **Leeds Castle**, and **St. Andrews Talks**, which produced varying degrees of success.

In May 2002 he became the first taoiseach in more than two decades to retain office following the return of his coalition government in that year's general election. In the autumn of 2006, he faced some criticism for accepting personal loans from business friends; however, public opinion seemed largely unconcerned by these revelations. By the end of 2006, he had become the longest serving taoiseach since Eamon de Valera. After the Irish general election of May 2007, he headed a coalition government led by FF but also included the PD and the Green Party.

**ALDERDICE, JOHN (1955– ).** Leader of the **Alliance Party of Northern Ireland** (APNI) and member of the **Independent Monitoring Commission** (IMC), John Alderdice was born in Ballymena, Co. Antrim, on 28 March 1955. The son of a Presbyterian minister, he was educated at Ballymena Academy; Queen's University, **Belfast** (QUB); and the Royal College of Psychiatrists. As a qualified psychiatrist, he worked in Belfast City Hospital. He joined APNI in 1978 and was a member of Belfast City Council from 1989 until 1997. Alderdice contested the East Belfast constituency in the **Westminster elections** of 1987 and 1992 and the European Parliament election in 1989 but failed to be elected. He was leader of APNI between October 1987 and 1998, becoming party leader before he was elected to Belfast City Council in 1989. He helped steer the party through the difficult post–**Anglo–Irish Agreement** (AIA) period and rejected **unionist** demands for the abolition of the AIA, although he supported calls for the review of its operation. He later led the APNI delegation in the **Brooke–Mayhew Talks**.

In February 1995, following the **Irish Republican Army** (IRA) ceasefire of the previous year, he led his party in their first formal talks with **Sinn Fein** (SF). He participated in the **Forum for Peace and Reconciliation** in Dublin (1994–96) and was elected to the **Northern Ireland Forum** (1996–98). He was also elected to the new **Northern Ireland Assembly** in 1998, although the party's performance, with 6.5 percent of the vote and six seats, was disappointing. In June 1998 he announced that he was retiring as leader of APNI (to the surprise of some of his colleagues) and subsequently accepted the nomination of **Mo Mowlam** to be speaker of the Assembly, a position he held throughout the Assembly's first term.

In October 2003 Alderdice was appointed a member of the IMC, which had been established to monitor the state of **paramilitary** activity in Northern Ireland. In February 2006 he resigned from APNI on the grounds that there might be a conflict of interest with his membership in the IMC. He received a life peerage in 1996 and took the title of Lord Alderdice of Knock in the city of Belfast.

**ALLIANCE PARTY OF NORTHERN IRELAND (APNI).** APNI, often referred to as Alliance, was formed in April 1970. From the outset it drew its support from across the religious divide and from those primarily seeking reform within Northern Ireland and an improvement in **community relations**. Although its base of support was middle class, it initially also gained the support of many former **Northern Ireland Labour Party** (NILP) voters.

In the **district council elections** of May 1973, APNI received almost 95,000 first-preference votes, 13.7 percent of the total, with only the **Ulster Unionist Party** (UUP) receiving more votes. In the

June 1973 **Northern Ireland Assembly** elections, however, it received approximately 66,500 first-preference votes, 9.2 percent of the total, and won eight seats in the Assembly. This result proved to be a more accurate reflection of the party's future electoral performances. In the Northern Ireland executive of 1974, party leader **Oliver Napier** and deputy leader Bob Cooper were responsible for law reform and manpower services, respectively.

In the Northern Ireland **Constitutional Convention** elections held on 1 May 1975, APNI received 9.8 percent of the vote and again won eight seats. In the Convention, Alliance proposed a system of government for Northern Ireland whereby Assembly committees, proportionate to the make up of the Assembly, would be responsible for the various Northern Ireland government departments.

At the time of the 1981 district council elections, APNI received 8.9 percent of the vote and clearly suffered from the polarization created by the **hunger strike** campaign. In the following year's Northern Ireland Assembly election, it received 9.3 percent of first-preference votes and won 10 seats; however with the advent of **Sinn Fein** (SF) in Northern Ireland electoral politics, and with some moderate Catholic voters rallying to the **Social Democratic and Labour Party** (SDLP), it found itself pushed into fifth place in the number of votes cast, and the party would in the future increasingly come to rely on vote transfers from other parties to maintain its position. In the wake of the **Anglo–Irish Agreement** (AIA), APNI's support for the agreement cost it the backing of some Protestant supporters, although the often sterile nature of **unionist** opposition to the AIA and associated violence saw much of this support return. In the June 1987 **Westminster** general election, the party received 10.0 percent of the vote. Despite this, APNI found itself increasingly based in the greater **Belfast** area and in predominantly Protestant constituencies.

As unionist anger against the AIA cooled and political discussions recommenced, APNI played an active role in the **Brooke–Mayhew Talks** of 1991–92 and in the Dublin **Forum for Peace and Reconciliation**, which was established in the wake of the **Irish Republican Army** (IRA) ceasefire of 1994. In the late 1980s, the party faced a challenge from Northern Ireland conservatives for part of its voter base, and in the 1990s, the emergence of the **Northern Ireland**

**Women's Coalition** (NIWC) also produced a challenge for votes. In the **Northern Ireland Forum** election of May 1996, the party received less than 50,000 votes (6.5 percent of the total) and had seven representatives in the Forum. Despite this disappointment the party played an important mediating role during the discussions that led to the **Good Friday Agreement** (GFA). In the subsequent Northern Ireland Assembly elections, the party again received 6.5 percent of votes and won six seats, although some commentators believed that the intervention of the NIWC had cost it two further seats.

In June 1998 the resignation of **John Alderdice** as party leader caused some disquiet within the party. His successor, Sean Neeson, had a short period as party leader, and following disagreements over party policy, such as whether to contest Westminster constituency elections against other pro-GFA parties, Neeson was in turn replaced by David Ford in October 2001.

In November 2001 during the Assembly crisis, which saw **David Trimble** fail to be reelected as first minister, three Alliance Assembly Members redesignated themselves as unionists in order to have Trimble reelected.

In the 2003 Northern Ireland Assembly election, APNI's share of first-preference votes fell to only 3.7 percent, but with the help of vote transfers from other parties, they managed to retain the six seats they had won in 1998. In the May 2005 Westminster general election, they took 3.9 percent of the poll, and in the district council elections held on the same day, they received 5.0 percent of first-preference votes and won 30 council seats. This included an extra seat on the Belfast City Council, where they retained the balance of power between the unionist and **nationalist** blocs.

Despite numerous attempts APNI has never won a Westminster seat, and from the mid-1990s the prospect of this has seemed increasingly unlikely. In April 2006 it was announced that party deputy leader Eileen Bell had been appointed by the secretary of state to be speaker of the Assembly in succession to John Alderdice.

In the March 2007 Northern Ireland Assembly election, APNI received 5.2 percent of first-preference votes and won seven seats. The election of APNI candidate Anna Lo to the Assembly marked the first time that someone born in China had been elected to a representative assembly anywhere in Europe.

**ANCIENT ORDER OF HIBERNIANS (AOH).** Often referred to as the **nationalist** equivalent of the **Orange Order**, the AOH can trace its origins back to at least the earlier 19th century, though some claims trace its antecedents back to two centuries earlier. The AOH was established to defend the Catholic faith and promote Irish nationalism, but with the growth of Irish **republicanism** in the south and partition, its political base of support was drastically restricted. The AOH holds its main annual parade on 15 August (the Feast of the Assumption) and to a lesser extent on 17 March (St. Patrick's Day), though the AOH occasionally suspended **parades** at times of high sectarian tension during **the Troubles**. It has an estimated membership of less than 5,000.

**ANGLO–IRISH AGREEMENT (AIA).** On 15 November 1985, after months of negotiation between British and Irish civil servants, the AIA was signed by Prime Minister **Margaret Thatcher** and Taoiseach **Garret FitzGerald** at Hillsborough Castle in Co. Down. As a result, the AIA was also initially referred to as the Hillsborough Agreement. The AIA stated that any change in the status of Northern Ireland would only come about with the consent of the majority of the people of Northern Ireland; however, the agreement failed to establish what the existing status of Northern Ireland was, leaving the document open to challenge.

The AIA established an Intergovernmental Conference (IGC) to meet regularly to deal with political matters, security and related matters, legal matters (including the administration of justice), and the promotion of cross-cooperation. Article 5 of the agreement dealt with the sensitive area of political matters. Article 5(a) stated that the IGC would look at measures to recognize and accommodate the rights and identities of the two traditions in Northern Ireland: protect human rights and prevent **discrimination**. Article 5(c) stated that, in the absence of a devolved administration, the Irish government could put forward views on proposals for legislation that were within the remit of the Northern Ireland departments in areas where the interests of the Catholic community were particularly affected. Under article 2(b) of the AIA, the British government was also committed to make determined efforts to resolve any differences arising with the Irish government within the IGC.

The Irish government and both **nationalists** and **unionists** in Northern Ireland interpreted the AIA as giving the Irish major input for the running of Northern Ireland, in effect approaching **joint authority**. For the British, however, the Republic of Ireland's role was to be merely consultative, and one of their main contributions, especially as far as Thatcher was concerned, should be to work to achieve improved security cooperation. Eventually both British and Irish expectations of what the AIA was intended to achieve would largely fail to be reached.

While the AIA failed to appeal to **republican** paramilitaries, who believed the agreement copper-fastened partition, the greatest degree of opposition came from unionists. Within days unionist-controlled **district councils** began adjourning in protest of the agreement, forcing the **Northern Ireland Office** (NIO) to set council rates. Secretary of State **Tom King** was attacked outside **Belfast** City Hall, and on 20 November 1985 an anti-AIA rally attended by approximately 200,000 unionists was held outside Belfast City Hall. Protests continued in the subsequent months, including attacks on the site of the Anglo–Irish secretariat at Maryfield near Belfast.

In December 1985, all 15 unionist Members of Parliament (MP) resigned their seats in protest of the agreement in order to create a minireferendum on the AIA. In the January 1986 by-**elections**, almost 420,000 votes were cast for candidates opposing the AIA, but the loss of the Newry and Armagh seat by the **Ulster Unionist Party** (UUP) to the **Social Democratic and Labour Party** (SDLP) made the exercise appear somewhat self-defeating.

In February 1986, **James Molyneaux** and **Ian Paisley** met Thatcher for discussions on the AIA, and there appeared to be agreement on a process for roundtable talks, which would lead to **devolution**; however, on their return to Belfast, it became clear that unionist grassroots would not consider talks while the AIA was in operation, and the idea was dropped. Unionist politicians continued to use the **Northern Ireland Assembly** as a vehicle for opposition to the agreement, and in June 1986 its closure was ordered by King. On the Assembly's final day, Paisley and 21 other Assembly members were forcibly removed from the building while Molyneaux declared that the AIA had made achieving any sort of democracy in Northern Ireland virtually impossible.

The agreement also led to a deterioration in the security situation. On 3 March 1986, a unionist "day of action" shut down commerce and industry in many parts of Northern Ireland and was followed by rioting in **loyalist** areas of Belfast. The AIA also heightened tensions around the tortuous issue of **parades** leading to riots. **Royal Ulster Constabulary** (RUC) officers also faced attacks on their homes by loyalists, adding further pressure to a strained police force. By late 1986 unionist opposition to the AIA still continued. On 10 November 1986, Paisley launched Ulster Resistance with the objective of destroying the AIA, while on 15 November 1986, another 200,000-strong anti-AIA rally was held at Belfast City Hall. Rioting broke out after the rally and continued in loyalist areas for two days.

By 1987 it had become clear to many political actors that the situation had reached a stalemate. Unionists could not destroy the AIA, but their opposition to it also made it largely unworkable. In January 1987 the **Ulster Defence Association** (UDA)–linked New Ulster Political Research Group (NUPRG) produced a series of proposals for a devolved government in Northern Ireland in a document titled "Common Sense." In February 1987, the UUP and **Democratic Unionist Party** (DUP) set up a taskforce to produce possible alternatives to the AIA. In July 1987, the taskforce report called for the opening of talks with the government to find an alternative to the AIA, and on 14 September 1987, Molyneaux and Paisley met King for "talks about talks" in the first meeting between unionist leaders and government ministers in 19 months.

In November 1988 on the third anniversary of the AIA, there were only minor protests by unionists but no sign of any progress toward devolution. Indeed, the AIA had produced the opposite effect and boosted unionist support for greater **integration** with Great Britain. In January 1990 King's successor as secretary of state, **Peter Brooke**, launched a fresh bid for interparty talks to lead to devolution, but this did not meet the unionist demand for the suspension of the AIA. In May 1990, Brooke conceded that political talks would consider an alternative to the agreement, and this opened the way for what would become the **Brooke–Mayhew Talks**.

The unionist cause in Britain had also been helped by British disillusionment with the Irish attitude toward **extradition** and by the outcome of the McGimpsey case in Dublin, which reaffirmed the objective of a united Ireland as a "constitutional imperative." Throughout the 1990s the replacement of the AIA continued to be a key unionist objective, and this was subsequently highlighted by **David Trimble** as one of the main achievements of the **Good Friday Agreement** (GFA) negotiations in 1998.

**ANGLO–IRISH INTERGOVERNMENTAL COUNCIL (AIIC).** The body established by Prime Minister **Margaret Thatcher** and Taoiseach **Garret FitzGerald** in November 1981 that would provide the framework for regular meetings between the British and Irish governments. The idea for the structure arose from a summit meeting involving Thatcher and then-taoiseach **Charles Haughey** in December 1980 but took another year to come to fruition. A parliamentary tier was envisioned as part of the overall structure, though **unionists** said they would not participate in such a body. In November 1985 the AIIC was effectively replaced by the **Anglo–Irish Agreement** (AIA).

**APPRENTICE BOYS OF DERRY (ABD).** One of the three main Protestant Loyal Orders, the ABD was formed in the 1850s to commemorate the siege of **Derry** of 1689, specifically the closing of the gates of Derry on the army of King James II by 13 apprentice boys, which instigated the siege of the city. The ABD is independent of the **Orange Order**, although some of its members are also members of Orange lodges. The organization has approximately 200 branch clubs in Northern Ireland, England, Scotland, and the **Republic of Ireland** and in 2007 claimed to have approximately 10,000 members. Its main **parade** is held on 12 August to celebrate the end of the siege, and a smaller demonstration is held on 18 December to commemorate the closing of the city gates. On this date an effigy of Colonel Lundy, who tried to negotiate the surrender of the city, is burned. The term *Lundy* is still used by **loyalists** to describe a traitor to their cause.

The ABD march of August 1969 sparked the outbreak of violence that led to the deployment of the **British Army** to the streets of Northern Ireland. The ABD march was then banned or, on some occasions, restricted by the ABD itself. The organization opposed the **Anglo–Irish Agreement** (AIA) of 1985, but an application from its leaders for a grant from the **International Fund for Ireland** (IFI, which was connected to the AIA) led to intense arguments within the organization. The IFI later offered a £250,000 grant, but this was refused by the ABD.

In 1995 in the wake of the **paramilitary** ceasefires, the first march by the ABD around the walls of Derry since 1969 took place; however, this was opposed by **republican** protestors, and there was a confrontation with the police. ABD marches in Derry and other areas were the scene of confrontations on a number of occasions in the following years. More recently the ABD has taken a less confrontational approach to decisions made by the **Parades Commission**, and it has been more willing than other loyal orders to work with **nationalist** resident groups to discuss parades issues. In 1999 it also agreed to move the date of the celebration of the closing of the gates of Derry after city traders said that the danger of conflict with nationalists over the event was hampering pre-Christmas sales in the city.

**ARMS CRISIS.** In May 1970 Taoiseach **Jack Lynch** fired Finance Minister **Charles Haughey** and Agriculture Minister Neil Blaney after revelations of a plot to smuggle arms imported into the **Republic of Ireland** to Northern Ireland. Haughey and Blaney were accused of conspiring to import £100,000 of weapons that would then be sent to the Provisional **Irish Republican Army** (PIRA) in Northern Ireland. The transportation of the weapons was called off when it was decided that they would be stopped by customs officials at the Dublin airport. A third minister, Kevin Boland, resigned from the government in protest of the firings. The minister of justice also resigned that May.

The firings caused divisions within **Fianna Fail** (FF), which endured until the end of Haughey's political career. Lynch won a vote of confidence over his decision and heightened his personal standing in the Republic. In May 1970 Haughey and Blaney appeared in court in connection with the plot. Both men denied any involvement and were released on bail. The defense argued that the guns had been imported as part of an officially sanctioned operation on behalf of the Irish army. Blaney was cleared of gun-running charges in July 1970 and Haughey in October 1970.

**ARMY.** *See* BRITISH ARMY.

**ATKINS, HUMPHREY (1922–96).** **Conservative Party** politician and Northern Ireland secretary of state, Humphrey Atkins was born on 12 August 1922 in Chalfont St. Peter, Buckinghamshire. His father was a former Indian Army officer who was later a coffee planter in Kenya. Atkins's father was killed by a rhinoceros, and the family subsequently returned to England. He was educated at Wellington College and joined the Royal Navy as a cadet in 1940, eventually becoming a lieutenant. During World War II, the destroyer on which he was serving was sunk while on convoy duty in the North Atlantic.

Atkins resigned from the navy in 1948 and initially worked in his father-in-law's law firm. He contested but lost the Scottish constituency of West Lothian in 1951. After the family moved to London, he contested and won the seat of Merton and Morden in 1955 and held it until 1970, when he transferred to the safe Conservative seat of Spelthorne, which he held until 1987. In opposition from 1967 and in the first years of **Edward Heath**'s premiership, he was a Conservative Party whip. In 1973 he became the party's chief whip, succeeding **Francis Pym**, in the post.

In May 1979 he was unexpectedly named Northern Ireland secretary by **Margaret Thatcher**. Compared to the high-profile Airey Neave, who had been murdered five weeks earlier, Atkins was largely unknown in public circles, and one Northern Ireland newspaper welcomed his appointment with the headline, "Humphrey Who?" Atkins's term as secretary of state was one of the most difficult of those to hold the post. He faced pressure from Thatcher and the army for swift action, **U.S.** interest in **the Troubles** was also increasing, and the American administration was looking for a fresh British initiative. He had replaced **Roy Mason**, who had been popular among **unionists**, and at the same time faced a growing crisis on the issue of political status for **paramilitary** prisoners.

Atkins's term as secretary of state was dominated by the **republican hunger strikes** of 1980 and 1981. During this period he followed the uncompromising approach taken by Prime Minister Thatcher that there would be no concessions on the issue of political status.

Attempts to restore devolved government to Northern Ireland also came to nothing as the **Atkins Talks** failed to square the circle for unionists that there be no **Irish dimension** with the **nationalist** insistence that there should be. In 1981 he proposed a 50-member advisory council of **elected** Northern Ireland representatives to assist the secretary of state in governing Northern Ireland, but this produced a lukewarm response.

He was also involved in early meetings between the British and Irish governments aimed at improving relations between the two and aiding progress in Northern Ireland. The discussions began in December 1980 and would eventually culminate in the **Anglo–Irish Agreement** (AIA) in 1985.

In September 1981 Atkins became lord privy seal and deputy foreign secretary; however, he resigned from the post in April 1982 in the wake of the Argentinean invasion of the Falkland Islands. He was knighted in 1983 and in 1984 became chairman of the commons select committee on defense. He retired from the House of Commons in 1987 and received a life peerage, taking the title Lord Colnbrook of Waltham St. Lawrence. Atkins died on 4 October 1996 as a result of cancer.

**ATKINS TALKS.** The Atkins Talks, more properly known as the Constitutional Conference, was organized by Secretary of State **Humphrey Atkins** and held at Parliament buildings, **Stormont**, between January and March 1980. In November 1979 the British government published a consultative paper aimed at achieving the highest level of agreement possible between the local parties. The paper ruled out discussion of the constitutional status of Northern Ireland. The proposals led to a split in the **Social Democratic and Labour Party** (SDLP) with **Gerry Fitt**, who wished to participate in the talks, resigning as party leader. The **Ulster Unionist Party** (UUP), influenced by the **integrationist Enoch Powell**, also declined to take part, claiming the talks were little more than a gimmick. **Democratic Unionist Party** (DUP), SDLP and **Alliance Party of Northern Ireland** (APNI) delegates did, however, meet privately under Atkins's chairmanship. While the SDLP and APNI advocated a **power-sharing** administration, the DUP demanded a return to majority (in effect **unionist**) rule, although they suggested there should be a "meaningful role" for other parties.

The conference did not deal with security matters, a prime concern of unionists, or with relations with the **Republic of Ireland**, which was central to **nationalist** concerns, and these issues were discussed in a parallel conference. In July 1980, with no agreed solution emerging from the discussions, Atkins proposed a number of fresh options that modified the main unionist and nationalist positions, but once again these proposals failed to win support. In November 1980 Atkins told the House of Commons that there was not enough agreement between the parties to justify bringing forward proposals for a devolved administration. Further proposals from Atkins for an advisory council made up of locally **elected** representatives were also dropped in 1981.

## – B –

**B SPECIALS.** *See* ULSTER SPECIAL CONSTABULARY (USC).

**BALLYKELLY BOMBING.** On 6 December 1982, an **Irish National Liberation Army** (INLA) bomb exploded at the Droppin' Well public house at Ballykelly, Co. Londonderry. The explosion killed 17 people, including 11 soldiers. The INLA targeted the bar because it was known to be frequented by soldiers from a local **British Army** base. Although the bomb used was comparatively small, it was placed beside a support pillar, which caused the bar's roof to collapse onto the 150 people packed into the building. In the House of Commons, **Margaret Thatcher** described the bombing as the "product of evil and depraved minds and the act of callous and brutal men."

**BANDIT COUNTRY.** The staunchly **republican** area of South Armagh, where the **Irish Republican Army** (IRA) campaign against the security forces was particularly intense. In relation to its population, the security forces suffered more casualties in Co. Armagh than any other part of Northern Ireland. Bombs and booby traps were often planted along roads, forcing the security forces to use helicopters as a means of transport in the area. Part of the reason for the success of the IRA in South Armagh was the experience of local members. Many of those who were active in the 1970s were still involved in the IRA's campaign 30 years later. One of the leading republican figures in the area is also believed to have played a role in the **Omagh bombing** of 1998. In September 2006 the demolition of Crossmaglen police and army base and the closure of Newtownhamilton security base as part of the "normalization" plan meant that there was no military presence in South Armagh. While this was welcomed by **nationalists**, it was criticized by **unionists**.

**BARR, GLEN (1932– ). Loyalist** politician and community worker. With a working-class background and experience as a trade union representative **Derry** man, Glen Barr joined the **Loyalist Association of Workers** (LAW) in the early 1970s. He was also associated with the **Ulster Defence Association** (UDA), although he claimed not to be a member of the organization. Viewed as the UDA's political spokesman, Barr was **elected** to the **Northern Ireland Assembly** in June 1973 as a member of the **Vanguard Unionist Progressive Party** (VUPP) for the constituency of Londonderry. His opposition to the **power-sharing** executive and the **Sunningdale** Agreement saw him assume an important position in the campaign against both. In May 1974 Barr assumed the role of chairman of the Coordinating Committee, which managed and conducted the **Ulster Workers' Council (UWC) strike**. In November 1974 he took part in a UDA delegation to **Libya** that examined the possibilities of Libyan financial support for an independent Northern Ireland or obtaining Libyan orders for Northern Ireland firms.

In 1975 Barr was elected to the Northern Ireland **Constitutional Convention**, and following the split in Vanguard over the issue of voluntary coalition, he served as its joint leader before the VUPP ceased to exist as a political party in 1978. Throughout 1978 and 1979, he worked with the New Ulster Political Research Group (NUPRG), which had close ties with the UDA, and he publicly supported its proposals for an independent Northern Ireland. He withdrew from politics in 1981 after the formation of the UDA-linked Ulster Loyalist Democratic Party (ULDP) and subsequently become involved in a variety of community projects. In 1997 he accepted an appointment to become a member of the **Parades Commission** but resigned in April 1998 because of local pressure.

In the late 1990s, Barr, along with former **Fine Gael** (FG) teachta dala (TD) Paddy Harte, played a leading role in the Journey of Reconciliation Trust (JORT). The Trust aimed to highlight the role of Irishmen who had served in the **British Army** in World War I, a role that had been down-played by the southern state in the decades after partition. Barr and Harte campaigned for a monument to the soldiers to be built at Messines in Belgium, where soldiers of the northern, mainly **unionist**, 36th Ulster division had fought beside men of the southern, largely **nationalist**, 16th Irish division. The plan received financial backing from both Northern Ireland and Irish government departments, and on 11 November 1998, the president of Ireland, **Mary McAleese**; Queen Elizabeth II; and the king of the Belgians attended a ceremony at Messines to officially open the memorial at the Peace Park and Irish Round Tower. As well as representing a symbolic reconciliation between nationalists and unionists, the memorial tower also highlighted a personal reconciliation between a leading northern loyalist and a southern nationalist.

**BATTLE OF THE BOGSIDE.** On 12 August 1969, severe rioting broke out on the edge of the Catholic Bogside area after an **Apprentice Boys of Derry** (ABD) march in Londonderry. Rioting continued for three days, leading the Northern Ireland prime minister **James Chichester-Clark** to call up the **Ulster Special Constabulary** (USC) to provide support to the **Royal Ulster Constabulary** (RUC). With police officers exhausted from three days of rioting, Chichester-Clark requested **British Army** support to maintain law and order, and at 5:15 p.m. on 14 August 1969, soldiers of the Prince of Wales Own Regiment and the Queen's Regiment were deployed to relieve the police.

The **Derry** Citizens' Defence Association, a local vigilante group, was involved in coordinating opposition to the police by erecting barricades, patrolling the streets, and helping counter the effects of tear gas. This eventually led to the development of the **no-go area** known as Free Derry.

**BELFAST.** The capital city of Northern Ireland. While the population of the greater Belfast area increased from approximately 650,000 in 1951 to nearly 730,000 in 2001, as with many other cities, there was a population movement away from the inner-city area and toward the suburbs. This movement was exacerbated by the outbreak of **the Troubles** and led to a greater movement out of the city than might otherwise have been the case. It is estimated that between 30,000 and

60,000 people in Belfast moved home as a result of the Troubles between August 1969 and February 1973. This movement of population also led to an increased number of areas in Belfast becoming either overwhelmingly Protestant or overwhelmingly Catholic.

During the course of the Troubles, Belfast was the location of nearly 1,700 **deaths** with almost two-thirds of these occurring from 1970 to 1977. The areas of Belfast that saw the greatest number of deaths were North and West Belfast. In North Belfast the intermixing of Protestant and Catholic residential areas made it relatively easy for **paramilitary** groups (and particularly **loyalist** groups) to attack members of the other community and escape. In West Belfast the existence of strongly **republican** neighborhoods made this one of the main areas of conflict between the **Irish Republican Army** (IRA) and security forces.

Belfast also suffered casualties as a result of bomb explosions, particularly from paramilitaries on public houses known to be frequented by members of the other community, and in attacks on economic targets such as the Europa Hotel in the center of the city. In the 1970s a ring of security barriers was erected in the city's main shopping area, and while this undoubtedly reduced the use of bombs in the area, it also had an adverse economic impact in itself by restricting the movement of shoppers.

Since the outbreak of the Troubles, there has also been a significant increase in the Catholic proportion of the city's population, leading to a situation where neither **unionists** nor **nationalists** have an overall majority on Belfast City Council.

**BELFAST AGREEMENT.** *See* GOOD FRIDAY AGREEMENT (GFA).

**BENNETT REPORT.** In June 1978 a three-member committee headed by Harry Bennett, Queen's Counsel (QC), was established by Secretary of State **Roy Mason** to investigate the interrogation procedures used by the **Royal Ulster Constabulary** (RUC) and the operation of the machinery that dealt with complaints. Demands for an official inquiry had grown after Amnesty International had examined 78 complaints of ill-treatment by individuals who had been held at the Castlereagh interrogation center in **Belfast** and at other centers. The

Bennett Report, published in March 1979, drew attention to cases where medical evidence showed injuries that had been received in police custody and that were not self-inflicted. The report recommended that close-circuit televisions should be installed in police interview rooms and that suspects should be permitted access to a solicitor after 48 hours. These and nearly all of the other report recommendations were accepted by the **Labour** government and by the incoming **Conservative** government.

**BIRMINGHAM BOMBS.** On 21 November 1974, **Irish Republican Army** (IRA) bombs exploded at the Mulberry Bush and Tavern in the Town public houses in Birmingham. Nineteen people were killed immediately and nearly 200 injured. Two other people died later. As with many of the worst atrocities of **the Troubles**, a warning was given but came too late for any effective action to be taken to prevent a major loss of life. The horror of the bombings sparked a wave of anti-Irish sentiment, with attacks on Irish community centers, bars, and businesses in England. In the wake of the attacks, the British government rushed the Prevention of Terrorism Act into law. The act included provisions for detention without charge for a period of seven days and expulsion from Great Britain to Northern Ireland or the **Republic of Ireland**.

**BIRMINGHAM SIX.** In 1975 six men from Northern Ireland, Hugh Callaghan, Paddy Hill, Gerry Hunter, Richard McIlkenny, Billy Power, and Johnny Walker, were sentenced to life imprisonment for causing the **Birmingham bombs** of November 1974. As time passed, however, doubts were increasingly cast on the convictions, and a broad range of Catholic, **nationalist**, and civil rights groups campaigned for the release of the Birmingham Six. After several failed appeals and 17 years in prison, the men were eventually released in March 1991, when the Appeal Court ruled that the convictions were unsafe. The decision led the British home secretary to announce a Royal Commission on Criminal Justice. In October 1993 the trial of three former policemen accused of perjury and conspiracy to pervert the course of justice in the case of the Birmingham Six was terminated because of what the judge described as saturation publicity surrounding their trial. On 21 May 2006, Richard McIlkenny died from cancer.

**BLAIR, ANTHONY (TONY) (1953– ). Labour Party** politician and prime minister, Tony Blair was born in Edinburgh, Scotland, on 6 May 1953. He was educated at Durham Choristers School; Fettes College, Edinburgh; and St. John's College, Oxford. Blair trained as a barrister and joined the Labour Party in 1975. He contested and lost the Beaconsfield by-**election** of 1982 but was elected to **Westminster** for the Sedgefield constituency in 1983. During Labour's period in opposition, he was on the modernizing wing of the party and held a number of positions in the shadow cabinet after 1988. Following the sudden death of Labour Party leader John Smith, Blair was elected leader of the party in July 1994 with the backing of his main party leadership rival **Gordon Brown**. Blair was central to the rebranding of the party as "new Labour," which assisted in the party's return to power in 1997. Subsequently, however, the party's concern with image has led to criticism that Blair's government has been more concerned with style than substance—a criticism that has also been made of its policy in Northern Ireland.

A major plank of Labour policy since 1997 has been constitutional reform involving, in part, **devolution** within the United Kingdom. This led to the establishment of the Scottish Parliament, the Welsh Assembly, and the **Northern Ireland Assembly**.

Under Blair's leadership Labour moved away from the policy of "unity by consent" in Ireland. On a visit to **Belfast** shortly after becoming prime minister, he stated that a united Ireland was unlikely to come about in his lifetime. In the following month, the government dropped the requirement for the **decommissioning** of **paramilitary** weapons before political talks could be held, opening the way for **Sinn Fein** (SF) to join talks, provided the **Irish Republican Army** (IRA) declared a ceasefire.

Following the declaration of a renewed IRA ceasefire in July 1997, Blair met SF leaders in Belfast in October 1997, becoming the first British prime minister to meet SF leaders since 1921. An attempt to do a balancing act on the same day by having Blair visit a shopping center in a **unionist** area backfired when Blair was barracked by unionist protestors and a visibly shaken prime minister was hustled into a nearby bank for his own protection. Blair, along with Taoiseach **Bertie Ahern,** played significant roles in the negotiations that were to lead to the **Good Friday Agreement** (GFA) in April 1998. A letter of support to **Ulster Unionist Party** (UUP) leader **David Trimble**, in which Blair stated that paramilitary decommissioning should commence immediately after the agreement was ratified, would later become one of the sources of dispute surrounding the interpretation of the GFA.

During the campaign for the referendum on the GFA, Blair sought to win over a reluctant Protestant electorate by making five handwritten promises in relation to the settlement. While these promises were sufficient to create a temporary upsurge in Protestant support for the agreement and thus help create a convincing vote in favor of the GFA, the subsequent perception that these promises were not fulfilled also played a part in undermining unionist support for the agreement.

As the agreement began to unravel as a result of problems in the interpretation of key elements, Blair's reputation in Northern Ireland began to decline. His reputation in Britain also went into sharp decline in the wake of Britain's participation in the war in Iraq. By late 2006 Blair's premiership seemed to be coming to a close and the plan to reestablish devolution in Northern Ireland, outlined in the **St. Andrews Agreement**, appeared to be an attempt by Blair to leave office on a positive note. On 10 May 2007, two days after he attended a ceremony at **Stormont** to mark a new period of devolution, he announced his decision to retire as prime minister. He resigned as prime minister on 27 June 2007 and also left the House of Commons. He was succeeded by Gordon Brown. In July 2007, he took up a new role as a special peace envoy in the Middle East.

**BLANKET PROTEST.** After the abolition of **special category status** in March 1976, the government and **paramilitary** prisoners almost inevitably headed toward conflict. The government wished to treat prisoners convicted of terrorist offenses in the same manner as all other prisoners, while the paramilitaries demanded that they be recognized as prisoners of war. Provisional **Irish Republican Army** (PIRA) member Ciaran Nugent was the first prisoner convicted of terrorist activities not to be accorded special category status. On 15 September 1976, when he entered the **Maze Prison**, he refused to wear a prison uniform and instead wrapped himself in a blanket to distinguish himself from those convicted of nonterrorist crimes. By 1978 more than 300 prisoners had joined the Blanket Protest. The issue of prison clothing would not be resolved until October 1981 when, following the **hunger strike** campaign of that year, Secretary of State **James Prior** announced that all prisoners would be allowed to wear their own clothing at all times.

**BLEAKLEY, DAVID (1925– ). Northern Ireland Labour Party** (NILP) politician, David Bleakley was born on 11 January 1925. After working in the **Belfast** shipyard, he continued his formal education at Ruskin College, Oxford, and Queen's University, Belfast (QUB). The best known member of the NILP, he was Member of Parliament (MP) for the East Belfast constituency of Victoria (1958–65) in the **Northern Ireland Parliament**. After losing the seat, he was a teacher and lecturer in Belfast. Under **Brian Faulkner** he was appointed minister of **community relations** in March 1971, as the **Ulster Unionist** prime minister attempted to broaden the government's base of support; however, as he was not then an MP, he could only hold the post for six months.

He was **elected** to both the **Northern Ireland Assembly** in 1973 and the **Constitutional Convention** in 1975 and on both occasions was the NILP's only representative. Bleakley stood in the East Belfast constituency in 1970 and in both the February and October 1974 **Westminster** general elections but was unsuccessful on all three occasions. He was also unsuccessful in the 1979 European Parliament elections, when he stood as a United Community candidate.

After leaving party politics, he was chief executive of the Irish Council of Churches (1979–92) and chairman of the Northern Ireland Standing Advisory Commission on Human Rights (1981–84). He was a member of the Labour group during the 1996 talks and stood as a Labour candidate in East Belfast in the 1998 Northern Ireland Assembly elections but received only 369 first-preference votes and was not elected.

**BLOODY FRIDAY.** On Friday, 21 July 1972, the Provisional **Irish Republican Army** (PIRA) detonated 26 bombs across **Belfast** in just over an hour. Nine people were killed and 130 injured. A car bomb at Oxford Street bus station killed four Ulsterbus workers and two soldiers. Two women and a schoolboy were killed by another car bomb on Cavehill Road in North Belfast. Some of the bodies were so badly mutilated that it was initially thought that a greater number of people had died. Although telephone warnings were given by the IRA, the emergency services could not cope with the number of bombs and bomb scares. Later, the day came to be called Bloody Friday.

One of those killed by the car bomb on Cavehill Road was Stephen Parker, the 14-year-old son of Rev. Joseph Parker. Rev. Parker was only able to identify his son's remains by his hands, a box of trick matches found in his son's trouser pocket, and a scout belt he had been wearing at the time of his death.

**BLOODY SUNDAY.** On 30 January 1972, 13 men were killed and another fatally wounded when soldiers from the **British Army**'s Parachute Regiment opened fire at the end of a civil rights march in **Derry** City. The illegal march had generally been peaceful until the end, when part of the crowd attempted to climb over a street barrier and was forced back by the army with rubber bullets and water cannons. More than 100 youths threw stones and iron bars at the soldiers, and a running battle continued for more than 10 minutes. The question of whether soldiers opened fire first or whether they were fired upon by **republican** gunmen or believed they were being fired upon remains a source of great controversy. Bloody Sunday was one of the key events of **the Troubles**. It hardened attitudes in the Catholic community and strengthened support for the **Irish Republican Army** (IRA), as well as damaged Britain's reputation internationally. In Dublin on 2 February 1972, anti-British demonstrations were followed by an attack on the British embassy and the burning of the building. Bloody Sunday also encouraged the British government to move toward taking full control of security policy in Northern Ireland, which in turn would lead to the introduction of **direct rule**.

A tribunal of inquiry, headed by Lord Chief Justice John Widgery, was quickly established to look into the events surrounding Bloody Sunday and produced a report in April 1972. The Widgery report stated that there would not have been any **deaths** if the organizers of the march had not created a dangerous situation. It stated that some soldiers showed a high degree of responsibility, but with others firing they bordered on reckless. Many **nationalists** viewed the report as an attempt to whitewash the guilt of the army in the incident, and anger surrounding the event continued.

Throughout the 1990s there had been renewed appeals for a fresh inquiry, and in January 1998 Prime Minister **Tony Blair** announced a new inquiry into Bloody Sunday. Nine years later, however, the inquiry team under Lord Saville had still not produced a final report. The cost of the Saville inquiry, in excess of £170 million, was also the source of much criticism. In October 2006 Lord Saville told relatives of those killed on Bloody Sunday that his final report was unlikely to be completed before 2008.

**BLOOMFIELD, KENNETH (1931– ).** A Northern Ireland civil servant, Kenneth Bloomfield was born in **Belfast** on 15 April 1931. He was educated at the Royal Belfast Academical Institute and St. Peter's College, Oxford. Joining the Northern Ireland Civil Service in 1952, he became secretary to the Northern Ireland cabinet from 1963 until 1972 and was a close advisor of **Terence O'Neill** during his time as prime minister of Northern Ireland. After the introduction of **direct rule**, he served in the **Northern Ireland Office** (NIO) and was the senior civil servant under the Northern Ireland executive of 1974. Between 1984 and 1991, he was head of the Northern Ireland Civil Service, a period that coincided with the **Anglo–Irish Agreement** (AIA) and subsequent **unionist** protests. Bloomfield later revealed that he considered resigning in protest of the agreement. In 1987 he was awarded a knighthood. In August 1988 the **Irish Republican Army** (IRA) detonated a bomb at his home, but he and his family escaped injury. After his retirement from the civil service, he held a number of positions, including the British Broadcasting Corporation (BBC) governor for Northern Ireland. As Northern Ireland **victims'** commissioner, he produced a report on the victims of **the Troubles** in May 1998. He subsequently became a member of the Independent Commission for the Location of Victims' Remains.

**BORDER POLL.** On 8 March 1973, a constitutional referendum was held in Northern Ireland on the question of whether Northern Ireland should remain part of the United Kingdom or join the **Republic of Ireland**. The number of votes in favor of remaining within the United Kingdom was 591,820, and the number voting to join the Republic of Ireland was 6,463. Many **nationalists** abstained from voting, as it was clear that a vote within Northern Ireland would return a clear majority in support of the U.K. option.

By conducting the referendum, the government hoped to build confidence within the **unionist** community that the constitutional future of Northern Ireland had been decided for the foreseeable future, thus encouraging them to participate in a cross-community **power-sharing** administration. However, the continuing high level of violence and the emphasis of nationalist parties on the need for movement toward a united Ireland helped undermine this plan. It was intended to run a similar poll every 10 years, but the process was never repeated.

In March 2002 **David Trimble** raised the possibility of a referendum on Northern Ireland's constitutional position being run in order to highlight the fact that there was still a clear majority in favor of maintaining the union; however, this did not take place.

**BRIGHTON BOMB.** On 12 October 1984, the Provisional **Irish Republican Army** (PIRA) detonated a bomb at the Grand Hotel, Brighton, which was being used by many senior **Conservative Party** members during the party's annual conference. The 20-pound bomb exploded just before 3:00 a.m., sliced four floors out of the middle of the building, and killed five people, including Sir Anthony Berry, Member of Parliament (MP), and Roberta Wakeham, the wife of the government chief whip. Norman Tebbitt, a close political ally of **Margaret Thatcher** and secretary of state for trade and industry, was one of more than 30 people injured in the explosion. Prime Minister Thatcher narrowly escaped injury. An IRA statement released shortly after the explosion said, "Today, we were unlucky. . . . but remember, we only have to be lucky once—you will have to be lucky always." IRA member Patrick Magee was later convicted of the bombing and given eight life sentences, while two of his five accomplices were also given life sentences. Magee was among those given early release from prison under the terms of the **Good Friday Agreement** (GFA).

**BRITISH ARMY.** Following the events of the **Battle of the Bogside** and the outbreak of sectarian rioting in **Belfast**, the **Northern Ireland government** asked for troops to be deployed in support of the police. On 14 August 1969, soldiers from the Prince of Wales Own

Regiment went on duty in **Derry**. Soldiers from the light infantry went on duty in Belfast the following day. The stated objective of the British Army in Northern Ireland was to support the police in the defeat of terrorism and maintain public order in order to assist the government in the objective of returning Northern Ireland to normalcy. The army's support role for the police during **the Troubles**, code-named Operation Banner, would eventually become the longest running operation in British Army history.

Initially the army was welcomed in many Catholic areas as providing protection against attacks by **loyalists**. However, as **Irish Republican Army** (IRA) operations increased, army activity in Catholic areas also increased, leading to a souring of the relationship. On 3–4 July 1970, a 34-hour-long curfew was imposed on the Catholic Lower Falls area of Belfast, covering an area of approximately 50 streets. House searches by the army uncovered a significant amount of arms and ammunition; however, damage caused by the soldiers during the course of the searches hurt relations between residents and the army. During the curfew gun battles broke out between the army and both the **Official Irish Republican Army** (OIRA) and the Provisional IRA (PIRA), resulting in five civilians being killed. The Falls curfew is viewed as a key turning point in the relationship between the army and the working-class Catholic community in Belfast.

There were also tensions between **unionists** and the army, with unionists pressing for the army to take stronger action against **republicans**. In February 1971 Gunner Robert Curtis, shot dead by the PIRA in Belfast, was the first member of the army to die on duty in Northern Ireland after the outbreak of the Troubles. In July 1971 the shooting **deaths** of two Derry men in disputed circumstances led to the withdrawal of the **Social Democratic and Labour Party** (SDLP) from the **Northern Ireland Parliament**. The introduction of **internment** in August 1971 heightened the conflict between republicans and the army.

In January 1972 the events of **Bloody Sunday**, when 14 men were shot dead by the army, had far-reaching consequences, leading to the suspension of the Northern Ireland Parliament and a continuing source of resentment within the **nationalist** community surrounding the event. As civil disorder and **paramilitary** activity intensified in the early 1970s, the number of soldiers serving in Northern Ireland increased. The period from August 1971 to 1974 also saw the army suffer its heaviest casualties (with the exception of 1979, which included the casualties suffered at **Warrenpoint**) and also led to a dramatic decrease in recruitment into the army.

During the course of the **Ulster Workers' Council (UWC) strike**, supporters of the **Sunningdale** deal believed that the army's unwillingness to take a more proactive stance against the loyalist strikers was a fundamental factor in the collapse of the **power-sharing** executive. In May 1977 army strength in Northern Ireland was again increased at the time of the **United Unionist Action Council (UUAC) strike**, though this was arguably aimed as much at reassuring mainstream unionists unsupportive of the strike that the army could increase its strength when required as it was in combating the strike itself. In the same year, the introduction of "police primacy" initiated a policy whereby the army was increasingly replaced by the **Royal Ulster Constabulary** (RUC) in many areas.

Initially army units served four-month tours of duty in Northern Ireland; however, this was gradually extended so that by the early 1980s, most soldiers served two-year-long tours. From 1976 the elite Special Air Service Regiment began to serve in Northern Ireland. This move was successful in countering increased paramilitary activity, but the secretive nature of their activities and operations, such as that at **Loughgall** in 1987, often led to controversy. In 1987 the army also established a series of observation posts as part of its surveillance system. These observation towers proved a source of antagonism for many nationalists, and their removal was an important demand of nationalists as the **peace process** progressed.

In 1988 the Royal Irish Rangers, based in Northern Ireland, were used for routine duties in the **province** for the first time during the course of the Troubles. In 1992, as part of overall army cuts following the end of the cold war, the regiment merged with the **Ulster Defence Regiment** (UDR) to form the **Royal Irish Regiment** (RIR).

In August 1979 the army suffered its largest number of casualties, 18, in the IRA ambush at Narrow Water near Warrenpoint, Co. Down. They also suffered significant casualties in February 1974, when 12 people, including 9 soldiers, were killed when a bomb exploded on a coach carrying soldiers and their families in Yorkshire. In July 1982,

11 cavalry members and bandsmen were killed by IRA bombs in Hyde Park and Regents Park, London. In September 1989 an IRA bomb at the Royal Marines School of Music at Deal in Kent killed 10 bandsmen. In February 1997 Stephen Restorick, killed by an IRA sniper, was the last soldier to be killed on duty in Northern Ireland.

The size of the British Army in Northern Ireland varied significantly during the course of the Troubles, with additional units being temporarily assigned to Northern Ireland during periods of increased instability. In June 1969, shortly before they were deployed on the streets, there were 2,700 soldiers based in Northern Ireland. By 1971 there were 11,800 soldiers, of which 4,000 belonged to the recently formed UDR. In July 1972, at the height of the Troubles, there were more than 30,000 soldiers based in Northern Ireland in more than 100 locations. This consisted of 21,800 members of British regiments and 8,500 UDR members. With the increasing size and prominence of the RUC, this was reduced to between 17,000 and 18,000 in the 1980s, with approximately 6,000 to 7,000 of these being UDR members. There were further reductions in size as the overall security situation slowly improved.

With the end of the cold war in 1989, a reduction in the overall size of the army meant that soldiers were spending comparatively longer periods of time in Northern Ireland. The ongoing requirement for troops to patrol in Northern Ireland also slowed the pace of army cutbacks. In August 2005, following the IRA's announcement that its campaign was over, the government announced that the number of troops in Northern Ireland would be reduced from 10,500 to 5,000 within two years. By September 2006 there were 9,000 troops based in Northern Ireland. Operation Banner was officially concluded on 31 July 2007.

The British Army was responsible for an estimated 302 deaths during the course of the Troubles and suffered 503 casualties in addition to 206 UDR and RIR casualties.

**BRITISH–IRISH COUNCIL (BIC).** Included as part of the **Good Friday Agreement** (GFA), the BIC provides an institutional link between the U.K. government, the **Republic of Ireland** government, the Welsh executive, Scottish executive, the Northern Ireland executive, and the Crown dependencies of the Channel Islands and the Isle of Man. Promoted by the **Ulster Unionist Party** (UUP) in the negotiations leading to the GFA, it was initially seen as a **unionist** counterbalance to the **North–South Ministerial Council** (NSMC) but has since attracted support elsewhere, particularly from the smaller areas represented in the BIC. The GFA specified that the summit meeting of the BIC, also referred to as "The Council of the Isles," should be held twice a year and regular sectoral meetings could be held by the relevant ministers.

The role of the BIC was to "exchange information, discuss, consult and use best endeavours to reach agreement on matters of mutual interest within the competence of the relevant administrations." As this concept was developed, a program of work and responsibilities was agreed upon among the various bodies. Tackling the issue of illegal drug use was allocated to the Irish government; social exclusion and an antipoverty strategy were taken on by Wales and Scotland; the Isle of Man and the Channel Isles were to examine the knowledge economy; the U.K. government was to take the lead on the environment, and the Northern Ireland executive was to lead on the development of a transport strategy for the islands. In practice, however, these plans have been severely hampered by the intermittent suspensions of the **Northern Ireland Assembly**. After the **devolution** of power to the Northern Ireland executive in May 2007, the BIC met at **Stormont** in July 2007, with **Gordon Brown** visiting Northern Ireland for the first time as prime minister.

**BRITISH–IRISH INTERPARLIAMENTARY BODY (BIIPB).** Although a proposal for a BIIPB had been made in 1981, it was not until 1990 that such a body was established. The aim of the body was to promote understanding between members of the British and Irish Parliaments; however, Northern Ireland matters have inevitably played a significant role in the activities of the body.

The BIIPB initially consisted of 25 members from each Parliament, with two plenary sessions each year at which ministers from the host country answered questions from members of the body. The BIIPB also debated recent political developments. Subcommittees examined issues of concern in European affairs; British–Irish matters; economic, environmental, and social affairs; and matters of common concern. It was intended that three of the **Westminster** representatives should come from Northern Ireland constituencies (two **unionists** and one **nationalist**), however unionist suspicions of the body meant that they did not attend.

In the wake of the **Good Friday Agreement** (GFA) provisions for a **British–Irish Council** (BIC), the BIIPB was expanded to include five members each from the Scottish Parliament, the Welsh Assembly, and the **Northern Ireland Assembly** and one each from the Isle of Man, Jersey, and Guernsey. In October 2004 the Nordic Council, representing the Scandinavian countries, was given observer status. While the Northern Ireland Assembly has been suspended, no Assembly member has attended the BIIPB. However, in April 2006 **Democratic Unionist Party** (DUP) deputy leader **Peter Robinson** gave a formal address to a meeting of the body in Killarney. In October 2006 the BIIPB met in **Belfast** for the first time.

**BROADCASTING BAN.** During the course of **the Troubles**, producing television news and documentary programs on controversial matters that were perceived as even-handed often proved a difficult prospect. In 1985 Prime Minister **Margaret Thatcher** warned that terrorists should be starved of the "oxygen of publicity," and the broadcasting of the British Broadcasting Corporation (BBC) documentary *At the Edge of the Union*, which featured an interview with **Martin McGuinness**, led to a heated dispute between the government and the BBC.

In 1988 Thames Television produced *Death on the Rock*, a documentary examining the events surrounding the shooting of three **Irish Republican Army** (IRA) members on **Gibraltar** by the Special Air Service. The documentary brought the program makers into conflict with the government, and on 19 October 1988, Home Secretary **Douglas Hurd** announced a ban on the broadcasting of statements by members of 12 organizations that supported the use of violence. The list included both the Provisional IRA (PIRA) and the **Official Irish Republican Army** (OIRA), **Sinn Fein** (SF), the **Ulster Volunteer Force** (UVF), and **Ulster Defence Association** (UDA). The broadcasting ban did not apply during the course of **election** campaigns, and elected representatives could be interviewed about matters of relevance to their constituencies. In practice the ban was often circumvented by having actors dub the words being spoken while the relevant interview footage was shown at the same time. The ban led to an increase in interest in the groups to which it applied, not least SF, and **Gerry Adams** benefited from the notoriety created by the ban during visits to the **United States.**

In the **Republic of Ireland**, section 31 of the Broadcasting Act of 1960 gave the Irish government power to ban any broadcast that "would tend to undermine the authority of the state," and in 1976 the **Dail** also passed legislation banning interviews with, or reports of interviews with, a list of **paramilitary** and political organizations. As the **peace process** developed, however, and paramilitary organizations moved toward ending their campaigns, broadcasting restrictions were also reexamined by the governments. In January 1994 the Irish government allowed the order banning SF from radio and television to lapse. In the United Kingdom, the broadcasting ban was lifted in September 1994, two weeks after the IRA announcement of a ceasefire.

**BROOKE, PETER (1934– ).** **Conservative Party** politician and secretary of state for Northern Ireland, Peter Brooke was born in London on 3 March 1934. The son of a former Conservative home secretary, he was educated at Marlborough School; Balliol College, Oxford; and Harvard Business School. He was a management consultant before being **elected** to the House of Commons for the constituency of the City of London and **Westminster** South in 1977. He held a number of junior ministerial posts before being appointed chairman of the Conservative Party (1987–89). As chairman he opposed calls for the Conservative Party to organize and contest elections in Northern Ireland.

In July 1989 he joined the cabinet when he succeeded **Tom King** as Northern Ireland secretary. As secretary of state, he engaged with **unionist** leaders in "talks about talks," attempting to find a formula that could involve unionists in discussions leading toward **devolution.** However, Brooke had to work within the constraints of the **Anglo–Irish Agreement** (AIA), to which **nationalists** and the Irish government were strongly attached. In April 1991 talks eventually got underway but soon stalled. Nevertheless, the fact that the talks occurred at all signified a thawing in political attitudes between the various **political parties.**

In November 1990 Brooke attempted to draw **republicans** toward a more political strategy by stating that Great Britain had no strategic or economic interest in Northern Ireland and that Britain would not stand in the way of Irish unification if it was achieved by peaceful constitutional means. The speech was strongly criticized by unionists and some Conservatives. In 1990, under Brooke, secret talks with **Sinn Fein** (SF) were undertaken, with the objective of discovering whether there was enough common ground to begin more in-depth negotiations. This "back channel" of communications would not be revealed until after Brooke had left Northern Ireland.

In January 1992 he sang on a Radio Telefis Eireann chat show hours after eight Protestant workmen had been killed by an **Irish Republican Army** (IRA) bomb at Teebane, Co. Tyrone. Brooke subsequently offered to resign as secretary of state, but his resignation was rejected by Prime Minister **John Major**.

Briefly out of government after the 1992 general election, he returned as heritage secretary in September of that year, holding the post until 1994. In July 1997 he was appointed chairman of the Northern Ireland Affairs Select Committee. He retired from the House of Commons in 2001 and was awarded a life peerage, becoming Lord Brooke of Sutton Mandeville. When he married for the second time in January 1991, he became the only serving Northern Ireland secretary to marry while in office.

**BROOKE–MAYHEW TALKS.** Between April 1991 and November 1992, political discussions between Northern Ireland **political parties** (excluding **Sinn Fein** [SF]) and the British and Irish governments were conducted with the objective of achieving a broadly based and widely accepted political settlement for Northern Ireland. The talks, named after successive Northern Ireland secretaries of state **Peter Brooke** and Sir **Patrick Mayhew**, were conducted during periods when meetings of the **Anglo–Irish Intergovernmental Council** (AIIC) were suspended as a way of meeting **unionist** concerns. The talks did not lead to an agreed package, partly because **Social Democratic and Labour Party** (SDLP) leader **John Hume** believed that an **Irish Republican Army** (IRA) ceasefire was essential for a political package to be successful, and he gave greater priority to his discussions with SF president **Gerry Adams**. The Brooke–

Mayhew Talks did, however, narrow the parameters around which an agreement would be reached on the basis of a **three strands approach**. Despite this, there continued to be significant differences between unionists and **nationalists** on such issues as amendments to the **Irish constitutional claim to Northern Ireland** and a **power-sharing** executive. The Brooke–Mayhew Talks did, however, see a number of important symbolic developments, including direct negotiations between unionist political leaders and the Irish government.

**BROWN, GORDON (1951– ). Labour Party** politician, chancellor of the exchequer, and prime minister, Gordon Brown was born in Glasgow, Scotland, on 20 February 1951. He was educated at Kirkcaldy High School and Edinburgh University, where he received an MA and later a PhD. He was a temporary lecturer at Edinburgh University in 1976 and a lecturer at Glasgow College of Technology from 1976 to 1980. From 1980 until 1983, he was a journalist and current affairs editor on Scottish Television.

In the 1979 **Westminster** general **election**, he contested and lost Edinburgh South as a Labour candidate but in 1983 won Dunfermline East and has retained the seat since that date. In opposition he held a number of posts in the Treasury and Ministry of Trade and Industry before being appointed opposition treasury secretary in 1992. Following the Labour Party victory in the general election of 1997, he was appointed chancellor of the exchequer and held the post for the following decade.

Although he was not known to have strong views on Northern Ireland, he visited **Belfast** in 2002 to announce the launch of a reinvestment and reform program and again in June 2006 to stress the need for agreement on a devolved government in Northern Ireland. In November 2006 he met politicians from the main Northern Ireland parties and announced a £50 billion financial package for Northern Ireland to accompany a political settlement. Independent observers estimated that £3 billion of this was additional money to what Northern Ireland might otherwise have expected to receive from the treasury. In March 2007 Brown had another meeting with local politicians and announced an additional £400 million for Northern Ireland, provided **devolution** took place. In May 2007, when **Tony Blair** announced his intention to retire as prime minister, Brown was viewed as the leading candidate to succeed him. He became leader of the Labour Party in June 2007 and prime minister of the United Kingdom on 27 June 2007.

**BRUTON, JOHN (1947– ). Fine Gael** (FG) leader and taoiseach, John Bruton was born in Co. Meath on 18 May 1947. He was educated at Clongowes Wood College, Naas, in Co. Kildare and University College, Dublin, where he received a BA in economics and politics. He subsequently qualified as a barrister but did not go into practice. In 1969 he was **elected** to the **Dail** as an FG member for the Meath constituency. At the age of 22, he was at that time the youngest person ever to be elected to the Dail.

He was a parliamentary secretary in the 1973–77 FG–**Irish Labour Party** coalition government and in opposition became FG spokesman on finance. He played a significant role in the 1981 Irish general election, which led to another FG–Labour coalition government, and was appointed minister for finance under **Garret FitzGerald**. In January 1982 Bruton's budget proposals were defeated in the Dail, leading to a collapse of the coalition and the advent of a **Fianna Fail** (FF) minority government. In the November 1982 FG–Labour coalition government, he was minister for industry, trade, commerce, and tourism. He was minister for finance once again in 1986; however, the coalition again collapsed over differences on the budget, and FG performed poorly in the general election the following year.

Bruton failed to win the party leadership in 1987, but after further poor electoral performances, Bruton became FG leader in 1990. After the 1992 general election, Bruton's strained relationship with Labour leader Dick Spring was viewed as one reason why an FG–Labour coalition government was not formed, and it was not until December 1994 that Bruton was able to form a coalition government with Labour and the Democratic Left. At the age of 47, Bruton became the youngest ever taoiseach.

Perceived as being right wing and unsympathetic to militant **republicans**, Bruton became taoiseach at a time when progress in Northern Ireland was stalled on the issue of whether **decommissioning** of **paramilitary** weapons was required before talks could begin. In February 1995 he jointly launched the abortive **Frameworks Documents** with **John Major**. Although he was viewed as being sympathetic to **unionists**, he developed a working relationship with **Sinn Fein**'s (SF) **Gerry Adams**. After the breakdown of the **Irish Republican Army** (IRA) ceasefire in February 1996 and the murder of Garda Jerry McCabe in June 1996, however, the relationship became strained, although contacts with SF were maintained. His criticism of the **Royal Ulster Constabulary** (RUC) for allowing an **Orange Order** march at **Drumcree** to proceed won him support from **nationalists** but alienated unionists.

Following the 1997 general election, Bruton was unable to form a government, and FG was forced into opposition. With no sign of a return to government, Bruton faced increased criticism from within the party and was forced to resign as leader in January 2001. In 2004 he retired from Irish politics and became the European Union ambassador to the **United States** in October of that year.

## – C –

**CALLAGHAN, JAMES (JIM) (1912–2005).** **Labour Party** politician and prime minister, James Callaghan was born in Portsmouth on 27 March 1912. Callaghan's father, a chief petty officer in the Royal Navy, died when he was nine, and although he attended Portsmouth Northern Secondary School, he could not afford to go to university. He took up a job with the Inland Revenue in 1929 but resigned in 1937 to become a full-time trade union official. In June 1940 he volunteered for the Royal Navy and later served in the Far East. Callaghan joined the Labour Party in 1931, and in 1945 he won the Cardiff South seat from the **Conservative Party**. Under Clement Attlee he held a number of junior positions in government. During the period of Conservative government from 1951 to 1964, he joined the shadow cabinet and became known as an able television performer. His affable manner would eventually help win him the nickname "Sunny Jim."

In 1963 he was unsuccessful in a challenge for the Labour Party leadership; however, when Labour returned to power in 1964, he was appointed chancellor of the exchequer under **Harold Wilson**. After the devaluation of sterling in October 1967, Callaghan offered his resignation. Wilson refused to accept this, but Callaghan insisted on leaving the treasury and was immediately appointed as home secretary.

While home secretary, Callaghan had some responsibility for Northern Ireland affairs. However, since the 1920s **Westminster** had strenuously avoided any deep involvement in Northern Ireland matters. With the growth of the civil rights movement and pressure from the **Campaign for Democracy in Ulster** (CDU), though, Callaghan began to exert pressure on the **Northern Ireland government** to speed up its program of reform. **Terence O'Neill**'s move toward reform increased party political and sectarian tensions within Northern Ireland, leading to the outbreak of widespread rioting in August 1969.

On 14 August 1969, Wilson and Callaghan agreed to **James Chichester-Clark**'s request for military assistance, and British troops were deployed to the streets of Northern Ireland in support of the **Royal Ulster Constabulary** (RUC). The deployment of troops inevitably meant an escalation of the involvement of Westminster in Northern Ireland affairs beyond purely security matters.

Callaghan was anxious to ensure that the **Ulster Unionist** (UUP) government in Northern Ireland moved forward with plans for the reform of public housing allocation and local government as quickly as possible. Besides this, Callaghan also influenced changes to policing that took place, including the abolition of the **Ulster Special Constabulary** (USC). Despite these changes the security situation continued to deteriorate, and it was during this period that the **Irish Republican Army** (IRA) reemerged and relations between the **British Army** and Catholics in the North deteriorated significantly. Callaghan considered the possibility of suspending the **Northern Ireland Parliament** and introducing **direct rule** from Westminster. However, this was seen as a measure of last resort that would drag Westminster even further into Northern Ireland affairs, and so this approach was initially rejected.

By the time Labour unexpectedly lost the June 1970 general **election, nationalist** expectations and **unionist** fears were already running ahead of reforms in Northern Ireland, but the worst years of **the Troubles** still lay ahead. Under the Conservative government of **Edward Heath**, the political and security situation deteriorated dramatically, and the Conservatives introduced direct rule.

When Labour returned to power in the wake of the February 1974 general election, the situation was utterly changed. The Labour government faced the impact of soaring oil prices, an ongoing dispute with mineworkers, and a political crisis surrounding the **Sunningdale** deal in Northern Ireland. As foreign secretary (1974–76) Callaghan had little direct contact with Northern Ireland affairs, but in April 1976 he was elected leader of the Labour Party and prime minister in succession to Wilson, becoming the only politician in the 20th century to hold all four of the major offices of state in the United Kingdom.

As prime minister, Callaghan's term of office was overshadowed by internal party disputes, a decreasing majority in the House of Commons, and industrial unrest leading to the "winter of discontent" in Britain in 1978–79. No major policy initiatives aimed at **devolution** were undertaken in Northern Ireland; however, the decision to increase the number of Northern Ireland Members of Parliament (MP) at Westminster (from 12 to between 16 and 18 seats, depending on acceptable boundaries) pleased unionists but angered nationalists.

In May 1979 Labour lost the general election, and in 1980 Callaghan stepped down as party leader. He remained an MP until 1987, when he received a life peerage, taking the title Lord Callaghan of Cardiff. James Callaghan died on 26 March 2005 on the eve of his 93rd birthday.

**CAMERON COMMISSION.** In January 1969 the **Northern Ireland government** established a commission under Lord Cameron to inquire into violence that had occurred since 5 October of the previous year. The findings of the commission were published in September 1969. The commission was critical of the Northern Ireland government and described its attitude as complacent. Among the causes of the outbreak of violence, the report highlighted the following: a sense of injustice among large sections of the Catholic community in regard to local authority housing allocation; religious **discrimination** in appointments; gerrymandering of local government boundaries to maintain **unionist** control in some areas; the failure of the Northern Ireland government to investigate complaints; resentment of Catholics toward the exclusively Protestant **Ulster Special Constabulary** (USC); resentment about the Special Powers Act; and fears among Protestants of a threat to unionist control of Northern Ireland because of an increasing Catholic population. The commission said the situation had been made worse by the hostile reaction of **loyalist** groups to the **Northern Ireland Civil Rights Association** (NICRA) and **People's Democracy** (PD), all of which helped create an atmosphere that easily led to violence. The report was also critical of the **Royal Ulster Constabulary** (RUC), the actions of which had, on occasion, been inept.

**CAMPAIGN FOR DEMOCRACY IN ULSTER (CDU).** A pressure group based in London that, in the late 1960s, worked for the introduction of reforms in Northern Ireland. It received significant support from members of the **Labour Party**, including the future **Northern Ireland Office** (NIO) minister Stanley Orme and future Labour opposition spokesman on Northern Ireland Kevin McNamara. Among its many roles, the CDU provided a forum in which the then West **Belfast** Member of Parliament (MP) **Gerry Fitt** highlighted areas of **discrimination** in public life in Northern Ireland.

**CAMPAIGN FOR EQUAL CITIZENSHIP (CEC).** One side effect of the **Anglo–Irish Agreement** (AIA) was to increase support within **unionist** circles for closer political links with Great Britain. As part of this strategy, the pressure group CEC was launched in May 1986 with the aim of achieving the full **integration** of Northern Ireland within the United Kingdom and having the **Conservative** and **Labour Parties** organize in Northern Ireland. The CEC argued that sectarianism in Northern Ireland could only be defeated by giving **electors** the opportunity to vote for parties based on economic interests.

While it drew a significant amount of its support from unionists, the CEC had a broader appeal because the electorate of Northern Ireland could not vote for either of the two political parties likely to form the government of the United Kingdom. Because the parties refused to organize in Northern Ireland, the electorate's rights as citizens of the United Kingdom were diminished. The leading figure of the CEC was **Robert McCartney**, Queen's Counsel (QC); however, he was increasingly viewed as articulating specifically unionist concerns by some, which helped distance him from some CEC members. As unionist fears concerning the AIA declined, the organization lost some support. Additionally, after the Conservatives voted to campaign in Northern Ireland in 1989, the CEC had achieved part of its objectives; however, the Labour Party has continued to oppose contesting elections in Northern Ireland.

**CAMPAIGN FOR SOCIAL JUSTICE (CSJ).** Established in January 1964, the CSJ organized a publicity campaign in Britain and internationally to highlight instances of **discrimination** in Northern Ireland. Based in Dungannon, Co. Tyrone, the CSJ sought to bring particular attention to discrimination in the areas of employment, public housing allocation, **electoral** practices, the gerrymandering of electoral boundaries, and public appointments. The leading spokespersons for the organization were Dr. Conn McCluskey and his wife, Councilor Patricia McCluskey. The efforts of CSJ were important in paving the way for the subsequent **Northern Ireland Civil Rights Association** (NICRA) campaign and helped establish links between civil rights campaigners in Northern Ireland and members of the British **Labour Party**.

**CENSUS.** The U.K. census is held once every 10 years. Although the census provides a wide range of information, in the context of **the Troubles**, it was most often scrutinized in terms of the religious makeup of the population, as this had implications in terms of changes in political support.

In 1971 the population of Northern Ireland was just over 1.5 million, with 31.4 percent Catholic, 26.7 percent Presbyterian, 22.0 percent Church of Ireland, 4.7 percent Methodist, 5.7 percent other denominations, and 9.4 percent no religious affiliation or did not reply to the question.

The 1981 census was conducted during the course of the **hunger strike** campaign of that year and was considered to be inaccurate, as many **republicans** refused to fill in the census form. A woman collecting census forms was shot and killed by the **Irish Republican Army** (IRA) in **Derry**. The uncorrected 1981 figures put the population of Northern Ireland at just under 1.5 million, with 28.0 percent Catholic, 22.9 percent Presbyterian, 19.0 percent Church of Ireland, 4.0 percent Methodist, 7.6 percent other denominations, and 18.5 percent no religious affiliation or did not reply.

In 1991 the census put the population of Northern Ireland at just under 1.6 million, with 38.4 percent Catholic, 21.4 percent Presbyterian, 17.7 percent Church of Ireland, and 3.8 percent Methodist. There were numerous other Protestant groups, including the Baptists, Brethren, and Free Presbyterian Church of Ulster as well as others, describing themselves merely as Protestant, making up 2.7 percent of the population. Other groups made up 5.0 percent. Those claiming no denomination made up 3.7 percent, and 7.3 percent did not state a religious affiliation.

The 2001 census gave the population of Northern Ireland at just under 1.7 million, with 40.2 percent Catholic, 20.7 percent Presbyterian, 15.3 percent Church of Ireland, 3.5 percent Methodist, 6.1 percent other Christian denominations, 0.3 percent other religions, and 13.9 percent no religion or did not reply.

**CENTRAL CITIZENS' DEFENCE COMMITTEE (CCDC).** Following the outbreak of major sectarian conflict in August 1969, a number of Catholic community organizations in West **Belfast** amalgamated to form the CCDC. The CCDC included local political representatives, such as **Paddy Devlin**, as well as Catholic clergymen. It opposed the use of violence against the security forces but saw them as **discriminating** against Catholics. Disputes of this sort were highlighted by incidents such as the Falls Road curfew of July 1970. In the early 1970s, the CCDC was routinely involved in discussions with the government and the British Army. In June 1973 it made an unsuccessful attempt to persuade the Provisional **Irish Republican Army** (PIRA) to end its campaign.

**CHICHESTER-CLARK, JAMES (1923–2002). Ulster Unionist Party** (UUP) politician and prime minister of Northern Ireland, James Chichester-Clark was born in Castledawson, Co. Londonderry, on 12 February 1923. He was educated at Selwyn House School in Kent and at Eton. Like his distant cousin **Terence O'Neill**, he was a member of one of the most famous families in Ireland. During World War II, he served in North Africa and Italy with the Irish Guards. He remained in the army until 1960, when he retired as a major. In the same year he was returned unopposed in a by-**election** for the **Stormont** seat of South Londonderry. Under Terence O'Neill, he was appointed junior minister in finance and chief whip of the Ulster Unionist Parliamentary Party (UUP Members of Parliament [MP] at Stormont) in 1963. In 1966 he became leader of the House of Commons and, in 1967, minister of agriculture.

As opposition to O'Neill began to increase within the UUP, Chichester-Clark was viewed as a possible successor. In April 1969 he resigned from the government on the grounds that reforms were being introduced too quickly and that this would increase political instability. Chichester-Clark's resignation further weakened O'Neill's tenuous position, and O'Neill resigned as prime minister less than a week later. Chichester-Clark subsequently defeated **Brian Faulkner** in a vote of UUP MPs at Stormont to become party leader and prime minister in May 1969. In some areas Chichester-Clark faced an even more difficult situation than O'Neill, and when the simmering political and sectarian tensions came to a head in August 1969, Chichester-Clark was forced to ask the British government to send troops to Northern Ireland in support of the overstretched **Royal Ulster Constabulary** (RUC). This development, however, also had the effect of involving the British government more directly in Northern Ireland affairs.

The growth of sectarian violence encouraged the development of **paramilitary** groups, not least the **Irish Republican Army** (IRA). As the IRA became more active, Chichester-Clark faced growing pressure from **unionists** to pursue a stronger security policy. On 18 March 1971, he met Prime Minister **Edward Heath** to ask for support of stronger security measures. Heath refused to support him, and Chichester-Clark resigned as prime minister of Northern Ireland two days later. In the same year, he received a life peerage and took the title of Lord Moyola. He died on 17 May 2002.

**CIVIC FORUM.** The concept of the civic forum as an element of the **Good Friday Agreement** (GFA) can largely be attributed to the efforts of the **Northern Ireland Women's Coalition** (NIWC). The NIWC wanted elements of civil society to be recognized within the overall political settlement and as such promoted the idea of a civic forum that would include representatives from businesses, trade unions, and the voluntary and community sectors. The civic forum was a novel attempt to give a formalized consultative role on social, economic, and cultural issues to important nonparty political sections of society. However, it also attempted to address fears within these sections of society that the return of a locally **elected** administration could work to their detriment as influence in policymaking areas shifted away from them toward the politicians.

In the medium term, a number of commentators have considered that the civic forum has underperformed in its role. This might be attributed partly to the forum's inability to establish a clear position for itself but may also be due to the greater accessibility of Northern Ireland executive ministers when compared to their **Northern Ireland Office** (NIO) counterparts under **direct rule**. As a result many groups that were expected to look to the civic forum to represent their interests instead found it more effective to take their case directly to the relevant executive minister. The civic forum was suspended in October 2002 at the same time as the **Northern Ireland Assembly**.

**CLINTON, WILLIAM (BILL) (1946– ).** President of the **United States**, Bill Clinton was born in Hope, Arkansas, on 19 August 1946. He graduated with a BSc in foreign service from Georgetown University and later a law degree from Yale Law School. He was a Rhodes Scholar at Oxford in 1968, where he developed an interest in affairs in Northern Ireland. In 1974, while lecturing in law at the University of Arkansas, he ran for the House of Representatives but was narrowly defeated. In 1976 he was **elected** attorney general of Arkansas and in 1978 governor of the state. He lost the office in the 1980 election but regained it in 1982. A skillfully managed campaign saw him win first the Democratic Party nomination and then the presidency in November 1992.

A significant factor in Clinton's success was the support of Irish American groups. His suggestion that he might send a presidential peace envoy to Northern Ireland had raised concerns among the British government and **unionists**. As president, with some notable exceptions, he pursued a pragmatic policy aimed at encouraging all political actors in Northern Ireland to reach agreement. He supported the **Downing Street Declaration** (1993) but outraged the British government by granting **Gerry Adams** a visa to the United States in January 1994. There was further criticism from Great Britain in March 1995 when he publicly shook hands with Adams at a function in

Washington. Such actions were, however, exceptions to a general policy of supporting the line taken by the British and Irish governments.

Clinton's appointment of **George Mitchell** as an economic envoy in 1994 was to have significant consequences through Mitchell's continuing role in the **peace process**. His arrival on a tour of London, **Belfast**, and Dublin in late November 1995 coincided with the launch of a twin-track policy outlining an approach to dealing with the issue of illegal weapons and political talks. Clinton's visit was widely viewed as politically balanced and providing a key moment in the developing peace process. When the **Irish Republican Army** (IRA) ended its ceasefire in February 1996, he refused demands to end visas to the United States for **Sinn Fein** (SF) members, but he encouraged **paramilitary** groups to end their campaigns.

After the IRA renewed its ceasefire in July 1997, he again encouraged parties to work toward agreement and spoke by telephone with some of the parties involved in talks on the final night of negotiations before the signing of the **Good Friday Agreement** (GFA). He threw his support behind the campaign in favor of the agreement and subsequently encouraged the **political parties** to work for its implementation. He visited Northern Ireland in September 1998 and again in December 2000, though with less impact than during his first visit. Unionists, disillusioned with the implementation of the GFA, began to question his evenhandedness with Northern Ireland over such issues as the apparent downplaying of IRA gun smuggling from Florida in 1999.

**COLLUSION.** The issue of the extent to which state forces assisted or participated in the murder of individuals for political reasons. The issue touched on the gray areas of intelligence gathering and counterterrorism and the question of whether agents of the state could operate on the fringes of the law in order to defeat terrorism. Although alleged cases of collusion included a number of incidents in the Republic, most referred to events in Northern Ireland and particularly those involving locally raised organizations such as the **Royal Ulster Constabulary** (RUC) and **Ulster Defence Regiment** (UDR) and **loyalist paramilitaries**.

The issue of collusion was investigated in the **Stevens Inquiry**, which found there was no institutional collusion between loyalists and the RUC. The issue was given renewed significance with the murder of solicitor Rosemary Nelson by loyalists in March 1999. In 2001 Peter Cory was appointed to examine several high-profile cases where collusion was alleged to have taken place, and the **Cory Reports** led to a number of inquiries being established. In November 2006 an independent report that examined 76 killings between 1972 and 1977 claimed that members of the security forces had colluded with loyalist paramilitaries in all but two of the **deaths**. In the same month, a report from a committee of the Irish Parliament also claimed that there had been significant collusion between loyalist paramilitaries and the security forces. In January 2007 a report from the police ombudsman stated that members of the RUC's special branch protected from prosecution an **Ulster Volunteer Force** (UVF) member who was a police informant despite his involvement in up to 16 murders. The ombudsman said that there was insufficient evidence to prosecute police officers involved in the event because evidence was either missing or had been destroyed. In March 2007 the ombudsman's report was in turn criticized by the Police Federation, the body that represents the views of police officers.

Debate on the issue within Northern Ireland helped demonstrate the high level of polarization between **unionists** and **nationalists** on the comparative importance of the events of **the Troubles**. Nationalists viewed the issue of collusion as one of equality and justice for Catholics in Northern Ireland; however, some unionists viewed the same issue as an attempt by **republicans** to demonize the security forces and highlight murders carried out by loyalists, while minimizing the greater number carried out by republican paramilitary organizations.

**COMBINED LOYALIST MILITARY COMMAND (CLMC).** The CLMC was an umbrella organization established by **loyalist paramilitary** organizations in April 1991 to coincide with the beginning of interparty talks in Northern Ireland. The CLMC included the **Ulster Volunteer Force** (UVF), **Ulster Freedom Fighters** (UFF), and Red Hand Commando. When the talks ended in July, the CLMC also ended its ceasefire. Even during this period, the CLMC sidestepped its own ceasefire by murdering **Sinn Fein** (SF) councilor Eddie Fullerton in Co. Donegal in the **Republic of Ireland.**

During the **Brooke–Mayhew Talks** of 1992, the CLMC did not repeat its ceasefire and appeared ready to use violence for tactical purposes whenever it felt it was necessary. As the **peace process** developed, it warned against any threat to the union with Great Britain but accepted the democratic pursuit of political and constitutional change.

Following the announcement of a ceasefire by the **Irish Republican Army** (IRA) in August 1994, the CLMC sought assurances from the British and Irish governments that no secret deal had been made with the IRA. Having received these assurances, on 13 October 1994, the CLMC announced a ceasefire, declared that the union was safe, and offered "abject and true remorse" to "innocent" **victims**.

In August 1995 it issued a statement saying it would "not initiate a return to war. There will be no first strike." However, it ruled out any discussion of **decommissioning** loyalist weapons while the IRA remained armed. Following the breakdown of the IRA ceasefire in February 1996, it largely maintained its ceasefire, though this was threatened by the crisis surrounding the controversy at **Drumcree** and the breakaway of the Portadown-based UVF group, which subsequently became the **Loyalist Volunteer Force** (LVF). The decision by the CLMC to expel **Billy Wright** and Alex Kerr and threaten them in August 1996 to leave Northern Ireland or face "summary justice" brought the situation to a crisis and also raised questions as to the democratic credentials of the **Progressive Unionist Party** (PUP) and **Ulster Democratic Party** (UDP).

Beyond this, relations between the **Ulster Defence Association** (UDA) and UVF also began to deteriorate. In October 1997 the failure of PUP representatives to appear at a UDA rally marking the third anniversary of the loyalist ceasefire highlighted tensions between the loyalist organizations, and the CLMC was formally disbanded later in the same month.

**COMMUNITY RELATIONS.** The strained relationship between the Protestant and Catholic communities in Northern Ireland was one of the, if not the, most significant features of **the Troubles**. Under pressure from then home secretary **James Callaghan** in October 1969, **Ulster Unionist Party** (UUP) **Stormont** Member of Parliament (MP) Robert Simpson was appointed as the first minister of community relations in the **Northern Ireland government**. Simpson was followed by the **Northern Ireland Labour Party**'s (NILP) **David Bleakley** (March–October 1971) and Basil McIvor of the UUP until the introduction of **direct rule** in March 1972, when the function was overseen by **Northern Ireland Office** (NIO) ministers. Under the **power-sharing** Northern Ireland executive of 1974, **Social Democratic and Labour Party** (SDLP) member and civil rights campaigner Ivan Cooper was minister of community relations but, after direct rule resumed, subsequently fell within the remit of the NIO minister responsible for education.

In 1990 the government established the Community Relations Council (CRC) as an independent body to promote better community relations. With the developing **peace process** and lower level of violence, this provided a more helpful environment within which the CRC could operate.

Under the Northern Ireland executive after December 1999, the task of reaching agreement on a community relations policy proved to be a protracted process. It was not until March 2005, again under the remit of NIO ministers, that the policy document for community relations titled "A Shared Future" emerged. This document was significant in stating that society in Northern Ireland should be integrated using shared resources and that appropriate policy actions should be taken to help create such a society. Within this remit the Northern Ireland Housing Executive launched the first mixed community social housing scheme at a site near Enniskillen in October 2006.

Although community relations in Northern Ireland have traditionally dealt with divisions between the Protestant and Catholic communities, the arrival of new ethnic groups in the early 21st century raised new issues. The expansion of the European Union (EU) in May 2004 and the arrival of larger numbers of asylum seekers led to a significant increase in the number of members of ethnic minority groups living in Northern Ireland and to the emergence of a new series of issues in community relations.

**COMPTON REPORT.** The report of a committee of inquiry that was established by the **Northern Ireland government** in August 1971 to look into allegations of the ill treatment of those who had been interned earlier in the month. The inquiry was headed by Sir Edmund Compton. The report was published in November 1971 and concluded that individuals had not suffered physical brutality but that there had been "ill treatment" of some of those interned. While there had not been torture, there had been "in-depth" interrogation. This involved hooding detainees, forcing detainees to stand with their arms against walls for long periods of time, and using "white noise" and food and sleep deprivation to cause confusion. The conclusions of the report were criticized in Great Britain and in Northern Ireland and led the British home secretary to establish a new inquiry under Lord Parker to examine whether such interrogation methods should be changed.

**CONSERVATIVE PARTY.** One of the two major **political parties** of the United Kingdom. During the course of **the Troubles**, the Conservatives formed the government from June 1970 until February 1974 under **Edward Heath**. The party returned to power in May 1979 under **Margaret Thatcher** and, from November 1990, **John Major**. Following internal party disputes, the party was heavily defeated in the 1997 general **election**, and it remained in opposition for the following decade. The Conservative Party was traditionally associated with the **Ulster Unionist Party** (UUP). During 1972–74 Robin Chichester-Clark, UUP Member of Parliament (MP) for Londonderry and brother of **James Chichester-Clark** served as a minister in the Conservative government.

Under the political and security pressures created by the Troubles, the relationship between the Conservatives and the UUP broke down, and UUP MPs were not offered the Conservative whip at **Westminster** after the February 1974 general election. As leader of the opposition after 1975, Margaret Thatcher appeared to favor UUP policies but, following the murder of Northern Ireland spokesman Airey Neave in March 1979, retreated to a more bilateral approach with the **Labour Party**.

The signing of the **Anglo-Irish Agreement** (AIA) in 1985 saw a breakdown in relations between **unionists** and the Conservative government, but only a minority within the party supported unionists' opposition to the AIA. Despite this an element of unionism reacted to the AIA by taking an **integrationist** approach and seeking closer ties with the Conservatives.

In 1988 the party's national union rejected an approach by a North Down "model" Conservative association to become affiliated to the party; however, a year later the Conservatives voted in favor of the principle of organizing in Northern Ireland.

In the 1992 Westminster general election, Conservative candidates contested 11 Northern Ireland constituencies but averaged only 5.7 percent of the vote in these areas. Under John Major the loose working relationship between the Conservatives and the UUP also appeared to work against the interests of Conservatives in Northern Ireland. In 1998 Northern Ireland became an area party within the national restructuring of the Conservatives, but by this time it retained only three councilors in Northern Ireland.

Since the 2001 **district council** elections, Conservatives have had no council representation. Despite this, internal disputes within the UUP, often associated with the implementation of the **Good Friday Agreement** (GFA), have led some UUP members to see the Conservative Party as a more appropriate political home.

In 2006 a number of UUP members left the party to join the Conservatives, including a former junior minister in the **Northern Ireland Assembly**, James Leslie, and later former leader **David Trimble**. In 2006 it was estimated that the Conservative Party in Northern Ireland had approximately 350 members.

In the March 2007 Northern Ireland Assembly election, the Conservatives received 0.5 percent of first-preference votes and failed to win any seats.

**CONSOCIATIONALISM.** A system of government in which the leaders of ethnic groups within a deeply divided society are represented in the governing (**power-sharing**) executive in an attempt to maintain political stability. The elements of a consociational settlement, outlined by the Dutch political scientist Arend Lijphart, include the following: a grand coalition executive, mutual veto, proportionality of representation in civic society (for example, in the police and civil service), and segmental autonomy. The idea of establishing a consociational form of government in Northern Ireland had a strong appeal to the British government after 1972, and elements of consociationalism appeared in the 1973 **Sunningdale** Agreement, 1982 **Northern Ireland Assembly**, and 1998 **Good Friday Agreement** (GFA). The

Sunningdale Agreement represented the political initiative that most closely followed the classic consociational framework. The collapse of the Northern Ireland executive in May 1974 in the face of **unionist** opposition led Lijphart to reexamine the theory in relation to the particular circumstances of Northern Ireland. The GFA of 1998 contains strong elements of consociationalism in its political structures but also includes aspects relating to security and other issues. As a result the GFA has been referred to as "consociation plus" by the political scientist Brendan O'Leary.

**CONSTITUTIONAL CONVENTION.** After the failure of the **Sunningdale** deal in May 1974, the British government put forward plans for a Constitutional Convention for Northern Ireland in which local politicians would attempt to reach agreement among themselves for a widely acceptable form of government throughout the community. **Elections** to the Convention were held on 1 May 1975, resulting in 47 **unionists** and **loyalists** being elected, giving them an overall majority in the 78-seat Convention.

Having defeated enforced **power sharing** a year earlier, unionists were unwilling to contemplate similar proposals in the Convention. While unionists offered at most representation for opposition parties at the departmental committee level, the **Social Democratic and Labour Party** (SDLP), **Alliance Party of Northern Ireland** (APNI), and **Northern Ireland Labour Party** (NILP) wanted power sharing at a Northern Ireland executive level. In September Vanguard leader **William Craig** attempted to break the deadlock by suggesting a temporary, voluntary coalition government. This was generally well received by the nonunionist parties but was rejected by the **United Ulster Unionist Council** (UUUC).

In November 1975 a majority report was presented by the unionists, but this was rejected by the government as not meeting the criterion of providing for a widely acceptable form of government. The Convention was recalled briefly in February 1976, but further meetings failed to produce proposals that the government found acceptable, and the Convention was dissolved on 3 March 1976.

**CONTINUITY IRISH REPUBLICAN ARMY (CIRA).** A **republican paramilitary** group commonly associated with **Republican**

Sinn Fein (RSF), although this connection is rejected by the RSF itself. CIRA became prominent after mid-1996, when it began a campaign of bomb attacks across Northern Ireland and in London. The organization is believed to consist of republican activists who have become disaffected by **Sinn Fein**'s (SF) role in the **peace process**. It is believed to be in possession of a small number of arms and explosives stolen by defectors from the **Irish Republican Army** (IRA). Estimates of the number of active members of CIRA range from 50 to 150. In October 2006 CIRA admitted responsibility for a series of firebomb attacks on shops in Northern Ireland.

**CORRIGAN-MAGUIRE, MAIREAD (1944– ).** Peace campaigner, Mairead Corrigan-Maguire was born on 27 January 1944. She was educated at a commercial college in **Belfast** and was the aunt of the three Maguire children who were killed when they were struck by a gunman's getaway car in West Belfast in August 1976. She subsequently joined with **Betty Williams** to organize marches and rallies in support of peace, leading to the formation of the Women's Peace Movement, later renamed the **Peace People**.

With Betty Williams she was awarded the Nobel Peace Prize in 1976 but later differed with Williams on how the prize money should be spent, as well as on other areas of strategy. After Williams left the Peace People, Corrigan remained close to the organization, becoming chairwoman in 1980. In 1980 her sister, Anne Maguire, who never fully recovered from the deaths of her children, committed suicide. A year later Mairead Corrigan married her sister's widower, Jackie Maguire. The couple subsequently had two sons of their own. As a Nobel Peace Prize winner, she has remained an influential figure, continuing to campaign on issues relating to Northern Ireland and on international issues, such as the Gulf War in 1991 and Iraq in 2003. In April 2007 she was injured by Israel Defense Forces while protesting against the erection of a security barrier between Palestinian and Israeli settlements.

**CORY REPORTS.** In the wake of the **Weston Park Talks** of July 2001, retired Canadian judge Peter Cory was appointed by the British and Irish governments to examine a number of allegations that members of the security forces had colluded with **paramilitary** groups to bring about the **deaths** of certain individuals. In Northern Ireland four cases involved **collusion** between the security forces and **loyalists** in the murders of Pat Finucane (1989), Robert Hamill (1997), and Rosemary Nelson (1999) and collusion with **republicans** in the death of **Billy Wright** (1997). In the Republic two cases involved possible collusion between **Garda Siochana** members and republicans in the murders of Lord Justice Maurice Gibson and his wife Cecily (1987) and **Royal Ulster Constabulary** (RUC) officers Chief Superintendent Harry Breen and Superintendent Robert Buchanan (1989).

In October 2003 Cory reported that he found no evidence of collusion in the Gibson case but recommended a public inquiry in the Breen and Buchanan case. The Irish government subsequently established the Smithwick Tribunal. Cory also recommended that inquiries be established for all four cases in Northern Ireland. The Rosemary Nelson inquiry was chaired by Sir Michael Morland, the Billy Wright inquiry by Lord MacLean, and the Robert Hamill inquiry by Sir Edwin Jowitt, while the Pat Finucane inquiry had yet to open in October 2006. In the same month it was announced that the inquiry into the murder of Rosemary Nelson, formally opened in May 2005, would be delayed for nine months to allow more time to prepare for hearings. In 2005 Peter Cory criticized legislation introduced by the British government that limited the scope of the inquiries.

**COSGRAVE, LIAM (1920– ). Fine Gael** (FG) leader and taoiseach, Liam Cosgrave was born in Co. Dublin on 13 April 1920. Educated at Castleknock College, he was the son of Irish revolutionary, politician, and taoiseach William T. Cosgrave. In 1943 he was **elected** as an FG member to the **Dail** for Co. Dublin, later Dun Laoghaire-Rathdown, and held the seat for the rest of his political career. He was a junior minister in the 1948–51 coalition government and minister for external affairs in the FG–**Irish Labour** coalition government of 1954–57. In 1965 he became FG leader in succession to James Dillon. Despite being criticized by some for a lack of personal charisma and socially conservative beliefs, he was able to become taoiseach in 1973 at the head of a FG–Labour coalition government.

As taoiseach the conflict in Northern Ireland was one of the most significant issues with which he had to deal. He led the Irish delegation at the **Sunningdale** Conference of December 1973 but declined to hold a referendum on the **Irish constitutional claim to Northern Ireland**, fearing that the vote would be lost. Attempts to find a compromise proved unsuccessful and helped undermine **unionist** support for Sunningdale. In the 1977 Irish general election, the coalition government lost power, and Cosgrave resigned as leader of FG. He retired from the Dail in 1981.

**CRAIG, WILLIAM (BILL) (1924– ). Unionist** politician, William Craig was born in Cookstown, Co. Tyrone, on 2 December 1924. He was educated at Dungannon Royal School, Larne Grammar School, and Queen's University, **Belfast** (QUB). During World War II, he served as a crew member with a Royal Air Force bomber squadron but also continued his legal studies. He qualified as a solicitor in 1952. After the war he joined the **Ulster Unionist Party** (UUP) and was a leading member of the Young Unionists. He was **elected** to the **Northern Ireland Parliament** for the Larne constituency in a 1960 by-election. He was government chief whip at **Stormont**, 1962–63, and under **Terence O'Neill** he was minister of home affairs, 1963–64; minister of health and local government, 1964–65; minister of development, 1965–66 and minister of home affairs for a second time, 1966–68.

He was critical of the **Northern Ireland Civil Rights Association** (NICRA), which he viewed as a front for the **Irish Republican Army** (IRA), and banned the 5 October 1968 civil rights march in **Derry**, the consequences of which helped bring about the outbreak of communal conflict in 1969. On 11 December 1968, he was dismissed by O'Neill; however, Craig continued to build a base of support in opposition to O'Neill, both inside and outside the UUP.

In 1971 he was narrowly defeated by **Brian Faulkner** for the leadership of the UUP. In February 1972, in anticipation of the introduction of **direct rule**, he launched **Ulster Vanguard** as a right-wing pressure group within the UUP and organized a number of mass rallies, at which he made several hard-line speeches. Amid heightened unionist fears of a British withdrawal from Northern Ireland, he promoted the idea of **independence** for Northern Ireland in preference to a united Ireland, and this alienated him from many mainstream unionists.

In March 1973, when the Ulster Unionist Council (UUC) voted not to reject British government proposals for the future administration of Northern Ireland, he left the UUP and formed the **Vanguard Unionist Progressive Party** (VUPP). In June he was elected to the **Northern Ireland Assembly** as a member for East Belfast. In December 1973 he joined other unionist political leaders in forming the **United Ulster Unionist Council** (UUUC) to oppose the **Sunningdale** Agreement and in February 1974 won the East Belfast seat in the **Westminster** general election of that month. He was the most prominent unionist politician in the **Ulster Workers' Council (UWC) strike** of May 1974 and the one most trusted by **loyalist paramilitaries** and the UWC.

In May 1975 he was elected to the Northern Ireland **Constitutional Convention**, where he broke with other members of the UUUC and proposed a temporary voluntary coalition government with **nationalists** as a possible way forward. Craig found himself isolated from the bulk of unionist opinion on the issue as well as instigating a split in his own party.

In 1978 he rejoined the UUP but narrowly lost his East Belfast seat to **Peter Robinson** of the **Democratic Unionist Party** (DUP) in 1979. He was appointed a member of the Council of Europe in 1976 and 1979. Given his controversial background, the appointment to what was perceived as a politically neutral position was the source of some criticism, particularly from nationalists. He was a candidate in the 1982 Northern Ireland Assembly election in East Belfast but was not elected and subsequently retired from public life.

**CROSSROADS ELECTION.** In December 1968 the then Northern Ireland prime minister **Terence O'Neill** went over the heads of **unionist** critics of his reformist policies by making a television appeal for support from the public. In this broadcast he stated, "Ulster stands at the crossroads. . . . What kind of Ulster do you want? A happy and respected province in good standing with the rest of the United Kingdom or a place continually torn apart by riots and demonstrations and regarded by the rest of Britain as a political outcast?" The broadcast won O'Neill much public support, but in the following months, the crisis deepened, and on 3 February 1969, O'Neill responded by calling a general **election** to the **Northern Ireland Parliament** for 24 February. By calling the election, he hoped to demonstrate the degree of public support for his policies and isolate his critics. Referring to

O'Neill's December 1968 speech, this election came to be known as the "crossroads election."

With a turnout of just under 72.0 percent, the election returned 39 unionists (24 official unionists and 3 unofficial unionists supporting O'Neill, 10 official **Ulster Unionist Party** [UUP] members opposing O'Neill, and 2 undecided), 6 members of the **Nationalist Party** (NP), 3 civil rights candidates, 2 republican **Labour** candidates, and 2 members of the **Northern Ireland Labour Party** (NILP).

Although O'Neill and his supporters won an overall majority of seats, he failed to see off his critics. Instead the election served mainly to demonstrate the divisions within the unionist political bloc. Official unionist supporters of O'Neill won 31.1 percent of the poll and unofficial unionist supporters of O'Neill a further 12.9 percent. However, anti-O'Neill official unionists won 17.1 percent of the poll. Signposting future developments, there was also a shift in voting in the **nationalist** bloc away from the NP toward individuals connected with the civil rights movement.

The election saw the emergence of a number of figures who were to dominate Northern Ireland politics for the next three decades, not least **John Hume** (who was elected for the Foyle constituency) and Rev. **Ian Paisley** (who provided a strong challenge but lost to O'Neill in Bannside).

**CURRIE, AUSTIN (1939– ). Nationalist, Social Democratic and Labour Party** (SDLP), and **Fine Gael** (FG) politician, Austin Currie was born in Coalisland, Co. Tyrone, on 11 October 1939. He was educated at St. Patrick's Academy, Dungannon, and Queen's University, **Belfast** (QUB), where he studied history and politics. In 1964, as a **Nationalist Party** (NP) candidate, he won a by-**election** for the **Northern Ireland Parliament** seat of East Tyrone and became the youngest person ever elected to the Northern Ireland Parliament. He retained the seat until the abolition of the Parliament in 1972. In June 1968 he took part in the sit-in at a council house in Caledon, Co. Tyrone, as part of a protest over the allocation of the house to an unmarried Protestant woman ahead of the claims of a number of Catholic families. He spoke regularly at civil rights events and helped organize the initial civil rights march from Coalisland to Dungannon in August 1968.

Currie was critical of the NP for its failure to modernize its image and structure, and he subsequently became a founding member of the SDLP in August 1970. As a member of the SDLP, he was elected to the **Northern Ireland Assembly** in 1973 (where he served as head of the Department of Housing, Planning, and Local Government in the 1974 Northern Ireland executive), the **Constitutional Convention** in 1975, and the 1982 Northern Ireland Assembly from the Fermanagh-South Tyrone constituency. He was the SDLP chief whip from 1974 until 1979 but resigned the position in order to contest the Fermanagh-South Tyrone **Westminster** constituency in the general election of that year against the wishes of his own party, which did not wish to split the nationalist vote in the constituency. Currie, standing as an independent SDLP candidate, failed to win the seat in any event. He remained the party's candidate for the same Westminster constituency in 1981 but did not contest the two by-elections of that year, which were won by **Bobby Sands** and Owen Carron. During the course of **the Troubles**, his home was attacked on more than 30 occasions. In one of these attacks in November 1972, his wife was badly beaten by **loyalists**.

In the late 1980s, there appeared to be little prospect of a return to **devolved** government in Northern Ireland for the foreseeable future. He participated in the **Duisburg Talks** in October 1988 but by 1989 had moved to the **Republic of Ireland** and was elected to the **Dail** as an FG member for the constituency of West Dublin.

In 1990 he was the FG candidate for the presidency of Ireland, and some observers believed that his Northern Ireland background was a factor in his comparatively poor showing in the election. In 1991 he became FG spokesman on communications and in 1994 spokesman on equality and law reform. Under **John Bruton** he was minister of state in the Departments of Health, Education, and Justice (1994–97), and in opposition he was FG spokesman on energy.

In 2002 he contested the Midwest Dublin constituency but failed to be elected and immediately announced his retirement from politics. As of 2007 he remains the only individual to have served in the elected assemblies of both Northern Ireland and the Republic.

**CUSHNAHAN, JOHN (1948– ). Alliance Party of Northern Ireland** (APNI) leader and **Fine Gael** (FG) Member of the European Parliament

(MEP), John Cushnahan was born in **Belfast** in on 23 July 1948. He was educated at Queen's University, Belfast (QUB), where he obtained a degree in education and subsequently worked as a teacher. He was an early member of APNI and its general secretary from 1974 until 1982. He was **elected** to Belfast City Council in 1977 and remained on the council until 1985. In 1982 he was returned to the **Northern Ireland Assembly** for the North Down constituency.

In September 1984 he succeeded **Oliver Napier** as leader of APNI and sought to develop closer links with the Liberal Party in Great Britain. Following the signing of the **Anglo–Irish Agreement** (AIA) in 1985, he and APNI generally supported the AIA, though this cost the party support from voters in the Protestant community. With the prospects for **devolution** frozen, however, he resigned as leader in September 1987 and subsequently moved to the **Republic of Ireland**. He joined FG and in 1989 was elected to the European Parliament for the Munster constituency. In 2004 he retired as an MEP.

## – D –

**DAIL EIREANN (THE DAIL).** The Lower House of the Oireachtas (Irish Parliament) from which the Irish government is drawn. The Dail has 166 members, known as Teachta Dala (TD), **elected** from multimember constituencies by the single transferable vote method of **proportional representation** (PR). General elections to the Dail are held at least once every five years. The taoiseach (prime minister) is elected by the Dail. The Upper House of the Oirechtas, Seanad Eireann (the senate), consists of nominated members and has substantially less power than the Dail. In January 2007 it was announced that a Dail committee was to be established that would examine Northern Ireland affairs.

**DARLINGTON CONFERENCE.** The first significant attempt after the introduction of **direct rule** to establish a framework for a new political settlement. The conference, called by Secretary of State **William Whitelaw**, was held in Darlington, England, between 25 and 27 September 1972 and attempted to reach agreement on a new form of government for Northern Ireland. Only the **Ulster Unionist Party (UUP)**, **Alliance Party of Northern Ireland** (APNI), and the **Northern Ireland Labour Party** (NILP) attended, while the **Nationalist Party** (NP), **Social Democratic and Labour Party** (SDLP), **Democratic Unionist Party** (DUP), and Republican Labour declined their invitations. Even the parties that did attend the conference, however, failed to reach agreement on what form a future **devolved** Northern Ireland administration should take.

**DEATHS.** Just as there is no definitive agreement on when **the Troubles** began or when they concluded, there is no agreement as to the number of deaths that resulted from the conflict. The most detailed analysis of those who died as a result of the Troubles, *Lost Lives* (McKittrick et al.), begins with the murder of John Scullion by the **Ulster Volunteer Force** (UVF) in June 1966 and concludes with the sectarian murder of Catholic schoolboy Michael McIlveen in May 2006. Of a total of 3,720 deaths, 3,453 occurred in Northern Ireland, with nearly half of these in **Belfast. Paramilitary** organizations suffered 562 casualties, the security forces 1,039, and all others 2,119. More than a third of all casualties, 1,259, were Catholic civilians, while 727 Protestant civilians were killed. Locally recruited members of the security forces, mostly Protestants, suffered 509 casualties, while the **British Army** suffered a further 503 casualties. **Republican** activists had 395 casualties, and loyalists, 167. A further 160 deaths did not fit into any of these categories.

Of those groups responsible for deaths, republican paramilitaries were the largest group, accountable for 2,152 killings. **Loyalists** were responsible for 1,112 deaths, and the security forces, 367. A number of murders could not be clearly attributed to a specific group. The Provisional **Irish Republican Army** (PIRA) alone was responsible for 1,768 deaths, almost half the total number of those killed.

**Police Service of Northern Ireland** (PSNI) figures give the number of people killed in Northern Ireland from 1969 until 2007 as 3,368, consisting of 302 police officers, 452 members of the army, 203 members of the **Ulster Defence Regiment** (UDR) or **Royal Irish Regiment** (RIR), and 2,411 civilians (including paramilitary members). The PSNI lists Francis McCloskey, a 67-year-old man from Dungiven who died on 14 July 1969 after being struck by a police baton, as the first victim of the Troubles. The year with the highest casualty figure was 1972, when 470 people were killed.

In 2006 the PSNI established the Historical Enquiries Team (HET) to examine all deaths attributable to the security situation between 1968 and 1998. The stated objective of the HET was to help bring a degree of resolution to outstanding cases. The HET was also required to work closely with the relatives of the murder **victims**.

**DECOMMISSIONING.** As **paramilitary** organizations began to scale down their campaigns, the **political parties** associated with them sought to be accepted as fully democratic parties. One of the major questions that this raised was what was to be done about weapons held by the paramilitary organizations. For **loyalist** organizations the issue, theoretically at least, should have been more easy to deal with than for **republicans** because the loyalist parties (the **Progressive Unionist Party** [PUP] and **Ulster Democratic Party** [UDP]) accepted being associated with their respective paramilitary groups (the **Ulster Volunteer Force** [UVF]and **Ulster Defence Association** [UDA]). **Sinn Fein** (SF), however, stated that it was not the **Irish Republican Army** (IRA) and did not accept that IRA activities should lead to any penalties on them. Furthermore, because the IRA claimed to be the legitimate army of Ireland, it felt under no obligation to disarm—particularly because such a move might be interpreted as the IRA accepting that it had been defeated militarily. In addition to this, both republican and loyalist paramilitaries faced practical difficulties in tracing all their weapons, as well as concerns about internal feuds or feuds with other paramilitary groups. There was also the broader question of whether these groups wished to keep their weapons as a way of retaining their control in certain areas.

In late 1993 and early 1994, there were disputes between the various political actors as to whether the decommissioning of weapons in connection with political negotiations had even been raised as an issue. The British insisted they had been clear on the need for decommissioning before talks, while republicans said no such preconditions had been mentioned.

By March 1995 the republican position had shifted somewhat, with SF president **Gerry Adams** stating that decommissioning would happen at the end of negotiations, not the beginning. In November

1995, after a long period of stalemate, a "twin track" approach was launched, with political talks to begin in February 1996, while an independent commission under Senator **George Mitchell** would examine the weapons issue. In January 1996 Mitchell suggested decommissioning begin during talks, but subsequent developments, such as Prime Minister **John Major**'s decision to hold **elections** that would lead to all-party talks, were not well received by republicans, and the IRA ended its ceasefire in February 1996 with the Canary Wharf bomb in London.

The arrival of the **Labour Party** to power in May 1997 was followed by the British government's dropping of the demand for decommissioning before talks and the IRA reinstatement of its ceasefire. In September 1997 SF signed the Mitchell Principles and joined the talks process. Later that month the **Independent International Commission on Decommissioning** (IICD) was launched; however, it made slow progress at best on the issue.

Even the signing of the **Good Friday Agreement** (GFA) in April 1998 failed to resolve the issue, with **Ulster Unionist Party** (UUP) leader **David Trimble** asking for, and receiving, a public written assurance from **Tony Blair** that the prime minister's view was that decommissioning should begin immediately. For the next 18 months, the UUP pursued a policy of "no guns, no government," that is, that the UUP would not enter government with SF until the decommissioning of IRA weapons had taken place. Decommissioning of loyalist paramilitary weapons was given less attention because loyalist parties had not won enough seats in the **Northern Ireland Assembly** to be represented in the executive. In December 1999 Trimble and the UUP moved its position and entered the executive with SF, though only on the basis that IRA decommissioning would commence by the end of January 2000. No IRA decommissioning took place, and in February 2000 Trimble used the threat of his resignation to force Secretary of State **Peter Mandelson** to suspend the institutions. In May 2000 an IRA statement said it was committed to putting its arms "completely and verifiably" beyond use, leading to the restoration of **devolution**. Although two IRA arms dumps were independently inspected the following month, there was no further movement on IRA weapons, and Trimble resigned as first minister over the issue in July 2001.

In October 2001 the IRA finally began to put its weapons "beyond use," though this was viewed as being at least partly due to the changed attitude of the **United States** toward paramilitary-terrorist groups holding weapons in the wake of the 11 September attacks. The arrest of three Irish republicans in Columbia in connection with the training of guerrilla groups in that country was also a contributing factor. The UUP reentered the executive, but the arms issue continued to be significant in turning **unionist** opinion against the GFA, under the terms of which, they believed, decommissioning should now have been completed.

In April 2002 the IRA put a second batch of its weapons beyond use; however, other IRA activity, such as intelligence gathering, continued leading to a further threat from the UUP to withdraw from the executive and another suspension of the institutions in October. In October, in conjunction with the announcement of fresh Northern Ireland Assembly elections, a third act of IRA decommissioning of weapons took place; however, a dispute surrounding details of the amount of weapons involved angered unionists and served to weaken Trimble's increasingly tenuous leadership of the UUP.

January 2004 saw the establishment of the **Independent Monitoring Commission** (IMC), which was perceived as taking a more proactive approach on the issue of paramilitary activity than the IICD. The IRA's principle of not decommissioning weapons had also now been breached, so that the question became one of when, rather than if, decommissioning would be completed.

In July 2005 the IRA announced an end to its armed campaign, and in September 2005 the IICD stated that the IRA had decommissioned all its weapons. The protracted nature of the issue of the decommissioning of IRA weapons, however, undoubtedly played a significant role in souring unionist–**nationalist** relations in the wake of the GFA and harming the prospects for devolution. Even after the completion of IRA decommissioning, the question of when loyalist paramilitaries would begin to move on the issue still remains to be dealt with.

**DEMILITARIZATION.** A term originally used by **republicans** but later used more widely to refer to the reduction of security force numbers and bases in Northern Ireland. While the **Irish Republican Army** (IRA) faced pressure to **decommission** weapons in the wake of the **Good Friday Agreement** (GFA), republicans preferred to present the argument in terms of the need for government security forces to be reduced as well. For republicans this was ideologically important, as they saw it as giving them equal legitimacy to the forces of the state. Inevitably demilitarization was criticized by **unionists** and others on precisely this point.

Given the mounting evidence that the IRA was ending its campaign, however, the government felt the need to respond by reducing security forces in Northern Ireland. There was also the practical concern of meeting British military commitments in Iraq, Afghanistan, and elsewhere, which were now more pressing than Northern Ireland. In August 2005, following the IRA announcement that it was ending its armed campaign, the government announced a reduction in the number of troops in Northern Ireland from 10,500 to 5,000, the closing of **British Army** bases, and defortification of police stations over a two-year period, provided the security situation remained stable. Unlike republicans, government sources referred to this as a process of "normalization." The reduction in security force numbers also led to the loss of 1,100 jobs for civilians employed by the Ministry of Defence in Northern Ireland.

**DEMOCRATIC UNIONIST PARTY (DUP).** The **unionist** political party founded by Rev. **Ian Paisley** and former **Ulster Unionist Party** (UUP) member Desmond Boal in October 1971. The party, formally known as the Ulster Democratic Unionist Party, stated that it would be on the right on constitutional issues and on the left on social issues. Initially the party drew its support from evangelical Protestants in rural areas linked to the **Free Presbyterian Church**, but also from working-class areas in **Belfast**. Ian Paisley has remained party leader since its inception.

In the 1973 **Northern Ireland Assembly elections**, it won 10.8 percent of the vote and eight seats as part of a **loyalist** coalition but was in competition with the **Vanguard Unionist Progressive Party** (VUPP) for the right-wing unionist vote. After the split within VUPP over the proposal for a voluntary coalition with the **Social Democratic and Labour Party** (SDLP); however, its only major rival for unionist votes was the UUP.

In the 1979 **Westminster** general election, the DUP won two seats in addition to Ian Paisley's, including **Peter Robinson** in East Belfast. The party also benefited from the personalized nature of the European

Parliament elections, with Paisley topping the poll in 1979 and continuing to do so until his retirement from the European Parliament in 2004. During the first decades of its existence, outside the European Parliament elections, it outpolled the UUP only in the 1981 **district council** elections held during the **hunger strike** campaign of that year.

The DUP is strongly in favor of a **devolved** executive for Northern Ireland, though only under what it considers to be appropriate conditions. The party strongly opposed the **Sunningdale** Agreement and **power-sharing** executive of 1973–74 but was equally strong in its support for the 1982–86 Northern Ireland Assembly. It opposed the **Anglo–Irish Agreement** (AIA) after 1985 and, as part of this campaign of opposition, did not oppose UUP candidates in the 1987 and 1992 Westminster general elections.

The DUP participated in the **Brooke–Mayhew Talks** but opposed the **Downing Street Declaration** as a threat to Northern Ireland's position within the United Kingdom. It participated in talks with the British and Irish governments but permanently withdrew from the talks process in July 1997 when **Sinn Fein** (SF) was admitted. In the 1998 referendum on the **Good Friday Agreement** (GFA), it campaigned against the GFA with the United Kingdom Unionist Party (UKUP) as the United Unionists. Although the referendum endorsed the GFA, the party performed well in the subsequent Northern Ireland Assembly elections, taking 18.1 percent of first-preference votes and winning 20 seats.

In the 1999 Northern Ireland executive, the party held the Ministries of Regional Development and Social Development. As the implementation of the GFA continued, the party capitalized on unionist disillusionment with the agreement and internal UUP disputes. A by-election win in South Antrim in 2000 was an indication of growing support for the DUP line. In the 2001 Westminster general election the, DUP won five seats, making it the second largest Northern Ireland party at Westminster.

In the 2003 Northern Ireland Assembly election, it became the largest party in Northern Ireland, receiving 25.6 percent of first-preference votes and winning 30 seats. In 2004 Jim Allister retained Paisley's seat in the European Parliament and again topped the poll for the DUP. In the May 2005 Westminster general election, the DUP won nine seats, with 33.7 percent of the vote, 30.0 percent of first-preference votes, and 182 councilors in the district council elections held on the same day. The results confirmed the DUP's standing as the largest party in Northern Ireland.

In November 2006 the party executive passed a motion neither backing, nor rejecting, the **St. Andrews Agreement**. The DUP maintained, however, that devolution should come about when the conditions were appropriate, not to meet a particular deadline. On 24 November 2006, Paisley said he would only become first minister under the appropriate conditions, however the speaker of the Assembly ruled this was a nomination. Senior members of the DUP subsequently released a statement denying this was the case.

In the March 2007 Northern Ireland Assembly election, the party received 30.1 percent of first-preference votes and was the largest party, with 36 seats. On 24 March 2007, the party executive voted to share power with SF in principle but wanted further assurances before nominating members to a Northern Ireland executive. On 26 March 2007, the DUP agreed to enter an executive with SF on 8 May 2007. The following day Member of the European Parliament (MEP) Jim Allister resigned from the party in protest. A number of councilors subsequently followed Allister by resigning from the party. In April 2007 the party chose Peter Robinson as minister of finance and personnel, **Nigel Dodds** as minister for enterprise trade and investment, former Ulster Unionist Arlene Foster as minister for the environment, and Edwin Poots as minister for culture, arts, and leisure in advance of devolution. In addition to this, Paisley was to be first minister, and Ian Paisley Jr. became a junior minister in the office of the first minister and deputy first minister.

**DERRY (LONDONDERRY).** The second largest city in Northern Ireland. In 2001 the population of the city was 90,000, of which 78.0 percent were Catholics and 21.0 percent Protestants. The gerrymandering of local government **electoral** boundaries by **unionists** in 1936 to produce an **Ulster Unionist Party** (UUP) majority in a city with a majority Catholic population was one of the largest grievances of **nationalists** and also helped inspire the **Northern Ireland Civil Rights Association** (NICRA).

The abolition of Londonderry Corporation by **Terence O'Neill** began the reform of local government in the city but did not stop the civil rights march in the city on 5 October 1968, which brought the political difficulties of Northern Ireland to the attention of the wider world and helped initiate the onset of **the Troubles**. In August 1969 an **Apprentice Boys of Derry** (ABD) march in the city led to rioting in the nationalist Bogside area, the **Battle of the Bogside**, and the establishment of the Free Derry **no-go area**. The violence in turn spread to **Belfast**, where there was open sectarian conflict leading to the introduction of the **British Army** on the streets of both cities to restore order.

In July 1971 the army shot two men dead in Derry, and the refusal of a request for an inquiry into the incident led the **Social Democratic and Labour Party** (SDLP) to withdraw from the **Northern Ireland Parliament**. **Bloody Sunday** in Derry in January 1972 proved to be one of the most significant incidents of the Troubles, leaving a legacy that had still not been resolved 35 years later. In May 1972 the kidnapping and murder by the **Official Irish Republican Army** (OIRA) of a Derry man serving in the British Army while he was on leave led the officials to declare a ceasefire.

In 1981 the SDLP gained overall control of the city council, and in 1983, following the increase in the number of Northern Ireland seats at **Westminster**, SDLP leader **John Hume** won the newly created seat of Foyle. During the 1990s the city continued to see an increase in **Sinn Fein** (SF) representation. There was also a continuing decline in the number of Protestants living in the area; during the course of the Troubles an estimated 15,000 Protestants left the city. There also continued to be disputes concerning the route and timing of ABD marches.

In the 1997 **district council** election, the SDLP lost its overall majority on the council but remained the largest single party, and this continued to be the case in both the 2001 and 2005 council elections. In 2005 there was speculation that SF would win the Westminster seat of Foyle following the retirement of John Hume; however, **Mark Durkan** retained the seat for the SDLP. Arguments surrounding the official name of the city have continued, and in January 2007 an attempt by nationalists to have the official name of the city changed from Londonderry to Derry was rejected in the High Court.

**DEVLIN (MCALISKEY), BERNADETTE (1947– ). Republican** politician, Bernadette Devlin was born in Cookstown, Co. Tyrone, on

23 April 1947. She was educated at St. Patrick's Girls Academy, Dungannon, and Queen's University, **Belfast** (QUB). During her final year at QUB, she became a prominent member of **People's Democracy** (PD) and was present at both the civil rights march in **Derry** on 5 October 1968 and the PD march of January 1969. In the **crossroads election**, she was defeated by **James Chichester-Clark** in South Londonderry but in March won a **Westminster** by-**election** for the Mid-Ulster seat, thus becoming the youngest woman ever elected to the House of Commons.

In August 1969 she became the focus of media attention during the **Battle of the Bogside**. In December 1969 she was sentenced to six months' imprisonment for incitement to riot and disorderly behavior. She began her prison sentence in June 1971, having retained her Westminster seat in the 1970 general election. In the aftermath of the events of **Bloody Sunday**, she slapped Home Secretary Reginald Maudling during a debate in the House of Commons. In April 1973 she married teacher Michael McAliskey. In the February 1974 general election, she lost her Mid-Ulster seat when a split in the **nationalist** vote allowed a **Vanguard Unionist Progressive Party** (VUPP) candidate to win, and she did not contest the seat in October 1974.

At the end of 1974, she became associated with the **Irish Republican Socialist Party** (IRSP) but was not a candidate in any further elections until 1979, when she stood as an independent in the European Parliament elections and received 5.9 percent of first-preference votes. During her campaign she highlighted the struggle of republican prisoners for political status. She and her husband were seriously injured on 16 February 1981 when they were shot and wounded by **loyalist** gunmen at their home near Coalisland, Co. Tyrone.

During the 1981 **hunger strike**, she was again a leading figure in the campaign in support of republican prisoners' objective of political status. She stood in both general elections in the Irish Republic in 1982 but was not elected. Since the 1980s she has continued to take a traditional republican stance in areas such as opposition to **extradition** and the **Good Friday Agreement** (GFA).

**DEVLIN, PATRICK (PADDY) (1925–99). Northern Ireland Labour Party** (NILP), **Social Democratic and Labour Party** (SDLP), and **Labour** politician, Paddy Devlin was born in **Belfast**

on 8 March 1925. He was a member of the **republican** movement and the **Irish Republican Army** (IRA) from a young age and was interned by the **Northern Ireland government** from 1942 until 1945. After World War II, he left the republican movement and in 1950 joined the **Irish Labour Party**. In 1958 Devlin moved to the NILP. He was the party's chairman in 1967–68 and in 1969 was **elected** to the **Northern Ireland Parliament** for the Falls constituency. He was a founding member of the **Northern Ireland Civil Rights Association** (NICRA) in 1967 and, in 1970, also became a founding member of the SDLP.

Devlin was elected to the **Northern Ireland Assembly** in 1973 and the **Constitutional Convention** in 1975 for the West Belfast constituency. In the Northern Ireland executive of 1974, he was head of the Department of Health and Social Services. His decision midway through the **Ulster Workers' Council (UWC) strike** to pay unemployment benefits to those who claimed to have been intimidated out of work by **loyalists** was seen as helping the strikers' position and was criticized by some pro-**Sunningdale** groups. Devlin himself had no regrets about his decision, which he viewed as helping those in need, irrespective of their political views.

After the end of the Constitutional Convention, he complained that the SDLP was becoming less socialist and was expelled from the party in 1977 after further disputes. He was elected to Belfast City Council in 1973 and held his position on the council until 1985, when he lost his seat due to the growing electoral strength of **Sinn Fein** (SF). He was district secretary of the Irish Transport and General Workers' Union, 1976–85, and during this period he promoted a new Labour party for Northern Ireland. In the 1979 European Parliament elections, he stood unsuccessfully as a United Labour Party candidate and in 1985 lost his Belfast City Council seat when standing as a Labour Party Northern Ireland candidate. Two years later he was vice chairman of another left-wing political party, Labour '87; however, this also failed to make any significant electoral impact. Paddy Devlin died on 15 August 1999 following a long period of ill health related to severe diabetes.

**DEVOLUTION.** Since the abolition of the **Northern Ireland government** in 1972, the primary objective of the British government has been to return responsibility for a range of matters, such as education, health, local economy, and (eventually) justice and policing, to a locally **elected** administration. There has generally been strong public support for the concept of a devolved administration within Northern Ireland. The 2003 Northern Ireland Life and Times survey found 52.0 percent preferred a form of devolved parliament or assembly for Northern Ireland, compared to 17.0 percent supporting an all-Ireland settlement, 12.0 percent supporting **direct rule**, and 9.0 percent supporting **independence** for Northern Ireland. The 2003 survey found 68.0 percent of Protestants favored a form of devolution, compared to 27.0 percent of Catholics and 56.0 percent of those giving no religion.

The difficulty in establishing a devolved administration has been in meeting the conflicting demands of **nationalists** and **unionists** as to the precise nature of the administration, which parties should be involved, and the relationship with the **Republic of Ireland**. The 1973–74, 1982–86, and post-1998 **Northern Ireland Assemblies** all failed to square this circle.

In 1997 a **Labour Party** government was elected in the United Kingdom, which had the objective of devolving power to Scotland, Wales, and Northern Ireland and to the regions within England. Significantly, and particularly for unionists, this meant that devolution within the United Kingdom would become the norm rather than the exception. Strenuous attempts to establish a stable devolved administration in Northern Ireland in the following decade proved unsuccessful.

In October 2006, in a further political initiative aimed at establishing a devolved administration in Northern Ireland, talks were held between Northern Ireland **political parties** and the British and Irish governments at **St. Andrews** in Scotland, with the aim of restoring a devolved administration. The failure to resolve differences between the **Democratic Unionist Party** (DUP) and **Sinn Fein** (SF) meant that on 24 November 2006, a supposed deadline for the nomination of ministers for a devolved executive had been reduced merely to the requirement for the parties to indicate who their choices for first and deputy first ministers might be in a devolved executive. While SF clearly nominated **Martin McGuinness** as deputy first minister, **Ian Paisley** made a conditional response. In the event, the speaker of the

Assembly ruled that the DUP had indeed made a nomination for the position of first minister, although this was disputed by some DUP members.

On 26 March 2007 another deadline for devolution was missed; however, the DUP and SF agreed to devolution coming into effect in May 2007. The government quickly introduced legislation to give effect to this decision. On 2 April 2007, the parties indicated their choice of ministerial posts and the chairs of Assembly committees the following day. On 8 May 2007, responsibility for local government departments was again devolved to the Northern Ireland Assembly.

**D'HONDT.** The method, named after the Belgian mathematician Viktor D'hondt, used after 1998 to allocate ministerial posts in the Northern Ireland executive and chairs and deputy chairs of departmental committees. In the post-1998 **Northern Ireland Assembly**, the political party with most Assembly seats has first choice of the ministerial posts available. Having made this choice, the party then rejoins the "queue" for ministerial positions at half this number. The party with the second highest number of seats has second choice. Having made its choice of ministerial post, it rejoins the line at half this value.

When a party gains a second post, the number of Assembly seats it holds is divided by three to determine its position in the line for post allocations. If a party gains a third post, its number of Assembly seats is divided by four to determine its position in line. If it gains a fourth post, the number of seats is divided by five. This process continues until all posts have been allocated.

Following the 1998 Assembly **election**, the **Ulster Unionist Party** (UUP) had 28 seats, **Social Democratic and Labour Party** (SDLP) had 24, **Democratic Unionist Party** (DUP) had 20, **Sinn Fein** (SF) had 18, **Alliance Party of Northern Ireland** (APNI) had 6, United Kingdom Unionist Party (UKUP) had 5, **Progressive Unionist Party** (PUP) had 2, **Northern Ireland Women's Coalition** (NIWC) had 2, and 3 other antiagreement **unionists** had the rest. This meant that the UUP and SDLP each had three executive posts, and the DUP and SF had two each.

In the March 2007 Northern Ireland Assembly election, the DUP won 36 seats, entitling the party to four posts in the executive (as well as the position of first minister). SF had 28 seats, earning them 3 executive positions (as well as the deputy first minister). The UUP had 18 seats (2 executive seats), and the SDLP had 16 seats (1 position in the executive) should devolution take place. On 2 April 2007, the parties made their selection of ministerial posts in advance of **devolution** in May 2007.

**DIPLOCK COURTS.** In December 1972 a commission headed by Lord Diplock reported that nonjury trials should be used in cases relating to terrorist offenses. The report argued that such cases should be heard by judges alone because of the threat of intimidation to jurors. The recommendation was later included in the 1973 Emergency Provisions Act. In 1985 the **Anglo–Irish Agreement** (AIA) raised the possibility of judges from the Republic sitting alongside those from Northern Ireland in Diplock cases (there would be three judges rather than one), but this proposal was not adopted. In August 2005 the **Northern Ireland Office** (NIO) announced that Diplock courts were to be phased out, and in August 2006 a further announcement stated that they would be ended by July 2007. In September 2006 the trial of a man in connection with the **Omagh bombing** was reported as being likely to be the last to be heard before a Diplock court.

**DIRECT RULE.** The system of government introduced in 1972 after the suspension of the **Northern Ireland Parliament**. Areas previously controlled by the **Northern Ireland government**, such as health and education, were now administered by the **Northern Ireland Office** (NIO), and legislation relating to these areas was also passed in the U.K. Parliament at **Westminster** rather than in Northern Ireland. Direct rule was initially seen as a temporary measure, and flaws in the system, such as the passing of most Northern Ireland legislation by the Order in Council method, which did not allow for any amendment, were initially overlooked.

As the failure to agree on the terms for **devolution** persisted, however, direct rule became the standard system of government by default, and attempts were made to give local political representatives some input through wider consultation. In practice most commentators accept that this still provides less accountability at the local level than a devolved system of government. In the period after 2003 when the British and Irish governments pushed local parties to agree to reestablish a devolved Northern Ireland executive, the NIO made a number of unpopular decisions in terms of domestic rates increases and the introduction of additional water charges. Many observers interpreted these policies as part of an attempt to pressure Northern Ireland parties into forming an executive in order to stop these decisions; however, this did not have the desired effect. Direct rule has always been a more popular fallback position for **unionists** than for **nationalists**, and during most of the conflict many unionists preferred this situation to one that required them to participate in an executive that would include **Sinn Fein** (SF).

**DIRTY PROTEST.** By late 1977, as part of the campaign to win back **special category status**, some **republican** prisoners were conducting a "dirty" or "no wash" protest in addition to the **Blanket Protest**. Prisoners refused to wash and smeared the walls of their cells with their own excreta. In February 1980, 30 female republican prisoners in Armagh Prison also joined the dirty protest. The propaganda aspect of the campaign was particularly important, and a great deal of effort was expended by republicans to convince the Irish American audience that the **Northern Ireland Office** (NIO) was responsible for the conditions of the cells.

In June 1980 a report from the European Commission on Human Rights (ECHR) rejected a case brought by Ciaran Nugent and three other former republican prisoners that claimed the conditions of the dirty protest were inhuman on the grounds that the conditions were self-inflicted; however, the report also said that the British government was being inflexible. In the wake of the report's release, the **Irish Republican Army** (IRA) stepped up attacks on prison officers, as well as street demonstrations.

**THE DISAPPEARED.** Although the term originated, and is more commonly associated with, South America, the name *Disappeared* has also been used in Northern Ireland. Unlike in South America, however, those who disappeared were not the **victims** of state violence but rather of **paramilitary** groups, primarily the Provisional

**Irish Republican Army** (PIRA). More specifically, the term *Disappeared* came to be used in relation to nine people from within the Catholic community who had been kidnapped and subsequently murdered by the IRA, although the organization continued to deny responsibility for these actions for many years. The most high-profile incident was that of 37-year-old Jean McConville, a mother of 10 children and widow who disappeared in March 1972 after being taken from her home in Divis Flats, **Belfast**, by an IRA gang. Some reports suggested that she was killed by the IRA because she had helped a British soldier who had been wounded by the IRA.

In the wake of the **Good Friday Agreement** (GFA), **republicans** came under pressure to demonstrate that their war was over, and the IRA offered to help locate the bodies. In July 2006 an investigation by the police ombudsman said there was no evidence that Mrs. McConville had given information to the security services; however, the IRA repeated their claims that this was the case.

In May 1999 the British and Irish governments passed legislation to allow information on the location of the bodies of the Disappeared to be passed to an independent commission, while any information obtained from the bodies as a result of information provided in this manner could not be used for criminal prosecutions. At the end of that month, the first body of one of the Disappeared was recovered. In June 1999 two more bodies were found, but it was not until August 2003 that the remains of Jean McConville were recovered. In October 2003 the IRA issued an apology for the grief suffered by the families of the Disappeared, however the issue remained open.

In July 2006 **Sinn Fein**'s (SF) **Martin McGuinness** again appealed to those with any relevant knowledge to help locate the bodies of the Disappeared. In November of the same year, **Ian Paisley** appealed for information to help find the body of Columba McVeigh, killed by the IRA in 1975, after a meeting with Mr. McVeigh's mother. In January 2007 appeals were made in Catholic churches throughout Ireland for information that might help lead to the recovery of the bodies of those who were still missing. In April 2007 a team of experts assembled by the Independent Commission for the Location of Victims' Remains launched a fresh initiative to recover the missing bodies.

**DISCRIMINATION.** In Northern Ireland the term has most frequently been used with regard to discrimination resulting from an individual's religious background or political opinion. The removal of discriminatory practices, which primarily affected Catholics, was one of the major issues in the period leading up to the outbreak of **the Troubles**. In 1967 the reforms advocated by the **Northern Ireland Civil Rights Association** (NICRA) were primarily aimed at ending abuses of power, mainly, although not exclusively, at local government level in employment and housing allocation, the gerrymandering of local government boundaries, and the introduction of a universal local government franchise.

From the outset some of these demands were perceived by **unionists** as an attempt to undermine Northern Ireland's position within the United Kingdom rather than a campaign for equal rights. In return many **nationalists** saw discriminatory practices as the inevitable outworking of **the Orange State**. This difference of opinion was arguably most evident in security-related issues, such as NICRA's call for the repeal of the Special Powers Act and abolition of the **Ulster Special Constabulary** (USC).

A series of reforms introduced by the **Northern Ireland government** in 1968 and 1969, partly as a result of pressure from the British government, did much to remove many of these issues to the edges of political debate by putting control of the area into the hands of independent bodies. Given the controversy surrounding the allocation of public housing, for example, the Northern Ireland Housing Executive, which was established in 1971, has been notable for the relative lack of criticism it has received on the issue of political or religious bias.

In November 2006 the Equality Commission for Northern Ireland reported that complaints about discrimination in the areas of disability and gender were now more common than those relating to religion or political opinion. Despite this, issues such as security and fair employment and the degree to which anti-Catholic discrimination continued in these areas, remain a source of contention.

**DISTRICT COUNCILS.** Plans for the reform of local government in Northern Ireland that were undertaken in the late 1960s led to the creation of 26 district councils in 1973. The councils, with a varying number of **elected** representatives depending on the population of the council area, are responsible for a range of services, including environmental health, building regulations, community service, refuse collection, street cleaning, parks, recreation facilities, and cemeteries. Councilors also serve on a range of other statutory bodies.

Despite their comparatively low-level responsibilities, council chambers were the scene of many heated debates during the course of **the Troubles**, particularly after **Sinn Fein** (SF) took their seats in the councils after 1985. In the wake of the **Enniskillen bombing** of 1987, however, relations between **unionists** and **nationalists** in Fermanagh improved, leading to the development of an unofficial **power-sharing** system in which the roles of mayor and council committee chairs were rotated. Although this system has since been adopted by many other district councils across Northern Ireland, there is no legislative requirement for them to do so. In 2005 plans for a review of public administration included the proposal for a reduction in the number of district councils to seven. Official proposals were released in November 2006.

**DODDS, NIGEL (1958– ). Democratic Unionist Party** (DUP) politician, Nigel Dodds was born in Londonderry (*see* DERRY) on 20 August 1958. He was educated at Portora Royal School, Enniskillen, and St. John's College, Cambridge. He trained as a barrister and was called to the Northern Ireland Bar in 1981. He was **elected** to **Belfast City Council** as a DUP member in 1985 and served as lord mayor of the city in 1988 and 1991. He served as the assistant to Rev. **Ian Paisley** in his role as a Member of the European Parliament (MEP). He contested East Antrim in the 1992 **Westminster** general election but lost to the **Ulster Unionist Party** (UUP) candidate. Dodds became general secretary of the DUP in 1993. In December 1996 a **Royal Ulster Constabulary** (RUC) officer guarding him was wounded by the **Irish Republican Army** (IRA) inside the Royal Belfast Hospital while Dodds was visiting his son there. He was elected to the **Northern Ireland Forum** for North Belfast in 1996 and to the **Northern Ireland Assembly** in 1998 and again in 2003. In 2001 he defeated the sitting UUP Member of Parliament (MP) to win the North Belfast seat at Westminster. He retained his Westminster seat in the 2005 general election. In the Northern Ireland executive, he was minister for social development from November 1999 until July 2000 and again from October 2001, when the **devolved** institutions were restored, until October 2002. In late October 2006, he caused controversy by suggesting that responsibility for policing might not be devolved to a Northern Ireland executive during his political lifetime and in November 2006 stated that the March 2007 deadline for devolution was not likely to be met. In March 2007 he was again returned to the Northern Ireland Assembly from North Belfast. In April 2007 it was announced that he was to be the minister responsible for enterprise, trade, and investment in the incoming executive.

**DONALDSON, JEFFREY (1962– ).** Unionist politician, Jeffrey Donaldson was born in Kilkeel, Co. Down, on 7 December 1962. He was educated at Kilkeel High School and Castlereagh College of Further Education. He joined the **Ulster Unionist Party** (UUP) at the age of 18 and was chairman of the Young Unionists in 1985 and 1986. He acted as **electoral** agent for **Enoch Powell** in the 1983 **Westminster** general election and 1986 by-election, with Powell being returned on both occasions. In October 1985 he became the youngest member of the **Northern Ireland Assembly** when he was returned in a by-election in South Down.

As the political assistant to UUP leader **James Molyneaux**, his profile within the party began to rise, and in 1988 he became honorary secretary of the Ulster Unionist Council (UUC), the ruling body of the UUP. He was a member of the UUP's negotiating team in the early 1990s and, following Molyneaux's retirement from politics in 1997, retained the Lagan Valley seat for the UUP.

Donaldson represented Lagan Valley in the **Northern Ireland Forum** and was again a member of the UUP's negotiating team in the talks that led to the **Good Friday Agreement** (GFA) in 1998. Donaldson refused to endorse the GFA, however, and withdrew from the negotiations. Initially he was viewed as a weathervane for the "soft no" unionist vote. However, as the implementation of the GFA continued, he became increasingly critical of the position taken by party leader **David Trimble** with regard to **Sinn Fein**'s (SF) participation in the Northern Ireland executive in advance of **Irish Republican Army** (IRA) **decommissioning** of weapons.

In September 2002 he was instrumental in a motion passed by the UUP confirming that the party would withdraw from the executive unless there were clear demonstrations by **republicans** that they would not return to violence. The UUP withdrawal was, however, preempted by **Stormontgate** and the government's suspension of the GFA institutions in October 2002. In June 2003 he and two other UUP Members of Parliament (MP) resigned from the UUP party whip at Westminster in protest to Trimble's policy. He rejoined the party group in October 2003 and in November 2003 was returned as a UUP member for Lagan Valley in the Northern Ireland Assembly elections. In December 2003 he and two other UUP members of the Legislative Assembly (MLA) resigned from the UUP and, in January 2004, joined the **Democratic Unionist Party** (DUP). In the May 2005 Westminster general election, he was again elected in Lagan Valley with a large majority and in March 2007 to the Northern Ireland Assembly.

**DOWNING STREET DECLARATION (1969).** On 19 August 1969, following two days of discussions in London between the U.K. and Northern Ireland governments, a joint policy statement, known as the Downing Street Declaration, was issued. The declaration reaffirmed that, despite recent events, Northern Ireland would not cease to be part of the United Kingdom without the consent of the people of Northern Ireland. It stated that the affairs of Northern Ireland were an entirely U.K. matter and that troops would be withdrawn when law and order had been restored. The U.K. government welcomed the reforms carried out by the Northern Ireland government with regard to the local government franchise, local government areas, the allocation of public housing, the creation of a parliamentary commissioner for administration, and administrative machinery for considering citizens' complaints. Both governments agreed that the momentum of internal reform should be maintained.

**DOWNING STREET DECLARATION (1993).** On 15 December 1993 in Downing Street, London, Prime Minister **John Major** and Taoiseach **Albert Reynolds** issued a Joint Declaration on Northern Ireland. The Downing Street Declaration proved to be one of the central documents of the **peace process**. The British and Irish governments committed themselves to work toward a new political framework founded on consent and encompassing arrangements within Northern Ireland, for the whole of Ireland, and between Great Britain and Ireland. The British government stated that it had no selfish strategic or economic interest in Northern Ireland and that its primary interest was to see peace, stability, and reconciliation established.

In the key section of the document, the British government stated that it was for the people of Ireland alone, by agreement between the two parts, to exercise their right of self-determination on the basis of consent, freely and concurrently given, North and South, to bring about a united Ireland, if that is their wish. The document provided a delicate balance between the **nationalist** objective of a united Ireland and the **unionist** demand for recognition of the right to remain part of the United Kingdom. The **Democratic Unionist Party** (DUP) perceived the declaration as weakening Northern Ireland's status within the United Kingdom, while **republicans** saw it as copper-fastening the unionists' right to prevent a united Ireland. For the most part, however, the declaration was welcomed as a workable compromise, and as such it continued to provide a point of reference in the developing peace process.

**DRUMCREE.** There had been a history of disputed **parades** for many years before the Drumcree crisis developed in 1995. In July 1985 a United Ulster Loyalist Front had been formed specifically to oppose the rerouting of Orange parades by the **Royal Ulster Constabulary** (RUC) in Portadown, Co. Armagh. A year later members of the **Orange Order** clashed with police while the RUC was attempting to prevent marchers from passing through the Catholic Obin Street area of the town.

On 9 July 1995, however, confrontations over Orange marches in the area reached a much higher level when the RUC prevented Orangemen from parading along the Catholic Garvaghy Road on the return route from a church service. The incident led to a standoff between police and Orangemen and widespread rioting in Protestant areas across Northern Ireland. On 11 July 1995, a compromise was reached between the police and Orangemen, allowing some of the marchers to walk along the road; however, this arrangement did not meet the demands of **nationalist** groups, who did not want any marchers in the area. In 1996 and 1997, the decision to allow the march to proceed led to rioting in nationalist areas. In 1998 the march was blocked and was followed by widespread rioting in **loyalist** areas. The **deaths** of three young Catholic brothers, aged 9 to 11, following a sectarian arson attack on their homes in Ballymoney, Co. Antrim, on 12 July 1998, led to a reduction in the level of violence.

The Drumcree dispute highlighted conflicting demands of **unionists** and nationalists in the area of civil rights. For nationalists the issue was one of freedom from sectarian harassment, but for unionists the issue was one of freedom to express their cultural identity. The dispute had an impact far beyond the individuals involved and the specific issue and was a significant factor in undermining support for the **Good Friday Agreement** (GFA). Although no march has taken place along the Garvaghy Road since 1997, the Drumcree dispute remains an issue of contention. In September 2006 Orangemen in Portadown held a commemoration to mark 3,000 days of protest of being banned from marching along the Garvaghy Road. In December 2006 members of the Orange Order offered to meet nationalist residents directly for the first time to resolve the dispute.

**DUBLIN AND MONAGHAN BOMBINGS.** On 17 May 1974, 33 people were killed and nearly 250 injured when 4 car bombs exploded in Dublin and in the town of Monaghan in the **Republic of Ireland**. Three car bombs, placed in Parnell Street, Talbot Street, and South Leinster Street in Dublin, exploded without warning within minutes of each other at approximately 5:30 p.m. As a result 26 people and an unborn child were killed. Just before 7:00 p.m., a fourth no-warning bomb exploded in Monaghan, killing seven more people. Two of the three cars used in the Dublin bombings had been stolen earlier in Protestant areas of **Belfast**, and all four cars had Northern Ireland registrations. Both the **Ulster Defence Association** (UDA) and **Ulster Volunteer Force** (UVF) denied responsibility for the bombings, however the UVF eventually admitted in July 1993 that it had carried out the attacks.

In 2004 an Irish parliamentary committee suggested that there had been collusion between **loyalist paramilitaries** and British security forces in relation to the Dublin and Monaghan bombs. The committee also suggested that a public inquiry into the bombings should be held in the United Kingdom.

In August 2006 the *Irish News* reported that it had obtained official documents relating to a meeting of British and Irish government officials in September 1974. At this meeting Northern Ireland secretary of state **Merlyn Rees** informed Irish ministers that the 25 people interned by the government during the **Ulster Workers' Council (UWC) strike** included those believed to be responsible for the Dublin bombings. In April 2007 during the winding down of the **Garda Siochana** investigation of the bombings, an Irish commission of investigation found no evidence of collusion.

**DUISBURG TALKS.** On 14 and 15 October 1988, representatives of the **Ulster Unionist Party** (UUP), **Democratic Unionist Party** (DUP), **Social Democratic and Labour Party** (SDLP), and **Alliance Party of Northern Ireland** (APNI) secretly met in Duisburg, in what was then West Germany, to find a system that would lead to formalized interparty talks. The talks attempted to reconcile **unionist** demands that the **Anglo–Irish Agreement** (AIA) be suspended before talks took place and the SDLP's view that the AIA continue to operate but that talks be held outside it. The views of the **republican** movement were presented in the talks by **Belfast** priest Fr. Alec Reid. Although the talks failed to produce agreement between the parties, they were significant in highlighting a willingness among the unionist parties to begin negotiations to find an alternative to the AIA.

**DURKAN, MARK (1960– ).** Social Democratic and Labour Party (SDLP) leader, Mark Durkan was born in the city of **Derry** on 26 June 1960. His father was a district inspector in the **Royal Ulster Constabulary** (RUC) but died before Durkan was a year old. Durkan was educated at St. Columb's College, Derry; Queen's University, **Belfast** (QUB), where he studied politics; and the University of Ulster, where he studied public policy. At QUB he was active in student politics, serving as deputy president of the students' union and subsequently deputy president of the Union of Students in Ireland (1982–84). During this period he joined the SDLP and in 1984 became an aide to **John Hume**. He organized the successful SDLP campaigns in Newry and Armagh in the **Westminster** by-**election** of

1986 and in the general election of 1987 in South Down. He became party chairman in 1990, and in 1993 he was elected to Derry City Council but stood down from the council in 2000.

Durkan was a delegate to the Dublin **Forum for Peace and Reconciliation** in 1994 and was elected to the **Northern Ireland Forum** for the Foyle constituency in 1996. He was a senior negotiator for the SDLP in the discussions leading to the **Good Friday Agreement** (GFA). In 1998 he was elected to the **Northern Ireland Assembly** from Foyle and, when power was **devolved** to the Northern Ireland executive in December 1999, became minister for finance and personnel.

In November 2001 he succeeded John Hume as SDLP leader and **Seamus Mallon** as deputy first minister in the Northern Ireland executive. He was deputy first minister at the time of the suspension of the devolved institutions in October 2002. In the Northern Ireland Assembly elections of 2003, he retained his seat, although his party lost six seats overall. In the May 2005 Westminster general election, he retained the Foyle seat for the SDLP despite speculation that it would be lost to **Sinn Fein** (SF).

## – E –

**EAMES, ROBIN (1937– ).** Church of Ireland primate of all Ireland, Robin Eames was born in **Belfast** on 27 April 1937. He was educated at Belfast Royal Academy and Methodist College, Belfast, and subsequently studied at Queen's University, Belfast (QUB), where he earned a law degree and later a PhD in ecclesiastical law. He attended divinity school at Trinity College, Dublin, between 1960 and 1963 and was appointed curate assistant at Bangor Parish Church, Co. Down, later that year. In 1966 he became rector of St. Dorothea's Church in a working-class area of East Belfast and witnessed the impact of the outbreak of **the Troubles** on the area. He was offered, but did not accept, the position of dean of Cork and in 1974 was appointed rector of St. Mark's Church (formerly the family church of the writer C. S. Lewis), also located in East Belfast. In 1975 he was appointed bishop of the diocese of **Derry** and Raphoe and invited his Catholic counterpart, Dr. Edward Daly, to the consecration ceremony.

In 1980 he became bishop of Down and Dromore and in 1986 head of the Anglican Church in Ireland as archbishop of Armagh.

While a student at QUB, Eames was briefly a member of the Young Unionists and, although he was later critical of some of the actions of the **Orange Order**, remained aware of grassroots **unionist** opinion. He was consulted by Taoiseach **Albert Reynolds** and Prime Minister **John Major** in the period leading up to the publication of the **Downing Street Declaration** in December 1993 and played a significant part in helping to draft the sections of the document dealing with Protestant concerns about the **Republic of Ireland**. He was awarded a life peerage in 1995. In March 1998 he received an apology from Secretary of State **Mo Mowlam** after he was mentioned in a leaked **Northern Ireland Office** (NIO) document listing individuals the NIO might use to help sell a political settlement to the general public in Northern Ireland.

One of the most difficult issues that Eames faced was in relation to the **parade** associated with **Drumcree** Parish Church. He appealed for mediation by those involved in the dispute and, in May 2001, told the Church of Ireland's general synod in Dublin that the **loyalist** march represented a cameo of the darker side of life in Northern Ireland.

In 2003 Eames was appointed chairman of the Lambeth Commission on Communion, which was established to examine challenges to unity in the Anglican Communion. The commission produced the Windsor Report in October 2004. In October 2006 he led a delegation of Church of Ireland clergymen in a meeting with **Gerry Adams**. He retired as archbishop of Armagh at the end of 2006. In June 2007, he was awarded the Order of Merit by the Queen.

**EIRE NUA.** A policy promoted by Provisional **Sinn Fein** (PSF) in the 1970s that called for a united Ireland with federal parliaments based in each of the four **provinces**. **Republican** leaders in the South saw this as a substantial concession to **unionists**, as it would give them significant influence, if not control, in the proposed nine-county Ulster Parliament. As the influence of Northern representatives grew within PSF, however, the more traditional republican approach of a unitary state gained support. At the party's 1981 ard fheis (conference), the Eire Nua policy was effectively abandoned despite opposition to the change from Southern leaders, and it was officially dropped by the party in 1982.

**ELECTIONS.** During the course of **the Troubles**, Northern Ireland voters participated in a wide range of elections for different types of representative bodies. The final general election to the **Northern Ireland Parliament**, the "**crossroads election**" of February 1969, returned 52 members from single-member constituencies using the plurality (first past the post) system.

U.K. elections also have single-member constituencies returned by the plurality method. Between the 1970 and 1979 **Westminster** general elections, Northern Ireland returned 12 Members of Parliament (MPs). From 1983 until 1992, Northern Ireland returned 17 MPs and, since the 1997 general election, 18 MPs. The first election where 18 constituencies were used, however, was for the Northern Ireland Forum election of 1996. Since 1968 there has been a number of highly significant Westminster by-elections, including those held in Mid-Ulster in 1969 (won by **Bernadette Devlin**), Fermanagh-South Tyrone in 1981 (**Bobby Sands** and Owen Carron), and South Antrim in 2000 (William McCrea of the **Democratic Unionist Party** [DUP]).

Elections to the **Northern Ireland Assemblies** of 1973, 1982, 1998, and 2003 have been by the single transferable vote (STV) system of **proportional representation** (PR) from multimember constituencies based on the same Westminster constituency. In 1973 and 1982, candidates were elected to a 78-member Assembly and, in 1998 and 2003, a 108-member Assembly. The election to the Northern Ireland **Constitutional Convention** in 1975 also returned 78 members from multimember constituencies using STV. The **Northern Ireland Forum** election of 1996 returned 110 members, with 90 being returned from a party list system based on the 18 Westminster constituencies. Two of the remaining 20 seats were then allocated to each of the 10 parties, with most votes across Northern Ireland.

Since 1973 elections to Northern Ireland's 26 **district councils** have been held every four years. Council elections also use the STV system of PR with multimember constituencies. The number of council seats has increased from 526 in 1973 to 582 in 2005.

The first direct election to the European Parliament was held in 1979, with subsequent elections being held every five years. Northern

Ireland is treated as a single constituency with three Members of the European Parliament (MEP) being returned by the STV method of PR.

Northern Ireland electors also participate in referendums, such as the **border poll** of 1973, the continuation of U.K. membership in the European Economic Community (EEC) in 1975, and the **Good Friday Agreement** (GFA) in 1998.

Since 1968 electoral results have shown a decline in the strength of the **unionist** bloc vote and an increase in the **nationalist** vote, reflecting the increasing Catholic proportion of the population within Northern Ireland.

**EMPEY, REGINALD (REG) (1947– ). Ulster Unionist Party** (UUP) leader, Sir Reg Empey was born on 26 October 1947. He was educated at the Royal School, Armagh, and at Queen's University, **Belfast** (QUB), where he studied economics. He was vice chairman of the Young Unionist Council but became disenchanted with the line being taken by the UUP and joined the **Vanguard Unionist Progressive Party** (VUPP), becoming chairman of the party in 1975. He was **elected** to the Northern Ireland **Constitutional Convention** from the East Belfast constituency and in the Convention served as secretary of the **United Ulster Unionist Council's** (UUUC) policy committee. When VUPP split Empey supported those who left to form the United Ulster Unionist Movement (UUUM) and later **United Ulster Unionist Party** (UUUP). He was deputy leader of the UUUP from 1977 until 1984. He stood in the 1982 **Northern Ireland Assembly** election but failed to be elected. With the demise of the UUUP, Empey rejoined the UUP and was elected to Belfast City Council in May 1985. He served two terms as lord mayor of the city in 1989–90 and 1993–94, and this helped raise his public profile.

Empey was a member of the UUP's negotiating team during the **Brooke–Mayhew Talks**, and in 1996 he was elected to the **Northern Ireland Forum** for East Belfast. In the talks leading to the **Good Friday Agreement** (GFA), he was one of the UUP's key negotiators. In the subsequent Northern Ireland Assembly elections of June 1998, he was again returned from East Belfast. In the Assembly he was a close ally of **David Trimble** and a strong defender of the line taken by the UUP on the issue of **decommissioning**.

When the Northern Ireland executive was established in December 1999, he was appointed minister of enterprise, trade, and investment, a post that was considered appropriate given his background in business. After Trimble resigned as first minister, between July and November 2001, Empey held the position on a temporary basis. In the May 2005 **Westminster** general election, he failed to defeat **Peter Robinson** in East Belfast. Following the disastrous electoral performance of the party in the 2005 elections, Trimble resigned as party leader and was succeeded by Empey the following month. As party leader he attempted to overcome the alienation of **loyalists**, and as part of this, he agreed to form a coalition in the Northern Ireland Assembly with **David Ervine** of the **Progressive Unionist Party** (PUP). This would also have given the UUP an extra seat in a new executive if it had been formed. However, the plan caused some unease within the UUP, as the **Ulster Volunteer Force** (UVF) remained active. The coalition was ruled out of order by the speaker of the Assembly. Empey was awarded a knighthood in 1999, and in March 2007 he was again returned to the Northern Ireland Assembly from East Belfast.

**ENNISKILLEN BOMBING.** On 8 November 1987, 11 people were killed and 63 injured when an **Irish Republican Army** (IRA) bomb exploded near the Enniskillen war memorial just before the annual Remembrance Sunday ceremony was due to commence. The attack was widely condemned, and the IRA subsequently expressed its regret for the event but suggested that the bomb could have been triggered by a security forces' electronic scanning device. Prime Minister **Margaret Thatcher** later attended the rescheduled memorial service in Enniskillen.

Unlike many of the atrocities of **the Troubles**, the Enniskillen bombing acted to bring the community together, and a number of programs were established to this end, including the Spirit of Enniskillen Trust, Enniskillen Together, and the Marie Wilson Voyage of Hope, a program for teenagers and named for the daughter of **Gordon Wilson** who had been killed in the explosion. In December 2000 Headmaster Ronnie Hill, who had been in a coma since the explosion, died becoming the 12th death resulting from the bombing.

**ERVINE, DAVID (1953–2007). Progressive Unionist Party** (PUP) leader, David Ervine was born in **Belfast** on 21 July 1953. He was educated at Orangefield Boys' Secondary School but left formal education at the age of 15. After the outbreak of **the Troubles** and communal violence, he joined the **Ulster Volunteer Force** (UVF). He claimed that the **Irish Republican Army** (IRA) bombing of Belfast on **Bloody Friday** was the specific event that led him to join the UVF.

In 1974 he was arrested while in possession of explosives and subsequently served six years imprisonment in the **Maze Prison**. During his term in prison, he was influenced by UVF leader **Gusty Spence** who encouraged **loyalist** prisoners to pursue a political strategy. After his release from prison in 1980, he became a member of the PUP, which was associated with the UVF. He stood in the **district council election** of 1985 but was not elected.

In the wake of **Combined Loyalist Military Command** (CLMC) ceasefire of 1994, however, loyalist politicians found themselves in a more hospitable political environment. Ervine proved to be one of the most eloquent of the new wave of loyalist politicians, and his opinions were well received in many areas of Northern Ireland, as well as in the **Republic of Ireland**. He was a member of the PUP delegation in the **Northern Ireland Forum** in 1996 and in the subsequent talks process. In the 1997 district council elections, he was elected to Belfast City Council.

Following the signing of the **Good Friday Agreement** (GFA) in April 1998, Ervine was a strong proponent of the GFA and of a *yes* vote in the referendum. In June 1998 he was returned to the **Northern Ireland Assembly** from the East Belfast constituency and consistently supported the GFA despite declining support for it within the broader **unionist** community. In April 2002 he succeeded Hugh Smyth as leader of the PUP.

Ervine retained his seat in the Assembly in the 2003 Northern Ireland Assembly elections and in the Belfast City Council in May 2005. In May 2006 Ervine announced that he was supporting the **Ulster Unionist Party** (UUP) group in the Assembly, a move that, under the **D'hondt** mechanism, potentially gave the UUP a third seat in a Northern Ireland executive. In September, however, the speaker of the Assembly ruled against this arrangement, leading an angry Ervine to complain that, although the Northern Ireland executive required a compulsory coalition between parties, a voluntary coalition was not permitted. He died following a heart attack and stroke on 8 January 2007.

**EUROPE.** The entrance of the United Kingdom and the **Republic of Ireland** into the European Economic Community (EEC) in 1973 received greater support from **nationalists** in Northern Ireland than **unionists** because nationalists believed that European integration could lead to a united Ireland; most unionists opposed Britain's involvement in Europe for the same reason. A significant proportion of Irish **republicans** also opposed Irish involvement in Europe, as they believed this compromised Irish **independence** and neutrality. In a 1975 U.K.-wide referendum on continued membership of the EEC, Northern Ireland voted in favor of the United Kingdom remaining in the EEC.

Direct **elections** to the European Parliament have taken place every five years since 1979, with three candidates being returned from Northern Ireland as a single constituency on the basis of the single transferable vote (STV) system. Within Northern Ireland, elections have largely been fought on local issues, and one **Democratic Unionist Party** (DUP), one **Ulster Unionist Party** (UUP), and one **Social Democratic and Labour Party** (SDLP) candidate have been returned in each election until 2004, when **Sinn Fein** (SF) won the seat formerly held by the SDLP.

In 1983 the political committee of the European Parliament established a committee under Danish liberal Nils Haagerup to investigate whether the EEC could help resolve Northern Ireland's economic and political problems. The creation of the committee was opposed by the British government and unionists, who saw it as interfering in internal U.K. affairs. The Haagerup report, which rejected the idea of British withdrawal from Northern Ireland, also stated that Northern Ireland was not entirely an internal U.K. problem. The report proposed a **power-sharing** administration for Northern Ireland and an integrated economic plan. The report was adopted by the European Parliament in March 1984, with only **Ian Paisley**, **John Taylor**, and Neil Blaney from the Republic of Ireland voting against it.

Northern Ireland has benefited from a range of funds from the European Union (EU), the successor to the EEC. It has also gained financially from programs run by the special EU programs body INTERREG (established 1989) and the Program for Peace and Reconciliation (1994), which cover Northern Ireland and the border counties of the Republic. These programs aim to promote reconciliation and build a more peaceful and stable society. As Northern Ireland became more prosperous and the EU faced fresh demands for financial support from poorer member states in Eastern Europe, the size of these funds were reduced. In its third phase, from 2007 to 2013, the amount available under the Peace Program would be reduced from £48 million per annum (2004–06) to £30 million. The goals outlined for the "Peace III" program include tackling sectarianism and racism, facilitating development of a shared community, reducing tensions at interface areas, acknowledging and dealing with the past, and supporting social and economic change. In December 2006 the president of the European Commission, Jose Manuel Barroso, wrote to the four largest Northern Ireland parties, inviting them to talks to discuss how the EU could support a **devolved** power-sharing administration in Northern Ireland. On 1 May 2007, Barroso met Paisley and **Martin McGuinness** and confirmed that £600 million of European funds would go to Northern Ireland and the border counties of the Republic of Ireland over the next six years.

The European Court of Human Rights has made a number of significant decisions in relation to affairs in Northern Ireland, particularly in relation to the treatment of **paramilitary** prisoners at the time of **internment** and during the 1981 **hunger strike** campaign. In 1995 the court ruled by a narrow majority that the killing of **Irish Republican Army** (IRA) activists by the **British Army** in **Gibraltar** had been unnecessary.

The IRA's campaign also extended to Europe, particularly to Germany, where a number of British bases and military personnel were targeted.

**EXTRADITION.** One of the issues that caused friction between the British and Irish governments during the course of **the Troubles** was that of the extradition of those suspected of terrorist activities from the **Republic of Ireland** to the United Kingdom. At the **Sunningdale** Conference of December 1973, **unionists** pressed the Irish government on the issue. However, the Irish government only considered the trial of those wanted for such crimes in the Republic through extraterritorial courts.

In December 1982, however, the Irish Supreme Court rejected the idea that any terrorist activity should be considered political, allowing the extradition of **Irish National Liberation Army** (INLA) leader Dominic McGlinchey to Northern Ireland. In 1985 McGlinchey's conviction in the North was overturned, and he was reextradited to the Republic to face further charges.

Following the escape of **Irish Republican Army** (IRA) prisoners from the **Maze Prison** in 1983, Irish courts refused to extradite three of the escapees. New extradition arrangements were introduced by the Republic in 1988, leading to a number of **republican paramilitary** members being extradited to Northern Ireland in the face of strong opposition from republicans. This did not mean that the issue was no longer a source of contention. In 1988 a British request to have Father Patrick Ryan extradited from Belgium in connection with alleged IRA activities failed, although Ryan was later extradited from Belgium to the Republic. In December 1988 **Margaret Thatcher** severely criticized **Charles Haughey** at a European Economic Community (EEC) summit meeting for the failure of the Irish government to extradite Ryan to the United Kingdom. Thatcher subsequently described the Irish attorney general's decision not to extradite on the grounds that Ryan would not receive a fair trial in Britain as a great insult to the British people.

In 1990 the Irish Supreme Court ruled against the extradition of former Member of Parliament (MP) Owen Carron on firearms offenses on the grounds that the offense was political. In 1990 republican suspect Desmond Ellis was extradited from the Republic to England but in Britain was charged with offenses not listed in the extradition request, causing anger in Ireland. After protests from the Irish government, the original charges were reinstated. Ellis was subsequently cleared of explosives offenses in 1991.

In September 1997 the **United States** attorney general halted the extradition of six IRA members at the request of U.S. secretary of state Madeleine Albright, who claimed that the suspension of the extraditions could help the **peace process**. In October 1998, however, an American appeals court overturned a decision not to return three Maze Prison escapees living in the United States to Northern Ireland.

## – F –

**FAIR EMPLOYMENT. Discrimination** against Catholics in employment was one of the issues that sparked the **Northern Ireland Civil Rights Association**'s (NICRA) campaign in the 1960s. While other disputed areas, such as the allocation of public housing and **electoral** boundaries, were largely resolved, fair employment remained a significant issue of contention until at least the late 1990s. In 1976 a Fair Employment Act established a Fair Employment Agency (FEA) to oversee the issue and made direct religious discrimination in employment illegal. However, the FEA relied on voluntary support from employers, and the act did not make indirect discrimination illegal.

In the late 1980s, a campaign for stronger legislation from within Northern Ireland, from the Anglo–Irish Intergovernmental Conference and from an Irish American lobbying group, led to a further Fair Employment Act in 1989. The 1989 act established the Fair Employment Commission (FEC) and gave it stronger powers than the FEA, not least giving it the power to require companies to undertake affirmative action programs to attract members from the underrepresented community. The 1989 act also introduced compulsory monitoring of workforces for companies with more then 25, and later 10, employees. The 1989 act also banned indirect religious discrimination. The major area of debate surrounding the 1989 act concerned whether the act had introduced a de facto quota system.

In 1998, in advance of the **Good Friday Agreement** (GFA), the Fair Employment and Treatment Order extended discrimination to cover the provision of services. The Northern Ireland act of 1998 subsequently created the Equality Commission for Northern Ireland (ECNI), which merged the quasi-governmental agencies dealing with discrimination in the areas of fair employment, race, gender, and disability.

In 2005 the ECNI reported that the religious imbalance in the Northern Ireland workforce had virtually disappeared. There was, however, underrepresentation for both communities in certain areas, such as some **district councils**. Catholics continued to be underrepresented in security-related jobs and Protestants in areas of the health and education sector. The issue still remained a topic of debate, however, and in September 2006 a report from the Committee on the Administration of Justice (CAJ) claimed that Catholics were still significantly overrepresented among those who were unemployed.

**FAULKNER, BRIAN (1921–77).** Ulster Unionist Party (UUP) politician, prime minister of Northern Ireland, and Northern Ireland chief executive, Brian Faulkner was born at Helen's Bay, Co. Down, on 18 February 1921. The son of a clothing manufacturer, he was educated at several boarding schools, including St. Columb's College, a Church of Ireland school in Dublin. He began studying law at Queen's University, **Belfast** (QUB), but after the outbreak of World War II, he began working in the family business. In 1949 he was **elected** to the **Northern Ireland Parliament** as the UUP Member of Parliament (MP) for East Down, and he retained the seat until 1972. In 1956 he was appointed government chief whip and in 1959 minister of home affairs. During this period he dealt with the **Irish Republican Army**'s (IRA) border campaign of 1956 to 1962. Under **Terence O'Neill** he became minister of commerce and was successful in attracting a number of new industrial concerns to Northern Ireland.

As demands for civil rights reforms grew, Faulkner, who was generally viewed as being on the right wing of the party, became increasingly critical of O'Neill's policies of reform. In January 1969 Faulkner resigned from the government in protest of the establishment of the **Cameron Commission**. Following O'Neill's resignation in April, Faulkner failed to win the UUP leadership and lost to **James Chichester-Clark** by one vote in a ballot of the UUP parliamentary party. Faulkner did, however, agree to serve in Chichester-Clark's cabinet and was appointed minister of development. Following Chichester-Clark's resignation March 1971, Faulkner finally became prime minister when he defeated **William Craig** in a ballot for the party leadership.

In August 1971, in an attempt to undermine **republican paramilitaries**, he introduced **internment**. The strategy proved completely counterproductive and initiated the most violent period of **the Troubles**. Following **Bloody Sunday** the British government finally decided to take full control of security policy in Northern Ireland, and when Faulkner's government rejected this, the Northern Ireland Parliament was suspended. Faulkner's initial response to this development was one of anger, and he accused the government of treating Northern Ireland like a "coconut colony." Following **William Whitelaw**'s decision to set up an advisory council, however, he was increasingly drawn toward the government's plans for a **power-sharing** administration as the best way to protect Northern Ireland's position within the United Kingdom. He participated in the talks at **Stormont** Castle in November 1973, which agreed on power sharing, and subsequently led the UUP delegation at **Sunningdale** in December. Faulkner, however, misjudged the degree of opposition within the **unionist** community to the concept of a Council of Ireland. On 4 January 1974, the ruling body of the UUP voted against the Council of Ireland, leading Faulkner to resign his position as party leader three days later.

Although Faulkner remained chief executive of the power-sharing executive, his support base within the unionist community was weak, and this was highlighted by the triumph of anti-Sunningdale unionist candidates in the U.K. general election of February 1974. The executive struggled on until late May, when the **Ulster Workers' Council (UWC) strike** led Faulkner to resign following **Merlyn Rees**'s decision not to negotiate with the strike leaders.

In the aftermath of the UWC strike, Faulkner launched the **Unionist Party of Northern Ireland** (UPNI). In May 1975 he and four other UPNI members were returned to the **Constitutional Convention**; however, it was clear that he now represented a minority within the unionist community. Following the failure of the Convention in 1976, Faulkner announced his intention to retire from politics. In 1977 he was awarded a life peerage and assumed the title of Lord Faulkner of Downpatrick. On 3 March 1977, however, he died in a horse-riding accident near his Co. Down home.

**FIANNA FAIL (FF).** The largest political party in the **Republic of Ireland**, with an estimated 55,000 members. FF (in English meaning "soldiers of destiny") was founded by Eamon DeValera in 1926, and it has dominated Irish political life for much of the time since then, forming the government during the periods of 1932 to 1948, 1951 to 1954, 1957 to 1973, and 1977 to 1981. Since the 1970s its dominance has declined. It was briefly in power in 1982 and was again in government from 1987 until 1994; however, in 1989 under **Charles**

**Haughey** the party broke with tradition and entered a coalition for the first time. FF has been in government since 1997 but always as the major partner in a coalition of parties.

The party has traditionally been viewed as more **republican** than its main political rival, **Fine Gael** (FG). However, in government it has generally taken a pragmatic approach in its policy toward Northern Ireland. In the early 1970s, under **Jack Lynch**, party unity was shaken by the events of the **arms crisis**, and continuing antagonism between Haughey and other leading FF figures produced an enduring legacy, not least when Des O'Malley and others left the party to form the Progressive Democrats (PD) in 1985.

After Haughey resigned amid a wave of controversy, he was replaced as party leader and taoiseach by **Albert Reynolds**. In coalition with the **Irish Labour Party**, Reynolds and Irish Labour leader Dick Spring worked with the British government under **John Major** as the **peace process** continued to develop. Significantly Reynolds and Major cosigned the **Downing Street Declaration** of December 1993. In November 1994, however, the FF–Labour coalition collapsed, and Reynolds resigned, leading to the advent of **Bertie Ahern** as the new party leader. After the June 1997 general **election**, FF entered government with the PD and found a renewed impetus in the Northern Ireland peace process, resulting from the election of a Labour government in Britain under **Tony Blair**. Both Ahern and Blair were closely involved in the negotiations that led to the **Good Friday Agreement** (GFA) in 1998.

Despite scandals surrounding the financial affairs of several senior party members, FF performed well in the 2002 Irish general election, although it failed to win an overall majority in the **Dail**. The party continued in office with the PD, with Ahern remaining as taoiseach. Despite the difficulties that have surrounded the implementation of the GFA, the FF government has continued to work closely with the Labour government in Britain in the **Weston Park**, **Leeds Castle**, and **St. Andrews Talks**. After the Irish general election of May 2007, FF led a coalition government formed in June 2007 that included the PD and the Green Party.

**FINE GAEL (FG).** The second largest party in the **Republic of Ireland**, FG was founded in 1933 by a coalition of those who had supported the treaty with Britain during the Irish Civil War and right-wing groups. By the late 1960s, a center-left-wing had developed in the party, though. Partly because of its protreaty history, FG continued to be perceived as being more hostile to radical **republicans** than **Fianna Fail** (FF).

In 1973 the party returned to power in coalition with the **Irish Labour Party**, with **Liam Cosgrave** as taoiseach. During this period it participated in the **Sunningdale** Conference, but the failure to deal with the **Irish constitutional claim to Northern Ireland** was an element in undermining **unionist** support for the deal. The government also faced criticism over the treatment of suspected republican activists by the **Garda Siochana** during this period. The party lost office in 1977, however, as a result of domestic issues, such as the poor economic performance of the Republic. Under **Garret Fitz-Gerald** the party took a more liberal approach, and during the lifetime of the FG–Labour minority coalition government of June 1981 to February 1982, FitzGerald launched his constitutional crusade, which was partly aimed at winning over Northern Protestants to support a united Ireland.

The 1981–82 minority government had to deal with the consequences of the 1981 **hunger strike**, and this was an issue that continued to be prominent when the FG–Labour government retained power with a secure majority in November 1982. Under FitzGerald, FG played a significant role in the **New Ireland Forum** and then in the **Anglo–Irish Agreement** (AIA), which helped strengthen constitutional **nationalists** in the wake of **Sinn Fein**'s (SF) entry to **electoral** politics in Northern Ireland. In January 1987 the Irish Labour Party withdrew from the coalition, and a subsequent general election saw FG again in opposition.

The poor performance of the party under FitzGerald's successor, Alan Dukes, combined with FF's new willingness to enter into coalition governments, saw the party out of office until December 1994 when it formed a "Rainbow Coalition" with the Irish Labour Party and Democratic Left. Under **John Bruton**, FG participated in government at an important point in the **peace process**. Bruton was a strong critic of the **Irish Republican Army** (IRA) but pursued a pragmatic balancing act in attempting to reconcile often conflicting demands from unionists, nationalists, and the British government.

Progress in the peace process was stymied by issues such as the controversy surrounding the **Drumcree** parade in 1995 and the end of the IRA ceasefire in February 1996, as well as the precarious position of the **Conservative** government in Great Britain. With the advent of the **Labour Party** government in Britain in May 1997, a fresh impetus was added to the peace process. However, an Irish general election in June 1997 saw FG out of power once more, despite gaining nine seats in the **Dail**.

Under Michael Noonan the party performed poorly in the 2002 general election, and Noonan was in turn succeeded by Enda Kenny. FG recovered its position slightly in 2004 when it won five of the Republic's European Parliament seats. In the period leading up to the 2007 general election, it worked closely with the Irish Labour Party with the objective of forming another coalition government after the election.

**FITT, GERARD (GERRY) (1926–2005).** Social Democratic and **Labour Party** (SDLP) leader and Northern Ireland deputy chief executive, Gerry Fitt was born in **Belfast** on 8 April 1926. He was educated at a Christian Brothers School but left at an early age to join the merchant navy, which he served in from 1941 until 1953. Upon his return to Belfast, he became involved in local politics in the Dock area. He was **elected** to Belfast Corporation in 1958 as an **Irish Labour** candidate and subsequently served on Belfast City Council from 1973 until 1981, when his opposition to the **hunger strikes** lost him votes in the Catholic community and cost him his council seat.

In 1960 he joined with another individualistic Belfast politician, Harry Diamond, to form the Republican Labour Party, and under this title he was elected as the Member of Parliament (MP) for the Dock area of Belfast to the **Northern Ireland Parliament** in 1962. In 1966 he won the West Belfast seat for **Westminster** and used this position to highlight instances of **discrimination** against Catholics in Northern Ireland. Fitt won the support of a number of British **Labour Party** MPs in his campaign for reforms but also succeeded in raising the profile of Northern Ireland as an issue at Westminster. He attended the **Derry** civil rights march on 5 October 1968, where he was struck on the head. The television images of Fitt wearing a blood soaked bandage had a major impact around the world.

In August 1970 he became a founding member and leader of the SDLP, although the political maverick was never completely at ease within the party. He was elected to the **Northern Ireland Assembly** in 1973 and was deputy chief executive in the **power-sharing** executive of 1974. Fitt's priority was to achieve a stable power-sharing executive, and he found himself at odds with much of the party, not least **John Hume**, over the need for a strong Council of Ireland.

He was a strong critic of the **Irish Republican Army** (IRA) and, in August 1986, defended himself and his family with his personal handgun when **republican** supporters broke into his home.

After the failure of the power-sharing executive and **Constitutional Convention** (to which he was also elected), the SDLP increasingly looked for a strong **Irish dimension** as part of a political settlement. As the **Atkins Talks** commenced, Fitt found himself at odds with the bulk of the party on this issue and resigned as party leader in November 1979 before subsequently leaving the party as well. He continued as an independent MP at Westminster, but his opposition to the republican hunger strikes in 1981 led him to lose his council seat in 1981 and his Westminster seat to **Gerry Adams** in 1983. Many of the 10,000 votes he received in the 1983 general election were cast in **unionist** areas of the constituency. Later in 1983 he was awarded a life peerage and took the title of Lord Fitt of Bell's Hill. In the lords he continued to speak on Northern Ireland matters. Fitt died on 26 August 2005.

**FITZGERALD, GARRET (1926– ). Fine Gael** (FG) leader and taoiseach, Garret FitzGerald was born in Dublin on 9 February 1926. The son of Desmond FitzGerald, the first foreign minister of the Irish Free State, he was educated at Belvedere College, Dublin, and University College, Dublin (UCD), where he received a first-class degree in history and French and a PhD in 1969. From 1947 until 1958, he worked for the Irish airline Aer Lingus but returned to UCD in 1959 and was a lecturer in economics until 1973.

FitzGerald was nominated to the Irish Senate by FG in 1965 and served until 1969. In the 1969 Irish general **election** he was returned to the **Dail** as an FG member for the Dublin Southeast constituency. In the FG–**Irish Labour Party** coalition government of 1973–77, he was appointed minister of foreign affairs by **Liam Cosgrave** and participated in the **Sunningdale** negotiations of December 1973. After the 1977 general election, FitzGerald replaced Cosgrave as FG leader and began a process of modernizing the party. In opposition he maintained an oversight on his party's policy on Northern Ireland. Following the June 1981 general election, he formed a minority FG–Labour government that lasted until January 1982. During this period he announced a "constitutional crusade" to try to make the Republic more attractive to Protestants in Northern Ireland. His meeting with **Margaret Thatcher** in November 1981 led to the decision to establish an **Anglo–Irish Intergovernmental Council** (AIIC). After the general election of November 1982, he formed another coalition government with Labour, which remained in power until 1987.

As was the case in FitzGerald's first term as taoiseach, Northern Ireland also proved to be a significant issue during his second term. The advent of **Sinn Fein** (SF) in party politics in 1982 was a significant factor in the decision to establish the **New Ireland Forum** in 1983 and, even more significantly, in the **Anglo–Irish Agreement** (AIA) of November 1985. In January 1987 the Irish Labour Party withdrew from the coalition, and the government collapsed. FitzGerald subsequently stood down as leader of FG, and he retired from the Dail in 1992. Out of office he has maintained an interest in and spoken frequently on Northern Ireland affairs.

**FORD, DAVID (1951– ). Alliance Party of Northern Ireland** (APNI) leader, David Ford was born in Orpington, England, on 24 February 1951. He was educated at Dulwich College, London, and Queen's University, **Belfast** (QUB), where he graduated with a BSc in economics. After postgraduate study he received a certificate in social work from the Ulster Polytechnic, Jordanstown, and began work as a social worker. He subsequently held various positions in the social service sector. His political career began in the 1980s when he joined APNI, and his first **electoral** contest came in the 1989 **district council** elections, when he stood unsuccessfully for a seat on Antrim Borough Council. In 1990 he became general secretary of APNI, helping to raise his political profile, and in 1993 he was elected to Antrim Borough Council. From 1996 until 1998, Ford was a member of the **Northern Ireland Forum** and represented APNI at the multiparty talks that culminated in the signing of the **Good Friday Agreement**

(GFA) in April 1998. In June 1998 he was elected to the new **Northern Ireland Assembly** for the constituency of South Antrim and became the party's chief whip from 1998 to 2001.

Following the resignation of the party leader, Sean Neeson, Ford became APNI leader in October 2001. At the election in November 2003 to the Northern Ireland Assembly under Ford, APNI managed to retain its six seats, although its share of the first-preference vote fell to 3.7 percent. Ford narrowly retained his seat in South Antrim, even though Martin Meehan claimed to have won the seat for **Sinn Fein** (SF). He contested the **Westminster** constituency of South Antrim for the first time in 1997 when he received 12.0 percent of the vote. In the 2001 general election, this fell to 4.5 percent, partly because some APNI voters chose to support the **Ulster Unionist Party** (UUP) candidate against the **Democratic Unionist Party** (DUP) in the electoral battle surrounding the GFA. In 2005 Ford's share of the votes in the general election recovered to 8.6 percent, though the South Antrim seat was won by the DUP. In March 2007 he was again returned to the Northern Ireland Assembly from South Antrim.

**FORUM FOR A NEW IRELAND.** *See* NEW IRELAND FORUM.

**FORUM FOR PEACE AND RECONCILIATION.** The forum was established by Taoiseach **Albert Reynolds** in the aftermath of the **Irish Republican Army** (IRA) ceasefire of August 1994, with the objective of strengthening the **peace process** by helping **republicans** become more deeply involved in democratic politics.

The forum opened in Dublin Castle on 28 October 1994 and received a range of submissions from political, business, trade union, voluntary, and prison group representatives. Although primarily **nationalist** in outlook, the forum did receive submissions from and was addressed by individuals from **unionist** and British backgrounds. In 1995 it heard from individuals on the issues of **victims'** rights and human rights and was addressed by South African deputy president F. W. De Klerk.

Early in 1996 a final report was being prepared that would have included recognition of the need for consent from the North before a united Ireland could come about. It appeared unlikely that **Sinn Fein** (SF) would have accepted this proposition. With the bombing of Canary Wharf in London and the end of the IRA ceasefire in February 1996, the forum appeared to be in limbo, and it was adjourned on 29 March 1996.

A meeting of the forum was held in December 1997, at which **Northern Ireland Women's Coalition** (NIWC) and Labour representatives from the North were present. However, plans for regular meetings were overtaken by the gathering pace of political negotiations and **elections**. In November 2002 the forum was again recalled in an attempt to bolster flagging support for the **Good Friday Agreement** (GFA), but this failed to have a significant impact.

**FRAMEWORKS DOCUMENTS.** In the wake of the **Downing Street Declaration** of December 1993, continuing negotiations between the British and Irish governments eventually led to the Frameworks Documents of February 1995. The Frameworks Documents included the British government's document titled "A Framework for Accountable Government in Northern Ireland" and "A New Framework for Agreement," drawn up jointly by the British and Irish governments and dealing with North–South and British–Irish relations.

Several weeks before the publication of the documents, **unionist** opinion had been unsettled by a London *Times* report that published leaked extracts from the documents and claimed that they brought a united Ireland closer than at any time since partition. Unionist complaints surrounding the documents owed as much to the **nationalist** rubric of the text as to the details of proposed structures. It soon became clear that unionists were not prepared to support the documents, and they were quietly dropped. Some members of the **Ulster Unionist Party** (UUP) blamed **James Molyneaux** for failing to stop the documents before they were published, and this loss of support was an element in his decision to resign as party leader later that year.

**FREE PRESBYTERIAN CHURCH OF ULSTER.** The Protestant denomination founded by Rev. **Ian Paisley** in Crossgar, Co. Down, in March 1951. Paisley was appointed as moderator of the Free Presbyterian Church and has remained so since then. The church, which is Conservative and evangelical in nature, has approximately 100 congregations, of which 60 are located in Northern Ireland.

Members of the church make up a section of the support for the **Democratic Unionist Party** (DUP); however, this is a clear minority of the DUP's **electoral** support at large. In November 2006 Free Presbyterian minister and former DUP Assembly member Rev. Ivan Foster stated that no Free Presbyterian would welcome the DUP's coalition with **Sinn Fein** (SF).

## – G –

**GADDAFI, MUAMMAR.** *See* LIBYA.

**GAELIC ATHLETIC ASSOCIATION (GAA).** Established in 1884 the GAA aims to promote specifically Irish sports, such as Gaelic football and hurling. From the outset the GAA was associated with Irish nationalism and later with Irish **republicanism** as well. Many GAA sports clubs, grounds, and trophies have been named after leading **nationalist** or republican figures. Many **unionists** in turn view the organization as being hostile to their interests, and this has encouraged attacks on GAA grounds and individuals associated with the GAA by some **loyalists**.

For much of its history, GAA members were banned from playing "foreign" sports, such as rugby or soccer, or using their grounds for those sports. Members of the British security forces were also banned from playing GAA sports. With new financial incentives and pressures, a change in Irish political culture, and a more relaxed political atmosphere in the wake of the **Good Friday Agreement** (GFA), however, these traditional restrictions have begun to break down. In November 2001 the ban on security force members was lifted, and in April 2005 the GAA congress voted to allow the Irish rugby team to play matches at the GAA stadium of Croke Park. However, a stronger traditional viewpoint remains within the Northern counties. In 2006 a **hunger strike** commemoration rally was held at Casement Park in **Belfast**, which was addressed by **Gerry Adams** and other leading **Sinn Fein** (SF) members. Although the GAA's Central Council in Dublin criticized the decision, the Antrim County Board insisted that the event was a commemoration and was therefore not political.

**GARDA SIOCHANA.** The police service of the **Republic of Ireland**. The name is Irish for Guardians of the Peace. In 2006 the force was approximately 12,200 strong. Twelve members of the Garda Siochana were killed during the course of **the Troubles**, all by individuals linked to **republican** organizations. The first was Garda Richard Fallon in January 1970 and the last Garda Jerry McCabe in June 1996. The refusal of the Irish government to give the killers of Garda McCabe early release from prison has been criticized by almost all of Northern Ireland's political parties as a failure of the government to meet its commitments to the **Good Friday Agreement** (GFA).

While there have been comparatively few accusations of **collusion** between the Garda Siochana and **paramilitaries**, an investigation by Peter Cory into the murders of two **Royal Ulster Constabulary** (RUC) officers in 1989 did lead to the establishment of the Smithwick Tribunal in 2003.

**GIBRALTAR.** On 6 March 1988, three unarmed **Irish Republican Army** (IRA) members on active duty were shot dead by the **British Army**'s Special Air Service (SAS) in Gibraltar. Although the IRA members, Sean Savage, Daniel McCann, and Mairead Farrell, did not have immediate access to a bomb when they were killed, plastic explosives were found two days later. Controversy surrounded the accuracy of the statement of events given by the British government and the issue of whether the IRA members could have been arrested rather than killed.

The European Commission of Human Rights (ECHR) ruled that the SAS had not used excessive force in killing the IRA members, but in 1995 the European Court of Human Rights ruled, by a 10–9 majority, that the killings were unnecessary.

The Gibraltar killings began a series of events that led to further **deaths** in the same month. On 16 March 1988, three mourners, including IRA member Kevin Brady, were killed at the funeral of the three IRA members at Milltown Cemetery, **Belfast**, by **loyalist paramilitary** Michael Stone. On 19 March 1988, two British Army corporals wearing civilian clothes were murdered by the IRA after their car was surrounded near the funeral cortege of Kevin Brady.

**GOOD FRIDAY AGREEMENT (GFA).** The agreement signed by the British and Irish governments and Northern Ireland **political parties** at **Stormont** on 10 April 1998. The GFA is also known, more properly, as the **Belfast** Agreement. The GFA contained proposals for both a political settlement based on the **three strands approach** outlined in the **Brooke–Mayhew Talks** and elements of a "peace" settlement dealing with prisoner releases, **decommissioning** of **paramilitary** weapons, police reform, and human rights.

For **Sinn Fein** (SF) two of the major difficulties were prisoner releases and decommissioning. In the final hours of negotiation, it was agreed to reduce the period by which all prisoners would be released from three years to two, while the language requiring decommissioning of paramilitary weapons was made less stringent. This, in turn led **David Trimble** to seek, and receive, a letter of assurance from **Tony Blair** effectively excluding those parties associated with paramilitary groups that had not decommissioned weapons (essentially SF) from office.

The GFA included a provision for a 108-member **Northern Ireland Assembly elected** by **proportional representation** (PR). The Assembly would be headed by an executive committee with legislative powers. The executive's first responsibility would be to establish a **North–South Ministerial Council** (NSMC) to direct cooperation on a number of issues. In the Assembly votes on important decisions would require a majority of both **unionist** and **nationalist** members voting in favor, or a weighted majority of 60.0 percent with 40.0 percent or more of both nationalists and unionists present voting in favor.

In the GFA the Irish government also agreed to amend the **Irish constitutional claim to Northern Ireland** to make the objective of a united Ireland aspirational rather than a constitutional imperative. The British government in turn agreed to replace the Government of Ireland Act. A **British–Irish Council** (BIC) was to be established, which would have representatives from all the major representative bodies in the British Isles. An independent policing commission was to report on future arrangements for policing. The number and role of armed forces in Northern Ireland would be reduced and emergency powers removed.

From the outset the GFA was rejected by those taking a hard-line traditional **republican** stance but also by a larger number of unionists. The **Democratic Unionist Party** (DUP), United Kingdom Unionist Party (UKUP), and other unionists campaigned against the GFA, and in the referendum held on 22 May 1998, it was estimated that only 55.0 percent of Protestants voted in favor of the agreement. Despite this, overwhelming Catholic support for the GFA saw a 71.0 percent vote in favor. In June the Northern Ireland Assembly election provided another worrying result, with nearly half the unionists who were elected being opposed to the GFA. This trend toward increasing opposition to or disillusionment with the GFA continued as elements of the agreement were implemented. Unionist discontent centered on issues such as police reform, **parades** disputes, lack of decommissioning while security force numbers were reduced, and the perceived inefficiency of the executive. Significantly, the Northern Ireland Life and Times survey found that the number of Catholics who believed their cultural tradition was always the underdog decreased from 31.0 percent in 1998 to 28.0 percent in 2001 and to 18.0 percent in 2003, while the number of Protestants increased from 17.0 percent in 1998 to 37.0 percent in 2001 before decreasing to 28.0 percent in 2003. Factors associated with the implementation of the GFA were clearly significant in this change, and survey results consistently showed that while Catholics perceived the GFA to be evenhanded, Protestants believed that nationalists had gained more than unionists from the deal. As a result the DUP campaigned on the issue of a "fair deal" to replace the GFA in the 2005 elections and was returned as the largest party. By late 2006, with the **St. Andrews Agreement** modifying elements of the GFA to accommodate the demands of the DUP and SF, only the **Social Democratic and Labour Party** (SDLP) appeared to support the GFA in the form in which it was initially envisioned.

**GUILDFORD AND WOOLWICH BOMBINGS.** On 5 October 1974, 5 people were killed and 54 injured when **Irish Republican Army** (IRA) bombs exploded without warning in 2 public houses in Guildford, Surrey. One of the pubs was regularly used by military personnel, and 4 of the 5 people killed were soldiers, all of them under 20 years old and 2 of them women. There were further bomb explosions in London during the same month. On 7 November 1974, another soldier and a civilian were killed and more than 20 others injured by an

IRA bomb explosion in a pub in Woolwich, London. The **Guildford Four** and the **Maguire Seven** were later wrongly convicted in connection with the bombings.

**GUILDFORD FOUR.** In October 1975 Paul Hill, Patrick Armstrong, Gerard Conlon, and Carole Richardson were found guilty of causing explosions in Great Britain a year earlier. After a long campaign, however, the convictions were finally overturned in October 1989. The Court of Appeal decided that the 1975 convictions were based on confessions that had been fabricated by the police. Claims were also made that the director of public prosecutions at the time also suppressed scientific evidence that conflicted with the confessions. When the convictions of the Guildford Four were overturned, fresh doubts were cast on those of the **Maguire Seven**, whom Conlon had allegedly named as the bomb makers for the Guildford Four. The Maguire Seven were cleared by the Court of Appeal in June 1991. In May 1993 three former detectives were cleared of the charge of conspiracy to pervert the course of justice by manufacturing the interview notes of one of the Guildford Four.

## – H –

**H BLOCKS.** *See* MAZE PRISON.

**HAIN, PETER (1950– ).** **Labour Party** politician and secretary of state for Northern Ireland, Peter Hain was born in Nairobi on 16 February 1950. He was educated at Pretoria High School in South Africa; Queen Mary's College, London; and the University of Sussex. In South Africa he and his family had been opponents of the apartheid regime and had left the country in 1966. In England he was a prominent campaigner against apartheid and helped organize protests against South Africa–related sports tours. More controversially, for his later Northern Ireland posting, he was also connected to the Troops Out Movement and was a proponent of a united Ireland, although he later stated that the **Good Friday Agreement** (GFA) changed the context in which he had held these views.

Initially he was a member of the Liberal Party, being national chairman of the Young Liberals (1971–73), before joining the Labour Party in the early 1980s. From 1976 until 1991, he worked as a research officer for the Union of Communication Workers and was also the press officer of the Anti-Nazi League from 1977 to 1980. In 1983 and 1987, he stood as a Labour candidate in the London constituency of Putney but lost on both occasions. In 1991, however, he won the seat of Neath in Wales.

In opposition he was a Labour Party whip and became the party's spokesman on employment in 1996. When the Labour Party returned to power in 1997, he became a junior minister in the Welsh Office (1997–99), a minister in the foreign office (1999–2000), and briefly with the department of trade and industry (2001) before returning to the foreign office (2001–02). Hain was secretary of state for Wales (2002–03) and leader of the House of Commons (2003–05).

In the wake of the May 2005 general election, Hain succeeded **Paul Murphy** as secretary of state; however, he was also secretary of state for Wales, and this double appointment was criticized in Northern Ireland, where it was felt he would not be able to carry out both positions effectively. His arrival in Northern Ireland coincided with the electoral confirmation that the **Democratic Unionist Party** (DUP) and **Sinn Fein** (SF) had become the two largest parties in Northern Ireland, arguably making his role in bringing about **devolution** in Northern Ireland more difficult. In September 2006, as **Tony Blair**'s leadership came under pressure, Hain announced his wish to be the next deputy leader of the Labour Party. On 26 March 2007, he welcomed the decision of the DUP and SF to enter a Northern Ireland executive together in May and said the failure to meet a deadline as a sideshow. He failed in his attempt to become deputy leader of the Labour Party but remained in the cabinet under **Gordon Brown** as secretary of state for Wales and for work and pensions when he left Northern Ireland on 28 June 2007. He was succeeded as Northern Ireland secretary by Shaun Woodward.

**HAUGHEY, CHARLES (1925–2006).** **Fianna Fail** (FF) leader and taoiseach of Ireland, Charles Haughey was born in Castlebar, Co. Mayo, on 16 September 1925. He was educated at St. Joseph's Christian Brothers' School, Dublin, and University College, Dublin, where he earned a degree in commerce. He subsequently worked as an accountant. His family came from the strongly **republican** town of Swatragh in Co. Londonderry, and his father had been an officer in the **Irish Republican Army** (IRA) and later the Irish army.

Haughey joined FF in 1948 and, after a number of failed attempts, was **elected** to the **Dail** in 1957 for Dublin Northeast. He held his seat in the constituency until 1992. From 1961 until 1964, he was minister for justice in the government of Sean Lemass, who was also his father-in-law, and gained a reputation as an efficient minister. In 1964 he became minister of agriculture, where his hard-line approach cost him the long-term support of many farmers. In 1966 he appeared to be the front runner to succeed Lemass as taoiseach; however, internal party rivalry with George Colley instead led to the appointment of compromise candidate **Jack Lynch** as FF leader and taoiseach. Lynch in turn appointed Haughey as minister for finance, a post he held until his firing as a result of the **arms crisis** in 1970.

As minister for justice, Haughey had played a role in the Irish government's response to the Border Campaign of 1956 to 1962; however, the outbreak of **the Troubles** in 1968 was of a much greater order and had a greater impact in the Republic. In May 1970, Haughey, fellow minister Neil Blaney, and others were charged with conspiracy to import arms. Haughey was removed from his ministerial position and, although subsequently acquitted, spent the next five years in the political wilderness. During this time, however, he built a base of support for himself at a grassroots level within FF.

In 1975 Lynch recalled him to be a party spokesman, and following the party's landslide win in 1977, he became minister for health. In 1979 Lynch resigned as taoiseach and was replaced by Haughey after he narrowly defeated Colley with the support of backbenchers. As taoiseach he was perceived to be someone who would make tough decisions but also had many political enemies. He was taoiseach from 1979 until 1981 and again, briefly, in 1982, but after this FF was in opposition until 1987.

Throughout this period, Northern Ireland remained a significant area of policy concern. His attitude was strongly antipartitionist but tempered by statements that a united Ireland could only be achieved by peaceful means. While his standpoint was generally welcomed by

**nationalists** in Northern Ireland, **unionists** saw his contribution as being almost entirely negative.

In December 1980 the British and Irish governments announced that a mechanism would be established to allow for joint studies in order to achieve a joint position between the governments in a number of areas. Topics to be studied included security, economic cooperation, and new governmental structures for Northern Ireland. Although serious disagreements between the two sides soon emerged, the process did mark the beginning of a long-term development in closer British–Irish relations.

While in opposition the **New Ireland Forum** report (1984) was a source of conflict between Haughey and his **Fine Gael** (FG) opposite, Taoiseach **Garret FitzGerald**, with Haughey insisting that the option of a unitary state be the first choice of the recommendations made by the forum's report. In 1985, following the signing of the **Anglo–Irish Agreement** (AIA), he was critical of areas of the agreement that guaranteed Northern Ireland's constitutional position within the United Kingdom. When he returned to power in March 1987 at the head of a minority government, he did not attempt to renegotiate the AIA but instead tried to use it to pursue nationalist objectives. In 1989 he abandoned one of FF's traditional principles and entered into a coalition with the Progressive Democrats (PD).

In February 1992 Haughey was forced to resign from office after allegations of misconduct concerning illegal telephone tapping of two political journalists, and he retired from active politics in November 1992. In the late 1990s, there were disclosures concerning Haughey's financial affairs, and a tribunal that investigated the matter concluded that he had compromised the office of the taoiseach and obstructed their work. The Moriarty Tribunal conducted further investigations into Haughey's financial affairs. In 2003 he sold several properties and agreed to pay 5 million Euro to the Irish Revenue Commissioners. Always a complex figure, Charles Haughey died from cancer on 13 June 2006.

**HEATH, EDWARD (1916–2005). Conservative Party** politician and prime minister, Edward Heath was born in Broadstairs on 9 July 1916, the son of a builder and a lady's maid. He was educated at

Chatham House School in Ramsgate and at Balliol College, Oxford from which he graduated with a degree in philosophy, politics, and economics. Heath had a distinguished military career, serving in northwest Europe during World War II, rising to the rank of lieutenant colonel, being awarded the military Member of the British Empire (MBE) and mentioned in dispatches. After the war he became a civil servant; in 1947, news editor of the *Church Times*; and in 1948, a trainee in a finance house. In 1949 he was defeated in a by-**election** in Bexley but won the seat in the following year's general election.

Heath held a number of junior government positions before entering the cabinet in 1959. As lord privy seal (1960–63), he had responsibility for Great Britain's negotiations for entry to the European Common Market. Although these proved unsuccessful, Heath remained ardently in favor of British entry to the Common Market, and this continued to be one of the abiding elements of his political career. In 1965, when Alec Douglas-Home stepped down, Heath became the first Conservative Party leader to be elected by a secret ballot of Members of Parliament (MP).

In June 1970, with **Labour**'s fortunes in decline, the Conservatives won a surprising victory in a **Westminster** general election leading to Heath becoming prime minister. Although Heath's premiership coincided with some of the worst years of **the Troubles** Northern Ireland remained something of a sideshow for Heath whose main concerns were with taking Britain into the Common Market and dealing with industrial relations. The impact of the Yom Kippur War in the Middle East and a strike by the National Union of Mineworkers in Britain added to the belief that, for Heath, Northern Ireland was largely a distraction from more important matters.

Like his contemporary, **Harold Wilson**, Heath appeared to be less than sympathetic to the **unionist** cause (if not pro-**nationalist**). In November 1971 he stated that the British government would not stand in the way of Irish unification if that was the desire of the people of Northern Ireland. In March 1972, in the wake of **Bloody Sunday**, he suspended the **Northern Ireland Parliament** in the face of unionist opposition, and his government attempted to introduce a cross-community **power-sharing** administration with an **Irish dimension** in its place. The latter objective was outlined in the **Sunningdale** Agreement of December 1973, although Heath's pressuring of the unionist negotiators into accepting what may have been an inherently unsalable deal has been criticized by some commentators. In February 1974 the Conservatives narrowly lost to Labour in a general election, and in 1975 Heath was replaced as party leader by **Margaret Thatcher**. Heath remained in the House of Commons until he retired at the general election of 2001. That Heath never held political office again was at least partly due to the personal antipathy between himself and Thatcher. In one of the last significant political events of his life, he gave evidence to the Bloody Sunday Inquiry while it was taking evidence in London. Edward Heath died on 17 July 2005.

**HERMON, JOHN (JACK) (1928– ).** Chief constable of the **Royal Ulster Constabulary** (RUC), John Hermon, usually known as Jack, was born in Larne, Co. Antrim, on 23 November 1928 and educated at Larne Grammar School. A career police officer, he joined the RUC in 1951 and, in 1963, became the first RUC officer to attend Bramshill Police Training College in England. Rising through the ranks, he became deputy chief constable in 1976 and, in January 1980, succeeded Sir **Kenneth Newman** as chief constable of the RUC.

During his term as chief constable, a number of controversial issues emerged; he had to deal with an upsurge in **republican** violence in the wake of the **hunger strikes**, and in 1982, there were accusations that the RUC was carrying out a **"shoot to kill"** policy against republican **paramilitary** suspects.

After the signing of the **Anglo–Irish Agreement** (AIA) in 1985, Hermon faced criticism from unionists in the way **unionist** protests were policed. The predominantly Protestant police force came under severe pressure at this time, and this was partly reflected in Hermon's choice for the title of his 1997 autobiography, *Holding the Line*. While he was a staunch defender of the RUC's reputation, his abrasive personality occasionally brought him into conflict with members of the force as well as with the police authority. He was awarded an order of the British Empire (OBE) in 1975 and a knighthood in 1982. He retired as chief constable in May 1989. He subsequently married Queen's University, **Belfast** (QUB) law lecturer Sylvia Paisley, who, as Lady Sylvia Hermon, won the North Down seat at **Westminster** for the **Ulster Unionist Party** (UUP) in 2001.

**HILLSBOROUGH AGREEMENT.** *See* ANGLO–IRISH AGREE-MENT (AIA).

**HUME, JOHN (1937– ).** Civil rights campaigner and **Social Democratic and Labour Party** (SDLP) leader, John Hume was born in **Derry** on 18 January 1937. He was educated at St. Columb's College, Derry, and at St. Patrick's College, Maynooth, where he received a BA degree before commencing work as a teacher. He first made a mark by helping found a credit union in the city. He was soon involved in the campaign for reform in Northern Ireland and was **elected** vice chairman of the Derry Citizens' Action Committee in the wake of the events surrounding the Derry civil rights march of 5 October 1968.

With this increased political profile, Hume won the Foyle seat at **Stormont** from the **Nationalist Party** (NP) leader Eddie McAteer in the **crossroads election** of February 1969. He was one of the co-founders of the SDLP in 1970 and deputy leader under **Gerry Fitt**. He was also recognized as one of the party's chief ideologues.

In 1973 he was elected to the **Northern Ireland Assembly** from the Londonderry constituency. He was one of the SDLP's negotiators in the Stormont Castle talks of November 1973 and at the **Sunningdale** Conference worked to achieve a strong **Irish dimension**. In the 1974 **power-sharing** executive, he was minister for commerce and was especially critical of the government's failure to take strong action during the **Ulster Workers' Council (UWC) strike** of May 1974. In 1975 he was returned to the **Constitutional Convention** from the Londonderry constituency but was again frustrated by what he perceived as the inability of **unionists** to compromise.

Increasingly Hume built on contacts that he had established with the Irish government and the Irish American lobby to create alliances that might address the Northern Ireland conflict in a wider perspective but that also worked to isolate unionists from him. These connections proved equally important in the 1980s in maintaining support for the constitutional **nationalist** position, which opposed using force to achieve a united Ireland.

Disagreements within the SDLP over the importance of the Irish dimension led to the resignation of Gerry Fitt as party leader in November 1979, with Hume becoming his successor. In June 1979, with

**Ian Paisley** and **John Taylor**, he was elected to the European Parliament and retained his seat until his retirement in 2004.

Under Hume the SDLP refused to participate in any political initiatives that dealt only with Northern Ireland affairs but did not address the Irish dimension. In the wake of the 1981 **hunger strike** and the entry of **Sinn Fein** (SF) to electoral politics, he played a significant role in promoting the **New Ireland Forum** to achieve a consensus among constitutional nationalist parties in Ireland. In 1983 he won the newly created **Westminster** constituency of Foyle, a seat he would hold until he retired from active politics in 2005.

In 1985 Hume welcomed the **Anglo–Irish Agreement** (AIA) and showed little sympathy for unionist criticisms of the AIA. Unionist opposition to the AIA nevertheless created a major obstacle to the achievement of a comprehensive political settlement. The other major difficulty in creating an overall political package lay in the ongoing **paramilitary** campaigns, particularly the **Irish Republican Army** (IRA) campaign.

In 1988 he commenced a series of intermittent discussions with SF president **Gerry Adams**, which eventually led to a joint series of proposals being sent to the Irish government in September 1993. Hume rejected critics of his approach, which downgraded attempts to achieve agreement between **political parties** within Northern Ireland in favor of negotiations that might lead to an IRA ceasefire. With the announcement of an IRA ceasefire in 1994, he believed his decision had been vindicated, and he rejected criticism that the ceasefire might not be permanent.

In 1996 Hume was elected to the **Northern Ireland Forum** but viewed it as an irrelevance to the main objective of all-party negotiations. In 1998 he signed the **Good Friday Agreement** (GFA) on behalf of the SDLP and was subsequently awarded the Nobel Peace Prize. In 1998 he was elected to the Northern Ireland Assembly but declined to stand for the position of deputy first minister. In August 2000 he announced his decision to retire from the Assembly and stood down as SDLP leader in September 2001. He retired from the European Parliament in 2004 and from Westminster in 2005.

**HUNGER STRIKE (1980).** As part of the campaign by **republican** prisoners to regain **special category status**, prisoners demanded the right to wear their own clothes rather than those issued by prison authorities. In October 1980 the prisoners rejected a **Northern Ireland Office** (NIO) proposal that they be allowed to wear "civilian style" clothes provided by the authorities and, on 27 October, seven H block prisoners began a hunger strike in protest. The prisoners' campaign had significant support in the Catholic community but faced strong opposition from the British government, led by **Margaret Thatcher**.

In early December three republican women prisoners in Armagh prison also joined the hunger strike. On 15 December with one of the original hunger strikers, Sean McKenna, apparently close to death, 23 more republican prisoners joined the hunger strike with a further 7 the following day. On 18 December the protest was called off after 53 days, following an appeal from Cardinal **Tomas O Fiaich** and hints from the government that there might be some movement toward political status. The republican prisoners claimed they received a document clarifying earlier proposals and, in effect, conceding all their demands. **Humphrey Atkins** rejected this assessment and said the document merely summarized changes that had been proposed since 4 December. The confused ending of the hunger strike reduced tension in Northern Ireland but left the prospect for a further confrontation on the issue, which actually occurred in the **hunger strike of 1981**.

**HUNGER STRIKE (1981).** Following the inconclusive end to the **1980 hunger strike** by **republican** prisoners, the relationship between the prisoners and prison authorities quickly broke down once again. On the fifth anniversary of the ending of **special category status**, 1 March 1981, the **Irish Republican Army** (IRA) leader in the **Maze Prison, Bobby Sands**, began a renewed hunger strike to regain special category status. Other republican prisoners subsequently joined the protest on a staggered basis. In practical terms the campaign involved recognition of the authorities of five demands by the prisoners: to wear their own clothing; not to undertake prison work; freedom of association; additional recreation facilities (including more visits and letters); and the restoration of remission of sentences lost as a result of the protest.

Outside the prison, the campaign in support of the protest was led by the National H Block/Armagh Committee, which had links with

**Sinn Fein** (SF). There was strong support for the campaign in the Catholic community at large, which viewed many of the restrictions as unjust and the attitude of the prison authorities and government as unreasonable. Attempts by representatives of the Catholic Church, including a papal envoy and cardinal **Tomas O Fiaich**, to mediate in the dispute proved unsuccessful, as did the efforts of the European Commission of Human Rights (ECHR) and the International Red Cross. During the course of the hunger strike, 10 prisoners died, beginning with Bobby Sands on 5 May and ending with Michael Devine on 20 August. Outside the prison 64 people died during the course of the campaign, including 30 members of the security forces.

Apart from the loss of life that took place during the campaign, the hunger strike had a significant political impact with Sands's **election** to the House of Commons in the Fermanagh-South Tyrone by-election in April (and subsequently Owen Carron's in August) and the election of two hunger strikers to the **Dail** in June. These successes encouraged republicans to move toward contesting elections throughout Ireland, though not initially to take seats that they might win in U.K.-based elections.

In September 1981 **James Prior** succeeded **Humphrey Atkins** as secretary of state. By this time, the relatives of some of those on hunger strike had already intervened in order to save the prisoners' lives, and the campaign was beginning to lose momentum. On 3 October the six prisoners still involved in the protest ended their campaign. On 6 October James Prior announced that prisoners could wear their own clothing at all times and that half of remission on sentences that had been lost would be restored. However, other demands made by the prisoners were not met.

**HUNT REPORT.** The report of the committee, headed by Lord Hunt and published on 10 October 1969. The report recommended widespread reforms to the security forces in Northern Ireland, including the disarming of the **Royal Ulster Constabulary** (RUC), the creation of an RUC Reserve, and the replacement of the **Ulster Special Constabulary** (USC) by a part-time force under the command of the **British Army**. The report was generally well received by **nationalists** but faced an angry response from some **unionists**, leading to serious rioting in Protestant areas of **Belfast**. On 11 October

1969, Constable Victor Arbuckle, the first police officer to die in **the Troubles**, was shot and killed by the **Ulster Volunteer Force** (UVF) during rioting on the Shankill Road.

**HURD, DOUGLAS (1930– ). Conservative Party** politician and Northern Ireland secretary of state, Douglas Hurd was born on 8 March 1930 and was educated at Eton and Trinity College, Cambridge. He served in the diplomatic service between 1952 and 1966 and subsequently in the Conservative Party's research department. He was elected to the House of Commons for the constituency of Mid-Oxfordshire in 1974 and was **Edward Heath**'s political secretary during Heath's period as prime minister.

After the Conservative Party returned to power in 1979, he held junior ministerial posts in the foreign office and at the home office. In September 1984 he succeeded **James Prior** as secretary of state for Northern Ireland but remained only until September of the following year before becoming home secretary (1985–89) and then foreign secretary (1989–95). He contested, but failed to win, the Conservative Party leadership in 1990 but was consistently a supporter of **John Major** during the intraparty disputes that later ravaged Major's government.

As Northern Ireland secretary of state, Hurd refused to meet **Sinn Fein** (SF) representatives, even though he had met **Gerry Adams** and Danny Morrison privately in 1978. Most significantly he played an influential role in the negotiations that led to the **Anglo–Irish Agreement** (AIA) in November 1985. His patrician manner and aloof personality, however, often appeared an ill fit for Northern Ireland politics, which often seemed to benefit from a more convivial approach.

The son of a life peer, he himself received a life peerage on his retirement from active politics in 1997, becoming Lord Hurd of Westwell.

– I –

**INDEPENDENCE.** Following the abolition of the **Northern Ireland Parliament** in 1972, some **loyalists** were attracted to the idea of either a unilateral declaration of independence or negotiated independence for Northern Ireland. Among the proponents of the idea in the 1970s were **Vanguard Unionist Progressive Party** (VUPP) leaders, including **William Craig** and **David Trimble**, and members of the **Ulster Defence Association** (UDA). For these groups independence was a preferable outcome to what they perceived to be the inevitable result of government policy at this time: a united Ireland. Whether for ideological reasons or for purely pragmatic ones, such as financial requirements and the difficulty of dealing with **nationalist** opposition within such a state, the idea of an independent Northern Ireland never achieved broad support within the Protestant community.

In the wake of the **Ulster Workers' Council (UWC) strike** of May 1974, in which the VUPP and the UDA were prominent, the government gave some consideration to the concept of "Ulster nationalism" and the idea of independence, but neither appeared to have significant support. Despite this, the UDA continued to promote the idea from time to time.

An Ulster Independence Party (UIP) was launched in 1977 but failed to have any **electoral** impact, and a decade later in early 1988, an Ulster Independence Committee was formed under the leadership of Rev. Hugh Ross, a Presbyterian minister. Like its predecessor the Ulster Independence Committee (Ulster Independence Movement after 1994) failed to have a significant electoral impact. In 1998 Ross contested the European Parliament election and received just under 8,000 votes (1.4 percent of the total). In 1998 it contested two **Northern Ireland Assembly** seats but failed to win either. In January 2000 the Ulster Independence Movement disbanded as a political party but has continued to operate as a pressure group.

**INDEPENDENT INTERNATIONAL COMMISSION ON DE-COMMISSIONING (IICD).** The IICD was established by an agreement signed by the governments of the United Kingdom and Ireland in August 1997. Commissioners from Canada, Finland, and the **United States** were appointed the following month. The head of the IICD was retired Canadian general John de Chastelain. The role of the IICD was to facilitate the voluntary **decommissioning** of weapons held by **paramilitary** groups.

In December 1998 the IICD witnessed the decommissioning of a small amount of weapons by the **Loyalist Volunteer Force** (LVF). It also witnessed three separate events where the **Irish Republican Army** (IRA) put weapons "beyond use" in October 2001, April 2002, and October 2003.

In October 2003 a prearranged sequence of statements and actions, including the announcement of **Northern Ireland Assembly elections** and the confirmation by the IICD that the IRA had put a further cache of weapons beyond use, was intended to lead to the reestablishment of a **devolved** Northern Ireland executive. The IRA did not permit the IICD to reveal precise details of the weapons included in this cache, and as a result the **Ulster Unionist Party** (UUP) felt they had been misled and the deal collapsed. In September 2005 the IICD stated that it believed the IRA had met its commitment to put all its arms beyond use. A further report in February 2006 reaffirmed this assessment.

**INDEPENDENT MONITORING COMMISSION (IMC).** The IMC was established by the governments of the United Kingdom and Ireland within the broader context of the **Good Friday Agreement** (GFA) on 7 January 2004. Its stated purpose is to help movement toward the establishment of a stable and inclusive **devolved** government within the context of a peaceful Northern Ireland. It aims to achieve this by reporting to the British and Irish governments on activity by **paramilitary** groups, on the normalization (i.e., the reduction) of security measures in Northern Ireland, and on claims by **Northern Ireland Assembly** parties that other parties, or ministers in a devolved Northern Ireland executive, are not living up to the standards required of them by the GFA.

The four commissioners are independent of both governments. The IMC commissioners are **John Alderdice**, former **Alliance Party of Northern Ireland** (APNI) leader and Assembly speaker; Joe Brosnan, former secretary general of the Irish department of justice; John Grieve, former deputy assistant commissioner in the metropolitan police, London; and Dick Kerr, former deputy director of the U.S. Central Intelligence Agency.

In the course of its work, the commission has stated that it has met the following categories of organizations of people in Northern Ireland and in the **Republic of Ireland**: **political parties**, government officials, police, community groups, churches, charities, pressure groups and other organizations, businesses, lawyers, journalists, academics, **victims**, private citizens (individuals and families), and former combatants. The IMC produced 15 reports between April 2004 and April 2007. Their assessments of the level of activity of paramilitary organizations have been notable for their lack of political "spin" and as a result have been carefully scrutinized by other political actors. In a number of reports, the IMC highlighted the fact that although "military" operations by paramilitary groups (i.e., attacks on security forces or rival groups) had been greatly reduced by the ceasefires, other criminal activity had continued and in some areas, such as punishment attacks, had substantially increased. In its 11th report, the IMC said that it believed that the **Irish Republican Army** (IRA) was committed to following a political path. Its 12th report repeated this opinion but noted that individuals from all the leading paramilitary groups were still involved in criminal activity. As the report came in the period of diplomatic pressure to agree to terms for a return to devolution, it was the subject of a high degree of "spin" from the major political actors, not least by the British and Irish governments. Its 14th report noted that the IRA had abandoned violence but that dissident paramilitary groups remained committed to terrorism. Its 15th report said that the IRA had not engaged in terrorism or crime since its previous report but the major loyalist paramilitary groups had all been involved in criminal activity.

**INTEGRATION.** The term used to describe the concept of Northern Ireland being run as an integral part of the United Kingdom, both legally and administratively. The idea of integration has always had a much stronger appeal to **unionists** than to **nationalists** because it appears to strengthen the union with Great Britain. In the mid- to late 1980s, in the wake of the **Anglo–Irish Agreement** (AIA), integration had a particular appeal to elements of the **Ulster Unionist Party** (UUP), while the **Campaign for Equal Citizenship** (CEC) also had a strong integrationist aspect to it. In contrast, the **Democratic Unionist Party** (DUP) has been a strong proponent of **devolution** for most of its existence. Following the advent of the **Labour Party** government in 1997, which has pursued a policy of devolution throughout the United Kingdom, the idea of integration has largely been off the political agenda.

**INTELLIGENCE AGENCIES.** The British Security Service, more widely known as MI5, has the task of protecting national security in areas relating to terrorism, espionage, foreign threats, and support of law enforcement agencies in the prevention and detection of serious crime. The way in which the Security Service operates in Northern Ireland is, almost inevitably, secretive and open to speculation. One theory suggests that in the 1970s some elements within MI5 believed **Harold Wilson** to be a Soviet agent and plotted to overthrow the **Labour** government. It as also suggests that the Security Service had encouraged the **Ulster Workers' Council (UWC) strike** as a means to undermine Wilson's authority in Great Britain.

Although MI5 has operated in Northern Ireland from the early 1970s, their role in Northern Ireland was only officially acknowledged in 1988. A particular area of activity involved operations intended to thwart **paramilitary** attempts to import weapons into Northern Ireland. Partly to reduce rivalry between intelligence services, MI5 was given overall responsibility for gathering intelligence in Northern Ireland around 1993. In June 1994, 29 passengers and crew were killed when a Chinook helicopter crashed in Scotland. Those onboard included **Royal Ulster Constabulary** (RUC) special branch, **British Army** intelligence, and MI5 officers, causing a significant loss of experience to the intelligence community.

A significant part of MI5's role during the course of **the Troubles** was intelligence gathering, and this continued during the **peace process**. In 1999 a listening and tracking device was found in a car owned by a senior **republican** that had been used by **Gerry Adams** and **Martin McGuinness**. In September 2004 electronic listening devices were found in **Sinn Fein**'s (SF) party headquarters. In December 2004 the head of MI5 confirmed that they had been responsible for placing the devices. In February 2005 it was announced that MI5 was to assume the lead role in intelligence gathering in Northern Ireland at the end of 2007. New MI5 headquarters were to be located in Holywood, Co. Down.

**Nationalists** remained concerned as to the precise role MI5 was to play in Northern Ireland. In January 2007 Prime Minister **Tony Blair** said that policing in Northern Ireland was solely the responsibility of the **Police Service of Northern Ireland** (PSNI) and that MI5 would have no role whatsoever in civic policing.

**INTERNATIONAL FUND FOR IRELAND (IFI).** Established in 1986 and administered by the governments of the United Kingdom and Ireland, the IFI was created to provide funds to Northern Ireland and border areas of the Irish Republic in order to encourage reconciliation. The **United States** provided $120 million in the period up to 1988, with further contributions coming under subsequent administrations. Canada, Australia, and New Zealand also made smaller contributions. In 1988 the European Community Commission proposed a contribution of just under £10 million per year for three years, and funding was continued in subsequent years.

The IFI was initially treated with deep suspicion by **unionists** because it was viewed as being linked to the implementation of the **Anglo–Irish Agreement** (AIA); however, these suspicions gradually began to break down. In 2005 it was decided that the IFI would cease operating in 2010. In January 2006 it was announced that IFI programs in its final years would center on four key areas: building foundations for reconciliation in marginalized communities, building bridges for contact between divided communities, moving toward a more integrated society, and ensuring sustainability in the longer term.

In October 2006 the European Commission, which had contributed more than one third of the total funds to the IFI since 1989, announced a further £40.5 million for the period 2007 to 2010 in support of the **peace process.** By late 2006 the IFI had distributed £580 million to some 6,000 social and economic projects in Northern Ireland and the Republic.

**INTERNMENT.** On 9 August 1971, "Operation Demetrius" saw the introduction of internment without trial. In an early morning operation by the army, 342 **republicans**, mainly from the **Official Irish Republican Army** (OIRA), were arrested from a list of 452 people sought. No **loyalists** were arrested. It soon became clear that security information on republican activists had proved hopelessly out of date. Of those who were arrested, 105 were released within two days, and a week after internment was introduced, the Provisional **Irish Republican Army**'s (PIRA) chief of staff claimed that only 30 of its members had been interned.

The introduction of internment was criticized by **nationalists** of all shades, as well as by civil rights organizations. Rather than reducing the level of violence, as **unionists** had hoped, there was a massive upsurge; 34 people died in Northern Ireland in 1971 before 9 August but 140 were killed in the rest of the year. The introduction of internment marked the beginning of the worst period of violence of **the Troubles**, which persisted until 1977. Even after this, the anniversary of the introduction of internment became associated with rioting in nationalist areas of Northern Ireland for many years afterward. The famous West **Belfast** Festival, which coincides with this date, was later established in part to provide more positive activities at this time of year.

As well as the negative political and security fallout, the treatment of internees was also a major issue of concern. In February 1972 a report from a committee of British privy councilors headed by Lord Parker reported on the use of five techniques used in "deep interrogation" and concluded that the methods could be justified under exceptional circumstances. Importantly, however, one member of the committee, Lord Gardiner stated that the interrogation techniques were not justifiable.

From November 1972 the Detention of Terrorists Order allowed suspects to be held for 28 days before a decision was made to release or detain them. In February 1973 the first loyalist **paramilitaries** were detained, leading to a loyalist strike that saw widespread violence and a halt to most industry in Northern Ireland. In August 1973 the Detention of Terrorists Order and Special Powers Act were replaced by the Emergency Provisions Act. In August 1975 an amendment to the act gave responsibility for detention orders to the secretary of state rather than commissioners.

In December 1975 Secretary of State **Merlyn Rees** announced that no further detention orders would be issued. By this time only, 73 people were still held under detention orders and 27 of these were also serving prison sentences. The last 46 detainees not serving sentences were released later in the same month. From August 1971 until December 1975, a total of 1,981 people had been detained, of these 107 were loyalists and the rest republicans. Although the power of detention remained on the statute book, it was not used again and was finally removed by the **Labour** government in 1997.

**IRELAND.** *See* REPUBLIC OF IRELAND.

**IRISH CONSTITUTIONAL CLAIM TO NORTHERN IRE-LAND.** Since the partitioning of Ireland in 1920, the status of Northern Ireland had been a source of dispute between the United Kingdom and **unionists** and **nationalists**. This dispute was reflected in the Irish Constitution of 1937, which asserted sovereignty over Ireland as a whole in articles 2 and 3 of the constitution. Although the claim made little practical difference in relations between the North and South, it did help provide militant **republicans** with a formal basis for their campaigns. The claim also made it difficult for unionists to accept formalized institutional links between the North and South, as this could be interpreted as accepting the legitimacy of the constitutional claim.

In 1973 the **Sunningdale** Conference failed to reach agreement on a joint view of the status of Northern Ireland and resulted in separate statements from the British and Irish governments. Even so, a case questioning the limited recognition given by the Irish government at Sunningdale was challenged, leading Irish courts to rule that the government had merely made a statement of policy and had not given formal recognition to Northern Ireland. This decision helped undermine the position of pro-Sunningdale unionists in Northern Ireland and hastened the end of the **power-sharing** executive.

As part of the **Anglo–Irish Agreement** (AIA) of 1985, the Irish government agreed that any change in status would only occur with the consent of a majority in Northern Ireland. This view was challenged in the Irish courts by **Ulster Unionist Party** (UUP) members Michael and Christopher McGimpsey and led the Irish Supreme Court to rule that reunification was a "constitutional imperative" for the Republic.

It was only in the **Downing Street Declaration** of December 1993 that a broadly acceptable consensus was reached. The Irish government agreed to remove the constitutional claim to Northern Ireland in the context of an overall settlement. The British government stated that it had no selfish or strategic interest in Northern Ireland and would facilitate reunification if it was supported by a majority in Northern Ireland.

The **Good Friday Agreement** (GFA) expanded on the principles laid out in the Downing Street Declaration. As part of the overall settlement, the Irish government proposed that articles 2 and 3 of the constitution be amended to an aspirational form. Significantly it included the statement that a "united Ireland shall be brought about only by peaceful means with the consent of a majority of the people, democratically expressed, in both jurisdictions in the island." The ratification of the GFA by referendum enabled these changes to come into effect, creating a more positive environment in which cooperation with unionists could take place.

**IRISH DIMENSION.** The term *Irish dimension* was first used officially in a British government consultative paper on Northern Ireland published in October 1972. Essentially the Irish dimension was intended to provide a structural political link between Northern Ireland and the **Republic of Ireland**, address the requirements of **nationalists** in the North, and raise the possibility that this could be developed at a future date. The difficulty, however, was that any Irish dimension had to address nationalists' demands in this area without unduly raising **unionist** fears that it provided an inevitable process leading to a united Ireland. The **Sunningdale** Agreement of 1973 singularly failed to find this balance, and unionist opposition to the Irish dimension was a significant element in the collapse of the agreement.

For the remainder of the 1970s, an institutionalized Irish dimension was largely off the political agenda. In the 1980s relations between the British and Irish governments gradually improved leading to the **Anglo–Irish Agreement** (AIA) of November 1985, in which the Irish dimension was preeminent. Again, however, unionist opposition meant that the AIA was unlikely to provide a stable political settlement, and the subsequent **Brooke–Mayhew Talks** broadened the scope to a **three strands approach**, which also included internal Northern Ireland relations and British–Irish relations.

Arguably the first document to succeed in balancing the differing requirements of the Irish dimension was the **Downing Street Declaration** of December 1993, which successfully addressed nationalist aspirations toward a united Ireland and unionist fears of the same objective. The **Frameworks Documents** of 1995 again failed to achieve the correct balance and were rejected by unionists. In the negotiations leading to the **Good Friday Agreement** (GFA) in 1998, the Irish dimension, somewhat surprisingly, proved one of the less contentious areas of negotiation. With the amendments to articles 2 and 3 of the Irish constitution, unionists were able to view all-Ireland bodies in a more pragmatic light than had earlier been the case rather than as being stepping stones toward a united Ireland. In 2006, however, unionists remained concerned that these bodies might be expanded in the absence of an agreement on the restoration of **devolution** and remained a potential source of conflict between unionists and the Irish government. With the restoration of a devolved administration on 8 May 2007, however, relations between Northern nationalists and unionists and the Dublin administration proved surprisingly amicable.

**IRISH INDEPENDENCE PARTY (IIP).** Formed in 1977 the IIP pursued the traditional **republican** agenda of seeking a British withdrawal from Northern Ireland. In the 1979 **Westminster** general **election**, the IIP fielded four candidates but failed to win a seat. In the Mid-Ulster constituency where there was a strong republican electoral base, the IIP candidate received more than 12,000 votes but still finished third. In the 1981 **district council** elections, it received 3.9 percent of first-preference votes and won 21 council seats.

With the advent of **Sinn Fein** (SF) in Northern Ireland politics in 1982, however, the IIP found itself increasingly sidelined by a larger party with similar objectives. In the 1985 district council elections, it received 1.1 percent of the vote and won four council seats. In 1989 it decided not to contest that year's district council elections and has been largely defunct since that time.

**IRISH LABOUR PARTY.** The left-wing political party established by James Connelly and others in 1912. It is the third largest party in the **Republic of Ireland** and has served in coalition with other parties but most often with **Fine Gael** (FG). The party proposed **Mary Robinson** for the role of president of Ireland, although she ran as an independent candidate. The party reached a high-water mark of **electoral** support in the November 1992 Irish general election when it won nearly 20.0 percent of the vote and 33 seats in the **Dail**. The Irish Labour Party subsequently formed a coalition with **Fianna Fail** (FF), with **Albert Reynolds** as taoiseach and Labour leader Dick Spring as tainaiste and minister for foreign affairs.

As minister for foreign affairs, Spring played a significant role in the developing **peace process**, not least in October 1993 when he outlined six democratic principles aimed at producing a sustainable peace. Spring initially promoted a policy of **paramilitary** arms **decommissioning** in advance of political talks but gradually softened this to one of all-party talks with decommissioning as a more long-term objective.

The government collapsed in November 1994 following controversy surrounding the appointment of a new president of the high court, leading to a new coalition government of FG, Labour, and the Democratic Left formed under **John Bruton** in December. Poor electoral performances in the general and Irish presidential elections in 1997 led to the resignation of Spring and the advent of Ruairi Quinn as party leader. In 1999 the party merged with Democratic Left but retained the name of Labour. In 2002 another poor performance in the general election led to the replacement of Quinn with former Democratic Left member Pat Rabitte as party leader. In the 2007 Irish general election, the party received 10.1 percent of the vote and won 20 seats; however, this was 1 less than in 2002.

**IRISH NATIONAL LIBERATION ARMY (INLA).** The **republican paramilitary** organization linked to the **Irish Republican Socialist Party** (IRSP), which emerged in December 1974 following a split within Official **Sinn Fein** (SF) and the **Official Irish Republican Army** (OIRA). Supporters of the INLA had become disenchanted with the OIRA after they declared a ceasefire in May 1972 and instead decided to follow a policy of paramilitary activity allied with Marxist politics.

The INLA soon came into conflict with the OIRA, with the first INLA member being killed by the OIRA in February 1975. In October 1977 Seamus Costello, one of the INLA's founding members, was killed in Dublin by the OIRA. The INLA conducted a policy of attacks on members of the security forces and in May 1979 was also responsible for the murder of **Conservative** Member of Parliament (MP), and the probable future Northern Ireland secretary, Airey Neave in London.

In 1980 several leading INLA/IRSP members were murdered by the **Ulster Defence Association** (UDA). In December 1982 the

INLA carried out the **Ballykelly bombing**, which killed 17 people, including 11 soldiers. In 1981 the INLA participated in the **hunger strike** campaign, and three of its prisoners subsequently died as a result of the campaign. In November 1983 INLA members attacked a Pentecostal hall at Darkley in Co. Armagh, shooting dead three church elders and wounding seven other members of the congregation during the Sunday church service. This attack was described by the leaders of the main churches in Ireland as an "act of sectarian slaughter on a worshipping community."

By this time the organization was increasingly becoming involved in criminality for financial gain, and this encouraged further splits. In 1986 and early 1987, the INLA became involved in a feud with the breakaway **Irish People's Liberation Organisation** (IPLO), which led to a dozen **deaths**. Following the arrest of INLA chief of staff Hugh Torney and three others in 1995, Torney announced a ceasefire on behalf of the INLA. However, as Torney did not have the authority to make such an announcement, the outcome was another internal feud in which Torney, one of his supporters, and the new INLA chief of staff were killed.

In December 1997 INLA prisoners in **Maze Prison** were responsible for the murder of **Loyalist Volunteer Force** (LVF) leader **Billy Wright**. The INLA did not support the **Good Friday Agreement** (GFA) but announced a complete ceasefire on 22 August 1998, stating that the will of the Irish people was clear. There have been continuing claims that the organization is involved in drug dealing, although this is strongly denied by the INLA itself. The INLA (including the IPLO) is estimated to have been responsible for 151 deaths during the course of **the Troubles**.

**IRISH PEOPLE'S LIBERATION ORGANISATION (IPLO).** The IPLO was a faction of the **Irish Republican Socialist Party** (IRSP) that attempted to force the IRSP and **Irish National Liberation Army** (INLA) to disband as a result of a campaign it conducted in 1986 and 1987. As part of this internal **republican** feud, 12 people were killed before a truce was arranged in March 1987. In 1987, under the cover name of Catholic Reaction Force, it murdered **loyalist** George Seawright, later claimed by the **Ulster Volunteer Force** (UVF) as a member. However, the apparently haphazard activities of the organization, along with claims of involvement in drug dealing, earned it the enmity of the **Irish Republican Army** (IRA). In March 1990 it was also declared an illegal organization in Northern Ireland. In 1991 the organization murdered five people, none of whom had a connection with the security forces.

At the end of 1991, it was reported that the IRA had ordered the IPLO to cease operations. In the summer of 1992, a split emerged within the IPLO between rival groups assuming the titles "Army Council" and "**Belfast** Brigade," leading to the murder of IPLO leader Jimmy Brown in August 1992. In October 1992 the IRA launched a major operation against the IPLO, leading to the death of one IPLO member and the wounding of several others. Within days, both IPLO groups announced that they were disbanding, and since that time the IPLO has essentially been inactive.

**IRISH REPUBLICAN ARMY (IRA).** By the mid-1960s, the IRA had become a small left-wing group. Following the outbreak of widespread civic unrest in August 1969, however, the organization reemerged as a vigilante group promoting itself as defending Catholics in Northern Ireland. A statement from the Provisional Army Council in late December 1969 signaled a split in the IRA over the issue of the recognition of the respective Parliaments in London, Dublin, and **Belfast**. The same statement criticized the existing IRA leadership for its failure to defend Catholics in Belfast. In January 1970 this split in the IRA between official and provisional wings was reflected in a similar split in **Sinn Fein** (SF). Almost from the outset, the self-stated objectives of defending the Catholic community in the North and ending British rule in Ireland were intermingled.

The campaign of the Provisional IRA, often referred to as PIRA by British security forces but more often as the "Provos" or later simply the IRA after the **Official Irish Republican Army** (OIRA) became largely inactive, moved through several different phases. Initially the PIRA highlighted their role in the defense of Catholic communities in the North following the introduction of **direct rule**, and particularly in the period following the **Ulster Workers' Council (UWC) strike**, they believed that Great Britain was considering withdrawal from Northern Ireland. However, during the course of **the Truce** of 1975, it became increasingly clear that this was unlikely to be the case. The IRA undertook its **long war** campaign, with the intention of causing economic damage in Northern Ireland and in Britain, as well as targeting British soldiers to increase public pressure for the withdrawal of troops. With the introduction of the policy of "Ulsterization," the **Royal Ulster Constabulary** (RUC) and **Ulster Defence Regiment** (UDR) became more prominent in activity against the IRA. Attacks on these locally raised and heavily Protestant security forces strengthened the belief of **unionists** that the IRA was engaged in a largely sectarian campaign.

Although the IRA has consistently maintained that it is not a sectarian organization, many of its actions contradicted this stance. In one of the IRA's most notorious actions, members of the organization murdered 10 Protestant workmen at Kingsmill, Co. Armagh, in January 1976 in retaliation for the **Ulster Volunteer Force** (UVF) murder of 6 Catholic men several days earlier.

In the early 1980s, the **hunger strike** campaigns drew republicans into the realm of party politics, with inevitable consequences for the IRA's campaign. While there was, to some extent, an overlap in membership, the political activity of SF began to give it a distinct identity from the IRA rather than it being a mere adjunct to the IRA. In October 1981 leading SF member Danny Morrison spoke of a "ballot box and Armalite strategy" for the **republican** movement to achieve power in Ireland, although increasingly greater emphasis was given to the ballot box side of the equation. From the early 1990s, republicans were again in contact with government officials, and these secret contacts formed a significant element in the early phrases of the **peace process**.

During the course of the long war, the IRA operated in a tight cell structure. While arms shipments, particularly those from **Libya** in the early 1980s, ensured that the IRA had sufficient materiel to continue its campaign, equally it appeared unable to achieve a significant military or political advantage. The ongoing IRA campaign was becoming increasingly unpopular within the Catholic community, and a number of high-profile "mistakes" added to this tendency.

In the summer of 1994, an IRA document was circulated internally that advocated a policy of the tactical use of the armed struggle (TUAS), which entailed using political pressure in Ireland and from the **United States** to force a British withdrawal from Northern

Ireland. The IRA subsequently called a "complete cessation of military operations" in August 1994. But this did not mean, as many had hoped, that all activity had ceased, and a number of alleged drug dealers and others were killed by the IRA under the cover name of Direct Action Against Drugs (DAAD).

In February 1996, with political negotiations stalled, the IRA ended its ceasefire by detonating a bomb at Canary Wharf in London. In July 1997 with a new **Labour** government in power and the requirements for the **decommissioning** of weapons before talks dropped, the IRA reinstated its ceasefire, and SF entered political negotiations.

As part of the **Good Friday Agreement** (GFA), **political parties** agreed to use their influence to have **paramilitary** organizations decommission weapons within two years. However, the IRA argued that this would be portrayed as a surrender by them, and no decommissioning occurred. The result was an ongoing dispute between unionists and republicans over the issue and recurring suspensions of the **Northern Ireland Assembly**. In October 2001 the IRA announced that it had put some of its weapons "beyond use," with further weapons being disposed of in April 2002 and October 2003.

In July 2005 the IRA announced a formal end to its armed campaign. This did not end the debate surrounding the fallout of earlier IRA activity, whether as a result of its campaign in general, the issue of **the disappeared**, or more recent controversies, such as the raid on the Northern Bank in December 2004 or the murder of **Belfast** man Robert McCartney in January 2005.

As one of the main protagonists of **the Troubles**, the organization was involved in many of the high-profile incidents of the conflict, including the attack on British soldiers at **Warrenpoint** in 1979; **Bloody Friday**; the **Birmingham**, **Guildford and Woolwich**, **Brighton**, **La Mon**, **Enniskillen**, and **Shankill bombs**; and the hunger strike campaigns in 1980 and 1981. The IRA also suffered casualties in incidents such as those in **Loughgall** and **Gibraltar**.

During the course of the Troubles, the IRA was responsible for 1,768 **deaths**, and 294 members of the IRA were killed.

**IRISH REPUBLICAN SOCIALIST PARTY (IRSP).** The IRSP was founded in December 1974 after a split within the **Official Irish Re-**

**publican Army** (OIRA). It holds the view that the aims of the reunification of Ireland and achieving a socialist society are interlinked. The IRSP's **paramilitary** wing is widely viewed as being the **Irish National Liberation Army** (INLA). It has been involved in intermittent feuds with other **republican** organizations, and its founder, Seamus Costello, was shot dead by the OIRA in Dublin in 1977.

During the 1981 **hunger strike**, the IRSP worked more closely with **Sinn Fein** (SF) and won two seats in the **district council elections** of the same year. Between 1983 and 1987, the organization was also disrupted by the impact of the **Supergrass trials**. In 1986 and 1987, the internal feud with the **Irish People's Liberation Organisation** (IPLO) faction, in which 12 people died, caused further damage. The IRSP opposes the **Good Friday Agreement** (GFA) on the basis that the GFA strengthens British involvement in Ireland.

– J –

**JOINT AUTHORITY.** A form of government proposed for Northern Ireland whereby the governments of the United Kingdom and Ireland would have equal authority over, and responsibility for, Northern Ireland. The main political proponents of this idea have been the **Social Democratic and Labour Party** (SDLP), who have argued, albeit intermittently, that this gives equal recognition to competing **unionist** and **nationalist** identities and political aspirations.

In practice such a policy was likely to create as many problems as it solved. **Republicans** viewed joint authority as being acceptable only if it eventually progressed to a united Ireland, while **unionists** of all shades were opposed to giving the Irish government a greater input in Northern Ireland affairs. In 1984 the **New Ireland Forum** report suggested joint authority as a possible political settlement. The **Anglo–Irish Agreement** (AIA) of 1985, which gave the Irish government the right to be consulted on Northern Ireland matters, was a small step along the path toward joint authority but brought a massive unionist campaign of opposition. In April 1988 a survey suggested that while 28.0 percent of Catholics would accept joint British–Irish authority over Northern Ireland, the comparable figure for Protestants was 4.0 percent.

## – K –

**KELLY, GERARD (GERRY) (1953– ). Republican** activist and **Sinn Fein** (SF) politician, Gerry Kelly was born in **Belfast** on 5 April 1953. He joined the **Irish Republican Army** (IRA) in 1972 and in 1973 was convicted of causing explosions and conspiracy to cause explosions in Britain, for which he received two life sentences. He campaigned for a transfer to a prison in Northern Ireland and, after taking part in a **hunger strike**, was transferred to the **Maze Prison** in 1975. He played a prominent role in the events surrounding the 1983 **Maze Prison escape**. In 1986 he and another IRA member were recaptured in Holland. Following his **extradition** he served the rest of his sentence in the Maze Prison and was released in 1989.

Kelly subsequently became a leading member of SF and was **elected** to the **Northern Ireland Forum** for the North Belfast constituency in 1996 and to the **Northern Ireland Assembly** in 1998 and 2003. In the 1997 **Westminster** general election, he came in third in the North Belfast constituency but in the 2001 and 2005 general elections came in second, behind the **Democratic Unionist Party** (DUP) candidate. In December 2006 he was warned by the police that he was likely to be attacked by dissident republicans. In March 2007 he was again returned to the Northern Ireland Assembly from North Belfast. In April 2007 he was named as SF's prospective junior minister in the office of the first minister and deputy first minister and took up the post in May 2007 following the devolution of power of the same month.

**KING, THOMAS (TOM) (1933– ). Conservative Party** politician and secretary of state for Northern Ireland, Tom King was born on 13 June 1933. He was educated at Rugby School and Emmanuel College, Cambridge. King was **elected** to the House of Commons for the constituency of Bridgewater in the 1970 general election. During the party's period in opposition between 1974 and 1979, he held a number of positions, including the Conservative spokesman on energy.

When the Conservatives returned to power in 1979, he served as a junior minister before becoming minister of the environment in January1983 and subsequently transport and then employment minister. He arrived in Northern Ireland in September 1985, two months before the signing of the **Anglo–Irish Agreement** (AIA), and the angry **unionist** reaction to the AIA would dominate most of his term as secretary of state. He himself was attacked by a crowd of **loyalists** outside **Belfast** City Hall on 20 November 1985. King attempted to reconcile unionists to the AIA. For example, in December 1985 he stated that the AIA meant that the Irish prime minister had, for all practical purposes, accepted that there would never be a united Ireland. This, however, led to a row between the British and Irish governments over the interpretation of the AIA, and King apologized for the statement in the House of Commons.

In June 1986 he wound up the **Northern Ireland Assembly** launched by **James Prior** in 1982 on the basis that it was being used solely as a unionist vehicle of opposition to the AIA and not serving its proper function. Restrictions on Orange **parades** helped address some **nationalist** concerns but served to further alienate unionists. Relations with Irish ministers on the Anglo–Irish Intergovernmental Conference were also often strained over differences on security issues.

In October 1988 three people were convicted of conspiracy to murder King; however, the convictions were overturned the following year on the basis that comments made by King about the alleged abuse of the right to silence had prejudiced the case.

King was appointed defense secretary in July 1989 before returning to the backbenches in 1992. He retired from the House of Commons at the 2001 general election and was subsequently awarded a life peerage, taking the title of Lord King of Bridgewater.

– L –

**LA MON BOMBING.** On 17 February 1978, 12 people, all of them Protestants, were killed and 23 injured by an **Irish Republican Army** (IRA) incendiary bomb at the La Mon House hotel in Castlereagh on the outskirts of **Belfast**. The **victims** included three married couples. Cans of petrol were attached to the bomb that sent fire sweeping through the hotel dining room. An anonymous telephone warning was given, and staff had begun clearing the hotel of the 400 people in the building when the bomb exploded on the windowsill outside the dining room. Many of the hotel guests escaped from windows with their clothes on fire. The **Royal Ulster Constabulary** (RUC) later distributed copies of a leaflet showing the badly burned remains of one of the victims.

**LABOUR PARTY.** One of the two major **political parties** of the United Kingdom. The Labour Party, under Prime Minister **Harold Wilson**, was in power at the outbreak of **the Troubles** in 1968 but lost the general **election** of June 1970 before returning to power after the February 1974 general election under Wilson and, from 1976, **James Callaghan**. Poor economic performance, industrial disputes, and internal party divisions saw the party lose the 1979 general election, and they remained in opposition until May 1997, when a landslide victory returned a Labour government under **Tony Blair**.

The Labour Party has generally been perceived as being more sympathetic to **nationalist** than **unionist** concerns, although in government the party has pursued a largely pragmatic policy. In opposition the Labour Party has been more overtly in favor of a united Ireland. In November 1971 Harold Wilson outlined a 15-point plan that could lead to a united Ireland within 15 years. Wilson's plan was based on winning over Protestant support for a united Ireland but made no detailed proposals as to how this would be achieved. In January 1976, however, Wilson stated that a united Ireland was neither a practical proposition nor a solution that any British party would wish to impose.

In September 1981, during the course of the **hunger strike** campaign, the Labour Party conference voted to campaign actively to achieve a united Ireland "by consent." In August 1985 the party's spokesman on Northern Ireland, Clive Soley, called for the harmonization of Northern Ireland with the **Republic of Ireland** as a prelude to reunification. In October 1994, however, the party leader, Neil Kinnock, said the Irish unification would not be achieved for many decades.

Kevin McNamara, the party's spokesman on Northern Ireland from 1987 until 1994, was perceived by some as the most pronationalist Labour spokesman. In 1988 he expressed the hope that he would be the last secretary of state for Northern Ireland, although he opposed calls for a withdrawal of troops from Northern Ireland. McNamara strongly opposed calls for the Labour Party to organize in Northern Ireland and supported the view that would-be Labour supporters in Northern Ireland should vote for the **Social Democratic and Labour Party** (SDLP). From the early 1990s, there were increasing demands from within Northern Ireland, supported by members of the Labour movement, to allow voters in Northern Ireland to join the party. While in September 2003 the Labour Party voted to allow supporters in Northern Ireland to join by 2007, Labour still did not contest Northern Ireland constituencies.

**LABOUR PARTY (IRELAND).** *See* IRISH LABOUR PARTY.

**LEEDS CASTLE TALKS.** Between 16 and 18 September 2004, talks involving the British and Irish governments and Northern Ireland **political parties** were held at Leeds Castle in Kent. The aim of the talks was to restore a **devolved** government to Northern Ireland by attempting to reconcile conflicting positions, especially between **Sinn Fein** (SF) and the **Democratic Unionist Party** (DUP), on **paramilitary** activity, arms **decommissioning**, and policing. The DUP also required changes to the way in which the Northern Ireland executive operated, so that ministers would have less scope to operate independently of executive control. The British and Irish governments put forward proposals that they regarded as an acceptable compromise, but these failed to break the deadlock.

**LIBERAL DEMOCRATS.** The British political party formed in 1988 by the merging of the Liberal Party and Social Democratic Party. It is the third largest political party in the United Kingdom. From 1988 until 1999, the party was led by Paddy Ashdown, who had family connections with Northern Ireland and had served in Northern Ireland while in the **British Army**. The Liberal Democrats organize in Northern Ireland but do not contest elections. The party works closely with the **Alliance Party of Northern Ireland** (APNI) and, in general, follows a similar line of policy on Northern Ireland affairs. APNI members of the House of Lords sit with the Liberal Democrats. The Liberal Democrat spokesman on Northern Ireland from 1997 until July 2007 was Lembit Opik, who was born and educated in Northern Ireland. On 4 July 2007 he was succeeded by Alan Reid.

**LIBYA.** Libya played a significant part in **the Troubles** through its role as a supplier of arms and weapons to the **Irish Republican Army** (IRA). Libya is believed to have begun smuggling weapons to the IRA, which it viewed as an anti-imperialist liberation organization, in 1972. In 1973 the Irish navy intercepted five tons of weapons from Libya onboard the ship *The Claudia*. Libyan president Muammar Gaddafi is also believed to have supplied the IRA with several million pounds in cash. The weapons supply was stopped in the mid-1970s, but in 1986, after Great Britain supported the **United States** in their bombing raids on Libya, Gaddafi recommenced supplies to the IRA. In October 1987 approximately 150 tons of weapons was intercepted by the French navy onboard *The Eksund*. Security experts suggest that three smaller shipments of weapons from Libya had already been smuggled into Ireland. By the early 1990s, Libyan supplies of weapons to the IRA seemed to have ended as Gaddafi sought to improve relations with the West.

In 1974 a delegation from the **Ulster Defence Association** (UDA), which included **Glen Barr**, visited Libya seeking financial backing to support the idea of an independent Northern Ireland, however, this failed to develop.

In November 2006 Gaddafi and senior members of the Libyan intelligence services were served with U.S. courts summons as part of a lawsuit by those who had suffered from IRA violence as a result of weapons being supplied by Libya to the IRA. Lawyers associated with the case suggested that more then 6,000 people had been killed or injured from weapons and training given to the IRA by Libya.

**LOCAL GOVERNMENT.** *See* DISTRICT COUNCILS.

**LONDONDERRY.** *See* DERRY (LONDONDERRY).

**LONG WAR.** The phrase used to describe the strategy pursued by the **Irish Republican Army** (IRA) from the collapse of **the Truce** in late 1975 until the development of the **peace process** in the early 1990s. Having failed to force British withdrawal from Northern Ireland by developing a broad base of support within the Catholic community, the Provisional IRA (PIRA) reorganized into a cell structure, with IRA activists conducting a war of attrition against the British state. Among the objectives of the long war strategy were the following: causing as many **deaths** as possible to increase support among the British public for a withdrawal from Northern Ireland, a bombing campaign to increase the economic cost of British involvement in Northern Ireland, making Northern Ireland ungovernable except by military means, winning support for the campaign both in Ireland and internationally by the use of publicity and propaganda, and maintenance of the campaign by physical attacks on opponents of the campaign.

As the long war continued, however, it became clear that the IRA had neither the support base nor the weapons required to defeat the British state and that their campaign had served to alienate Protestants and a significant number of Catholics. As the peace process developed, emphasis on political activity became increasingly incompatible with the long war, and the IRA's declaration of a cessation of operations in 1994 marked the effective end of the long war.

**LOUGHGALL.** A Co. Armagh village where, on 8 May 1987, eight **Irish Republican Army** (IRA) members were shot dead by the **British Army**'s Special Air Service (SAS) when they attacked the local **Royal Ulster Constabulary** (RUC) station. A civilian caught in the firing was also killed. British intelligence agents discovered that the IRA was planning a bomb attack on the local police station, and an operation involving 40 SAS members was set up to ambush the IRA active service unit. SAS members were positioned inside the station and in a nearby wood and others were assigned to cut off the IRA unit if it tried to escape.

The IRA unit attacked the station with a mechanical digger carrying a 200-pound bomb, which was detonated and destroyed part of the police station. The SAS fired more than 100 rounds of ammunition into the digger and a van carrying other members of the IRA unit. The civilian was killed when he drove through one of the SAS groups. The ambush effectively destroyed the IRA's East Tyrone unit and was the organization's highest **death** toll in any single incident.

In January 1999 a meeting between a **Northern Ireland Office** (NIO) minister and relatives of the IRA members killed in the incident was criticized by relatives of those murdered by the IRA in the area.

**LOYALIST.** An individual or group that expresses loyalty to the British Crown and to the union between Great Britain and Northern Ireland. In the period before the outbreak of **the Troubles**, the term was often used interchangeably with the word *unionist*, but with the fragmentation of the unionist political bloc in the 1970s, *loyalist* increasingly referred to the more militant or working-class section of the unionist community. Protestant **paramilitary** groups are always referred to as loyalist rather than unionist. Unlike their Catholic counterparts, loyalist **political parties**, such as the **Progressive Unionist Party** (PUP) and **Ulster Democratic Party** (UDP), have not enjoyed significant **electoral** success.

**LOYALIST ASSOCIATION OF WORKERS (LAW).** The LAW was a **loyalist** group that emerged in 1971 in the months leading up to the introduction of **internment**. Led by Harland and Wolff shipyard trade unionist Billy Hull, it had its main support in the heavy industries of the **Belfast** area. It was heavily influenced by the **Ulster Defence Association** (UDA) and was also later closely linked with **Ulster Vanguard**. The organization also played a role in a 48-hour loyalist strike held to protest the introduction of **direct rule**.

In February 1973 LAW was involved in another loyalist strike that was organized to protest the internment of two UDA members. The level of violence associated with this strike did much to undermine the reputation of LAW, as did subsequent revelations about the misuse of funds. The organization was still nominally in existence in May 1974 at the time of the **Ulster Workers' Council (UWC) strike**, but during the course of the strike, it was effectively replaced by the UWC.

**LOYALIST VOLUNTEER FORCE (LVF).** The **loyalist paramilitary** organization that emerged in 1997 after a split in the **Ulster Volunteer Force** (UVF). In July 1996, during a period of increased tension surrounding the **Drumcree parade**, a Catholic taxi driver was murdered in the area of Lurgan, Co. Armagh. The murder breached the UVF's ceasefire, and the Mid-Ulster brigade of the UVF was subsequently disbanded by the organization's leadership in **Belfast**. In 1997 the former UVF members formed the LVF under **Billy Wright**.

In May 1997 the murder of **Gaelic Athletic Association** (GAA) official Sean Brown from Bellaghy reemphasized the LVF's willingness to attack individuals from any section of the Catholic community. The organization was declared illegal in June 1997. In December 1997 Billy Wright was killed by **Irish National Liberation Army** (INLA) prisoners inside the **Maze Prison**, and the LVF responded by murdering a number of Catholic civilians. In the period leading up to and following the signing of the **Good Friday Agreement** (GFA), the LVF gained some support from a number of those who opposed the **peace process**. In May 1998 it declared a ceasefire that was accepted by the **Northern Ireland Office** (NIO) in November. In December 1998 it handed over a small number of weapons to the International **Decommissioning** Body. In 2002 Wright's successor as LVF leader, Mark Fulton, committed suicide in Maghaberry prison.

Throughout its existence the LVF has been involved in an intermittent feud with the UVF. In July and August 2005, four people were killed during a feud with the UVF. An element of the feud surrounded the LVF's heavy involvement in drug trafficking. In October 2005, following the **Irish Republican Army**'s (IRA) decommissioning of weapons the previous month, the LVF announced that it was standing down. In July 2006 LVF supporters were forced out of a housing estate in East Belfast by **Ulster Defence Association** (UDA) and UVF members.

**LYNCH, JOHN (JACK) (1917–99).** Fianna Fail (FF) leader and taoiseach, Jack Lynch was born in Cork on 15 August 1917. He was educated at St. Vincent's, North Mon, before beginning work as a civil servant in the Department of Justice in Dublin in 1936. He later qualified as a barrister and was called to the bar in 1945. Before entering politics Lynch had made his name as a sportsman, playing Gaelic football and hurling for County Cork.

In 1948 Lynch was **elected** to the **Dail** as an FF teachta dala (TD) representing a seat in Cork City (1948–81). He became a junior government minister in 1951 and joined the cabinet in 1957 as minister of education (1957–59). He subsequently held the posts of minister for industry and commerce (1959–65) and for finance (1965–66) before succeeding Sean Lemass as party leader and taoiseach

(1966–69). While minister for industry and commerce, he helped improve economic relations with Northern Ireland and conducted talks with his Northern Ireland counterpart, **Brian Faulkner**. After becoming taoiseach he had talks with **Terence O'Neill** at **Stormont** in December 1967.

With the outbreak of **the Troubles**, comments by Lynch, which supported the claims of Catholic grievances in the North, were welcomed by Catholics but heightened the antagonism of Protestants, who viewed such statements as an unwarranted interference in Northern Ireland affairs. Most significant in this area were Lynch's comments in a broadcast made on 13 August 1969, when he stated, "It is clear also that the Irish government can no longer stand by and see innocent people injured and perhaps worse." He also called for a United Nations peacekeeping force to intervene in Northern Ireland and announced that Irish army field hospitals would be set up along the border. **Unionists** blamed Lynch for inflaming an already dangerous situation, while **nationalists** felt betrayed by his failure to become more involved.

In 1970 the situation in Northern Ireland brought further difficulties, and Lynch was forced to fire two members of his cabinet after allegations that they had been involved in a plot to illegally import arms for use by nationalists in Northern Ireland. The **arms crisis** highlighted divisions within FF, but Lynch managed to retain leadership of the party.

Following the Irish general election of 1973, FF lost power for the first time since 1957. In opposition, FF appealed more openly to its more **republican** wing, and in 1975 the party issued a policy document calling for a British withdrawal from Northern Ireland. In the 1977 Irish general election, FF was returned with a significant majority. Despite this, relations with Great Britain remained cool, particularly with security cooperation, although Lynch pursued a more pragmatic course on Northern Ireland when in office than had been suggested in opposition. In any event, social and economic conditions in the Republic were a more pressing concern of Lynch's government in this period. Toward the end of 1979, pressure was increasing within FF for a change of leadership, and in December he was replaced by **Charles Haughey** as FF leader and taoiseach. In 1981 he retired from active politics. Jack Lynch died on 20 October 1999.

# – M –

**MAGINNIS, KENNETH (KEN) (1938– ).** Ulster Unionist Party (UUP) politician, Ken Maginnis was born in Co. Tyrone on 21 January 1938. He was educated at the Royal School, Dungannon, and Stranmillis Teacher Training College, Belfast. A teacher by profession, he also served in the **Ulster Special Constabulary** (USC) and later the **Ulster Defence Regiment** (UDR), in which he was a parttime major. Over the course of his career, he survived a number of attempts on his life by **republican paramilitary** groups.

He was **elected** to Dungannon **district council** in May 1981 as a UUP candidate and in August 1981 was the party's candidate in the Fermanagh-South Tyrone by-election but was defeated by the anti–H blocks candidate, Owen Carron. In the 1983 Westminster general election, the **nationalist** bloc vote was split between Carron and the **Social Democratic and Labour Party** (SDLP) candidate, and Maginnis won the seat. He represented the Fermanagh-South Tyrone constituency until 2001, when he did not contest the seat.

In 1982 Maginnis was elected to the **Northern Ireland Assembly** from Fermanagh-South Tyrone. He was UUP spokesman on security from 1982 until 2001. In the wake of the **Anglo–Irish Agreement** (AIA), he refused to pay car tax in protest, and this led to his serving a brief prison sentence in 1987. He was one of the main UUP negotiators during the **Brooke–Mayhew Talks**. In 1995 he contested the leadership of the UUP, but despite being the most popular of the candidates within Northern Ireland, he was viewed as too much on the liberal wing of the party and lost to **David Trimble**. He was returned to the **Northern Ireland Forum** in 1996 and was a member of the UUP negotiating team in the talks leading to the **Good Friday Agreement** (GFA). In the wake of the GFA, he was a strong supporter of the line taken by Trimble. Following his retirement from the House of Commons in 2001, he was awarded a life peerage, becoming Lord Maginnis of Drumglass. In May 2005 he lost his seat on the Dungannon district council as part of a general swing from the UUP toward the **Democratic Unionist Party** (DUP).

**MAGUIRE SEVEN/FAMILY.** Along with the **Birmingham Six** and **Guildford Four**, the Maguire family case was one of a series of miscarriages of justice that occurred in England and were associated with **the Troubles**. In March 1976 Annie Maguire, five other members of her family, and a family friend were jailed for possessing explosives. In December 1974 Giuseppe Conlon arrived in London to speak with solicitors defending his son Gerry on charges relating to the **Guildford and Woolwich bombings** and, while in England, visited the Maguire family.

On the basis of scientific tests, police decided that the family had passed on nitroglycerine to the Guildford bomb makers. The Maguire Seven were later arrested and convicted of possessing explosives. All of the Maguire family members served their sentences of between 4 and 10 years and were released, with the exception of Giuseppe Conlon who died in prison. Their convictions were overturned in 1991, however, when the Court of Appeal ruled that the evidence used in the convictions was inadmissible. In February 2005 Prime Minister **Tony Blair** issued an apology to both the Maguire family and the Guildford Four for their wrongful imprisonment.

**MAJOR, JOHN (1943– ). Conservative Party** politician and prime minister, John Major was born in London on 29 March 1943, the son of a retired theatrical performer and businessman. He was educated at Rutlish School but left school to begin work at the age of 16 due to a family financial crisis. He worked as a general laborer for two years before joining a banking firm, of which he eventually became head of corporate affairs. Major won a seat on Lambeth Council in London for the Conservatives in 1968 and, although defeated in 1971, built a reputation as an effective councilor. He contested, but lost, the safe **Labour** seat of St. Pancras in London in the 1974 general **election** but won the seat of Huntingtonshire in 1979.

In the following years, he held a number of junior government positions before becoming foreign secretary between July and October 1989 and chancellor of the exchequer from October 1989 to November 1990. As the various factions within the Conservative Party argued over who should replace **Margaret Thatcher**, John Major emerged, partly through political skill and partly good fortune, to claim the party leadership and premiership.

Although the Conservatives surprisingly won the 1992 general election, their parliamentary majority was seriously reduced and would continue to diminish in the following five years. This would prove to be an important factor in all the party's decisions during the course of the Parliament, not least, in matters relating to Northern Ireland.

Major's government of 1992 to 1997 was characterized by internal faction fighting (particularly over Britain's role in Europe), allegations of sleaze, and crises over the value of sterling. In June 1995, in a tactic aimed at silencing his critics, Major resigned as party leader but stood in, and comfortably won, the subsequent leadership contest and was reelected as party leader. Although the move bought him another two years as prime minister, it was clear to all that the Conservative's period in power since 1979 was drawing to a close. It came as little surprise that the Conservatives were resoundingly defeated in the May 1997 general election, though few predicted the extent of the Conservative defeat. Major resigned as Conservative leader almost immediately afterward.

In Northern Ireland the years of Major's premiership saw significant progress. As with his ascent to the office of prime minister in November 1990, this was partly due to political skill and partly a case of being in the right place at the right time. Like President **Bill Clinton**, the resolution of the Northern Ireland conflict also offered the prospect of a positive achievement for posterity.

Major's premiership arguably coincided with the most crucial years of the **peace process**, including, most significantly, the **Downing Street Declaration** of December 1993 and the **loyalist** and **republican** ceasefires of the following year. Political progress in the final year of his premiership was slowed by the fact that the Conservatives were widely viewed as a lame duck government. Major was also hampered by his party's declining support in the House of Commons, leading to the Conservatives intermittent reliance on **Ulster Unionist Party** (UUP) votes to pass legislation. The significance of this was perhaps in the perception among **nationalists** that Major was more sympathetic to **unionists** than was in fact the case.

In February 1996 the **Irish Republican Army** (IRA) ended its ceasefire in an attempt to force the British government toward a more republican agenda in the peace process. While this proved to be largely unsuccessful, by the time the ceasefire was reinstated, Major was no longer in office. He retained an interest in Northern Ireland affairs, however, and actively campaigned in favor of a *yes* vote in the referendum on the **Good Friday Agreement** (GFA) in May 1998. Major retired from active politics in 2001.

**MALLON, SEAMUS (1936– ). Social Democratic and Labour Party** (SDLP) politician and deputy first minister, Seamus Mallon was born in Markethill, Co. Armagh, on 17 August 1936. He was educated at the Abbey Christian Brothers' School in Newry and at St. Joseph's Teacher Training College in **Belfast**. He was chairman of the Mid-Armagh Antidiscrimination Committee from 1963 until 1968 and joined the SDLP shortly after it was formed in 1970.

In 1973 he was **elected** to the Armagh **district council** (serving until 1989) and was also elected to the **Northern Ireland Assembly** for the Armagh constituency in 1973 and the **Constitutional Convention** in 1975. In the October 1974 and 1979 general elections, he failed to win the **Westminster** seat of Armagh, and in 1983 he narrowly failed to be elected for the new seat of Newry and Armagh because of split in the **nationalist** vote, which allowed the **Ulster Unionist Party** (UUP) to win the seat. Mallon won Newry and Armagh in the January 1986 by-election and retained it until he retired from politics in 2005.

When **John Hume** became leader of the SDLP in 1979, Mallon was elected as deputy leader. In May 1982 he was appointed to the senate in the **Republic of Ireland** by Taoiseach **Charles Haughey**. However, he was also elected to the Northern Ireland Assembly later in the same year, and this led to a challenge from the UUP in an election court, which led to Mallon losing his Assembly seat.

As the SDLP's spokesman on justice, after 1979 he was a severe critic of some of the policies pursued by the security forces, including **"shoot to kill,"** but Mallon was also strongly critical of **paramilitary** groups, not least the **Irish Republican Army** (IRA), and did not always appear to be convinced of the value of John Hume's dialogue with **Gerry Adams** of **Sinn Fein** (SF).

Mallon was one of the SDLP's delegates to the **New Ireland Forum** and consistently supported the line that any political settlement would require a significant input from the Republic. He was elected to the **Northern Ireland Forum** in 1996 and was the SDLP's chief negotiator in the multiparty talks after September 1997. In 1998 he was again elected in Newry and Armagh to the Northern Ireland As-

VICARAGE STREET

SINCE THE SIGNING OF THE GOOD FRIDAY AGREEMENT IN APRIL 1998
THE FOLLOWING CONCESSIONS HAVE BEEN GIVEN :—

| REPUBLICANS | LOYALISTS |
|---|---|
| · PRISONERS RELEASED <br> · SEATS IN GOVERNMENT <br> · FACILITIES AT WESTMINSTER <br> · VISAS TO THE USA <br> · ARMY-POLICE STATIONS CLOSED <br> · HOME BATTALIONS OF THE RIR DISBANDED <br> · ON THE RUNS ALLOWED TO RETURN <br> · COLUMBIA 3 REMAIN AT LIBERTY <br> · BIAS AGAINST PROTESTANTS IN EMPLOYMENT PRACTICES <br> · SEAN KELLY CHILD MURDERER SET FREE <br> · INCREASED IN INVESTMENT <br> · ACCESS TO SHARED ROADS DENIED <br> · LOYALIST CULTURE ERODED <br> · £26·5 MILLION-PAY OFF | · PRISONERS RELEASED <br> · VISAS TO THE USA <br><br> THE LOYALIST PEOPLE OF EAST BELFAST DEMAND :— <br> · EQUALITY <br> · PARITY OF ESTEEM <br> · SHARED ACCESS TO MAIN ARTERIAL ROUTES <br> · NO BIAS IN EMPLOYMENT PRACTICES <br> · CULTURAL EQUALITY <br> · EQUAL INVESTMENT <br> · EFFECTIVE ACCOUNTABLE POLICING |

This is not equality -This is not parity of esteem-This is not What the Good Friday Agreement was meant to deliver.

Belfast Wall mural. Loyalists criticize the Good Friday Agreement.

Remains of one of the huts in which prisoners were first kept after internment was introduced in 1971. Maze Prison.

External walls surrounding the H Blocks at the Maze Prison.

Loyalist paramilitary mural showing support for the Ulster Freedom Fighters.

Loyalist mural remembering the Ulster Defence Regiment and Ulster Special Constabulary.

Loyalist wall mural highlighting republican paramilitary attacks.

Republican wall murals calling for the withdrawal of British soldiers and highlighting the issue of collusion.

Parliament Buildings, Stormont. Location of the Northern Ireland Assembly.

Bobby Sands mural on the side of Sinn Fein headquarters in Belfast.

sembly, and when John Hume declined the role, he became the deputy first minister designate.

In June 1999 the slow progress in the implementation of the **Good Friday Agreement** (GFA) led him to offer his resignation as deputy first minister. However, he took up the position when power was **devolved** in December 1999 before retiring from the post in November 2001. He did not stand in the Northern Ireland Assembly election in 2003 and stood down as a Westminster Member of Parliament (MP) in 2005.

**MANDELSON, PETER (1953– ).** **Labour Party** politician and secretary of state for Northern Ireland, Peter Mandelson was born in London on 21 October 1953. He was educated at Hendon Senior High School and St. Catherine's College, Oxford, where he majored in philosophy, politics, and economics. With a strong Labour family background, there was a certain inevitably about his involvement in party politics. After graduating from Oxford, Mandelson worked in the Trades Union Congress's economic department (1977–78), served on Lambeth Borough Council (1979–82), and was subsequently a television producer (1982–85).

As Labour's director of campaigns and communications (1985–90), Mandelson was an influential figure in the rebranding of the Labour Party. After two years as an industrial consultant, he was elected to the House of Commons in 1992 for the constituency of Hartlepool. A close political associate of **Tony Blair**, he held a number of junior opposition posts after 1994 but was most influential as Labour's election campaign manager from 1996 to 1997. He was a member of the Labour cabinet in 1997 but resigned in late 1998 after controversy surrounding a personal loan from a party colleague. He was appointed secretary of state for Northern Ireland in October 1999 in succession to **Mo Mowlam** but resigned again in February 2001 as a result of another (non–Northern Ireland related) controversy.

As secretary of state, he presided over the restoration of **devolution** in December 1999 and the radical reform of the police service. In February 2000 he aroused the anger of **republicans** by suspending the executive after interparty negotiations had failed to resolve the issue of the **decommissioning** of **paramilitary** weapons. In 2004 he was appointed to the European Commission and had responsibility for trade. In an interview with *The Guardian* in March 2007, he criticized Blair for being overly sympathetic to republican demands in the **peace process**.

**MARCHES.** *See* PARADES.

**MASON, ROY (1924– ).** **Labour Party** politician and secretary of state for Northern Ireland, Roy Mason was born near Barnsley, Yorkshire, on 18 April 1924. He was educated at Carlton and Royston Elementary Schools but left school at the age of 14 to become a coalminer. He was later a National Union of Mineworkers' branch official (1947–53). In 1953 he was elected as Member of Parliament (MP) for Barnsley.

Under **Harold Wilson** he held a number of junior government posts after 1964 before being appointed to the cabinet as president of the Board of Trade in 1969. When Labour returned to power in March 1974, he was defense secretary and became secretary of state for Northern Ireland in September 1976, holding the post until the general election of May 1979. In April 1974, as defense secretary, he had caused concern by stating that pressure was mounting for troops to be withdrawn from Northern Ireland.

Mason's period as secretary of state was characterized by an absence of high-profile political initiatives and a decline in the level of violence, which had a much greater appeal to **unionist** sensibilities than to **nationalists**, and Mason has remained the secretary of state most admired by Protestants. Under Mason there was a continuation of the policy of "Ulsterization," with an expanded **Royal Ulster Constabulary** (RUC) and **Ulster Defence Regiment** (UDR) increasingly taking the lead role in security matters rather than the **British Army**. He astutely handled the **loyalist United Unionist Action Council (UUAC) strike** of May 1977 by addressing some of the concerns of the power workers and other groups that may have given their backing to the strikers.

Economic initiatives proved less successful, in particular the high-profile collapse of the DeLorean Motor Car company in West **Belfast**. Mason retired as an MP in 1987 and received a life peerage, taking the title Lord Mason of Barnsley. In 1992 his name was found on a list of individuals being targeted by the **Irish Republican Army** (IRA).

**MAYHEW, PATRICK (1929– ). Conservative Party** politician and secretary of state for Northern Ireland, Sir Patrick Mayhew was born on 11 September 1929. He was educated at Tonbridge and Balliol College, Oxford. His father had had a distinguished military career, winning the military cross, and Mayhew himself would serve in the 4/7 Royal Dragoon Guards. As a lawyer he was called to the bar in 1956 before entering politics. He contested, but lost, the Camberwell and Dulwich seat as a Conservative candidate in 1970 before winning Tunbridge Wells in February 1974. He would hold this seat until 1997.

When the Conservatives returned to power in 1979, he served as a junior minister in employment (1979–81) and in the home office (1981–83). Following the 1983 general **election**, he became solicitor general (he received a knighthood in the same year) and, in 1987, attorney general. As attorney general he made a number of decisions that were not well received by **nationalists** in Northern Ireland or by the Irish government.

In April 1992 Mayhew was appointed secretary of state for Northern Ireland. Under other circumstances this might have been seen as a demotion, but Mayhew had long expressed an interest in Northern Ireland affairs and had campaigned for the appointment. The longest serving secretary of state, his time in the office coincided with a crucial period in the **peace process**. He made efforts to restart the party talks that had stalled under **Peter Brooke**, and although these broke up without agreement in November 1992, there was a distinct narrowing of the gap between the parties. A month later, amid a climate of increasing violence, he angered **unionists** by stating that soldiers could be withdrawn from the streets and **Sinn Fein** (SF) would be included in future political talks if the **Irish Republican Army** (IRA) ended its campaign.

In April 1993 he did not condemn **Social Democratic and Labour Party** (SDLP) leader **John Hume** for meeting SF president **Gerry Adams** for talks while IRA violence was continuing but said the government would not talk to SF until violence ended. In November 1993, however, *The Observer* newspaper revealed that British officials had been in contact with SF for three years and in regular contact since February. The revelation could hardly have come at a worse time for Mayhew as, in the previous month, 27 people had died as a result of **the Troubles**, the worst figure for any month since October 1976. Although close to resigning, Mayhew received the backing of Prime Minister **John Major** and most of the House of Commons and stayed in his post.

The political situation improved significantly in December 1993 with the publication of the **Downing Street Declaration**. The declaration, for the first time, successfully balanced the needs of most unionists and nationalists and laid the foundation for much of what was to follow. After a prolonged period involving **republican** demands for clarification of the declaration, the IRA announced a ceasefire in August 1994 followed by a **loyalist paramilitary** ceasefire in October. Further significant progress was delayed by the controversy surrounding the issue of the **decommissioning** of weapons by paramilitary groups.

In October 1995, on the eve of a visit by U.S. president **Bill Clinton**, a "twin-track" approach was launched, which, it was hoped, would lead to political negotiations running parallel with the process of decommissioning. However, this again failed to produce any movement by paramilitary groups to get rid of their weapons. In February 1996 the IRA returned to a bombing campaign, leading to the exclusion of SF from multiparty talks in June. By this time, however, there was a growing belief that the Conservatives' period in government was coming to a close, and this, along with the continuing IRA campaign, helped stall further significant progress while Mayhew was in office. In May 1997 he retired as a Member of Parliament (MP) and was awarded a life peerage, taking the title of Lord Mayhew of Twysden.

**MAZE PRISON.** Officially Her Majesty's Prison, the Maze Prison is more often referred to as the Maze or, by **republicans** and **loyalists**, as the older name of Long Kesh (or occasionally colloquially as "the Kesh"). The prison, which played a significant role in the history of **the Troubles**, was located on a 360-acre site outside the city of Lisburn in Co. Antrim. Following the introduction of **internment** in August 1971, internees were initially kept in Nissen huts at the former air force base at Long Kesh. However, when **special category status** was ended in 1976, those convicted of terrorist offenses were housed in eight H blocks (so called because of the shape of the building). The relocation of prisoners, linked to the change in their status, meant that the H blocks became associated with the campaign to regain special category status. In 1980 and 1981, the prison was the location of **hunger strikes** aimed at winning political status for republican prisoners, which ended with the **deaths** of 10 prisoners but with many of their demands being conceded by the government.

In March 1997 a 40-foot-long tunnel dug by **Irish Republican Army** (IRA) prisoners was discovered, leading to concerns that security in the prison was lax. In December 1997 **Loyalist Volunteer Force** (LVF) leader **Billy Wright** was shot dead by **Irish National Liberation Army** (INLA) prisoners inside the prison.

In January 1998 Secretary of State **Mo Mowlam** visited the prison to encourage loyalist prisoners to support the **peace process**. After the endorsement of the **Good Friday Agreement** (GFA), approximately 430 prisoners were given early release on license, and at the end of September 2000, the last 4 prisoners were transferred, and the prison closed.

In January 2003 official debate began on how the site should be used, and in 2006 the government released its detailed proposals. It suggested there could be a sports stadium, offices, houses, and an International Center for Conflict Transformation. The International Center for Conflict Transformation would have links with other areas of conflict around the world. It would provide visitor and educational facilities and be located close to some of the former prison buildings. Public responses to the proposals were at best lukewarm; there was much opposition to siting a major sports stadium outside the **Belfast** area, and the wisdom of locating the stadium close to such a politically controversial site was also strongly debated. The first phase of demolition of the former prison buildings began in October 2006, with the exterior wall being demolished in April 2007.

**MAZE PRISON ESCAPE.** On 25 September 1983, 38 **Irish Republican Army** (IRA) inmates at the **Maze Prison** used guns and knives to threaten wardens and then seized a lorry, which was delivering prison meals inside the compound, in an attempt to escape from the prison. One warden died and another was seriously wounded during the escape. Nineteen of the prisoners were recaptured afterward but the rest escaped. By August 1992, 5, including **Gerry Kelly** and

Brendan McFarlane, had been recaptured; 3 had been killed by the army; and the remaining 11 were still on the run. In June 1991 **Belfast** High Court awarded £47,500 compensation to 12 prisoners who were assaulted by wardens after they were recaptured.

**MCALEESE, MARY (1951– ).** President of Ireland, Mary McAleese (nee Leneghan) was born in **Belfast** on 27 May 1951. She was educated at St. Dominic's High School, Belfast; Queen's University, Belfast (QUB); and Trinity College, Dublin. She became a barrister in 1974 and was professor of criminal law at Trinity College, Dublin, between 1975 and 1979 and again between 1981 and 1987. While in Dublin she also worked as a television presenter and journalist with Radio Telefis Eireann (RTE). In 1987 she was appointed director of the Institute of Professional Legal Studies at QUB (1987–97) and in 1994 became the first female pro–vice chancellor at the university.

In September 1997, when she became **Fianna Fail**'s (FF) candidate for the presidency, she received some criticism for allegedly being overly sympathetic to **Sinn Fein**'s (SF) position but won the election to become the first Irish president from Northern Ireland. In November 1998 she met Prince Philip during his first official visit to the Republic and in the same month jointly opened a memorial to the Irish dead of World War I with Queen Elizabeth at Messines in Belgium.

In January 2005 she made a controversial speech in Germany in which she stated that some people in Nazi Germany "gave to their children an irrational hatred of Jews in the same way that people in Northern Ireland transmitted to their children an irrational hatred, for example, of Catholics." As the statement appeared, to some, to compare **unionist** attitudes with Nazis, it had a damaging effect on her relations with Protestants. The statement was also criticized by members of the Jewish community. In 2006 a speech she gave commemorating the Easter Rising was also criticized for providing what was viewed by some as an unduly rosy interpretation of the event.

**MCALISKEY, BERNADETTE.** *See* DEVLIN (MCALISKEY), BERNADETTE (1947– ).

**MCCARTNEY, ROBERT (BOB) (1936– ).** Barrister and politician, Robert McCartney was born in the Shankill area of **Belfast** on 24

April 1936. He was educated at Grosvenor High School and at Queen's University, Belfast (QUB). McCartney became a solicitor in 1962, was called to the bar in 1968, and became a member of the Queen's Counsel (QC) in 1975. In 1982 he was elected to the **Northern Ireland Assembly** as an **Ulster Unionist Party** (UUP) member for the North Down constituency. During this time he was associated with the **integrationist** wing of the UUP and was unenthusiastic about the prospect of a **devolved** assembly.

Between 1986 and 1988, McCartney was president of the **Campaign for Equal Citizenship** (CEC), an integrationist organization that had at least partly developed as a response to the **Anglo–Irish Agreement** (AIA). He disagreed with the UUP's tactical response to the AIA, which aimed to highlight **unionist** unity in opposing the AIA, and, in May 1987, split with the UUP when he refused to stand down against the sitting independent unionist candidate for the **Westminster** constituency of North Down in that year's general **election**. McCartney stood as a "real unionist" candidate in the election but failed to unseat the sitting member of Parliament (MP), James Kilfedder. In June 1995 a by-election arose in North Down following Kilfedder's death, and McCartney won the seat, albeit on a low turnout.

In the 1990s McCartney was increasingly opposed to the direction in which the **peace process** was developing. In 1996 he formed the United Kingdom Unionist Party (UKUP) to contest the elections to the **Northern Ireland Forum** and was elected to the forum along with two party colleagues. His participation in the subsequent party talks was intermittent, and he and his party withdrew on several occasions in protest of the direction the talks were taking.

In 1997, when **Sinn Fein** (SF) entered political discussions before the **decommissioning** of **Irish Republican Army** (IRA) weapons had commenced, McCartney and his party representatives joined with the **Democratic Unionist Party** (DUP) in formally withdrawing from negotiations. Although he had been a strong critic of Rev. **Ian Paisley** in the past, he worked with the DUP in the United Unionist campaign, which called for a *no* vote in the referendum on the **Good Friday Agreement** (GFA) in May 1998. In the elections to the new Northern Ireland Assembly, he was one of five UKUP members returned to **Stormont**. However, differences in the tactics that the party should use to oppose the GFA led to a split in January 1999 with his four colleagues, then forming the Northern Ireland Unionist Party (NIUP).

Although he had retained his Westminster seat in 1997, he lost to Lady Sylvia Hermon of the UUP in June 2001. Part of the reason for this defeat was that the **Alliance Party of Northern Ireland** (APNI) chose not to field a candidate, and some of these voters undoubtedly switched to Hermon instead. In 1999 he ran for the European Parliament but was not elected, receiving 2.9 percent of first-preference votes in Northern Ireland. In November 2003 he was again returned to the Northern Ireland Assembly for North Down, but where he had topped the poll in 1998, he was only the fifth highest polling candidate in 2003. Part of the decline in McCartney's support was undoubtedly due to his continued promotion of a policy of integration, which, in the light of the **Labour** government's policy of devolution throughout the United Kingdom after 1997, seemed increasingly impractical. In the March 2007 Northern Ireland Assembly election, he stood in six constituencies but was not elected in any.

**MCGUINNESS, MARTIN (1950– ). Republican** activist and **Sinn Fein** (SF) member, Martin McGuinness was born in **Derry** on 23 May 1950. He left school at the age of 15 and worked as a butcher's assistant. After the outbreak of **the Troubles**, he initially joined the **Official Irish Republican Army** (OIRA) but quickly switched to the Provisional **Irish Republican Army** (PIRA). At the time of **Bloody Sunday** in January 1972, he was second in command of the PIRA in the city. In July 1972, following the introduction of **direct rule**, he was part of a high-level IRA delegation that met Secretary of State **William Whitelaw** for talks in London. In 1973 he was convicted by a special criminal court in the **Republic of Ireland** for possession of explosives and ammunition and sentenced to six months imprisonment. He was later also convicted of IRA membership in the Republic. From the 1980s McGuinness was the chief link between the PIRA and British officials, and this partly led to intermittent claims that he had given information to British intelligence sources. McGuinness has always strongly refuted such claims.

In the wake of the 1981 **hunger strike** campaign, he worked closely with **Gerry Adams** and others to develop SF's political strategy. In 1982, running on an abstentionist policy, he was **elected** to the

**Northern Ireland Assembly** from the Londonderry constituency, coming second in the poll behind **John Hume**. In 1983 he came in third in the Foyle constituency in the **Westminster** general election. More significantly in the same year, he was elected vice president of SF, with Gerry Adams assuming the role of party president. At the 1986 SF ard fheis, he gave a keynote speech in favor of the party, ending its abstention from the **Dail**.

In November 1993 the *Observer* newspaper revealed that the British government had secretly been in contact with SF and the IRA since 1990, with McGuinness as the chief contact. After the British government published details of the discussions, McGuinness challenged the accuracy of some of the British assertions. In August 1993 a television documentary claimed that he had played a part in the murder of an alleged informer against the IRA and raised the issue of McGuinness's continued involvement in the organization.

In the wake of the IRA ceasefire of 1994, he led an SF delegation in preliminary discussions with British officials. When the IRA ended its ceasefire in February 1996, he blamed the British government for undermining the **peace process**. The breakdown of the ceasefire did not damage McGuinness's electoral fortunes, however. In 1996 he was elected to the **Northern Ireland Forum** from the Foyle constituency and in May 1997 won the Mid-Ulster seat in the Westminster general election from the **Democratic Unionist Party** (DUP).

After the announcement of a new IRA ceasefire in July 1997, SF participated in the party talks that led to the **Good Friday Agreement** (GFA), with McGuinness acting as the party's chief negotiator. He was elected to the Northern Ireland Assembly from Mid-Ulster in 1998 and reelected in 2003. During this time he acted as SF's main contact with the **Independent International Commission on Decommissioning** (IICD). In December 1999, following the **devolution** of power, McGuinness became minister of education in the Northern Ireland executive. Although he was widely viewed as a competent minister, he caused controversy as he was leaving office by introducing a measure banning the selection of pupils for grammar schools. He retained his Mid-Ulster seat at Westminster in the 2001 and 2005 general elections.

In May 2006 he was proposed as deputy first minister by Gerry Adams as part of an attempt to elect a new Northern Ireland executive.

In November 2006 the publication of a photograph taken in the 1970s showing McGuinness in IRA uniform aroused fresh controversy over his **paramilitary** background. In the same month, he was again nominated in the Northern Ireland Assembly for the position of deputy first minister. In March 2007 he was again returned to the Northern Ireland Assembly from Mid-Ulster. When power was devolved on 8 May 2007, he became deputy first minister of Northern Ireland.

**MCGURK'S BAR BOMBING.** On 4 December 1971, a 50-pound **Ulster Volunteer Force** (UVF) bomb exploded in McGurk's Bar in **Belfast**, killing 15 people, all Catholics, and injuring a dozen more. Among those killed were the owner's wife and 14-year-old daughter. For some years after the event, there continued to be a dispute as to whether the bombing had been conducted by **loyalists** or was the result of the premature explosion of an **Irish Republican Army** (IRA) bomb. The explosion reduced the building to rubble and local people, rescue services personnel, and members of the security forces used their bare hands to pull away debris. The incident was the greatest loss of civilian life in any one incident of **the Troubles** until the **Omagh bomb** of 1998. Despite this, the incident has, somewhat surprisingly, never received as much attention as other incidents with fewer casualties.

**MCWILLIAMS, MONICA (1954– ).** Academic and politician, Monica McWilliams was born in Kilrea, Co. Londonderry, on 28 April 1954. She was educated at Loreto College, Coleraine; Queen's University, **Belfast** (QUB); and the University of Michigan. She became professor of women's studies and social policy at the University of Ulster in 1998. McWilliams was a founding member of the **Northern Ireland Women's Coalition** (NIWC) in 1996, was **elected** to the **Northern Ireland Forum**, and participated in the political talks of 1996 to 1998.

In the negotiations leading to the **Good Friday Agreement** (GFA), she was a strong supporter of the idea that any agreement should be as inclusive as possible. She campaigned actively for a *yes* vote in the referendum on the GFA, and in June 1998 she was one of two NIWC members to be elected to the new **Northern Ireland Assembly**, being returned in the South Belfast constituency.

When the NIWC held its first party conference in November 1998, she was selected as leader. As disillusionment with the GFA grew, however, support for the NIWC also declined, and in the November 2003 Assembly election, she lost her seat. In June 2005 she was appointed chief commissioner of the **Northern Ireland Human Rights Commission** (NIHRC).

**MITCHELL, GEORGE (1933– ). United States** Democratic Party politician and mediator, George Mitchell was born in Waterville, Maine, on 20 August 1933. From a working-class background, he was educated at Bowdoin College, Maine, and Georgetown University. A lawyer by profession, he was the U.S. attorney for Maine (1977–79) and the U.S. district judge for North Maine (1979–80). He was initially appointed to the Senate as a replacement for Senator Edmund Muskie but was later **elected** to the U.S. Senate for Maine in 1980 and served until 1995, being Senate majority leader from 1988 until 1995.

Mitchell became President **Bill Clinton**'s economic envoy to Ireland in 1994, and this role subsequently led the British and Irish governments to ask him to head up the international body established to deal with the issue of the **decommissioning** of **paramilitary** weapons. He became chairman of the International Commission on Decommissioning (also referred to as the Mitchell Commission) in November 1995.

The international body reported in January 1996 that there was a commitment by paramilitary groups to decommission illegal weapons but that this would not happen in advance of all-party talks. The report recommended that the decommissioning of weapons take place at the same time as talks.

The Mitchell Report also included a number of principles that participants in all-party talks might be expected to endorse. The Mitchell Principles suggested that those involved in all-party negotiations affirmed their commitment to democratic and exclusively peaceful means of resolving political issues and to the total disarmament of all paramilitary organizations; that disarmament should be verified to the satisfaction of an independent commission; that the parties renounce for themselves and oppose any efforts by others to use force, or threaten to use force, to influence the course or the outcome of all-party negotiations; that they agree to abide by the terms of any agreement reached in all-party negotiations and to use only democratic and exclusively peaceful means in trying to alter any aspect of that outcome with which they might disagree; and that they urge that punishment killings and beatings stop and take effective steps to prevent such measures. Among a number of possible confidence-building measures, the report suggested that an elected body with an appropriate mandate might be established. This latter suggestion would help lead to the creation of the **Northern Ireland Forum**.

Mitchell was appointed to chair all-party talks in June 1996, against the objections of some **unionists**, but the talks stalled partly because **Sinn Fein** (SF) was excluded due to the renewed **Irish Republican Army** (IRA) campaign and the perception that the **Conservative** government was in its final days. The return of a **Labour** government in May 1997 and a renewed IRA ceasefire in July 1997 added a fresh incentive to the talks process. SF entered the talks in September 1997, but it was not until April 1998 that agreement was reached in the form of the **Good Friday Agreement** (GFA).

In December 1998 Mitchell was awarded an honorary knighthood in recognition of his contribution, but as implementation of the GFA became more fraught, he returned to chair a review of the GFA in September 1999, helping to pave the way for the functioning of the Northern Ireland executive in December.

In May 2001 Mitchell was the chairman of a United Nations commission aimed at making progress in the Israeli–Palestinian peace process. He has subsequently continued his connection with Ireland through the George Mitchell scholarships, which sponsor postgraduate study for Americans in Ireland, and as chancellor of Queen's University, **Belfast** (QUB).

**MOLYNEAUX, JAMES (1920– ). Ulster Unionist Party** (UUP) leader, James Molyneaux was born in Co. Antrim on 27 August 1920. He was educated at Aldergrove School and left school to work on a family farm. In 1941 he joined the Royal Air Force and, during World War II, served in Europe after D-Day, being among the earliest British servicemen to enter the Belson concentration camp after it was liberated. After the war he returned home to manage the family farm. Conservative in nature and in politics, he joined the UUP and was involved in local party matters. It was not until 1970, however, that he became the UUP candidate for South Antrim and was elected to **Westminster** in the general **election** of that year.

Molyneaux was an opponent of the **Sunningdale** Agreement and **power sharing**. In January 1974 he stood for the leadership of the UUP following the resignation of **Brian Faulkner** but lost to **Harry West**. After the February 1974 general election, he was secretary of the coalition of **unionist** Members of Parliament (MP) at Westminster and in October 1974, when West lost his seat, became leader of the UUP at Westminster. The October 1974–79 Parliament also saw UUP MPs move away from their traditional role as supporters of the **Conservative Party** at Westminster and toward a closer working relationship with the **Labour** government.

In 1979 Molyneaux became UUP leader and had to mediate between those within the party who favored **devolution** and those who favored **integration**. He was elected to the 1982 **Northern Ireland Assembly** for the South Antrim constituency but was skeptical of the Assembly leading to a devolved administration. In 1983, after the increase in the number of Northern Ireland seats at Westminster, the UUP had 11 MPs, but this did not prevent continuing discussions concerning Northern Ireland between the British and Irish governments. Molyneaux was criticized in some unionist circles for not having done more to prevent the **Anglo–Irish Agreement** (AIA), but he joined with other unionists in the campaign to oppose the AIA. After the long political stalemate of the post-AIA period he, along with **Democratic Unionist Party** (DUP) leader **Ian Paisley**, was involved in "talks about talks" with Secretary of State **Tom King**.

As the **peace process** developed in the 1990s, he was critical of the **John Hume–Gerry Adams** proposals but, unlike Paisley, gave a guarded welcome to the **Downing Street Declaration** of December 1993. After the release of the **Frameworks Documents** in 1995, however, his support within the party began to decline, as it was felt he had again failed to prevent the emergence of a pro-**nationalist** document as government policy.

Molyneaux fought off a leadership challenge but retired as UUP leader in August 1995 at the age of 75. He received a knighthood in 1996 and a life peerage on his retirement from the House of Commons in 1997, entering the House of Lords as Lord Molyneaux of

Killead. He subsequently campaigned against the **Good Friday Agreement** (GFA) and criticized the decision of his successor, **David Trimble**, to take part in a power-sharing executive including **Sinn Fein** (SF) before the complete **decommissioning** of weapons by the **Irish Republican Army** (IRA).

**MOWLAM, MARJORIE (MO) (1949–2005). Labour Party** politician and Northern Ireland secretary of state, Mo Mowlam was born in Watford, Hertfordshire, on 18 September 1949. She was educated at Coundon Court Comprehensive School, Coventry; the University of Durham, where she studied sociology and anthropology; and later the University of Iowa, where she received an MA and PhD. A member of the Labour Party from 1969, she worked as a research assistant to both the radical Labour Member of Parliament (MP) Tony Benn and distinguished American writer Alvin Toffler in the early 1970s. She was a lecturer at the University of Wisconsin (1976–77), Florida State University (1977–78), and the University of Newcastle (1979–83).

In the 1987 general **election**, she won the Redcar seat for Labour. Mowlam held a number of positions in opposition before becoming Labour spokesperson on Northern Ireland in 1994. In the wake of the Labour landslide victory in the May 1997 general election, she became the first woman to hold the post of secretary of state for Northern Ireland. Ironically, given the importance it was to have to her reputation, she is believed to have refused the Northern Ireland post at least three times.

Mowlam arrived in Northern Ireland amid expectations that the new Labour government would give momentum to the stalled **peace process**. Mowlam's unpretentious approach to the position marked a radical change in attitude toward her predecessor, the patrician Sir **Patrick Mayhew**. Mowlam's unassuming attitude was generally well received, particularly among grassroots Labour Party members, much of the general public in Great Britain, and the voluntary and community sectors in Northern Ireland. However, she could also be seen as behaving in an undignified manner, and this was the view of some of her civil servants and among many **unionists**. The personal antagonism between Mowlam and a number of senior unionists would prove to be a difficulty in the period leading up to the signing of the **Good Friday Agreement** (GFA), when she was effectively sidelined in favor of the prime minister's staff. Some, including Mowlam herself, believed that 10 Downing Street saw her popularity as a threat to the prime minister. Despite this, her achievement was all the more remarkable for the fact that she conducted her duties while undergoing treatment for a brain tumor.

Mowlam's early months in office were dominated by the dispute surrounding her decision to permit an Orange march to take place along the Garvaghy Road in Portadown. Local **nationalist** residents claimed that Mowlam had said she would inform them in advance whether the **parade** would be allowed to proceed. In the end, the march went ahead without the residents group being informed, and **republicans** accused Mowlam of duplicity.

In January 1998 she was both praised and criticized in Northern Ireland after she visited **loyalist paramilitary** prisoners in the **Maze Prison** to encourage them to support the peace process at a time when terrorist activity was increasing. In the wake of the signing of the GFA, however, Protestant support for the agreement began to slip, and Mowlam was increasingly perceived by unionists as being too sympathetic to nationalist concerns.

In the autumn of 1999, largely against her wishes, she was moved to the cabinet office, where she was minister and chancellor of the duchy of Lancaster until her retirement as an MP in 2001. While she remained a popular public figure, her health was in decline, and she died from brain cancer on 19 August 2005.

**MURALS.** Wall murals are one of the most common forms of imagery associated with the conflict in Northern Ireland. **Loyalist** murals can be dated back to the early 20th century. These early murals were of William of Orange (popularly referred to as King Billy) at the Battle of the Boyne in 1690. This remained the case until well after the outbreak of **the Troubles** in 1968, suggesting that the political fragmentation of the **unionist** community was not reflected in the appearance of new political imagery in murals.

Within the **nationalist** community, the **hunger strike** campaign of 1981 was to be the major catalyst for the emergence of a new wave of political imagery. Slogans painted on walls in support of the hunger strikers' demands, gradually became more ornate and included into wall murals. The 1981 hunger strike also marked **Sinn Fein**'s (SF) entry into electoral politics, and subsequent wall murals reflected political issues of particular concern to **republicans**, such as security issues, justice, and conflicts elsewhere in the world.

In the wake of the **Irish Republican Army**'s (IRA) 1994 ceasefire, and particularly from 1996, republican murals were often aimed at convincing their grassroots supporters of the need to participate in the **peace process** and reform the political system. Murals encouraging opposition to the **decommissioning** of IRA weapons also appeared.

Opposition to Orange marches also provided the inspiration for many murals, particularly in areas such as Garvaghy Road in Portadown and lower Ormeau Road in **Belfast**. Republican murals also commented on issues given greater importance by the developing peace process (e.g., policing) and the related issue of **collusion** between the police and loyalist **paramilitaries**, while calling for the reduction of security force numbers. At the same time, murals related specifically to the armed struggle largely disappeared and were often replaced by memorials to IRA members killed during the conflict. A number of murals relating to the 1981 hunger strike also appeared around the time of the 20th anniversary of the event in 2001 and again on the 25th anniversary in 2006. In both instances these images commemorated the persons or events involved but also placed them in a context that suggested they were now part of the past.

There has generally been less political management in the type of loyalist wall murals that have appeared until recently. To some extent this can be attributed to the divisions within unionism and conflicts between paramilitary organizations, resulting in a less focused political message in loyalist murals than their republican counterparts. Aggressive militaristic murals have persisted more so than for republicans reflecting loyalist insecurity and for maintaining paramilitary support in local areas.

Murals can also be used to mark out territory, not just between loyalist and republican areas, but also between conflicting loyalist paramilitary groups. As well as murals featuring prominent loyalist paramilitary individuals, there have been (as is the case with republicans) murals depicting historical or mythological events or figures. The mythological figure of Cuchulainn has been adopted by both republicans, as a defender of Ireland, and by the **Ulster Defence Association** (UDA), as a defender of Ulster.

The painting of a wall mural in the Shankill area of Belfast in September 2002 was also significant in sparking an intraloyalist feud. The mural, painted at the behest of loyalist paramilitary leader Johnny Adair, showed his "C" Company and the **Loyalist Volunteer Force** (LVF) as "brothers in arms" at a time when the LVF and the rest of the UDA were in conflict. The mural was seen as a challenge to the UDA leadership by Adair and helped lead to his expulsion from the UDA.

In the last few years there have been efforts within the loyalist community to produce less threatening murals. Partly as a result of this, a greater number of loyalist murals with a historical or cultural theme have appeared, although some maintain a military, if not necessarily paramilitary, theme. In July 2006, the government announced that £3.3 million would be allocated to an art scheme aimed at replacing paramilitary murals with more positive images.

**MURPHY, PAUL (1948– ). Labour Party** politician and secretary of state for Northern Ireland, Paul Murphy was born in Gwent, Wales, on 25 November 1948. He was educated at St. Francis Roman Catholic School, Abersychan; West Monmouth School, Pontypool; and Oriel College, Oxford. He was a lecturer in government and history at Ebbw Vale College of Further Education from 1971 and a member of Torfaen Borough Council from 1973 until 1987, when he was elected to **Westminster** for the Torfaen constituency.

Murphy was an opposition spokesman on a number of areas after 1988, including on Northern Ireland (1994–95). Following the Labour landslide win of 1997, he was minister of state at the **Northern Ireland Office** (NIO) under **Mo Mowlam** before being appointed secretary of state for Wales in July 1999. As minister of state, Murphy was responsible for political development and was closely involved in the negotiations leading to the **Good Friday Agreement** (GFA). His quiet, unfailingly polite attitude made him one of the most liked ministers ever to serve in the NIO and at times provided a useful counterpoint to Mowlam's exuberance.

In October 2002 he returned to Northern Ireland as secretary of state, and his period in office was characterized by further progress on the **decommissioning** of **Irish Republican Army** (IRA) weapons and continuing **loyalist** and **republican** activity. Political negotiations at **Leeds Castle** in September 2004 failed to achieve a breakthrough, although the ground between **Sinn Fein** (SF) and the **Democratic Unionist Party** (DUP)—by now the largest parties—appeared to have narrowed before the Northern Bank robbery in December 2004 and the murder of **Belfast** man Robert McCartney in January 2005 again stalled political progress. In May 2005 Murphy was succeeded by **Peter Hain**. He was subsequently appointed cochairman of the **British–Irish Interparliamentary Body** (BIIPB).

## – N –

**NAPIER, OLIVER (1935– ). Alliance Party of Northern Ireland** (APNI) leader, Oliver Napier was born on 11 July 1935. He was educated at St. Malachy's College, **Belfast**, and Queen's University, Belfast (QUB), where he earned a degree in law. He subsequently opened his own practice as a solicitor. He first became involved in politics through the **New Ulster Movement** (NUM), which subsequently played a significant part in the creation of APNI. He joined APNI in 1970 and became party leader in 1972. He was **elected** to the **Northern Ireland Assembly** in 1973 for the East Belfast constituency and played an important role in the Castle Talks and **Sunningdale** Conference later that year. He was a fervent, but not uncritical, supporter of the Sunningdale Agreement and warned the Irish government of the need to give full recognition to Northern Ireland if the agreement was to succeed.

In the **power-sharing** executive of January to May 1974, he was head of the Office of Law Reform. In 1975 he was again elected from East Belfast to the **Constitutional Convention** and was also returned to the 1982 Northern Ireland Assembly from the same constituency. He was elected to Belfast City Council in 1977 and remained on the council until 1989. He remained leader of APNI until 1984 and in 1985 was awarded a knighthood.

Napier represented the party in East Belfast for the 1979 and 1983 **Westminster** general elections and 1986 by-election and North Down in the 1995 by-election and 1997 general election but failed to be elected. In 1996, however, he was elected to the **Northern Ireland Forum** from North Down and was subsequently a member of the APNI delegation that participated in the all-party talks that led to the **Good Friday Agreement** (GFA) in 1998. From 1988 until 1992, he also served as chairman of the Standing Advisory Commission on Human Rights (SACHR).

**NATIONAL IDENTITY.** One of the areas in which **the Troubles** had most impact was in how individuals perceived their national identity. Protestants had largely seen themselves as British and Catholics as Irish, but in the years before the outbreak of the Troubles, there was still some overlapping between the two. In a survey conducted in 1968, on the eve of the outbreak of violence, only 39.0 percent of Protestants described themselves as British, but 20.0 percent of Catholics also said they were British. In the same survey, 76.0 percent of Catholics said they were Irish, but so did 20.0 percent of Protestants. Additionally, 32.0 percent of Protestants described their national identity as "Ulster," while 5.0 percent of Catholics did the same (Rose, 1971).

By the time another major survey was conducted in 1978, the worst years of the Troubles had taken place, and there had been 2,000 **deaths** as a result of the conflict. This clearly led to a hardening of attitudes, not least in how people described their national identity, particularly among Protestants, who largely rejected an "Irish" identity. In 1978, 67.0 percent of Protestants described themselves as British, though 20.0 percent of Catholics still did so as well. The numbers of Protestants calling themselves Irish had fallen to 8.0 percent, but so had the number of Catholics—to 69.0 percent. Twenty percent of Protestants now gave their identity as Ulster, as did 6.0 percent of Catholics (Moxon-Browne, 1983).

In 1989 the social attitudes survey showed further movement toward the axioms of "Protestant equals British" and "Catholic equals Irish." In the 1989 survey, 68.0 percent of Protestants said they were British, compared to 8.0 percent of Catholics. Only 3.0 percent of Protestants said they were Irish, compared to 60.0 percent of Catholics. Ten percent of Protestants described themselves as Ulster, compared to 2.0 percent of Catholics. There was, however, a surprising amount of support for the choice of "Northern Irish"—16.0

percent of Protestants described themselves as Northern Irish, as did 25.0 percent of Catholics.

If the most obvious reason for the decline in Protestants identifying themselves as Irish was **paramilitary** violence, then the decline in the number of Catholics who described themselves as British in the early 1980s was almost certainly a result of the political fallout from the **republican hunger strikes** of 1981. Whereas 20.0 percent of Catholics had still called themselves British in 1978, by 1986 this had dropped to 9.0 percent (Whyte, 1991).

The division in attitudes between Protestants and Catholics toward national identity has also been reflected in attitudes toward the law and violence—reflecting a traditional Protestant support for the political institutions and Catholic indifference, or opposition to, the same institutions. In 1990, at the beginning of the **peace process**, the social attitudes survey posed the statement "The law should always be obeyed, even if a particular law is wrong." The responses showed a clear difference between Protestant and Catholic attitudes, with 49.0 percent of Protestants agreeing but only 28.0 percent of Catholics giving the same response. Similarly, while 71.0 percent of Catholics opposed the use of the death penalty for terrorism, only 19.0 percent of Protestants were opposed. These results highlighted the fact that religious and national identity also had an impact on attitudes toward many other issues directly or indirectly associated with the conflict (Moxon-Browne, 1983).

By 2003 the level of violence in Northern Ireland was at a much reduced level; however, the same general pattern of national identity still existed; two thirds of Protestants considered themselves British and two thirds of Catholics saw themselves as Irish. An interesting development was that 24.0 percent of people now saw themselves as "Northern Irish," and this consisted of roughly equal percentages of Protestants, Catholics, and those giving no religion. If the Northern Irish identity could be viewed as a more unifying one, then another cause for optimism was the fact that this description was most common among 18- to 24-year-olds, with one-third describing themselves as Northern Irish.

**NATIONALIST.** An individual, or group, supporting the unification of Ireland as a single independent state. In Northern Ireland almost all nationalists are members of the Catholic community, though not necessarily practicing members of the Catholic Church. The term can also be used to refer to those who support the use of nonviolent constitutional methods to obtain the political objective of a united Ireland. The term is also used to refer to the political party of the same name, which was the main expression of Catholic political opinion in Northern Ireland until the 1970s.

**NATIONALIST PARTY (NP).** At the time of the outbreak of **the Troubles** in 1969, the NP was the main political party representing Catholic political opinion in Northern Ireland. Inherently conservative, ideologically its main support base was in rural areas. In the **crossroads election** of 1969, the party won six seats, but the trend of events was signposted by the fact that they lost Mid-Londonderry to Ivan Cooper and Foyle to **John Hume**, two future leading members of the **Social Democratic and Labour Party** (SDLP). An attempt had been made to restructure and modernize the NP in the early 1960s, and some of this group had subsequently broken away to form the National Democratic Party (NDP). Significant figures in the NDP included future SDLP Members of Parliament (MP) at **Westminster**, Eddie McGrady and Alasdair McDonnell. With the formation of the SDLP in 1970, however, Catholic political support largely swung behind the new party. When the NP contested the **Northern Ireland Assembly elections** in 1973, they received 1.2 percent of first-preference votes but failed to win any seats.

**NEEDHAM, RICHARD (1942– ). Conservative Party** politician and the longest serving **Northern Ireland Office** (NIO) minister, Richard Needham was born on 29 January 1942. He was educated at Eton College. His family had long connections with Northern Ireland, and he inherited the Irish title of the Earl of Kilmorey (an area in South Down), while his first job had been with a **Belfast** tobacco company.

He was **elected** to the House of Commons for the constituency of Chippenham in 1979 and had worked with **James Prior** while he was Northern Ireland secretary of state. He held a number of junior ministerial positions before being appointed to the NIO in 1985. At the

NIO his responsibilities covered a wide range of areas, initially environment, health and social services, and, after 1988, economic development and environment. Inevitably, during his term in office in Northern Ireland, he came into conflict with most shades of political opinion; however, there was also general recognition of his strong personal commitment to improving the economic and political situation in Northern Ireland.

After the 1992 general election, against his own personal preference to stay in Northern Ireland, Needham became minister of state at the Department of Trade and Industry. He retired to the backbenches in 1995 but maintained connections with some Northern Ireland companies. In 1997 he stood down as Member of Parliament (MP) and received a knighthood. In 1998 he returned to Northern Ireland in order to campaign in favor of a *yes* vote for the referendum on the **Good Friday Agreement** (GFA).

**NEW IRELAND FORUM.** More correctly referred to as the Forum for a New Ireland, in May 1983 it was made up of what were then the four main **nationalist** parties in Ireland: **Fianna Fail** (FF), **Fine Gael** (FG), the **Irish Labour Party**, and the **Social Democratic and Labour Party** (SDLP). The forum had been inspired by SDLP leader **John Hume**, who sought a united nationalist approach to achieving the reunification of Ireland. The entry of Provisional **Sinn Fein** (PSF) into party politics in the North, at a time when the **Irish Republican Army**'s (IRA) campaign was continuing, gave a particular impetus to the nationalist parties to outline a nonviolent route toward a united Ireland.

The forum held its first meeting in Dublin in May 1983 and produced its report in May 1984. The parties stated their preference for a unitary 32-county state but also suggested the alternatives of a federal arrangement or joint British–Irish authority over Northern Ireland. While the report represented a significant development in nationalist thinking, it remained a nationalist document that presented a nationalist perspective, and inevitably it was rejected by **unionists** and by the British government. In November 1984 Prime Minister **Margaret Thatcher** rejected the report's three proposals by saying each was "out." This led to an angry reaction from nationalists who believed their work had been too readily dismissed by Thatcher.

**NEW ULSTER MOVEMENT (NUM).** A moderate reformist movement that emerged in early 1969 and was one of the first groups to press for a range of reforms, including the creation of a **community relations** body, the installation of a central housing executive for Northern Ireland, and the abolition of the **Ulster Special Constabulary** (USC). In 1971 the NUM advocated a **power-sharing** administration for Northern Ireland. Later in the same year, the NUM called for the suspension of the **Northern Ireland Parliament**. Many of its members later became associated with the **Alliance Party of Northern Ireland** (APNI).

**NEWMAN, KENNETH (1926– ).** Chief constable of the **Royal Ulster Constabulary** (RUC), Kenneth Newman was born on 15 August 1926. He was educated at the University of London and joined the Palestine Police in 1946 and the London Metropolitan Police in 1948. He was a commander at New Scotland Yard before becoming deputy chief constable of the RUC in 1973 and chief constable from 1976 until 1979. He received a knighthood in 1978.

Newman's period in Northern Ireland coincided with the introduction of the policy of "Ulsterization" and police primacy, along with an expansion in the size of the RUC. He established regional crime squads and improved relations with the **British Army** in the area of **intelligence** gathering. Criticism of police interrogation methods at this time was addressed by the **Bennett Report** of 1979, and a number of reforms were introduced. After leaving Northern Ireland, he became commandant of the Police Staff College at Bramshill and, from 1982 until 1987, was commissioner of the London Metropolitan Police.

**NO-GO AREAS.** A term applied to urban areas in Northern Ireland where state security forces were unable to operate between August 1969 and July 1972. In these areas, **paramilitary** organizations often had a greater degree of control than the state. The most high-profile no-go areas were the Bogside, Brandywell, and lower Creggan area of **Derry**, known as "Free Derry," which had developed after the **Battle of the Bogside** in August 1969. There were other **Republican** no-go areas in parts of West **Belfast**. These areas often produced their own news sheets and even illegal radio stations. **Loyalists** sought to pressure the government, particularly after the introduction of **direct rule**, into ending no-go areas and therefore set up their own areas in East and West Belfast and Portadown. At the end of July 1972, **Operation Motorman** ended no-go areas, though these often remained areas in which security forces found it difficult to operate.

**NORMALIZATION.** *See* DEMILITARIZATION.

**NORTH–SOUTH MINISTERIAL COUNCIL (NSMC).** Within "strand 2" of the **Good Friday Agreement** (GFA), a NSMC was established, which was to have a minimum of two members from the Northern Ireland executive and one from the Irish Republic's government. There would also be a secretariat and implementation bodies to advance matters of common interest in specific areas between Northern Ireland and the Republic.

In December 1998 agreement was reached between the parties on six areas in which new implementation bodies were to be established and a further six areas in which cooperation would take place between existing bodies in Northern Ireland and the Republic. It was envisaged that plenary sessions of the NSMC, involving members of the Northern Ireland executive and Irish government, would take place twice a year and sectoral meetings, which would be attended by one **unionist** and one **nationalist** minister from Northern Ireland and a minister from the Republic, would take place each quarter.

Given the controversial nature of previous attempts to establish North–South bodies, such as the Council of Ireland in 1973, the NSMC proved comparatively uncontroversial. During the life of the first **Northern Ireland Assembly** after 1998, **Democratic Unionist Party** (DUP) ministers refused to take part in NSMC meetings. Unionists criticized the level of funding given by the North–South Language Body to the Irish language in comparison to Ulster–Scots, while **David Trimble**'s attempt to ban **Sinn Fein** (SF) ministers from attending NSMC meetings in 2000 in response to the **Irish Republican Army**'s (IRA) failure to **decommission** weapons also brought the NSMC to public attention. While the executive was suspended, the secretariat continued progress on a program of work outlined by the executive. Although this risked the possibility of heightening unionist fears of increased North–South cooperation without their consent, by early 2007 this had not become a major issue. On 17 July 2007, DUP ministers attended a meeting of the NSMC for the first time.

**NORTHERN IRELAND (NI).** The **six counties** of Ireland—Antrim, Armagh, Down, Fermanagh, Londonderry, and Tyrone—that remained part of the United Kingdom after partition. Traditionally **nationalists** have refused to accept the political legitimacy of Northern Ireland and often refer instead to Northern Ireland as the "North" or the "North of Ireland." Geographically neither term is completely accurate as Co. Donegal, in the northwest, is part of the **Republic of Ireland**.

**NORTHERN IRELAND ASSEMBLY.** Since the abolition of the **Northern Ireland Parliament**, there have been three Northern Ireland assemblies, all located at Parliament buildings in **Stormont**. The Northern Ireland Constitution Act of 1973 established a 78-member assembly that was **elected** by **proportional representation** (PR) in June 1973. Following negotiations at Stormont Castle and **Sunningdale** in December 1973, a **power-sharing** executive involving **Social Democratic and Labour Party** (SDLP), **Alliance Party of Northern Ireland** (APNI), and **unionist** members took office on 1 January 1974. The executive was hampered by internal disputes concerning Sunningdale and by **loyalist** and unionist opposition—the majority of unionists in the Assembly being opposed to power sharing and the proposed Council of Ireland. In February 1974 the **Westminster** general election showed a clear majority of unionists opposed to the Sunningdale Agreement, and the **Ulster Workers' Council (UWC) strike** of May 1974 brought the Assembly to a dramatic conclusion. Chief Executive **Brian Faulkner** and other unionist ministers resigned on 28 May 1974, effectively ending the Assembly.

The Northern Ireland Assembly of 1982–86 also began in difficult circumstances. The October 1982 election was the first major electoral test for **Sinn Fein** (SF), and their entry into party politics also pressured the SDLP into taking an abstentionist stance with the Assembly. With no **nationalist** representation and intermittent boycotts by the **Ulster Unionist Party** (UUP), the Assembly, which was partly based on the premise of **rolling devolution**, failed to develop fully.

Following the signing of the **Anglo–Irish Agreement** (AIA) in November 1985, unionists increasingly used the Assembly as a vehicle for opposition to the AIA. In December APNI withdrew from the Assembly, and in subsequent months the **Northern Ireland Office** (NIO) withdrew support from the Assembly before the Assembly was dissolved in June 1986.

The Northern Ireland Assembly of 1998 was elected in a more optimistic atmosphere than its predecessors. However, of the 108-member Assembly elected in June 1998, nearly half of the unionists returned were opposed to the **Good Friday Agreement** (GFA), which raised questions for the future stability of political arrangements. Disputes over **Irish Republican Army** (IRA) weapons delayed the **devolution** of power to the new Northern Ireland executive until December 1999, and the failure to resolve the issue led to further intermittent suspensions of the executive before the Assembly was dissolved in October 2002. Assembly elections, scheduled for May 2003, were postponed until November when the **Democratic Unionist Party** (DUP) and SF were returned as the two largest political parties. The issues of IRA weapons, IRA activity, and SF lack of support for the police continued to frustrate agreement on the terms for a return to a functional assembly and devolution.

In May 2006 the Assembly met, but an attempt to elect a new executive failed due to unionist opposition. On 24 November 2006, an attempt to nominate a first and deputy first minister ended in some confusion when **Ian Paisley** stated that the conditions did not yet exist for the DUP to nominate a first minister; however, the speaker of the Assembly ruled that this was a nomination. The intent appeared to be to allow the Assembly to continue to exist, as a ruling that no nomination had been made would have led to the Assembly being dissolved. Further confusion was added to the events of the day by the arrest of loyalist Michael Stone at the doors of Parliament buildings. Stone was carrying weapons when he was detained.

In December 2006 the Assembly established six subcommittees, including one on policing and justice, to help overcome areas of difficulty in reestablishing a devolved administration. The Assembly was dissolved at the end of January 2007, with fresh elections held on 7 March 2007. In March 2007, 36 DUP members, 28 SF members, 18 UUP members, 16 SDLP members, 7 APNI members, 1 **Progres-**

sive **Unionist Party** (PUP) member, 1 Green Party member, and 1 independent were elected to the Assembly.

**NORTHERN IRELAND CIVIL RIGHTS ASSOCIATION (NICRA).**
Established in early 1967 and with a constitution similar to the London-based National Council for Civil Liberties, the NICRA sought reform within Northern Ireland. Its first committee members represented a broad range of interests, including the **Campaign for Social Justice** (CSJ), the Ulster Liberal Party, trade **unionists**, the **Northern Ireland Labour Party** (NILP), the Republican Labour Party, the Wolfe Tone Society, and the Young Unionists at Queen's University, **Belfast** (QUB). The basic objectives of the organization were as follows: one man, one vote for council **elections**; the ending of gerrymandered electoral boundaries; the creation of official offices to prevent **discrimination** by public authorities and to deal with complaints; fair allocation of public housing; the repeal of the Special Powers Act; and the disbanding of the **Ulster Special Constabulary** (USC; B Specials).

NICRA organized a protest march (*see* PARADES) at Dungannon, Co. Tyrone, on 24 August 1968 at the suggestion of **Stormont Nationalist Party** Member of Parliament (MP) **Austin Currie**. The next NICRA march, in **Derry** on 5 October 1968, was banned by the **Northern Ireland government**, led to clashes with the **Royal Ulster Constabulary** (RUC), and brought the protest campaign in Northern Ireland to the attention of the world. It was the conflict surrounding this march that many view as the beginning of **the Troubles**. The organization was criticized by unionists as being a front for the **Irish Republican Army** (IRA), and while some of its members were **republicans**, it did not follow an exclusively republican agenda in its early years.

With the introduction of **internment** in August 1971, NICRA became increasingly associated with **nationalist** objectives. It promoted a civil disobedience campaign that led to the nonpayment of rent and rates but found itself in conflict with the **Social Democratic and Labour Party** (SDLP) in 1974 when the party called for an end to the rent and rates strike.

**NORTHERN IRELAND CONSTITUTIONAL CONVENTION.**
*See* CONSTITUTIONAL CONVENTION.

**NORTHERN IRELAND FORUM.** Following the publication of the report of the commission headed by **George Mitchell** in January 1996, British prime minister **John Major** announced an **election** to a Northern Ireland Forum as a way of balancing the contentious issues of political talks and the **decommissioning** of **paramilitary** weapons. The proposal received a hostile reception from **nationalists**, partly because the idea was perceived to have come from the **Ulster Unionist Party** (UUP) and partly because they believed this was an attempt to slow progress in the talks process. By late February, however, the Irish government had decided to accept the proposal.

The elections to the forum, held in May 1996, took a novel form, with a number of candidates being elected on a constituency basis and the rest on the basis of representation for the 10 most successful parties across Northern Ireland. This system gave representation to the five major parties as well as the recently formed United Kingdom Unionist Party (UKUP), **Northern Ireland Women's Coalition** (NIWC), and a Labour group. The **loyalist Progressive Unionist Party** (PUP) and **Ulster Democratic Party** (UDP) were also represented, and it might be argued that the system used for the election was largely created to ensure these two groups were represented in the talks that ran parallel to the forum.

**Sinn Fein** (SF) contested the election but did not attend meetings of the forum. Following a summer recess during which the dispute surrounding the **Drumcree** march dominated events, **Social Democratic and Labour Party** (SDLP) members withdrew from the forum. By September 1996 the forum was an overwhelmingly **unionist** body, and many of its subsequent decisions reflected this. It met for its final session in April 1998.

**NORTHERN IRELAND GOVERNMENT.** The government established after partition in 1921 and responsible for **devolved** powers in Northern Ireland until the suspension of the **Northern Ireland Parliament** in 1972. The Northern Ireland government reflected the **unionist** majority in Northern Ireland as a whole and was made up almost entirely of members of the **Ulster Unionist Party** (UUP) throughout its entire lifetime. With the return of the **Labour Party** to power at **Westminster** in the mid-1960s, it came under pressure to end **discriminatory** practices that disadvantaged Catholics; however, when these reforms were undertaken, they came too late to appease **nationalists**, while at the same time increasing opposition to reform from unionist critics. Following the outbreak of **the Troubles**, some attempts were made to broaden the government's base of support with the appointment of **Northern Ireland Labour Party** (NILP) member **David Bleakley** as minister of **community relations** and G. B. Newe, a Catholic, as a minister of state in the prime minister's office in 1971. These appointments made little impact in the face of the worsening political and security situation.

The deployment of troops on the streets of Northern Ireland inevitably entailed an increased interest in Northern Ireland affairs by the British government, and this came to a head after **Bloody Sunday**. In March 1972 the British government decided to take control of security matters in Northern Ireland. However, the Northern Ireland government refused to accept this decision, leading Prime Minister **Edward Heath** to suspend the Northern Ireland Parliament and introduce a system of **direct rule** by the British government.

**NORTHERN IRELAND HUMAN RIGHTS COMMISSION (NIHRC).** A statutory body established under the terms of the **Good Friday Agreement** (GFA) and Northern Ireland Act of 1998 and came into existence on 1 March 1999. Its role is to promote awareness of human rights in Northern Ireland, review existing laws and practices, and advise the secretary of state and Northern Ireland executive on steps that may be required to protect human rights in Northern Ireland. It was given the specific responsibility of drafting a bill of rights for Northern Ireland to supplement the European Convention on Human Rights. The NIHCR also has the power to conduct investigations, assist individuals in court proceedings, or bring proceedings itself.

NIHRC's first chief commissioner was Professor Brice Dickson, who was succeeded by Professor **Monica McWilliams** in June 2005. In its first term, there was much debate about the content of the proposed bill of rights, and suggestions failed to win widespread support. There was also criticism, most notably from the broad **unionist** community, about the makeup of the commission itself and the degree to which it was representative of Northern Ireland society as a whole. Some critics also suggested that the government had stifled the NIHRC by failing to provide it with adequate resources and powers.

**NORTHERN IRELAND LABOUR PARTY (NILP).** The Northern Ireland political party associated with, but not part of, the British **Labour Party**. It largely drew its support from working-class areas of **Belfast** and, between 1958 and 1965, had four Members of Parliament (MP) in the **Northern Ireland Parliament**. In the 1970 **Westminster** general **election**, it polled nearly 100,000 votes (12.6 percent of the total) but failed to win a seat. After the outbreak of **the Troubles**, increasing polarization saw the NILP and its support begin to fragment. **Paddy Devlin**, a leading member, joined the **Social Democratic and Labour Party** (SDLP), and by the 1973 **district council** elections, the party received less than 17,500 first-preference votes (2.5 percent of the poll). For those not willing to vote for **unionist** or **nationalist** groups, the **Alliance Party of Northern Ireland** (APNI) was also perceived as the major party to support, and this also worked to the detriment of the NILP.

In the 1973 **Northern Ireland Assembly** election, the NILP received just over 18,500 first-preference votes (2.6 percent of the poll), but only **David Bleakley** was elected. In the Assembly the party supported **power sharing**, but following the collapse of the executive in May 1974, it opposed both the Council of Ireland and formalized power sharing.

In the February 1974 Westminster general election, the NILP received approximately 17,500 votes (2.4 percent), but in the general election of October 1974, this declined to 11,500 (1.6 percent). David Bleakley was elected to the Northern Ireland **Constitutional Convention** in May 1975, but the NILP as a whole received only 9,000 first-preference votes (1.4 percent), and by the time of the next district council elections in 1977, the party was receiving less than 1.0 percent of first-preference votes. In the 1979 Westminster general election, the NILP received less than 4,500 votes (0.6 percent). In 1987 the remnants of the NILP were absorbed into a new political party, Labour '87.

**NORTHERN IRELAND OFFICE (NIO).** The department of government established by the U.K. Parliament in March 1972, which took control of those responsibilities formally held by the **Northern Ireland government**. The NIO was headed by a secretary of state, who was a member of the British cabinet, with varying numbers of junior ministers having responsibility for individual Northern Ireland departments that oversaw such areas as health, education, and economic development. During periods in which **devolution** returned power to a **Northern Ireland Assembly,** many of the NIO's responsibilities were assumed by Northern Ireland executive ministers, and the number of NIO ministers was reduced. Even in these periods, however, the NIO kept control of certain areas, such as security and the administration of justice, which could be considered for devolution at a future date. After **Gordon Brown** became prime minister in June 2007, the subsequent cabinet reshuffle left only two ministers at the NIO. Shaun Woodward became secretary of state and Paul Goggins had responsibility for security and prisons.

**NORTHERN IRELAND PARLIAMENT.** The Northern Ireland Parliament was established by the Government of Ireland Act of 1920 and came into existence in 1921. It was suspended in 1972 and abolished by the Northern Ireland Constitution Act of 1973. Although the Parliament consisted of two chambers, the House of Commons and the Senate, the makeup of the Senate reflected the composition of the Commons in being overwhelmingly **unionist.** It was, therefore, largely uncontroversial, if also arguably ineffective. **Elections** to the 52-member House of Commons were initially by **proportional representation** (PR), however this was changed to the "first past the post" (or plurality) system, with single-member constituencies in 1929. The main objective of this change was to prevent the fragmentation of support for the **Ulster Unionist Party** (UUP) rather than to reduce **nationalist** representation.

In 1932 the Northern Ireland Parliament relocated to the newly constructed Parliament buildings at **Stormont** on the eastern outskirts of **Belfast**. The same buildings have subsequently been used for the various **Northern Ireland Assemblies**.

Nationalists were wary of giving credibility to the Parliament, as this could have been interpreted as an acceptance of partition, and it was not until 1965 that the **Nationalist Party** (NP) accepted the role of official opposition in the Parliament.

With the outbreak of **the Troubles,** the turmoil on the streets began to be reflected in the Parliament. The 1969 Northern Ireland general election saw a fragmentation of the UUP and the election of candidates associated with the civil rights movement to be followed by **Ian Paisley** and a fellow Protestant Unionist member in subsequent by-elections. In July 1971 the **Social Democratic and Labour Party** (SDLP), now the main nationalist party, withdrew from the Parliament when the unionist government refused to conduct an inquiry into the actions of the **Royal Ulster Constabulary** (RUC) in **Derry**. Following the events of **Bloody Sunday** in January 1972, the U.K. government moved to assume control of all aspects of security policy in Northern Ireland, and when the unionist government opposed this move, the Northern Ireland Parliament was suspended in March 1972 before being superseded by the Northern Ireland Assembly in 1973.

**NORTHERN IRELAND WOMEN'S COALITION (NIWC).** In 1996, in the period leading up to the **Northern Ireland Forum election, women** from the voluntary and community sectors in Northern Ireland lobbied local **political parties** on their policies on women's representation and other issues closely associated with women. Uninspired by the responses they received, they decided to run their own candidates in the forum election on 30 May 1996. The nature of this election was such that by running candidates across Northern Ireland, they could win enough votes to become one of the top 10 parties and thus be represented in the forum talks.

The NIWC candidates stood on a policy of "reconciliation through dialogue, accommodation, and inclusion" and promoted the participation of women in Northern Ireland politics and society in general. With 7,731 votes (1.0 percent), the NIWC was the ninth most successful party, and this enabled them to participate in the multiparty talks that began in June 1996.

During the talks process, the NIWC strongly advocated an inclusive approach, and this was reflected in elements of the **Good Friday Agreement** (GFA) in April 1998. The NIWC campaigned strongly for a *yes* vote in the referendum on the GFA, and in the subsequent elections to the **Northern Ireland Assembly** in June 1998, they received 1.6 percent of the vote and won two seats (**Monica McWilliams** and Jane Morrice). In the 1998–2003 Assembly, the NIWC strongly supported the GFA, and this was to be illustrated in November 2001 when the party's two Assembly members redesignated themselves as a

**unionist** and **nationalist** (rather than "other") to allow for the reelection of **David Trimble** as first minister.

At the Assembly elections in November 2003, the NIWC polled 0.8 percent of the vote and lost its two seats. In 2005 the party received only 738 votes across Northern Ireland (0.1 percent) and failed to have any representatives returned at **district-council** level. In May 2006 the NIWC announced that it was disbanding. Former member of the legislative assembly (MLA) Jane Morrice blamed the polarization of politics and disillusionment with the GFA for the decline in the NIWC's electoral fortunes.

## – O –

**O BRADAIGH, RUAIRI (1932– ).** **Republican** activist and president of **Sinn Fein** (SF) and **Republican Sinn Fein** (RSF), Ruairi O Bradaigh was born in Longford on 2 October 1932. He was educated at St. Mel's College and University College, Dublin, where he received a bachelor's degree in commerce. From a strongly republican family, he joined SF in 1950 and the **Irish Republican Army** (IRA) in 1951. In 1954 he became part of the IRA's military council, which was planning attacks against **Royal Ulster Constabulary** (RUC) barracks. In August 1955 he was part of an IRA group that raided a **British Army** barracks near Arborfield, Berkshire, and stole 60 weapons and 90,000 rounds of ammunition.

During the Border Campaign of 1956–62, O Bradaigh was second in command of an IRA unit in the west of Ireland. In December 1956 he was arrested in the Republic after a raid on an RUC barracks in Fermanagh and was subsequently imprisoned for six years. In the Irish general **election** of 1957, while still a prisoner, he was elected to the **Dail** from the Longford-Westmeath constituency. O Bradaigh lost the seat in the 1961 general election. On completing his jail sentence, he was immediately interned by the Irish government but escaped in September 1958. In October 1958 he became IRA chief of staff but was recaptured the following year and imprisoned once again. He was again IRA chief of staff in 1961–62 and played a significant role in the ending of the border campaign. He resumed his career in teaching in 1962 but remained a member of SF and the

IRA's Army Council. In the 1966 U.K. general election, he stood as an independent republican in Fermanagh-South Tyrone and received nearly 20.0 percent of the vote but was not elected.

In January 1970, when the SF ard fheis voted to end abstentionism and take seats in the **Belfast**, London, and Dublin Parliaments, O Bradaigh led the walkout of those who opposed the change in policy. He was subsequently elected president of Provisional Sinn Fein (PSF) and retained the position until 1983. In 1972 he was arrested in the Republic and immediately began a **hunger strike** in protest; however, two weeks later the charges were dropped, and he was released. In 1972 he developed the **Eire Nua** policy with his colleague, Daithi O Conaill, which proposed an all-Ireland federal system of government. In December 1972 he was arrested once again and, in January 1973, became the first person to be convicted under the Offenses against the State Act of 1972. In 1974 he undertook a promotional tour of the **United States** but later had his entry visa revoked.

In December 1974 O Bradaigh participated in the Feakle Talks with Protestant clergymen, which led to a ceasefire and **the Truce** of 1975. However, this collapsed in late 1975 when it became clear to republicans that the British government had no imminent plan to withdraw from Northern Ireland. Despite this, he was part of a republican group that continued to have talks with British government representatives in 1975–76. In 1976 and 1977, he was involved in secret negotiations with **loyalist paramilitary** members on the issue of negotiated **independence** for Northern Ireland, but the talks ended when they were publicly revealed by Irish minister **Conor Cruise O'Brien**.

In the late 1970s, republicans from Northern Ireland became increasingly influential within the republican movement. Northern republicans were particularly critical of the Eire Nua policy, which was dropped by the party in 1982, and O Bradaigh and O Conaill resigned their party positions in 1983.

In November 1986, when SF voted to end abstention from the Dail, O Bradaigh and opponents of this move withdrew from the ard fheis and established RSF, with O Bradaigh becoming president. RSF subsequently adopted much of the Eire Nua policy. Since the 1990s he has remained a critic of the policy pursued by SF in the **peace process**. In October 2006 he was again refused a visa to enter the United States.

**O FIAICH, TOMAS (1923–90).** Catholic cardinal of Ireland, Tomas O Fiaich was born on 3 November 1923 at Cullyhannagh in Co. Armagh. He was educated at Creganduff Public Elementary School and St. Patrick's College, Armagh. In 1940 he entered St. Patrick's College, Maynooth, and graduated with a first-class degree in Celtic studies. He subsequently studied for the priesthood and was ordained at St. Peter's College, Wexford, in 1948. In 1950 he received an MA in medieval Irish history from University College, Dublin, and then undertook further historical research at the University of Louvain in France. In 1953 he was appointed as a lecturer in modern history at Maynooth, becoming a professor in 1959. He became president of Maynooth College in 1974. He was a fluent Irish speaker and writer and strong proponent of the use of the language.

In August 1977 O Fiaich was, somewhat unexpectedly, appointed archbishop of Armagh, becoming a cardinal in June 1979. His strongly **nationalist** views brought him into conflict with **unionist** politicians, not least in January 1984 when he stated that people could be morally justified in joining **Sinn Fein** (SF) with the intention of becoming involved in community activities.

O Fiaich's most overtly political stance came in his strenuous opposition to **internment**. He opposed the 1981 **hunger strike** campaign but supported the prisoners' demand for political status. He sought to mediate between the prisoners and the government, but almost inevitably this approach was rejected by the government. During the course of a pilgrimage to Lourdes, Tomas O Fiaich suffered a heart attack and died on 8 May 1990.

**O'BRIEN, CONOR CRUISE (1917– ).** Politician, diplomat, and academic, Conor Cruise O'Brien was born in Dublin on 3 November 1917. He was educated at Sandford Park School and Trinity College, Dublin, where he graduated with a BA and later a PhD. Although O'Brien was from a nominally Catholic family, his first wife was from a **Belfast** Presbyterian background. He joined the Irish Department of External Affairs in 1944 and served in France and at the United Nations before holding academic posts in Ghana (1962–65) and in New York (1965–69). As a special representative of the United Nations, he was at the center of a crisis in the Congo in 1961 but resigned after pressure from a number of international interests.

In 1969 O'Brien was **elected** to the **Dail** as an **Irish Labour Party** member for the Dublin Northeast constituency. In the 1973–77 **Fine Gael** (FG)–**Labour** coalition government, he was minister for posts and telegraphs under **Liam Cosgrave**. Already a critic of traditional Irish **republicanism**, O'Brien became one of the most vocal opponents of the **Irish Republican Army** (IRA) and as minister banned interviews with **Sinn Fein** (SF) and IRA members from being broadcast on Irish radio and television.

In the 1977 Irish general election, O'Brien lost his seat in the Dail but was subsequently elected to the Irish Senate (1977–79). From 1979 until 1981, he was editor in chief of the *Observer* newspaper in Britain and held numerous academic positions in Ireland, Britain, the **United States**, and, more controversially, in apartheid South Africa. He opposed the **Anglo–Irish Agreement** (AIA) and by the early 1990s was increasingly pro-**unionist** in opinion.

Despite his politically maverick past and hostility to Irish republicanism, it was still something of a surprise when O'Brien joined **Robert McCartney**'s United Kingdom Unionist Party (UKUP). He was elected to the **Northern Ireland Forum** in 1996 as a UKUP representative and participated in political discussions. In 1998, however, he was forced to resign from the party after suggesting that unionists should accept the idea of a united Ireland to outmaneuver SF politically.

The author of a significant number of publications, O'Brien played an important ideological role in helping move Irish political identity toward a more internationalist perspective and away from the often more introspective traditional republican view. His attempts to perform a similar role with some unionists proved less successful.

**OFFICIAL IRISH REPUBLICAN ARMY (OIRA).** The **republican paramilitary** organization that emerged after the split in the republican movement in December 1969. The OIRA retained its Marxist political attitude, while the Provisional **Irish Republican Army** (PIRA) gave greater prominence in its rhetoric to its role as defender of the Catholic population in Northern Ireland. In Northern Ireland the PIRA quickly became the larger organization, but the OIRA remained a significant force in some areas of **Belfast**.

Inevitably there were intermittent feuds with the PIRA, which continued long after the OIRA declared a ceasefire in May 1972. Those killed by the OIRA were, in general, more clearly linked to the state than the PIRA's **victims**. Despite this, nearly half of the more than 50 people killed by the OIRA were civilians.

In September 1971 the OIRA murdered **Ulster Unionist Party** (UUP) senator Jack Barnhill and wounded UUP minister **John Taylor**. In the aftermath of **Bloody Sunday**, it also claimed responsibility for a bomb at Aldershot Barracks in England, the base of the Parachute Regiment, which killed seven people. In May 1972 the OIRA kidnapped and killed a local man serving in the **British Army** who was home on leave in **Derry**. The outcry against the murder from within staunchly republican areas was such that the OIRA subsequently announced a ceasefire.

After the **Irish Republican Socialist Party** (IRSP) split from the OIRA in 1975, another feud developed, leading to eight **deaths**. Since the 1980s the organization appears to have been largely inactive as the OIRA wing of the republican movement concentrated on political activity. Despite this, the existence of the OIRA was a major element in the split within the **Workers' Party** (WP) and emergence of the Democratic Left in 1992. During the course of **the Troubles**, the OIRA was responsible for 57 deaths.

**OFFICIAL SINN FEIN (OSF).** *See* SINN FEIN (SF).

**OMAGH BOMB.** On 15 August 1998, a car bomb planted by the **republican** splinter group the **Real Irish Republican Army** (RIRA) exploded in Omagh, Co. Tyrone, killing 28 people and injuring 360 others. One victim died from his wounds three weeks later. The 300- to 500-pound bomb went off on a Saturday afternoon during the town's civic festival, with many of those killed being women and children. The police received a telephone warning but were given the wrong location for the bomb, inadvertently directing people toward the car bomb instead of away from it. The Omagh bomb was the largest number of **deaths** of any single event in **the Troubles**.

Among those killed in the explosion were a 20-month-old baby girl, 2 Spanish visitors, a grandmother and her daughter and granddaughter, and unborn twins. Controversy later emerged as to whether the **Royal Ulster Constabulary** (RUC) could have done more to prevent the explosion. In September 2006 a man went on trial for charges connected with the Omagh bombing.

**O'NEILL, TERENCE (1914–90).** Ulster Unionist Party (UUP) leader and prime minister of Northern Ireland, Terence O'Neill was born in London on 10 September 1914. He was a member of one of the most famous landed families of Ireland. His father, the **unionist** Member of Parliament (MP) for Mid-Antrim, was killed in action in November 1914. O'Neill was educated at West Downs School, Winchester, and Eton. Much of his youth was spent in England or abroad, with visits to Ireland during summer holidays. In World War II, he served with the Irish Guards and became a captain. He was wounded in September 1944 and evacuated back to England.

In late 1945 O'Neill and his family settled in Northern Ireland, and in 1946 he was **elected** to the **Northern Ireland Parliament** in a by-election for the safe unionist seat of Bannside. He retained the seat until his retirement from active politics in 1970. He held a number of junior positions in the **Northern Ireland government** before being appointed minister of home affairs in 1955. Less than a year later, he became minister of finance and held this position until he became prime minister in March 1963 following the retirement of Lord Brookeborough.

As prime minister O'Neill undertook a series of economic reforms aimed at replacing jobs lost in Northern Ireland's declining heavy industries. He also sought to improve relations with the **Republic of Ireland** and with Catholics within Northern Ireland. In January 1965 Taoiseach Sean Lemass made an unannounced visit to **Stormont**, which angered some right-wing unionists. O'Neill was somewhat unfortunate in that his efforts at reform also coincided with the 50th anniversary of the 1916 Easter Rising in Dublin, which saw heightened **republican** rhetoric and increased unionist fears. This led, in part, to the emergence of the **loyalist paramilitary Ulster Volunteer Force** (UVF) in 1966.

From 1967 O'Neill encountered another challenge with the **Northern Ireland Civil Rights Association** (NICRA), which pressed for the immediate ending of **discriminatory** practices against Catholics.

O'Neill faced the difficult prospect of balancing reform while maintaining the support of his party with increasing protests and counter-protests on the streets. The problem was clearly revealed on 5 October 1968, when the **Royal Ulster Constabulary** (RUC) overreacted to the **Derry** civil rights march (*see* PARADES). O'Neill decided to press ahead with reforms despite opposition within his own party and government. In December 1968 he fired Minister of Home Affairs **William Craig** but also appealed to demonstrators to end street protests. A five-point program of reforms was introduced addressing many of the issues raised by NICRA.

At the end of 1968, O'Neill appeared to have public opinion behind him and decided to challenge his unionist critics in a Northern Ireland general election. The result of the **crossroads election** in February 1969 failed to give O'Neill the overwhelming endorsement he had hoped for, while the civil rights campaign continued to press for further reforms. Amid continuing antagonism in the UUP, O'Neill resigned as prime minister on 28 April 1969. In 1970 he was awarded a life peerage and assumed the title of Lord O'Neill of the Maine. He continued to speak on Northern Ireland issues in the House of Lords. O'Neill died on 12 June 1990.

**OPERATION MOTORMAN.** The codename for the largest British military operation since the Suez in 1956, Operation Motorman ended **no-go areas** in **Belfast** and **Derry**. On 31 July 1972, 12,000 soldiers with bulldozers and tanks smashed their way into the no-go areas as part of the effort to restore government control to hard-line **republican** and **loyalist** areas. In Belfast the **Ulster Defence Association** (UDA) helped soldiers dismantle barriers in loyalist areas, while some Catholics assisted in dismantling barricades in their areas. The **British Army** was reported to have prepared for up to 40 civilian casualties as a result of resistance to the operation, and in the event 2 youths were shot dead and 2 injured in Derry during gun battles. No soldiers were injured. Despite a series of raids by the army, no **Irish Republican Army** (IRA) members were captured, although 24 people were arrested for possession of illegal arms and explosions.

**ORANGE ORDER.** The largest of the Protestant Loyal Orders, the Loyal Orange Institution, more commonly known as the Orange

Order, was founded in 1795 after a sectarian battle in County Armagh. Initially a militant working-class organization, it was adopted by members of the gentry in the early 19th century. However, the upper classes abandoned the organization following sectarian conflicts surrounding Orange demonstrations.

In the late 19th century, **unionist** leaders aligned with the Orange Order in the campaign against home rule for Ireland, and the Order played a leading part in the formation of the Ulster Unionist Council (UUC) in 1905. After the foundation of Northern Ireland, the Order had an influential role through its membership on the UUC and its strong association with leading **Ulster Unionist Party** (UUP) members. Only three UUP Members of Parliament (MP) at **Westminster** have not been members of the Orange Order: **Enoch Powell, Ken Maginnis**, and Lady Sylvia Hermon. Many people refer to Northern Ireland as **the Orange State**, and the main Orange celebration of **the Twelfth** of July was a state event during the period from 1921 until 1972, when the Northern Ireland Parliament was suspended.

With the outbreak of **the Troubles**, the organization came under pressure for opposing reasons. Some **loyalists** had believed that the Orange Order would function as a **paramilitary** organization in times of crisis and viewed the Order as ineffective. Others, generally middle-class unionists, believed the organization was too closely associated with political hardliners. A number of Orange marches became associated with controversy or sectarian conflict, most significantly at **Drumcree** in July 1995. Despite the controversy aroused by the Drumcree **parade**, the Orange Order actually saw an increase in its membership after 1995.

Politically the organization has been on the right wing of unionism. It was opposed to the **Sunningdale** Agreement in 1973, the **Anglo–Irish Agreement** (AIA) in 1985, and **Good Friday Agreement** (GFA) in 1998. As the implementation of the GFA continued, the Orange Order became increasingly alienated from the UUP, and in March 2005 the organization voted to end its connection with the party.

During the course of the Troubles, there were numerous sectarian attacks by **republicans** on members of the Orange Order and on Orange Order property. In 2005 an unofficial estimate claimed that 304 members of the Orange Order had been murdered by the **Irish Republican Army** (IRA) during the course of the Troubles, of whom

156 were members of the **Royal Ulster Constabulary** (RUC), the **Ulster Defence Regiment** (UDR), or the prison service and 148 were civilians (Cargo, 2005). The Orange Order is estimated to have as many as 100,000 members.

**THE ORANGE STATE.** A phrase used by some **nationalists** and left-wing critics to refer to Northern Ireland, particularly in the period leading up to the suspension of the **Northern Ireland Parliament**. Before 1972 all of the prime ministers and almost all of the ministers of the **Northern Ireland government** were members of the **Orange Order**. The Orange Order also had representatives on the **Ulster Unionist Party**'s (UUP) ruling body, the Ulster Unionist Council (UUC), while the **Ulster Special Constabulary** (USC) was also composed almost entirely of members of the Orange Order. The Protestant and **unionist** ethos of the Orange Order was also viewed by nationalists as permeating the entire political culture of Northern Ireland, creating a state that was inherently **discriminatory** and anti-Catholic. After the abolition of the Northern Ireland government, some critics continued to refer to Northern Ireland as the Orange State on the basis that the administrative structure remained largely unchanged despite the introduction of **direct rule**. With the levers of power in the hands of the British government after 1972, continued reforms, and the fragmentation of the unionist political bloc, however, this argument became more difficult to sustain.

**ORDE, HUGH (1958– ).** Chief constable of the **Police Service of Northern Ireland** (PSNI), Hugh Orde was born on 27 August 1958. He was educated at the University of Kent, where he earned a BA in public administration and management. He joined the London Metropolitan Police in 1977 and worked his way through the ranks to become deputy assistant commissioner in 1999. He became chief constable of the PSNI in 2002. He has been responsible for the implementation of the police reforms recommended by the **Patten Report**. In November 2006 he said that although the **Irish Republican Army**'s (IRA) command structure was still in place, the organization did not pose a threat to national security. In January 2007 he announced that plastic baton rounds would no longer be used in public order situations. In the same month, he said that the cost of inquiries dealing with past murders was a drain on financial resources. At the end of January 2007, he criticized **nationalist** politicians for using policing as a "political football." An enthusiastic marathon runner, he was awarded a knighthood in June 2005.

## – P –

**PAISLEY, IAN (1926– ). Democratic Unionist Party** (DUP) leader, Ian Paisley was born in Armagh City, Co. Armagh, on 6 April 1926. The son of a Baptist minister, he was educated at Ballymena Model School, Ballymena Technical High School, the South Wales Bible College, and the Reformed Presbyterian Theological College in **Belfast**. He was ordained as a Baptist minister in 1946 but, in 1951, formed the **Free Presbyterian Church of Ulster**.

Initially his Protestant fundamentalist views attracted greater attention than his politics, and he was a strong opponent of growing links between the Catholic and Protestant Churches. Increasingly, however, his religious views intruded into the world of politics, and he became a fierce critic of **Terence O'Neill**'s reformist policies, which he attacked as undermining Northern Ireland's position within the United Kingdom. To oppose O'Neill's policies and the growing campaign of the **Northern Ireland Civil Rights Association** (NICRA), he helped instigate the Ulster Constitution Defence Committee (UCDC) and Ulster Protestant Volunteers (UPV), which were prominent in counterdemonstrations against civil rights marches (*see* PARADES).

In November 1968 Paisley was arrested in Armagh during a protest of a civil rights march, and he was subsequently sentenced to six weeks imprisonment. At the Northern Ireland general **election** of 1969, standing as a Protestant **Unionist** candidate, he had a strong electoral showing but lost to Terence O'Neill in the Bannside constituency. In April 1970, however, he won the same seat in the by-election brought about by O'Neill's retirement from politics. There was further evidence of support for Paisley in June 1970 when he won the North Antrim seat at **Westminster**, a seat he has retained since that time.

In September 1971, with former **Ulster Unionist Party** (UUP) member Desmond Boal, Paisley launched the DUP. After the introduction of **direct rule** in 1972, he initially appeared to support an **integrationist** approach but for the rest of his political career has favored **devolution** for Northern Ireland. The DUP was excluded from the 1973 **Stormont** Castle and **Sunningdale** Talks, and Paisley was a staunch and vocal critic of the Sunningdale deal. He was in Canada at the start of the **Ulster Workers' Council (UWC) strike** but soon returned and worked with other unionist politicians, **loyalist** workers, and **paramilitaries** to bring about the collapse of the **power-sharing** executive.

In the **Constitutional Convention**, Paisley briefly appeared to consider some form of power sharing, but this was opposed by most of the DUP, and his party benefited from the subsequent fragmentation of the **Vanguard Unionist Progressive Party** (VUPP) on the issue. In May 1977 he was at the forefront of the **United Unionist Action Council (UUAC) strike** and said he would retire from politics if the strike failed. Although he later insisted that the strike had not failed, his political prestige undoubtedly suffered a temporary setback.

In 1979 Paisley topped the poll in the first direct elections to the European Parliament and continued to do so in subsequent elections until his retirement from the European Parliament in 2004. In October 1988 he interrupted a speech by Pope John Paul II in the European Parliament, claiming that the Pope was the antichrist, before he was removed from the chamber.

In November 1981 Paisley was ordered out of the House of Commons after criticizing Secretary of State **James Prior** over the **Irish Republican Army** (IRA) murder of Rev. Robert Bradford, Member of Parliament (MP). His promotion of a quasi vigilante "third force" to protect Protestants living in isolated areas in late 1981 led to his being banned from the **United States** at the urging of Irish American congressmen. He was a strong supporter of the 1982 **Northern Ireland Assembly** and relished his role as chairman of the Agriculture Committee. In the wake of the **Anglo–Irish Agreement** (AIA), he was a leading figure in unionist opposition to the AIA. In November 1986 he participated in a rally held by Ulster Resistance, a paramilitary-style organization formed to oppose the AIA. As the organization became more associated with loyalist paramilitaries, however, Paisley disassociated himself from it.

With **James Molyneaux** he took part in "talks about talks" with **Tom King**. He led his party in the **Brooke–Mayhew Talks** and later met members of the Irish government for discussions in 1992. He was critical of the **Downing Street Declaration** of December 1993 and saw it, and the IRA ceasefire of 1994, as part of a wider scheme to undermine Northern Ireland. He was elected to the **Northern Ireland Forum** in 1996, again in North Antrim, and participated in subsequent talks; however, his party withdrew in July 1997 when **Sinn Fein** (SF) entered negotiations.

Paisley opposed the **Good Friday Agreement** (GFA) and campaigned for a *no* vote in the referendum. He was elected to the Assembly in 1998 and saw his party capitalize on unionist disillusionment with the GFA to win increasing electoral support. Following the November 2003 Assembly elections, he became the leader of the largest party in the Assembly. For a period he appeared to be in ill health, and in 2004 he stepped down from the European Parliament.

In May 2006, shortly after Paisley celebrated his 80th birthday, **Gerry Adams** proposed that Paisley be elected first minister and **Martin McGuinness** deputy first minister in an attempt to establish a new Northern Ireland executive. In October 2006 he met the head of the Catholic Church in Ireland in his role as leader of the DUP. In November 2006 there was confusion in the Assembly as to whether he had indicated that he would accept the position of first minister if SF clearly supported the police and the justice system. In March 2007 he was again returned to the Northern Ireland Assembly from North Antrim. On 26 March 2007, he met Adams directly for talks for the first time, and on 4 April 2007, he met, and shook hands with, Bertie Ahern while in Dublin for talks. When power was devolved on 8 May 2007, he became first minister of Northern Ireland.

**PARADES.** Parades have been an often controversial feature of life in Ireland for five centuries. Parading was illegal in Ireland from 1832 until 1845 and from 1850 until 1872. In the late 19th century, parades were increasingly associated with the **Orange Order** and with marching bands. This trend increased after the foundation of Northern Ireland in 1921, while at the same time, parades associated with **nation-**

**alism** were curtailed in Northern Ireland. Parades by the Protestant Loyal Orders in predominantly Catholic areas were perceived by nationalists as displays of **unionist** triumphalism and created an atmosphere in which there was often the possibility of violence.

In the 1960s, marches by the **Northern Ireland Civil Rights Association** (NICRA) were similarly viewed by some unionists as a nationalist encroachment into neutral or unionist territory. It was not a coincidence that the outbreak of **the Troubles** was associated with the violence connected to three parades: by the civil rights movement in **Derry** in October 1968, by **People's Democracy** (PD) at Burntollet in January 1969, and by the **Apprentice Boys of Derry** (ABD) in Londonderry in August 1969. In 1985 and 1986, the parading issue became particularly controversial as a number of Orange parades were rerouted by the **Royal Ulster Constabulary** (RUC). The issue increased unionist antagonism for the **Anglo–Irish Agreement** (AIA) and the Irish government, which was believed to have pushed for changes to parades by the Loyal Orders.

In the 1990s, residents' groups in nationalist areas became increasingly active in opposing Orange parades, with the most prominent dispute occurring around the **Drumcree** parade in Portadown. By the early 21st century, there were approximately 3,500 parades each year in Northern Ireland. While most of these were uncontroversial, a number still had the potential to lead to outbreaks of sustained violence. In July 2005 approximately 500 nationalists attacked police following an Orange parade in North **Belfast**. The rerouting of another Orange parade in North Belfast in September 2005 led to several days of severe rioting in **loyalist** areas across Belfast. The "marching season," in which various loyalist organizations parade, often accompanied by bands, begins in March and continues through September. The main period of activity is in July, which includes the Orange Order demonstration on **the Twelfth**, and in August. In April 2007 the government announced that a new body chaired by former **Liberal Democrat** leader Lord Paddy Ashdown would undertake a strategic review of the parades issue.

**PARADES COMMISSION.** The issue of contested **parades** was highlighted by the events at **Drumcree** in 1995. As a response the government established an independent body under Dr. Peter North to review the issue in July 1996, with the Report of the Independent Review of Parades and Marches (the North Report) being presented in January 1997. The most significant recommendation of the report was the creation of an independent Parades Commission, with members to be appointed by the secretary of state for Northern Ireland. Where agreement was not reached in relation to a particular parade, the commission would determine whether conditions should be imposed. Many of the report's recommendations were included in the Public Procession Acts of 1998.

The Parades Commission has the power to ban a march; to impose conditions, such as whether music is played; or to determine the route of the parade. The ruling of the commission is enforced by the **Police Service of Northern Ireland** (PSNI) or by parade stewards. The commission has been the source of much criticism, particularly from the **unionist** community and especially from the **Orange Order**.

In 2005, with several notable exceptions, there was a reduction in violence associated with parades. By 2006 the Parades Commission was making approximately 170 formal determinations on parades each year. More than 50 of these were reapplications from the Orange Order relating to a march at Drumcree.

In October 2006 Parades Commission chairman Roger Poole expressed his hope that agreement on parades could be reached between those parties involved and that the Parades Commission could go out of business in several years time.

**PARAMILITARY.** A vigilante organization, or member of an organization, that is prepared to use illegal means, including the use of violence, to achieve political objectives. There are both **republican** and **loyalist** paramilitary organizations, the most significant of which have been the Provisional **Irish Republican Army** (PIRA), the **Ulster Defence Association** (UDA), and the **Ulster Volunteer Force** (UVF). Each of these organizations has used cover names to disguise their activities on occasion, and all have been involved in illegal activities beyond the use of violence, such as extortion, robbery, drug dealing, and counterfeiting. Although the IRA and UVF trace their ancestry back to an earlier period, the paramilitary groups that developed during **the Troubles** were largely the result of the outbreak of community conflict that took place in 1969 and the development of vigilante groups in working-class areas for the defense of their communities. A number of groups, such as the **Irish National Liberation Army** (INLA) and the **Loyalist Volunteer Force** (LVF), emerged as the result of schisms within organizations, while the most significant paramilitary group of the Troubles, the PIRA, was itself the result of a split with the **Official Irish Republican Army** (OIRA). The paramilitaries were the main protagonists of the Troubles in terms of casualties, responsible for nearly 90.0 percent of all **deaths** resulting from the conflict.

**PATTEN, CHRISTOPHER (CHRIS) (1944– ). Conservative Party** politician, Chris Patten was born on 12 May 1944. He was educated at Balliol College, Oxford. He was a research officer with the Conservative Party and, from 1974 until 1979, was head of the party's research department. In the 1979 general **election**, he was elected as Member of Parliament (MP) for Bath and subsequently worked as a speech writer for **Margaret Thatcher**.

Although Patten was perceived to be one of the party's most talented MPs, he was always seen as being on the left wing of the Conservative Party and was not ideologically close to Thatcher. In 1983 he was appointed to his first government position as a junior minister in the **Northern Ireland Office** (NIO). In Northern Ireland his most controversial decision was allowing the name change from Londonderry to **Derry** City Council, which was welcomed by **nationalists** but opposed by **unionists**.

In 1985 he left Northern Ireland to become a minister at the department of education. He was minister for overseas development from 1986 until 1989, secretary of state for the environment from 1989 to 1990, and chairman of the Conservative Party from 1990 to 1992. Although the Conservatives won the 1992 general election, Patten lost his seat.

A close political ally of **John Major**, Patten was appointed governor of Hong Kong in 1992 and oversaw the handover of power to China in 1997. Following the signing of the **Good Friday Agreement** (GFA), he was appointed to chair the independent commission on the future of policing. The report of this committee was published in September 1999. In 1999 Chris Patten was appointed to the European Commission and had responsibility for foreign affairs and external relations, holding the post until 2004. In 2005 he entered the House of Lords as Lord Patten of Barnes.

**PATTEN REPORT.** In line with the requirements of the **Good Friday Agreement** (GFA), **Chris Patten** was invited by Prime Minister **Tony Blair** to chair an independent commission into the future of policing in Northern Ireland. The Independent Commission on Policing for Northern Ireland, composed of six men and two women, was established on 3 June 1998 to carry out a fundamental review of policing and recommend proposals for future policing structures and arrangements. The objective of the commission was to "depoliticize policing" and to create a police service that would be effective, impartial, accountable, and representative of the community and would protect human rights. The commission undertook a broad consultation process but faced the difficult challenge of meeting **nationalist** demands for the disbandment of the **Royal Ulster Constabulary** (RUC) or major changes to the force and **unionist** demands for minimal changes to what they viewed as an effective organization.

In September 1999 the commission produced its final report, which made 175 recommendations, including changing the name of the RUC, changing the badge and symbols to make them free from either the British or Irish states, recruiting 50.0 percent Catholic officers—50.0 percent others, and replacing the Police Authority with a Police Board consisting of a majority of elected **Northern Ireland Assembly** members holding the responsibility for policing, to be **devolved** to the Northern Ireland executive as soon as possible.

While nationalists believed that the reforms recommended by the Patten Report did not go far enough, the proposals were universally attacked by unionists, and the subsequent implementation of many of the recommendations in the Police (Northern Ireland) Act 2000 was a factor in the decline of unionist support for the GFA.

**PEACE LINES/WALLS.** Following intense sectarian rioting between individuals from the Catholic Falls Road and Protestant Shankill Road areas of **Belfast** in the summer of 1969, a barrier was erected by the **British Army** in September of that year to prevent further rioting. In the following years, peace lines became both more widespread and more sophisticated in construction. By 2006 there were 40 peace walls in Belfast stretching 13 miles in total length. Despite the **peace process** and the signing of the **Good Friday Agreement** (GFA) in 1998, intercommunal relations on the ground often continued to be strained, and there appeared little prospect of the removal of peace lines for the foreseeable future. In April 2007 the government stated that there were 46 walls or fences and 11 gates separating Protestant and Catholic communities in Northern Ireland.

**PEACE PEOPLE.** On 10 August 1976, two of Anne Maguire's children were killed and a third fatally injured when a car driven by an **Irish Republican Army** (IRA) member, who had been shot dead by the **British Army**, crashed into the children. On 12 August 1976, more than 1,000 women held a demonstration for peace in the **nationalist** area of Andersonstown in **Belfast**. Further rallies followed, leading to the creation of the Women's Peace Movement, which later became the Peace People.

The movement attracted support from both Protestants and Catholics and organized a series of rallies throughout Northern Ireland and in Liverpool, Glasgow, and Dublin in late 1976. The leading figures in the Peace People were **Betty Williams**, **Mairead Corrigan-Maguire**, and Ciaran McKeown, with Williams and Corrigan subsequently being awarded the 1976 Nobel Peace Prize. Following the initial period in which it organized mass rallies, it increasingly focused on improving cross-**community relations** and was often critical of the role played by politicians in Northern Ireland.

In the early 1980s, a number of the Peace People's leading members, including Betty Williams, left the organization following internal disagreements. The Peace People also faced a continuing difficulty in working to promote peace due to criticism from **republicans** that the Peace People were promoting government policy. The support of the government for the Peace People's work only served to strengthen this argument from republicans.

**PEACE PROCESS.** The term used to describe the scaling down of **paramilitary** activity and reciprocal moves by the British and Irish governments alongside negotiations to achieve a widely accepted political settlement. Commentators have emphasized various aspects of the peace process and as a result there is no generally accepted date at which the process began. A number of important events can, however, be highlighted. The discussions between **Social Democratic and Labour Party** (SDLP) leader **John Hume** and **Gerry Adams**, president of **Sinn Fein** (SF), led to a document in September 1993 that they said could lead to peace in Ireland. The Hume–Adams document, in turn, influenced the **Downing Street Declaration** of December 1993, although Hume–Adams was significantly modified by the declaration in key areas, such as the need for the consent of the people of Northern Ireland for a united Ireland. The British government also conducted talks with SF through a secret "back channel," and this provided another line of contact. Similar contacts were also established with **loyalists** by both the British and Irish governments.

Much of the premise of the peace process was built on the assumption that if the **Irish Republican Army** (IRA), as the most active paramilitary group in the conflict, ended its campaign, then the consequent reduction in the level of violence would make a political settlement easier to achieve. The difficulty in this approach was that the British, and to a lesser extent Irish, governments could only go so far to meet the needs of **republicans** without alienating **unionists** and also raising loyalist paramilitary activity.

A crucial element of the peace process was the decision by republican leaders that the **long war** was ineffective and that political cooperation with the SDLP, the Irish government, and Irish Americans would be a more effective method of achieving a united Ireland. Following this path, which inevitably included the declaration of a cessation of operations, proved to be a double-edged sword, however, and while the gradual transition to constitutional politics reaped significant benefits for SF, the question of whether it had brought a united Ireland any closer was open to debate. During this transitional period, SF leaders faced the difficult task of maintaining grassroots republican and IRA support. In this they were generally successful, although the slow pace of progress toward talks was a major element in the breakdown of the IRA ceasefire in 1996 and in the breaking away of some republicans to form dissident groups in the period following the ceasefires.

For loyalist paramilitaries the main issue was the security of the union of Great Britain and Northern Ireland and the fear that the British government had made a secret deal with the IRA to achieve a ceasefire. Having been convinced that no such deal had been made by the British and Irish governments, loyalist paramilitaries announced their own ceasefire in October 1994. In comparison with the IRA, however, the loyalist paramilitary groups were more prone to fragmentation, and this proved to be another destabilizing element in the peace process.

As well as dealing with the security situation, the British and Irish governments had to strive toward achieving a political settlement. The **Brooke–Mayhew Talks** had gone some way toward achieving this agreement but had ultimately failed. Despite this, it provided a basis from which further talks could continue.

In the wake of the 1997 general **election**, the **Labour** government dropped the demand for **decommissioning** of weapons before parties linked to paramilitary groups could participate in negotiations. After the IRA renewed its ceasefire in July 1997, SF entered negotiations, but the **Democratic Unionist Party** (DUP) and United Kingdom Unionist Party withdrew. The negotiations eventually led to the **Good Friday Agreement** (GFA) in April 1998, which enjoyed widespread support, as demonstrated by the referendum on the GFA, but with a significant section of political unionism and militant republicanism opposed to it.

Disillusionment with the GFA quickly began to develop, particularly among unionists. In this, security-related issues were key factors. Paramilitary prisoners were released, security forces reduced, and major changes to policing were recommended without the decommissioning of paramilitary weapons. Primarily as a result of the failure to resolve the decommissioning issue, power was not **devolved** until December 1999, and ongoing disagreements on the issue led to intermittent suspensions of the **Northern Ireland Assembly**.

In October 2002 the **Stormontgate** affair led to the indefinite suspension of the Assembly. In 2003 the Northern Ireland Assembly election returned the DUP and SF as the two largest parties, seemingly making the prospects for devolution even less likely. Despite this, the security situation continued to improve, with normalization and decommissioning both making significant headway. In July 2005 the IRA announced an end to its campaign, and in September 2005 the **Independent International Commission on Decommissioning** (IICD) stated that the IRA had decommissioned all its weapons. The normalization of security was due to be completed in August 2007. By late 2006 the political situation remained deadlocked, and another "final" deadline of November 2006 for establishing a Northern Ireland executive was pushed back to March 2007. Although this deadline was not met, devolution was agreed for 8 May 2007, and the Northern Ireland executive assumed responsibility on that date.

**PEOPLE'S DEMOCRACY (PD).** In the aftermath of the events of the **Derry** civil rights march of 5 October 1968, a group of students at Queen's University, **Belfast** (QUB), organized a march to Belfast city hall on 9 October 1968 to protest against the police response in Derry. The student march was blocked by a counterdemonstration led by **Ian Paisley,** and the students in turn held a sit-down protest. Later that day some of the students involved formed PD. A radical leftwing group, PD played a significant role within the broader civil rights campaign. However, where the aim of the **Northern Ireland Civil Rights Association** (NICRA) was reform within Northern Ireland, PD aimed to overthrow the state and, as such, was more clearly in line with Irish **republican** objectives than was NICRA. On 1 January 1969, against the advice of NICRA, PD members began a protest march from Belfast to Derry. On 4 January 1969, the marchers were attacked by **loyalists** (including off-duty members of the **Ulster Special Constabulary** [USC]) at Burntollet Bridge near Derry and received little protection from police officers accompanying the marchers. The march was an important event in the descent toward **the Troubles.** For many nationalists the perception was that the **Northern Ireland government** was incapable of providing equal rights to Catholics, while, for unionists, the view was that the campaign for civil rights was merely a cover for a plot to undermine the existence of Northern Ireland. As the Troubles broke out in full force in August 1969, PD was increasingly perceived as being associated with republicanism and was largely overshadowed by larger forces.

**POLICE SERVICE OF NORTHERN IRELAND (PSNI).** In 1999 the report of the Independent Commission on Policing (the **Patten Report**) made 175 recommendations aimed at providing a new beginning to policing in Northern Ireland. The report included recommendations on the composition, size, and structure of the police service and laid heavy emphasis on the need for human rights and community policing to underline the work of the police. The report led to a new name, badge, and uniform for the police force, with the **Royal Ulster Constabulary** (RUC) becoming the PSNI in November 2001. Structures that were established to ensure that the police service was accountable included the Policing Board, the Police Ombudsman's Office, and 29 district policing partnerships. An oversight commissioner also reports on the progress made toward implementing the recommendations of the Patten Report. The role of oversight commissioner from May 2000 until December 2003 was performed by Tom Constantine, the former head of the **United States** Drugs Enforcement Agency.

By late 2006 one of the significant outstanding issues surrounding the **peace process** was a commitment of support from **Sinn Fein** (SF) for the PSNI. In January 2007 a special SF voted ard fheis to support the PSNI. It was also revealed that 12.0 percent of applications in a recruitment drive held two months earlier had come from Polish candidates.

In October 2006 there were 4,400 regular officers, 686 full-time reserve officers, and 768 part-time reserve officers serving in the PSNI.

**POLITICAL PARTIES.** Most of Northern Ireland's political parties are locally based and organized. **Sinn Fein** (SF) organizes on an all-Ireland basis, while Conservatives in Northern Ireland are affiliated to the British **Conservative Party**. Additionally, a number of locally based parties have links with parties outside Northern Ireland: the **Social Democratic and Labour Party** (SDLP) with the **Irish Labour Party** and **Fianna Fail** (FF) and the **Alliance Party of Northern Ireland** (APNI) with the **Liberal Democrats** in Great Britain.

As with other aspects of society, the outbreak of **the Troubles** had a dramatic impact on political parties; SF split into the official and provisional wings in January 1970, and APNI was founded in April 1970, the SDLP in August 1970, and the **Democratic Unionist Party** (DUP) in October 1971. Equally some parties that predated the conflict, such as the **Nationalist Party** (NP), the **Northern Ireland Labour Party** (NILP), and the Ulster Liberal Party, faded from the political scene.

Major political initiatives also had a dramatic effect on party politics. The **Sunningdale** deal encouraged the fragmentation of the **Ulster Unionist Party** (UUP) and the creation of the **Vanguard Unionist Progressive Party** (VUPP) and later the **Unionist Party of Northern Ireland** (UPNI). The **election** to the **Northern Ireland Forum** in the midst of the **peace process** saw the formation of the United Kingdom Unionist Party (UKUP) and the **Northern Ireland Women's Coalition** (NIWC), and the peace process encouraged a temporary increase in support for the **Progressive Unionist Party** (PUP) and **Ulster Democratic Party** (UDP). Disillusionment with the implementation of the **Good Friday Agreement** (GFA) after 1998, however, saw many of these parties go into decline or vanish completely. Only the UUP, the party of government from 1921 to 1972, remained largely intact during the course of the Troubles, though **unionist** opposition to the GFA saw the party reduced to become only the third largest in Northern Ireland by late 2003.

**POPULATION.** *See* CENSUS.

**POWELL, ENOCH (1912–98). Conservative** and **Ulster Unionist Party** (UUP) politician, Enoch Powell, the son of a schoolmaster, was born in Birmingham on 16 June 1912. One of the most controversial politicians of his generation, he won a scholarship to King Edward's School, Birmingham, and another to Trinity College, Cambridge. He graduated with first class honors in classics and seemed destined for a distinguished academic career after becoming a fellow of Trinity College at the age of 22. In the winter of 1938, still only 25, he became professor of Greek at the University of Sydney.

On the outbreak of World War II, however, Powell immediately returned to England and joined the **British Army**. Throughout the war Powell was largely restricted, against his wishes, to planning and intelligence roles. He attended the Casablanca Conference in 1943 and subsequently believed that the **United States'** main war aim was to destroy British imperial power. After serving for nearly three years in India, he returned to England in 1946, having reached the rank of brigadier general. He joined the Conservative Party and served in the party's research department. Although shocked by the decision to concede independence to India in 1947, and previously a staunch imperialist, he then became strongly anti-imperialist, seeing no need for the empire after India became independent.

Powell contested, but lost, a by-**election** in a safe **Labour** seat but won the Wolverhampton Southwest seat in 1950. In 1952 he was offered a ministerial post in the home office but turned it down on the basis that he was only interested in working in a ministry with economic responsibilities. In 1955 he was appointed to the ministry of housing and, in January 1957, became financial secretary to the treasury. A year later he resigned when Prime Minister Harold Macmillan refused to back spending cuts. In 1960 he returned as minister for health, joining the cabinet in this position in 1962 but leaving office in 1963 when Alec Douglas-Home became prime minister. He was also an early Conservative proponent of the liberal economic theories that would later influence **Margaret Thatcher**.

In opposition he was spokesman on transport and was unsuccessful in his challenge for the party leadership in 1965. He accepted the post of opposition spokesman on defense under **Edward Heath** but caused alarm with speeches advocating a reduced defense role for Great Britain. In April 1968 he caused outrage when he warned that unrestricted immigration to Britain could lead to widespread violence. Heath decided the tone of the speech was racist and fired Powell the next day. While the general public gave Powell support, he was attacked by the left wing and by the media.

After 1968 Powell was an increasingly regular visitor to Northern Ireland, supporting the **unionists'** right to remain within the United Kingdom and strongly opposing the introduction of **direct rule** in 1972. After the United Kingdom's entry into the European Economic Community (EEC) and a change in the government's economic policy, Powell's opposition to Heath turned to outright rebellion. He refused to stand as a Conservative candidate in February 1974 but was approached by the UUP to stand in South Down in the **Westminster** general election held in November of the same year. He subsequently won the South Down seat and retained it for 13 years.

During the late 1970s, Powell encouraged his UUP colleagues to support the minority Labour government at key moments. This in turn led the government to agree to increase the number of Northern Ireland seats in the House of Commons. The return of a Conservative government with a clear majority in 1979, however, meant that the

UUP no longer held the balance of power. Initially cool toward Margaret Thatcher, he strongly supported her campaign to retake the Falkland Islands after the Argentinean invasion in 1982 and subsequently had regular meetings with the prime minister. However, Powell's connection with Thatcher also led him, and by extension the UUP, to underestimate the planned extent of the **Anglo–Irish Agreement** (AIA).

Powell retained his seat in the January 1986 by-elections held by unionist Members of Parliament (MP) as a protest of the AIA, but a growth in the Catholic electorate within the constituency saw him lose the seat to the **Social Democratic and Labour Party** (SDLP) in 1987. Throughout this period he was a strong proponent of full legal and administrative **integration** of Northern Ireland within the United Kingdom, dividing the UUP on the issue of **devolution**.

After losing his seat in 1987, Powell rejected the offer of a life peerage but continued to produce academic work and to speak publicly into the 1990s. He was diagnosed with Parkinson's disease in 1994 and died on 8 February 1998.

**POWER SHARING.** The popular name for the **consociational** form of government advocated by the U.K. government since 1972 as the model for a Northern Ireland executive. The consociational model in Northern Ireland requires that **elected** representatives from the major communities within a divided society be represented in the governing executive in proportion to their electoral strength. The first formal statement of this policy by the British government came in October 1972 in a discussion paper, *The Future of Northern Ireland.* While this has remained the objective of the British government since then, and subsequently also of the Irish government, the practical difficulty has been in reconciling the constitutional objectives of **nationalist** and **unionist** representatives within such a framework. The 1973–74 **Northern Ireland Assembly**, 1982–86 Assembly, the post-1998 Assembly, and the **Anglo–Irish Agreement** (AIA) all envisioned a power-sharing executive for Northern Ireland; however, all of these initiatives had at best only partial success.

**PRIOR, JAMES (1927– ). Conservative Party** politician and secretary of state for Northern Ireland, James Prior was born on 11 October 1927 and educated at Charterhouse School and Pembroke College, Cambridge. He held a commission in the Royal Norfolk Regiment in 1946 and served in India and West Germany. He was **elected** to the House of Commons for the constituency of Lowestoft in 1959 and remained a member of the House until 1987.

Prior held a number of junior government posts before becoming minister of agriculture in 1972 and subsequently leader of the House of Commons from 1972 to 1974. In opposition he was Conservative spokesman on employment and, when the Conservatives returned to power in 1979, was secretary of state for employment under **Margaret Thatcher** (1979–81), though his political views soon put him in conflict with her. In September 1981 he became secretary of state for Northern Ireland, but his apparent reluctance to accept the post did much to create the widely held view that the post was one given to politicians out of favor with the prime minister. It is also debatable whether Prior ever won over public opinion in Northern Ireland, given his widely reported reluctance to come to the **province**. He left the cabinet in 1984 and received a life peerage in 1987, becoming Lord Prior of Brampton.

Prior's main achievement in Northern Ireland was helping to bring about a resolution to the ongoing **republican hunger strike**. In this he was aided by the fact that he was a new, apparently more pragmatic, face in the post and also by the fact that the protest appeared to be running out of steam. Notably, Prior visited the **Maze Prison** on his first day in Northern Ireland as secretary of state. The aftermath of the hunger strike was, however, to witness an upsurge in republican **paramilitary** activity. In November 1981, when the **Ulster Unionist Party** (UUP) Member of Parliament (MP) Rev. Robert Bradford was murdered by the **Irish Republican Army** (IRA), Prior received a hostile reception from members of the congregation when he attended the funeral service.

Despite the inauspicious omens provided by the security situation, Prior decided to press ahead with a political initiative. Prior's plan for a new **Northern Ireland Assembly** centered on the idea of **rolling devolution** had few enthusiasts in government and was hampered by unfavorable circumstances within Northern Ireland. In the wake of the hunger strike, both **nationalists** and republicans boycotted the Northern Ireland Assembly, while the UUP was also less than committed to the new Assembly. Indeed, more attention was focused on the fact that Provisional **Sinn Fein** (PSF) contested the elections to the Assembly, held in October 1982, than on the powers of the body itself. On his retirement from active politics, Prior concentrated on his business interests, but as late as January 1992, he was the target of an IRA bomb that was placed at a block of flats where he lived in London.

**PROGRESSIVE UNIONIST PARTY (PUP).** The political party associated with the **Ulster Volunteer Force** (UVF). It was established by **Belfast** city councilor Hugh Smyth in 1978 as the Independent Unionist Group before assuming the name of PUP in 1979. Smyth, who was elected to both the 1973 **Northern Ireland Assembly** and to the **Constitutional Convention**, in 1994 became the first PUP member to hold the office of lord mayor of Belfast. His term of office coincided with the declarations of both the **Irish Republican Army** (IRA) and **Combined Loyalist Military Command** (CLMC) ceasefires, the latter announced by PUP member **Gusty Spence**. The party's chief spokespersons increasingly came to be **David Ervine** and Billy Hutchinson, both former UVF prisoners and perceived as effective public speakers and political negotiators.

In the 1996 **Northern Ireland Forum elections**, they won 3.5 percent of the vote and were the seventh largest party. In the period leading up the **Good Friday Agreement** (GFA), they were strongly in favor of reaching a settlement and were very critical of anti-GFA **unionists** in the wake of its signing. In the 1998 Northern Ireland Assembly election, they won 2.6 percent of first-preference votes and took two seats. The following year Ervine was fifth in the European Parliament election, finishing ahead of **Robert McCartney** and Sean Neeson of the **Alliance Party of Northern Ireland** (APNI). As unionist disillusionment with the GFA began to grow, however, the party's electoral fortunes also went into decline. Support for the PUP was also undermined by continuing UVF activity, not least the intermittent **loyalist** feuds with the **Ulster Defence Association** (UDA) and **Loyalist Volunteer Force** (LVF). In July 2001 the party withdrew from the **Weston Park Talks** on the grounds that **republicans** had refused to set terms for **decommissioning**.

In the next significant electoral test, the 2003 Assembly elections the PUP polled only 1.2 percent of first-preference votes and retained only one seat, that of new party leader David Ervine. In 2005 the party discussed ending its relationship with the UVF but rejected this option. In 2006 Ervine attempted to form an alliance with the **Ulster Unionist Party** (UUP) in the Northern Ireland Assembly, but this was overruled by the speaker. In March 2006 PUP chairperson Dawn Purvis was appointed as an independent member of the Policing Board. In January 2007 the party suffered a significant loss with the sudden death of Ervine. Later in the same month, Dawn Purvis was elected as the new party leader.

In the March 2007 Northern Ireland Assembly election, the party received 0.6 percent of first-preference votes; however, Purvis retained the Assembly seat formerly held by Ervine.

**PROPORTIONAL REPRESENTATION (PR).** The single transferable vote (STV) system of PR is used in **Northern Ireland Assembly**, **district council**, and European Parliament **elections** in Northern Ireland. Electors vote for individual candidates, ranking them in order of preference. After first-preference votes have been counted, a quota for election is established, and a process of election or elimination of candidates is then conducted until all the seats in the constituency have been filled.

PR was reintroduced to Northern Ireland elections in 1973 on the basis that it was more proportionate (and therefore more fair) than the "first past the post" (plurality) system used for **Westminster** elections. The introduction of PR was also intended to break up the **unionist** and **nationalist** voting blocs and provide electoral opportunities for smaller parties. Although the British government believed that introducing PR would benefit moderate parties, in practice it has also helped smaller extremist parties win political representation. While PR was initially met with some skepticism, particularly from unionist parties, the system has become almost universally accepted as an equitable way of conducting elections.

**PROVINCE.** A term used to describe one of the traditional four provinces of the island of Ireland: Ulster, Munster, Leinster, and Connacht. In the context of Northern Ireland politics, the term can have a particular subtext in that while **unionists** may refer to the **six counties** of Northern Ireland as the "Province," **nationalists** may use the same term for the traditional nine counties of Ulster—the six counties of Northern Ireland as well as Cavan, Monaghan, and Donegal.

**PROVISIONAL IRISH REPUBLICAN ARMY (PIRA).** *See* IRISH REPUBLICAN ARMY (IRA).

**PROVISIONAL SINN FEIN (PSF).** *See* SINN FEIN (SF).

**PUNISHMENT BEATINGS.** The phrase used to describe physical attacks by **paramilitary** groups on individuals who are judged by the paramilitaries to have taken part in antisocial behavior, such as theft or the stealing and driving of cars ("joy riding"). Paramilitary groups have often excused such attacks by claiming that they have been demanded as a form of retribution by local communities. However, the use of punishment attacks also serves to reinforce paramilitary groups' control of certain areas.

In the wake of the 1994 ceasefires, there was a decrease in the number of punishment shootings, such as "knee capping" by paramilitary organizations, but a massive increase in the number of beatings carried out by these groups. Since 1998 a significant majority of all punishment attacks have been conducted by **loyalist** as opposed to **republican** groups. In 2005, however, there were still 85 punishment shootings, 74 by loyalist groups, and 89 punishment beatings, 60 by loyalist groups. In September 2006 an 18-year-old teenager had a leg amputated following a punishment shooting in the Falls area of **Belfast**. He had been beaten with hammers in an earlier attack. In 2006, as a whole, the number of attacks fell to approximately half of the 2005 figure.

**PYM, FRANCIS (1922– ). Conservative Party** politician and Northern Ireland secretary of state, Francis Pym was born in Abergavenny, Wales, on 13 February 1922. He was educated at Eton and Magdalene College, Cambridge. He served with the **British Army** during World War II, winning the military cross and bar. A businessman and landowner, he became a member of Herefordshire County Council but failed to win the Rhondda West seat in 1959 before being **elected** for Cambridgeshire in a 1961 by-election. The son of a Conservative

Member of Parliament (MP), he was MP for Cambridgeshire and later Cambridgeshire Southeast until 1987.

Conservative Party chief whip under **Edward Heath** from 1970, Pym became Northern Ireland's shortest serving secretary of state in December 1973, when **William Whitelaw** was recalled to London by Heath to deal with a coalminers' strike. During the three months in which he was secretary of state, he participated in the **Sunningdale** Conference but saw **unionist** support for the deal quickly evaporate. He argued against a general election being called in February 1974, fearing, correctly, that the outcome would undermine the Northern Ireland executive. The result of the election was a clear victory for anti-Sunningdale unionists but also sent the Conservatives into opposition.

Under **Margaret Thatcher** Pym was agriculture minister, secretary of state for defense (1979–81), leader of the House of Commons, lord president of the council (1981–82), and foreign secretary (1982–83). In 1982 he was one of the few enthusiastic supporters of **James Prior**'s plan for **rolling devolution** in Northern Ireland. His reluctance to pursue the Falklands War outside the exclusion zone alienated him from Thatcher, and he was replaced in 1983. In 1987 he retired from the House of Commons and was awarded a life peerage, becoming Lord Pym of Sandy in the County of Bedfordshire.

# – R –

**REAL IRISH REPUBLICAN ARMY (RIRA).** The RIRA emerged in the period leading up to the signing of the **Good Friday Agreement** (GFA) of 1998. It consisted of **republican** activists, mainly from the **Irish Republican Army** (IRA) in south Armagh, who had become disaffected with the mainstream republican movement because of the involvement of **Sinn Fein** (SF) in the **peace process**. The organization's alleged leader was Michael McKevitt, who was jailed on charges of directing terrorism in August 2003. The organization was responsible for the **Omagh bomb** of August 1998, which killed 29 people. The RIRA announced a ceasefire in the aftermath of the Omagh bomb but carried out a number of bomb attacks in England in 2001. Since then a number of sporadic attacks have been carried out by the RIRA within Northern Ireland, though these have had limited political impact. Although the RIRA, which is estimated to have less than 150 members, is reputed to be the military wing of the **Thirty-two County Sovereignty Movement**, the movement does not accept this assertion. In October 2006 the **Garda Siochana** found explosives belonging to the RIRA that they believed were to be used to increase political tension in the lead-up to the November deadline for a return to **devolution** in Northern Ireland. Three firebomb attacks on shops in **Belfast** were also claimed by the RIRA.

**REES, MERLYN (1920–2006).** **Labour Party** politician and secretary of state for Northern Ireland, Merlyn Rees was born in Cilfynydd, Wales, on 18 December 1920. Descended from a long line of coalminers, he was educated at Harrow Weald Grammar School, Middlesex; Goldsmiths' College, London; London School of Economics; and London University. After 1941 he served in the Royal Air Force, mostly in southern Italy as a spitfire pilot, leaving the service as a squadron leader in 1946.

Between 1949 and 1960, Rees was a teacher at Harrow Weald School and later taught economics at Luton College of Technology (1962–63). On three occasions in the 1950s, he failed to win a seat in the House of Commons, but he was well known and liked within the Labour Party. In 1963 he contested and won Leeds South, the constituency formerly held by Labour leader Hugh Gaitskell who had died unexpectedly. In Parliament he was associated with **James Callaghan** and was viewed as being on the moderate wing of the party. He was a junior minister in defense (1965–68) and the home office (1968–70) before Labour lost power in the 1970 general election. In 1972 he was appointed opposition spokesman on Northern Ireland.

Rees arrived in Northern Ireland as secretary of state in March 1974 amid gathering **unionist** opposition to the **Sunningdale** Agreement. Rees initially underestimated the significance of the **Ulster Workers' Council (UWC) strike** when it was called on 14 May 1974, and the government's response proved too late to defeat the **loyalist** stoppage. Rees was subsequently criticized by supporters of Sunningdale for this perceived failure on his part.

In July 1974 Rees launched a fresh political initiative, proposing an elected **Constitutional Convention** for Northern Ireland politicians to develop their own structures for Northern Ireland. Although the Constitutional Convention (May 1975–March 1976) failed to reach an accommodation between unionists and **nationalists**, the idea of a voluntary coalition briefly provided a possible area of agreement, and this concept would continue to reappear in subsequent years.

Renewed government contacts with the Provisional **Irish Republican Army** (PIRA) led to them calling a ceasefire in February 1975. However, **the Truce** was based on a fundamental misconception by **republicans** of the British government's intentions and, when added to continuing loyalist and republican **paramilitary** activity, saw the eventual corrosion of the Truce. In November 1975 Rees ordered the closure of the incident centers intended to monitor the ceasefire.

Rees's term as secretary of state saw significant developments in security. He began the policy of "Ulsterization" and "police primacy," which promoted Northern Ireland–raised forces on the forefront of the campaign against terrorism. He also ended **special category status** in November 1975 and **internment** the following month, although this would also have long-term effects in sowing the seeds for future republican **hunger strikes**.

In September 1976, when Callaghan became prime minister, Rees was appointed home secretary and held the position until the 1979 general election. During this period he set up the Commission on Criminal Procedure, which provided the foundation for recording police interviews and the improved surveillance of police prosecution and conduct. After Labour lost power in 1979, he was opposition spokesman on energy but returned to the backbenches in 1983. He retired from the Commons in 1992 and received a life peerage in the same year, taking the title Lord Merlyn-Rees of Morley and South Leeds and of Cilfynydd. He remained an active member of the House of Lords and retained an interest in Northern Ireland affairs until his death on 5 January 2006.

**REID, JOHN (1947– ).** **Labour Party** politician and secretary of state for Northern Ireland, John Reid was born on 8 May 1947 and was educated at St. Patrick's Senior Secondary School, Coatbridge, and

Stirling University. He later received a DPhil in economic history. Reid was a researcher for the Labour Party in Scotland (1979–83) and an advisor to Labour Party leader Neil Kinnock (1983–85) before becoming Scottish organizer for the Trades Union Congress (1985–87). In 1987 he won the Motherwell North constituency in the House of Commons and became an opposition spokesman, first on children and then on the armed forces. When Labour returned to power in 1997, he became a junior minister in defense, minister for sport in 1998 and 1999, and secretary of state for Scotland before becoming Northern Ireland secretary in January 2001 in succession to **Peter Mandelson.**

Reid's time in Northern Ireland was characterized by a crisis in support for the **Good Friday Agreement** (GFA), particularly within the **unionist** community. By the summer of 2001, **Ulster Unionist Party** (UUP) members were threatening to resign from the Northern Ireland executive because of the failure of the **Irish Republican Army** (IRA) to **decommission** weapons. Political negotiations at **Weston Park** in England failed to break the deadlock, and on 10 August 2001, Reid announced a 24-hour suspension of the **Northern Ireland Assembly**, which permitted a further six weeks of negotiation before Reid would be legally obliged to call new **elections** to the Assembly. The fear in British and Irish government circles was that these elections would strengthen the positions of the **Democratic Unionist Party** (DUP) and **Sinn Fein** (SF), making a return to **devolution** more difficult.

The discussions that followed the first suspension failed to make progress and, on 21 September 2001, Reid was forced to make a second 24-hour suspension of the Assembly. Events and the change in public opinion in the **United States** in the aftermath of the attacks of 11 September 2001, however, also had an impact in Northern Ireland, with **republicans** facing renewed pressure to begin decommissioning their weapons.

Although progress began on decommissioning, both unionists and **nationalists** continued to look as each other as begrudging supporters of the **peace process**. In the spring of 2002, the UUP again threatened to resign from the executive if republicans did not complete decommissioning. This crisis was, however, preempted by the emergence of the **Stormontgate** affair. On 14 October 2002, Reid suspended the devolved institutions, his last major decision in Northern Ireland, before assuming the role of Labour Party chairman later that month. Reid's career continued to develop after leaving Northern Ireland. He became leader of the House of Commons in 2003 and health secretary later that same year. In May 2005 he was appointed home secretary. In June 2007 he left the cabinet after **Gordon Brown** became prime minister.

**REPUBLIC OF IRELAND.** After Ireland was partitioned in 1921, the 26 southern counties formed the Irish Free State, while the six Northeastern counties became **Northern Ireland**. In 1937, under **Fianna Fail** (FF), a new constitution effectively made the state a republic, although it was not officially declared so until 1948. Until 1998 the Irish constitution required Irish governments to work toward achieving a united Ireland; however, no sustained effort was made in this regard. In practice the main thrust of Irish government policy toward Northern Ireland was to protect the Catholic minority in the North. During the heated period of the early years of **the Troubles**, in particular, what action this might entail was open to interpretation, as the **arms crisis** highlighted. While **nationalists** felt that successive Irish governments did not do enough to support Catholics in Northern Ireland, **unionists** believed that the Republic of Ireland was unduly lenient on **republican paramilitaries**, particularly on issues such as **internment** and **extradition**. In January 2007, for the first time, the Irish government allocated £800 million over a six-year period from the Republic's budget toward the cost of infrastructure improvements in Northern Ireland.

The population of the Republic of Ireland grew from just under 3 million in 1971 to 4.2 million in 2006.

**REPUBLICAN.** The term used to refer to an individual or group supporting the objective of a united, independent Irish Republic. Most republicans also support the view that this should be a socialist and unitary state. The term is often applied to those prepared to use violence to achieve this objective. The name "republican movement" is often used when referring to both the political and **paramilitary** wings of the mainstream republican community, that is, **Sinn Fein** (SF) and the **Irish Republican Army** (IRA).

**REPUBLICAN SINN FEIN (RSF).** The breakaway organization that emerged in 1986 after a **Sinn Fein** (SF) ard fheis voted to end its abstention from the **Dail**. The leading figures in RSF were veteran Southern activists **Ruairi O Bradaigh** and Daithi O Conaill. It opposed the **peace process** and supported the traditional **republican** objectives of achieving a British withdrawal from Northern Ireland by the use of force and establishing an all-Ireland socialist republic. RSF denies having a **paramilitary** wing but is alleged to have links with the **Continuity Irish Republican Army** (CIRA), which became active in 1996. RSF opposed the **Good Friday Agreement** (GFA) in 1998 and has continued to be critical of the peace process, particularly SF's role in it.

**REYNOLDS, ALBERT (1932– ). Fianna Fail** (FF) leader and taoiseach, Albert Reynolds was born in Rooskey, Co. Roscommon, on 3 November 1932. He was educated at Summerhill College, Sligo, but left school at an early age and developed a career as an independent businessman. Reynolds was **elected** to Longford County Council in 1974 as a member of FF and, three years later, was elected to the **Dail**. He became a close political ally of **Charles Haughey**, and when Haughey became taoiseach in 1979, Reynolds was appointed as minister for posts and telegraphs (1979–81). He had a brief period as minister for industry and energy in 1982; however, FF then went out of office. When they returned to power in 1987, Reynolds was appointed minister for industry and commerce (1987–88) and then minister for finance (1988–91). In November 1991 he was fired from the cabinet after he supported a leadership challenge against Haughey. In early 1992 Haughey was forced to resign as taoiseach and leader of FF, and Reynolds was elected as his replacement by the party.

As taoiseach Reynolds was constrained by the fact that he headed a coalition government with the Progressive Democrats (PD). The coalition collapsed in late 1992, but a general election failed to give FF an overall majority, and Reynolds returned in January 1993 at the head of another coalition, this time with the **Irish Labour Party**. Although Reynolds' term as taoiseach was comparatively short, it coincided with an important period in the Northern Ireland **peace process**.

Reynolds developed a good working relationship with Prime Minister **John Major**, which was important to developments in Northern

Ireland, and was also able to develop contacts with **John Hume** and **Gerry Adams** as the Hume–Adams talks progressed. As part of the effort to end **paramilitary** violence, he also began secret discussions between the Irish government and both **loyalist** and **republican** paramilitary groups. Further negotiations with the British government led to the **Downing Street Declaration** in December 1993. Reynolds was subsequently more amenable to the idea of providing "clarification" of the meaning of the declaration to republicans than the British government.

In private he continued to work with others to try to secure an **Irish Republican Army** (IRA) ceasefire, which he welcomed when it came in August 1994. In an effort to tie in the republican movement more strongly to the peace process, he sought to involve **Sinn Fein** (SF) in the **Forum for Peace and Reconciliation**, which met for the first time on 28 October 1994. In November 1994, however, his choice for the position of president of the high court caused a rift with his Labour Party coalition partners, leading Reynolds to resign as taoiseach. He continued to comment on the developing peace process in the following years but retired from the Dail at the 2002 general election.

**ROBINSON, MARY (1944– ).** Lawyer, politician, and president of Ireland, Mary Robinson was born in Ballina, Co. Mayo, on 21 May 1944. She was educated at Trinity College, Dublin, and Harvard University. Robinson won an international reputation as an expert in the field of human rights. A strong proponent of women's rights, she campaigned for the liberalization of Ireland's laws, which prohibited divorce and abortion. She was appointed professor of criminal law in Trinity College, Dublin, when she was 25 years old. In 1969 she won a seat in the Irish Senate as a representative of the University of Dublin and held the seat until 1989.

Campaigning as a member of the **Irish Labour Party**, she twice failed to be **elected** to the **Dail** but was surprisingly elected as an independent candidate to the presidency in 1990 after the favorite, Brian Lenihan of **Fianna Fail** (FF), was fired as tainaiste by **Charles Haughey** following charges of corruption.

Robinson's election is viewed as a turning point in Irish politics. She was the first woman to hold the office, and her outward-looking, liberal views matched a rapidly changing Irish society that was entering the economic boom era of the "Celtic tiger." Her election to the role of president also coincided with a developing **peace process** in Northern Ireland. In addition she was well placed to help improve relations with **unionists** in the North; her husband was a Protestant, and she had resigned from the Irish Labour Party in a protest against the **Anglo–Irish Agreement** (AIA).

Although she was constrained by her role as guardian of the Irish constitution, unionists were cautious of the Irish president playing too large a role in Northern affairs, but she was able to play a part in improving North–South relations. In May 1993 she met the Queen at Buckingham Palace, the first meeting between the British and Irish heads of state but, a month later, was strongly criticized by unionists after she met **Gerry Adams** in West **Belfast**. This, however, was part of a careful balancing act aimed at preventing any group from feeling alienated, and she met a wide range of political and religious groups to this end.

Robinson also continued to take a number of important symbolic actions. In June 1996, for example, she became the first Irish head of state to make an official visit to Great Britain. In September 1997 she resigned as president to take up the post of United Nations High Commissioner for Human Rights. In 2006 she was president of the organization Realizing Rights: The Ethical Globalization Initiative.

**ROBINSON, PETER (1948– ). Democratic Unionist Party** (DUP) politician, Peter Robinson was born in **Belfast** on 29 December 1948. He was educated at Annadale Grammar School, Belfast, and Castlereagh College of Further Education. He began work as an estate agent but soon joined the DUP and worked as the party's full-time general secretary from 1975 until 1979.

He failed to win a seat in East Belfast in the 1975 **Constitutional Convention election** but in 1977 was elected to Castlereagh Borough Council, a council area that covered the southeastern suburbs of Belfast. In the 1979 **Westminster** general election, he organized an astute campaign that saw him win the East Belfast seat from **William Craig** by 64 votes, however he subsequently made the constituency a safe DUP seat.

Robinson was appointed deputy leader of the DUP in 1979 and, although he became one of the most recognized Northern Ireland politicians, inevitably remained in the shadow of the charismatic **Ian Paisley**. In 1982 he was elected to the **Northern Ireland Assembly**, but the latter part of the Assembly's life was dominated by **unionist** opposition to the **Anglo–Irish Agreement** (AIA). In 1986 he retained his seat in the Westminster by-elections brought about by the resignation of unionist Members of Parliament (MP) in protest against the AIA. In August 1986 Robinson was arrested in the village of Clontibret, Co. Monaghan, when he and several hundred **loyalists** "invaded" the village in the Republic as a protest against the AIA. In a court in Drogheda, he subsequently pleaded guilty to unlawful assembly and was fined Irish £15,000. His refusal to pay the fines imposed by courts in Northern Ireland resulting from protests against the AIA also led to his imprisonment in Northern Ireland for short periods of time. At one point in 1988, both he and his wife Iris (elected as the DUP MP for Strangford in 2001) were imprisoned at the same time.

Robinson was coauthor of a report outlining a way forward for unionist politics in 1987 and resigned as deputy leader for three months, apparently because no action was taken on the report. In 1988 he participated in the **Duisburg Talks**. He was part of the DUP's delegation in the **Brooke–Mayhew Talks** and strongly supported the objective of **devolution** for Northern Ireland, though only under certain conditions. He was critical of the **Downing Street Declaration** in 1993 and skeptical of the **Irish Republican Army** (IRA) ceasefire in 1994. In 1996 he was elected to the **Northern Ireland Forum** for East Belfast and participated in the early part of the subsequent talks process but withdrew with his party colleagues in July 1997 when **Sinn Fein** (SF) entered negotiations.

Robinson was critical of the **Good Friday Agreement** (GFA) and helped orchestrate his party's campaign to capitalize on unionist disillusionment with the implementation of the GFA. He was elected to the Northern Ireland Assembly from East Belfast in 1998 and again in 2003 and 2007. During the course of the 1998 Assembly, the DUP followed a policy of rotating members as ministers. He served as minister for regional development in the periods from December 1999 to

July 2000 and November 2001 to October 2002. Robinson is viewed as the most likely successor to Ian Paisley for the role of DUP party leader. In April 2007 it was announced that he was to be the minister responsible for finance and personnel in the incoming executive.

**ROLLING DEVOLUTION.** A scheme proposed in the government policy document of April 1982, *Northern Ireland: A Framework for Devolution*, which proposed that a 78-member **Northern Ireland Assembly** should be elected with the task of reaching agreement on how **devolved** powers should be exercised. If 70.0 percent of Northern Ireland Assembly members could reach agreement, necessitating support from both **unionists** and **nationalists**, then powers would be devolved at the discretion of the secretary of state. Control of local functions, such as health and education, could be devolved on a department-by-department basis, provided there was agreement within the Assembly. The scheme thus acquired the name of "rolling devolution." In the aftermath off the 1981 **hunger strike**, however, with **Social Democratic and Labour Party** (SDLP) and **Sinn Fein** (SF) boycotts of the Assembly, cross-community agreement on the devolution of powers was not possible, and the plan for rolling devolution failed to develop.

**ROYAL IRISH REGIMENT (RIR).** The **British Army** regiment that came into existence with the merging of the **Ulster Defence Regiment** (UDR) and the Royal Irish Rangers in July 1992. The merging of the two regiments was presented by the ministry of defense as part of an overall reduction in the size of the British Army following the end of the cold war. At the time the two bodies merged, the UDR had a strength of 6,000, and members continued to serve in home service (or resident service) battalions. The two former Royal Irish Ranger battalions were reduced to one general service battalion that served both in Northern Ireland and abroad. The first member of the new regiment to be killed was an off-duty sergeant who was shot dead by the **Irish Republican Army** (IRA) in October 1992.

Following the IRA's end to its campaign in July 2005, it was announced that the resident service battalions, numbering 3,000, were to be disbanded in August 2007. September 2006 saw the end of the deployment of RIR soldiers on the streets of Northern Ireland. In October 2006 it was announced that 70 soldiers had transferred from the resident service to the general service battalion of the RIR. On 6 October 2006, Queen Elizabeth awarded the regiment the conspicuous gallantry cross. The home service battalions were disbanded with the end of the British Army's Operation Banner (supporting the police in Northern Ireland) at the end of July 2007.

**ROYAL ULSTER CONSTABULARY (RUC).** The police force of Northern Ireland that was established in 1922. The RUC initially had a significant Catholic membership, but as former Catholic members of the Royal Irish Constabulary who had transferred to the RUC retired, their numbers were not replaced, and the force was increasingly made up of members of the Protestant community.

During the **Irish Republican Army** (IRA) border campaign of 1956–62, seven members of the RUC were killed, but the force faced a much more difficult challenge after 1968. In July 1969 the first **deaths** of **the Troubles** occurred after two Catholic men, Francis McCloskey and Samuel Devenney, were beaten by members of the RUC in separate incidents. In August 1969, at the outbreak of serious intercommunal violence, the RUC was undermanned and underresourced, having a strength of just over 3,000. By 1991 this would have increased to 8,500 members, with a full-time reserve of 3,000 and a part-time reserve of 1,500.

Following the **Battle of the Bogside** and the outbreak of sectarian rioting in **Belfast** in August 1969, the **British Army** was called in to support the RUC; they would continue this role until 2007. In the wake of the **Hunt Report**, the RUC was disarmed, but in the face of the killing of police officers by **paramilitary** groups, this decision was soon reversed. Although the vast majority of RUC officers killed during the Troubles were killed by **republicans**, the first RUC member to die, Constable Victor Arbuckle, was shot dead by the **Ulster Volunteer Force** (UVF) in October 1969 during protest riots by **loyalists** against the Hunt Report.

Following the introduction of **direct rule** in 1972, the **Northern Ireland Office** (NIO) assumed responsibility for the RUC. From the mid-1970s, the government pursued a policy of "Ulsterization" and "police primacy," which saw the RUC expanded to take over many of the duties previously undertaken by the army.

In 1982 the shooting deaths of a number of republicans by members of the RUC raised questions of whether a **"shoot to kill"** policy was being undertaken as well as the accountability of the force. Further questions emerged as a result of the Stalker Inquiry. In February 1985 nine RUC officers were killed as the result of an IRA mortar bomb attack on a police station in Newry, Co. Down, bringing the greatest number of police casualties in one incident.

In the wake of the **Anglo-Irish Agreement** (AIA), the RUC came into direct conflict with a significant section of the **unionist** community. At the same time, RUC members and their homes were attacked by loyalists, forcing more than 150 families to move from their houses. In the 1990s the force faced controversy on the issue of **collusion** with loyalist paramilitaries and was at the center of controversy associated with the **Drumcree parade** after 1995.

In the wake of the **Good Friday Agreement** (GFA), the **Patten Report** recommended significant changes to policing in Northern Ireland. The change of name and badge became a source of heated debate between **nationalists** and unionists. In November 2001 the RUC was replaced by the **Police Service of Northern Ireland** (PSNI).

During the course of the Troubles, 303 RUC officers were killed and more then 9,000 injured. Nearly 280 of these officers were killed by the Provisional IRA (PIRA). The RUC was responsible for an estimated 51 deaths. In 1999 the Queen awarded the George Cross medal to the organization.

## – S –

**SANDS, ROBERT (BOBBY) (1954–81).** Bobby Sands was born in **Belfast** on 9 March 1954. His family lived in the Rathcoole estate on the northern outskirts of Belfast. Initially the estate housed both Protestant and Catholic families, but after the outbreak of **the Troubles**, the estate became increasingly Protestant and **loyalist**, and the Sands family was forced to move to the Catholic Twinbrook estate in West Belfast in 1972.

Sands joined the **Irish Republican Army** (IRA) and was arrested in 1973 for firearms offenses, for which he served five years in the **Maze Prison**. He was released in 1976 but rearrested for possession of weapons in 1977 and subsequently sentenced to a further 14 years imprisonment. By this time the campaign to regain **special category status** for prisoners was underway. During the 1980 **hunger strike**, he became leader of IRA prisoners in the H blocks, and when it emerged that this campaign had ended without special category status having been conceded by the government, Sands launched another hunger strike campaign on 1 March 1981.

During the course of Sands's hunger strike, the sitting Member of Parliament (MP) for Fermanagh-South Tyrone died, leading to a by-**election**. In a straight contest against **Ulster Unionist Party** (UUP) leader **Harry West** on 9 April 1981, Sands won 30,492 votes to 29,046 on a turnout of nearly 87.0 percent. The result provided the H block campaign with enormous publicity and encouraged some leaders within the **republican** movement to support the idea of greater involvement in party politics. However, the result also did further damage to relations between Protestants and Catholics, as **unionists** viewed the result as widespread **nationalist** support for terrorism over democracy. Despite appeals from politicians and clergymen, Sands continued his hunger strike and died on 5 May 1981 on the 66th day of his fast. More than 100,000 people attended his funeral.

**SHANKILL BOMB.** On 23 October 1993, 10 people, including 1 who planted the bomb, were killed and 58 others were injured when an **Irish Republican Army** (IRA) bomb exploded at a fish shop on Shankill Road in **Belfast**. The IRA claimed (inaccurately) that they had targeted the shop because the **Ulster Freedom Fighters**' (UFF) leadership was holding a meeting in a room above the shop. **Sinn Fein** (SF) president **Gerry Adams** faced widespread criticism when he carried the coffin of IRA bomber Thomas Begley several days later. The bombing was followed by a wave of sectarian murders by **loyalist paramilitaries** claiming retaliation for the Shankill bombing. This included the murder of seven people at the Rising Sun Bar in Greysteel, Co. Londonderry, on 30 October 1993. With 27 murders in the month, October 1993 saw the greatest number of **deaths** since October 1976.

In July 2000 Shankill bomber Sean Kelly was released under the terms of the **Good Friday Agreement** (GFA), but he was returned to jail in June 2005 after it was claimed that he had become reinvolved in terrorism. Kelly was again released on 28 July 2005 on the day the IRA ordered an end to its campaign. **Unionists** criticized Kelly's release as being a bribe for **republicans**.

**SHANKILL BUTCHERS.** A **loyalist** gang linked to the **Ulster Volunteer Force** (UVF) that operated in the Shankill area of **Belfast** in the 1970s. The most notorious of the murders committed by the gang included the abduction of seven Catholics and their murders with cleavers, axes, and butcher knives. In February 1979, 11 members of the gang were convicted of 19 murders. In October 1977 Lenny Murphy, the gang's leader, had been imprisoned for possession of firearms, but Murphy himself was never convicted of murder. Murphy was shot dead by the **Irish Republican Army** (IRA) in November 1982 shortly after he was released from prison. In June 1997 Robert Bates, another former member of the gang, was murdered in an internal loyalist dispute.

**"SHOOT TO KILL."** The name given to a policy allegedly pursued by the security forces in the early 1980s. The claims followed the killing of a number of **republican** activists in disputed circumstances. In November 1982 three **Irish Republican Army** (IRA) members were shot and killed by the **Royal Ulster Constabulary** (RUC) near Lurgan, Co. Armagh. The RUC claimed that they had driven through a police checkpoint. In the same month, one man was killed and another wounded by an RUC patrol observing a farmhouse near Craigavon, Co. Armagh. In December 1982 two **Irish National Liberation Army** (INLA) members were shot dead by the police at a checkpoint near Armagh city.

The incidents were investigated by Deputy Chief Constable John Stalker from Manchester. However, he was controversially removed from the investigation and replaced by Chief Constable Colin Sampson from West Yorkshire. In 1988 the then attorney general Sir **Patrick Mayhew** stated that there was evidence to pervert the course of justice but that police officers would not be prosecuted on the grounds of national security. A report from Staffordshire chief constable Charles Kelly led to disciplinary charges being made against 20 junior RUC officers, but there were no charges against senior officers. The controversy served to raise questions about some of the gray areas of security policy pursued by the state during the course of **the Troubles** without providing any clear answers. In July 2007 the government asked the police ombudsman for Northern Ireland to examine the Stalker files in response to concerns raised by the Council of Europe.

**SINN FEIN (SF).** The party founded in 1905 with the objective of achieving the political separation of Ireland from Great Britain. In the 1918 **Westminster** general **election**, SF (Irish for "we ourselves" or "ourselves alone") became the largest political party in Ireland. Following the Anglo–Irish Treaty of 1921, which ended the War of Independence, SF split into pro- and antitreaty factions, with the antitreaty forces retaining the SF name. A further split in the antitreaty side led to the formation of **Fianna Fail** (FF) in 1926. The remaining element of SF maintained a policy of refusing to recognize the legitimacy of the states in both the North and South of Ireland. In the 1960s the party became increasingly Marxist in outlook.

On 11 January 1970, a majority of delegates at an SF ard fheis (conference) voted to overturn the party's abstentionist policy and take seats in the London, Dublin, and **Belfast** Parliaments. Those in favor of ending abstention became known as Official Sinn Fein (OSF), and those who were opposed, Provisional Sinn Fein (PSF; the name reflected the phrase "provisional government of the Irish Republic" used by **republicans** in the Easter Rising of 1916). The associated **paramilitary** wings became known as the **Official Irish Republican Army** (OIRA) and Provisional **Irish Republican Army** (PIRA). A significant subtext in the split was the impact of **the Troubles**, with a large percentage of those supporting the PSF coming from the North, where the impact of sectarian conflict on the Catholic community provided a more pressing motivation than Marxist theory.

In 1977 OSF became known as SF: The **Workers' Party** (WP) in the **Republic of Ireland** and, following another name change in 1982, the WP. In Northern Ireland the party campaigned under the name Republican Clubs, becoming the WP: Republican Clubs in 1981 but also adopting the WP name in 1982. This change effectively left the SF name to the PSF wing, which was increasingly referred to merely as SF.

In the 1970s SF was largely viewed as an adjunct of the PIRA, but following the successes of **Bobby Sands** and Owen Carron in the Fermanagh-South Tyrone by-elections and the winning of two **Dail** seats by republican prisoners in 1981, the republican movement made a strategic decision to contest future elections throughout Ireland. The change in strategy was dramatically illustrated by leading Belfast republican Danny Morrison's speech at the 1981 ard fheis, when he stated, "Will anyone here object if, with a ballot paper in one hand and the Armalite in the other, we take power in Ireland?"

In 1982 the party contested the **Northern Ireland Assembly** election and won 10.1 percent of first-preference votes but failed to attract significant transfers from other parties and so won only five seats. In the 1983 Westminster general election, the party won 13.4 percent of votes cast, and **Gerry Adams** won the West Belfast seat. The election of Adams as party president in November indicated a swing in power from Southern republicans to the North. The advent of SF to electoral politics was also a significant factor in the creation of the **Anglo–Irish Agreement** (AIA), which was partly intended to bolster the electoral position of the **Social Democratic and Labour Party** (SDLP) against SF. The entry of SF councillors in significant numbers into **district councils** after 1985 also led to heated arguments with **unionists** in some council chambers, not least in Belfast.

In 1986 the party made another significant policy change by voting to end abstention from the Dail. This decision led those who were opposed to withdraw from the party and form **Republican Sinn Fein** (RSF). In the late 1980s and early 1990s, the party's electoral support remained at approximately 11.0 percent, with Gerry Adams losing the West Belfast Westminster seat to the SDLP in 1992. In 1987 the party launched a document titled *Scenario for Peace*, which, while presenting an essentially traditionally republican interpretation, also indicated that the party was open to negotiation. The developing **peace process**, in which SF played a central role, proved to be popular with **nationalist** voters at large, and the party began to capitalize on this factor, particularly after the IRA ceasefire of 1994. The higher profile of the party also led to them being targeted by **loyalist** paramilitaries, and a number of SF members were murdered by loyalists in the early 1990s.

In the 1996 **Northern Ireland Forum** election, SF won 15.5 percent of the vote. In the 1997 Westminster election, they increased their vote again, with Gerry Adams winning back West Belfast and **Martin McGuinness** winning the Mid-Ulster seat. Following the 1997 general election, a change in policy by the new **Labour** government allowed SF to enter all-party negotiations after the IRA renewed its ceasefire.

The party participated in the negotiations that led to the **Good Friday Agreement** (GFA), and in May 1998 a special ard fheis voted overwhelmingly to canvas for a *yes* vote on the GFA in the referendums in Northern Ireland and the Republic. The ard fheis also voted to allow party members elected to the Northern Ireland Assembly to take their seats. In the 1998 Northern Ireland Assembly election, it received 17.6 percent of first-preference votes and won 18 seats. In the Northern Ireland executive after 1999, the party held the education and health ministries.

Throughout the controversy surrounding the **decommissioning** of IRA weapons, SF maintained that it was a separate organization from the IRA and was not responsible for the IRA's actions. However, this was not an argument accepted by nonrepublicans. The success of the peace process from a nationalist perspective along with an efficient party organization saw continuing electoral gains for SF. In the 2001 Westminster general election, the party won four seats and 21.7 percent of the vote, overtaking the SDLP, which received 21.0 percent.

In the 2003 Northern Ireland Assembly elections, SF received 23.5 percent of first-preference votes and 24 seats, making it the largest nationalist party in the Assembly. In the 2004 European Parliament election, Bairbre de Brun was elected on the first count, effectively taking the seat from the SDLP. In the May 2005 district council elections, SF won 23.0 percent of first-preference votes and had 126 councillors elected. The 2005 Westminster general election held on the same day saw SF take 24.3 percent of the poll and win five seats. The 2005 results confirmed SF's position as the largest nationalist party and the second largest in Northern Ireland.

In March 2005 the U.S. government banned SF fund-raising activities in the **United States** in the wake of the Northern Bank robbery and murder of Belfast man Robert McCartney. The fund-raising ban was lifted in November 2005 after SF gave conditional approval to the **St. Andrews Agreement**. On 24 November 2005, the party nominated Martin McGuinness as deputy first minister in the Northern Ireland Assembly. In December 2006 a party delegation led by Gerry Adams met **Police Service of Northern Ireland** (PSNI) chief constable **Hugh Orde** to discuss policing issues. In January 2007, at a special ard fheis, 90.0 percent of those voting favored giving support to the PSNI following **devolution**.

In the March 2007 Northern Ireland Assembly election, the party received 26.2 percent of first-preference votes and won 28 seats. Later that month SF agreed to participate in a Northern Ireland executive. In April, in advance of devolution, the party selected the three departments of education (Catriona Ruane), regional development (Conor Murphy), and agriculture (Michelle Gildernew) for their prospective ministers. In the same month, a party delegation met the Policing Board for the first time.

**SIX COUNTIES.** A term used by **nationalists** and **republicans** to refer to the six counties of **Northern Ireland**. The use of the term has an important political subtext in that it denies the political legitimacy, and even existence of, Northern Ireland as a distinct political entity. In contrast **unionists** and British government sources are more likely to refer to Northern Ireland as the **Province**.

**SOCIAL DEMOCRATIC AND LABOUR PARTY (SDLP).** The SDLP was formed in August 1970 by a coalition of seven **Stormont** Members of Parliament (MP) from the **Nationalist Party** (NP), Republican Labour, **Northern Ireland Labour Party** (NILP) and independents associated with the civil rights campaign in Northern Ireland. The first leader of the SDLP was **Gerry Fitt**. The party sought to achieve a united Ireland by constitutional methods and on other policies was generally on the center-left. In 1972 the party's first major policy document, *Towards a New Ireland*, effectively advocated joint British–Irish authority over Northern Ireland pending reunification. The party also promoted a rent and rates strike, which had a significant impact within the Catholic community, after the introduction of **internment** in August 1971.

In the 1973 Assembly **election**, SDLP received 22.1 percent of first-preference votes and won 19 of the 78 seats. At the **Sunningdale**

Conference in December 1973, there were differences of emphasis on the importance of a strong **Irish dimension** at leadership level, and Fitt subsequently blamed those who supported a strong Irish dimension as part of the settlement for the collapse of the **power-sharing** executive in May 1974. While in office the SDLP also faced criticism from within **nationalist** ranks for the decision to end the rent and rates strike, not least because the emotive question of internment had not been resolved. The experience of the Sunningdale experiment convinced others, however, of the need to seek a political settlement that would extend beyond Northern Ireland alone.

In 1979 the demands from the majority of the party for an Irish dimension in the **Atkins Talks** led Fitt to resign and **John Hume** becoming party leader. Under Hume the SDLP maintained its position as the chief political client in the North of the Irish government as well as developing support in Europe and the **United States**. This was particularly significant during the 1981 **hunger strike** and aftermath when it was feared that the Catholic community would throw its support behind the **Irish Republican Army** (IRA) military campaign. During the course of the hunger strike, the SDLP supported concessions to some of the prisoners' demands but not political status.

The advent of **Sinn Fein** (SF) to electoral politics in Northern Ireland caused widespread concern in official circles, and this was a significant factor in the creation of the **New Ireland Forum** and subsequently in the **Anglo–Irish Agreement** (AIA). The SDLP boycotted the 1982 **Northern Ireland Assembly**, partly due to concerns about being politically outflanked by SF. The SDLP share of votes fell to under 19.0 percent in the Assembly election; however, while the IRA's military campaign continued, SF did not significantly challenge the SDLP as the main party supported by Catholic voters. The party participated in the **Brooke–Mayhew Talks**, but John Hume gave greater emphasis to his discussions with **Gerry Adams** in an attempt to find a viable political settlement. There was some concern within the party leadership to Hume's approach, but Hume felt vindicated by the announcement of an IRA ceasefire in August 1994.

As the **peace process** developed, SF began to make inroads into the SDLP's electoral lead over them. Initially this was interpreted as encouragement for SF's role in the peace process. However, as the SDLP vote began to decline, it became clear that a more long-term change was taking place, with SF being perceived as a more effective advocate of nationalist concerns than the SDLP. The SDLP won 21.4 percent of the vote in the **Northern Ireland Forum** election but withdrew in July 1996 during the controversy surrounding the **Drumcree parade**.

The SDLP was one of the strongest advocates of the **Good Friday Agreement** (GFA), and in the 1998 Northern Ireland Assembly election, it received more first-preference votes than any other party (22.0 percent of the poll) as a result of splits in the **unionist** vote. However, with vote transfers they won fewer seats in the Assembly. In the Northern Ireland executive, the party held the posts of deputy first minister and the ministers of finance and personnel, higher and further education, training and employment (later employment and learning), and agriculture. In the 2001 **Westminster** general election, SF received more votes than the SDLP (21.7 percent of the poll to 21.0 percent) and won four seats to the SDLP's three.

In the 2003 Northern Ireland Assembly elections, the SDLP took 17.0 percent of first-preference votes and won 18 seats. Significantly this was six seats less than SF, confirming that SF was now the dominant nationalist party. In the 2004 European Parliament elections, they received 15.9 percent of first-preference votes and lost the seat formerly held by John Hume to SF. The **district council** and Westminster elections of May 2005 confirmed this trend; in the council elections, the SDLP received 17.0 percent of the vote and had 101 councilors elected and in the Westminster elections took 17.5 percent of the vote and won 3 seats. In Newry and Mourne, the party lost retiring former deputy leader **Seamus Mallon**'s seat to SF, but **Mark Durkan**, SDLP leader from November 2001, retained the seat formerly held by Hume.

As negotiations to reestablish **devolution** continued in 2006, the SDLP found themselves sidelined as the British and Irish governments appeared to concentrate on meeting the concerns of the **Democratic Unionist Party** (DUP) and SF. In the March 2007 Northern Ireland Assembly election, the party received 15.2 percent of first-preference votes and won 16 seats. In early April they chose the department for social development for their minister (Margaret Ritchie) on the Northern Ireland executive, which assumed power on 8 May 2007.

**SPECIAL CATEGORY STATUS.** In June 1972 Secretary of State **William Whitelaw** conceded special category status to prisoners convicted of terrorist or politically motivated crimes. In practice this meant that **paramilitary** prisoners were not required to do prison work; were allowed more visits, letters, and parcels than normal; and could wear civilian clothes. The decision laid the seeds for much of the conflict surrounding prisons and prisoners that followed. From an ideological perspective, the decision allowed **loyalist** and particularly **republican** inmates to claim that they were prisoners of war or political prisoners. Increasingly, however, the British government wished to treat such prisoners in the same way as any other, whether their actions and convictions were the result of **the Troubles** or not; this policy was referred to as one of "criminalization."

In 1973 there were 379 special category prisoners, representing 42.0 percent of the prison population. By March 1976, however, this had increased to 1,498 prisoners, representing 68.0 percent of the total. In March 1976 special category status was withdrawn for those convicted after that date, meaning that those convicted of politically motivated offenses would be treated in the same way as other prisoners. The first **Irish Republican Army** (IRA) member to be imprisoned after these changes, Ciaran Nugent, refused to accept these rules and in September 1976 refused to wear a prison uniform thus initiating the **Blanket Protest**.

In March 1980 Secretary of State **Humphrey Atkins** announced the ending of special category status for all prisoners, including the 443 convicted before March 1976, bringing a further increase in tensions between the government and prisoners.

**SPENCE, AUGUSTUS (GUSTY) (1933– ).** **Paramilitary** leader and community worker, Gusty Spence was born in the **loyalist** Shankill Road area of **Belfast** on 28 June 1933. He left school at an early age and worked in a number of manual jobs before joining the **British Army** in 1957. Poor health led him to leave the army in 1961. In the mid-1960s, the **Ulster Volunteer Force** (UVF) paramilitary group was formed, and Spence soon became a member. In October 1966 he was sentenced to life imprisonment for the murder of a Catholic barman outside a public house on Shankill Road. Spence has consistently denied committing the crime.

Following the outbreak of **the Troubles** and his transfer to the **Maze Prison**, Spence became UVF commander in the prison, where he encouraged UVF prisoners to think along political lines. In 1977 he called for reconciliation in Northern Ireland and condemned the use of violence to achieve political aims, subsequently resigning as UVF leader in the Maze. He was released from prison in December 1984. Following his release he remained active in community politics and was a leading member of the **Progressive Unionist Party** (PUP).

Spence's standing within loyalist circles was highlighted by the fact that he was chosen to read out the **Combined Loyalist Military Command** (CLMC) statement announcing a ceasefire in October 1994. He supported the developing **peace process** and the **Good Friday Agreement** (GFA) that emerged from it. Even his reputation did not exclude him from the impact of intraloyalist disputes, however, and in August 2000 his home was attacked during the course of a feud between the UVF and **Ulster Defence Association** (UDA) centered in the Shankill area.

**ST. ANDREWS AGREEMENT.** On 13 October 2006, following three days of negotiations involving the British government, Irish government, and Northern Ireland **political parties**, the governments produced a set of proposals aimed at reestablishing a **devolved** executive in Northern Ireland. These proposals were dubbed the "St. Andrews Agreement." At its core the agreement required the **Democratic Unionist Party** (DUP) to share power in the executive with **Sinn Fein** (SF) and SF to give support to the **Police Service of Northern Ireland** (PSNI), although responsibility for policing and justice would not be devolved to the **Northern Ireland Assembly** until May 2008 at the earliest.

The parties were given until 10 November 2006 to consult with their members to see whether they supported the agreement. If support was forthcoming, the Assembly would then meet to elect the first minister and deputy first minister on 24 November 2006. Between then and 26 March 2007, when the restoration of the executive was proposed, a preparation for government committee would meet to agree on details of ministerial responsibilities. The restoration of the executive would, however, have to be supported by a popular mandate in the form of a referendum or Assembly election to be held in March 2007

In addition to the main proposals and modifications to the way in which the Assembly worked, there was also a range of recommendations dealing with specific issues in areas such as education, rates charges, and an economic support package. The St. Andrews Agreement received a guarded welcome from most areas, although the most difficult challenge appeared to lie with SF in winning over its constituency to support the PSNI.

In November 2006 an attitude survey conducted for British Broadcasting Corporation (BBC) Northern Ireland found 54.3 percent support the agreement in Northern Ireland, with 22.8 percent opposed. Of **unionists** surveyed, 48.5 percent were in favor and 26.1 percent were opposed, while 61.8 percent of **nationalists** supported the agreement and 19.5 percent were opposed. Among the major parties, the highest level of support came from the **Social Democratic and Labour Party** (SDLP; 71.6 percent) and the lowest from the DUP (46.6 percent). The survey also suggested that the DUP had the highest percentage of those who opposed the St. Andrews Agreement (31.9 percent).

On 16 November 2006, the government outlined plans for legislation based on parts of the St. Andrews Agreement. The legislation envisaged a transitional Northern Ireland Assembly from 25 November 2006 to 26 March 2007; a pledge requiring all ministers to endorse the PSNI and criminal justice system, making all ministers accountable to the executive as a whole as well as participating in the **North–South Ministerial Council** (NSMC); provision for SF members to join district policing partnerships; and proposals on the role of MI5 in Northern Ireland. Ministers would also be required to report back to the secretary of state in a year on progress toward transferring policing and justice powers to the executive. The secretary of state would have the power to dissolve the Assembly until March 2007. It also required an election to the Northern Ireland Assembly on 7 March 2007. Legislation reflecting these proposals was rushed through Parliament in advance of the meeting of the Northern Ireland Assembly, which was held on 24 November 2006.

**STALKER-SAMPSON INQUIRY.** Following the murders of six Catholic men by the **Royal Ulster Constabulary** (RUC) in 1982 and allegations of a **"shoot-to-kill"** policy, Manchester deputy chief constable John Stalker was appointed to investigate the killings. In September 1985 Stalker submitted an initial report on the issue to RUC chief constable Sir **John Hermon**.

In June 1986 Stalker was removed as the officer in charge of the investigation and replaced by the chief constable of West Yorkshire, Colin Sampson. Stalker was suspended and faced charges of associating with "known criminals;" however, he was subsequently cleared of the charges. Despite this, he resigned from the police in December 1986.

In January 1988 the then attorney general, Sir **Patrick Mayhew**, announced that there would be no prosecutions arising from the inquiry on the grounds of national security. In February 1988 Stalker said that he had been removed from the inquiry because it would have led to a number of high-level resignations. He stated that although the RUC officers involved had shot and killed the six men and then fabricated stories to cover the truth, there was no official policy to kill suspects rather than arrest them. A week later the Irish government temporarily halted meetings between the **Garda Siochana** and the RUC as a mark of protest. In September 1994 the **Belfast** coroner abandoned the inquests into the **deaths** of the six men because of the refusal of the RUC chief constable to provide the inquest with the Stalker–Sampson Report.

**STEVENS INQUIRY.** In August 1989 the murder of Catholic man Loughlin Maginn by the **Ulster Freedom Fighters** (UFF) was followed by claims that members of the security forces had provided information that had led to the murder. The controversy led to the appointment of John Stevens, deputy chief constable of the Cambridgeshire police force, to head an inquiry into how security information came to **loyalist paramilitaries**. In January 1990 a number of **Ulster Defence Association** (UDA) members were arrested at the request of the Stevens inquiry team, including Brian Nelson, who the press then revealed had been working for **British Army intelligence**.

In May 1990 a summary of the Stevens report stated that there had been **collusion** between the security forces and loyalist paramilitaries but that this had occurred on an individual basis and was not institutionalized. During the course of the inquiry, 58 people were charged with offenses, including 10 **Ulster Defence Regiment** (UDR) members and 32 loyalist paramilitaries. In July 1991 five men charged as a result of the Stevens inquiry into intelligence leaks to loyalists were imprisoned for between four and seven years. In March 1992 two UDR members were convicted, with a third man, of aiding the murder of Loughlin Maginn.

Stevens conducted a second inquiry into the issue of security forces' collusion with loyalists in Northern Ireland in 1993 and a third in 1999. The third report examined the role of UDA member William Stobie in the murder of solicitor Pat Finucane. Stobie claimed he had warned the RUC that Finucane was about to be attacked. In November 2001 Stobie went on trial but was shot dead by other members of the UDA in December.

In May 2002, following the Corey Reports, the government announced an inquiry into the Finucane murder, leading Stevens to announce that his report would be delayed. In September 2002 **Hugh Orde**, who was in charge of the day-to-day running of the Stevens inquiry, stepped down following his appointment as chief constable of the **Police Service of Northern Ireland** (PSNI). The third Stevens Report was published in April 2003.

**STORMONT.** The name of the estate on the eastern edge of **Belfast** containing a number of government buildings. Most notably these include the **Northern Ireland Assembly** buildings, still popularly referred to as Parliament buildings because it was the location of the **Northern Ireland Parliament** for most of its existence. The Stormont estate also includes Stormont Castle, where the offices of the secretary of state for Northern Ireland are located, as well as Castle buildings, where much of the interparty negotiations that led to the signing of the **Good Friday Agreement** (GFA) were conducted.

Although the name Stormont is often associated with the **unionist**-dominated **Northern Ireland government** of 1921–72, more recently it has also come to refer to any **devolved** assembly or executive operating from that location. Although **republicans** had some concerns about working in a building closely associated with the unionist regime, many of these have been overcome. The question of symbolism remains an issue, however, with a statue of the unionist leader Sir Edward Carson in front of the building and another of the unionist prime minister Lord Craigavon in the Great Hall.

Partly as a result of a policy encouraged by former Secretary of State **Mo Mowlam**, recent years have seen the grounds opened up to the public for a range of nonpolitical events, such as popular and classical music concerts. In December 2005 the Great Hall was the location for a funeral service for the Northern Ireland soccer star George Best. In November 2006 **loyalist** Michael Stone was detained at the doors of Parliament buildings when he was found to be carrying weapons.

**STORMONTGATE.** On 4 October 2002, **Police Service of Northern Ireland** (PSNI) officers raided **Sinn Fein** (SF) party offices in the **Northern Ireland Assembly** buildings. The PSNI claimed that the **Irish Republican Army** (IRA) was operating a spy ring from **Stormont**. Three men, including SF's Northern Ireland Assembly office administrator Denis Donaldson, were subsequently arrested. Although documents were discovered at Donaldson's home, only two computer disks were reportedly taken from the SF offices, and these were later returned. SF members claimed that the raid had been instigated by the special branch and by "securocrats" in an attempt to undermine the **peace process**.

The PSNI raid and associated events, nicknamed "Stormontgate," increased hostility between **unionists** and **nationalists** in the Assembly. The **Ulster Unionist Party** (UUP) had already threatened to withdraw from the Northern Ireland executive because of continuing IRA activity, including the suspicion of IRA involvement in a break-in at Castlereagh police station in March and the failure of the IRA to **decommission** weapons. The police action against an alleged **republican** spy ring operating in Stormont was, therefore, effectively the final straw for unionists. In the wake of the raid, **David Trimble** demanded **Tony Blair** exclude SF from the Northern Ireland executive or UUP ministers would resign. The government refused to take such a course and instead suspended the **devolved** institutions on 14 October 2002.

On 8 December 2005, the Northern Ireland Public Prosecution Service announced that charges against the three men had been dropped because they were "no longer in the public interest." The announcement brought conflicting claims from unionists and republicans as to whether it was a concession to republicans in the wake of IRA decommissioning or the fact that there was no evidence against the three. A week later, however, **Gerry Adams** revealed that Donaldson had been an MI5 informant for more than two decades, raising questions of whether more highly placed informants were still active within the republican movement. Donaldson subsequently moved to a cottage in Co. Donegal but was found shot dead there on 4 April 2006.

**SUNNINGDALE.** The Civil Service Staff College at Sunningdale Park, Berkshire, which was the location of the tripartite conference of 6–9 December 1973. It was the first conference since 1925 to be attended by heads of government from the United Kingdom, Northern Ireland, and the **Republic of Ireland**. The aim of the conference was to flesh out the concept of an **Irish dimension**, which was a prerequisite for **Social Democratic and Labour Party** (SDLP) participation in the Northern Ireland executive. Agreement was reached on the formation of a Council of Ireland that would have representatives from Northern Ireland and the Republic and would consist of a Council of Ministers and a Consultative Assembly. A permanent secretariat would "supervise the carrying out of the executive and harmonising functions and the consultative role of the council."

During the negotiations **Ulster Unionist Party** (UUP) representatives pressed the Irish government for changes to articles 2 and 3 of the Irish constitution (which claimed jurisdiction over Northern Ireland) but failed to achieve a clear commitment on this issue. The Irish government also rejected **unionist** calls for the **extradition** of terrorist suspects from the Republic to the North. The fact that the Council of Ireland was portrayed as a prototype all-Ireland government by some **nationalists** while UUP negotiators failed to achieve their objectives meant that unionist opinion was generally opposed to the Sunningdale Agreement from the outset.

Unionist opponents of the deal included those who objected to the Council of Ireland, some who opposed a **power-sharing** executive that included the SDLP, and some who opposed the settlement as a whole. As unionist opposition to the proposed settlement grew, however, the entire package came to be referred to as Sunningdale.

**SUPERGRASS TRIALS.** In April 1983, at the end of the first of a series of trials based on evidence given by informers, 14 **Ulster Volunteer Force** (UVF) members were jailed on the evidence of "supergrass" Joseph Bennett. Bennett was offered immunity from prosecution for his own crimes in return for evidence against other UVF members. In August 1983, in another high-profile case, 22 alleged **Irish Republican Army** (IRA) members were imprisoned on evidence given by Christopher Black. During the course of the supergrass trials, the **Irish National Liberation Army** (INLA) kidnapped the wife of Harry Kirkpatrick, while the IRA held the father of Raymond Gilmour in an attempt to force them to withdraw their evidence. Both were later released.

In December 1985, 25 people were convicted on the evidence of INLA informer Harry Kirkpatrick. By this time the confessions of nearly 30 informers from various **paramilitary** groups had led to almost 300 people being charged. There was, however, concern over the fact that many people had been convicted exclusively on evidence provided by informers who often received financial incentives and immunity from prosecution for their own offenses in return. By the end of the Kirkpatrick case, the convictions of 14 people jailed as a result of the Joe Bennett UVF case in 1983 had already been overturned. In 1986 the Court of Appeal overturned the convictions of those imprisoned on the evidence of Christopher Black, and this effectively ended the supergrass system.

## – T –

**TARTAN GANGS.** In March 1971 three off-duty soldiers from Scotland were lured from a public house in **Belfast** and shot dead by the **Irish Republican Army** (IRA) on the outskirts of Belfast. The incident produced a strong reaction in public opinion but also helped give an identity to gangs of **loyalist** youths, who adopted tartan scarves as a "uniform" in memory of the Scottish soldiers. The gangs adopted their own distinctive tartan, and such gangs as the Woodstock Tartan from East Belfast were involved in clashes with rival gangs of Catholic youths (some of which also adopted tartans) and attacks on Catholic homes and property in many areas of Northern Ireland. Confrontations with the security forces and attacks on the homes of police officers were also routine events.

At the height of the Tartan Gangs' strength during a five-day period in late April and early May 1972, there were continuous clashes in East Belfast between gang members and both Catholic youths from the Short Strand area and the **Royal Ulster Constabulary** (RUC). By the end of the year, the gangs were increasingly coming under the influence of the **Ulster Defence Association** (UDA) and effectively a youth wing of that organization. During the **Ulster Workers' Council (UWC) strike** of 1974, Tartan Gang members operated under the direction of the UDA to participate in blocking roads but also to help in the distribution of food.

**TAYLOR, JOHN (1937– ).** **Ulster Unionist Party** (UUP) politician, John Taylor was born in Armagh on 24 December 1937. He was educated at the Royal School, Armagh, and at Queen's University, **Belfast** (QUB), where he graduated with a BSc degree. At QUB he joined the Young Unionists and was chairman of the Ulster Young Unionist Council (1961–62). In 1965 he became the youngest UUP Member of Parliament (MP) at **Stormont** when he was returned for the South Tyrone constituency. He held this seat until the suspension of the **Northern Ireland Parliament** in 1972.

At Stormont Taylor was skeptical of **Terence O'Neill**'s policy of moderate reform and, in February 1969, was one of 12 UUP MPs who signed a statement calling for a change in leadership to unite the party. Despite this, he was appointed as parliamentary secretary at the ministry of home affairs in May 1969 and in August 1970 became a member of the Northern Ireland cabinet as minister of state in the same department.

In February 1972 Taylor was wounded in an **Official Irish Republican Army** (OIRA) ambush in Armagh. The OIRA had targeted Taylor because they believed that he was one of the chief advocates of **internment**. In 1973 he was **elected** to the **Northern Ireland Assembly** as a member for Fermanagh-South Tyrone and was one of the leading opponents of the **Sunningdale** deal within the UUP. After the collapse of the **power-sharing** executive, Taylor was again elected to the **Constitutional Convention** in 1975, this time for the North Down constituency.

In 1976 Taylor became UUP spokesman on the European Community and in 1979 was returned to the European Parliament in the first direct elections to that body. He was again returned to the European Parliament in 1984 but did not contest the election in 1989. As one of the UUP's senior members, he was also elected to the Northern Ireland Assembly of 1982–86 from North Down and in 1983 won the newly created **Westminster** seat of Strangford, which he held until 2001. In addition to this, he also served on Castlereagh Borough Council between 1989 and 1997.

With the developing **peace process** in the early 1990s, Taylor remained generally in favor of talks with other parties but was critical of the **John Hume–Gerry Adams** discussions, which he viewed as an attempt to create a pan-**nationalist** front to isolate **unionists**. He was cautiously optimistic on the **Downing Street Declaration** and **paramilitary** ceasefires but warned of the dangers of trying to impose another Sunningdale-type settlement.

Following the resignation of **James Molyneaux** as UUP leader in August 1995, Taylor contested the party leadership but lost, somewhat surprisingly, to **David Trimble**. He subsequently became the party's deputy leader. In May 1996 he was elected to the **Northern Ireland Forum** for Strangford and remained an ally of Trimble during the negotiations that led to the **Good Friday Agreement** (GFA) in April 1998, subsequently defending the GFA.

Taylor was again returned from Strangford to the new Northern Ireland Assembly in June 1998 and continued to be a key supporter of Trimble at Stormont. Early in 2001 he announced that he would not contest the forthcoming Westminster general election, and he was awarded a life peerage, assuming the title Lord Kilclooney of Armagh. In October 2001 he became one of three UUP representatives on the newly created Northern Ireland Policing Board, remaining on the board until 2006.

**THATCHER, MARGARET (1925– ). Conservative Party** politician and prime minister, Margaret Thatcher was born in Grantham, Lincolnshire, on 13 October 1925, the younger daughter of shopkeeper Alfred Roberts. She was educated at Grantham Girls' High School and later won a scholarship to Somerville College, Oxford. She graduated with a degree in natural science and subsequently worked as an industrial research chemist. She also began to study for the bar and in 1954 began to practice as a barrister.

While at Oxford she had been president of the university's Conservative Association and was later accepted as the party's candidate for the Deptford constituency; however, it was not until 1959 that she was **elected** to Parliament when she won the seat of Finchley. She married Denis Thatcher in 1951. She was a junior minister in pensions and national insurance from 1961 until 1964 and a member of the shadow cabinet from 1967 until 1970. Under **Edward Heath** she served as minister of education but was increasingly influenced by free-market economic theories and antipathy to state intervention in the economy. In 1975, in the wake of two general election defeats the previous year, Thatcher caused some surprise by defeating Heath and **William Whitelaw** to become Conservative Party leader.

In 1979 the Conservatives won the general election with a small majority, and Thatcher subsequently began to cut support to what the right wing looked on as "lame duck" industries. Thatcher's strong-willed and strong-headed approach would be both her greatest strength and also her greatest weakness. Her often uncompromising approach to issues, whether on the economy (notably the coalminers' strike of 1984), on foreign affairs (most notably the Falklands conflict), or in Northern Ireland made her both admired by her supporters and equally detested by her opponents.

Thatcher had always been a strong vocal proponent of maintaining the position of Northern Ireland within the United Kingdom. In opposition she appeared to support the views of her Northern Ireland spokesman Airey Neave that **power sharing** was not a practical proposition, but with the assassination of Neave (the first of a number of Conservative politicians close to her to be murdered by **republican paramilitaries**) in March 1979 and once in power, tentative moves were made toward achieving a power-sharing **devolved** administration. Under her first secretary of state for Northern Ireland, **Humphrey Atkins**, political talks between Northern Ireland parties failed to make significant progress, but under **James Prior** a **Northern Ireland Assembly** made a limited contribution, given that it was boycotted by all **nationalist** representatives.

Thatcher was vilified by nationalists and republicans for her uncompromising approach to the republican **hunger strikes** of 1980 and 1981. She equally caused anger in Irish government circles from her dismissive reaction to the report of the **New Ireland Forum** in 1984 and outrage among **unionists** by signing the **Anglo–Irish Agreement** (AIA) in 1985. Her unflappable attitude in the face of adversity, as in the wake of the **Brighton bomb** explosion in 1984, were important elements of her character. However, despite some of the high policy decisions on Northern Ireland (including dabbling with the idea of repartition) and issuing a number of memorable phrases, the impression remained that Northern Ireland was something of a distraction for Thatcher, who saw her role as being an actor on a world stage.

In the latter years of her premiership, her government was increasingly perceived as being arrogant and unresponsive to public opinion—the ill-conceived council poll tax or "community charge" proved her political undoing. In November 1990, with another general election looming, she was unceremoniously replaced as leader of the Conservative Party by the less colorful **John Major**. In July of the same year, another of her close political colleagues, Ian Gow, had been killed by an **Irish Republican Army** (IRA) bomb. In 1992 she was awarded a life peerage and became Baroness Thatcher of Kesteven.

**THIRTY-TWO COUNTY SOVEREIGNTY COMMITTEE.** An organization formed in Dublin in December 1997 by **republicans** opposed to the developing **peace process**. Its 15-member committee included Bernadette Sands-McKevitt, sister of **hunger striker Bobby Sands**. It is often viewed as the political wing of the dissident republican **paramilitary** group the **Real Irish Republican Army** (RIRA), although it does not confirm this opinion. It has subsequently changed its name to the Thirty-two County Sovereignty Movement. While it opposes the **Good Friday Agreement** (GFA), it stresses that it is not a political party and does not intend to contest **elections**. In July 2002 it broadened the range of issues on which it would express an opinion beyond that of Irish independence to include issues that opposed colonialism and imperialism.

**THREE STRANDS APPROACH.** In March 1991 Secretary of State **Peter Brooke** outlined the structure that the forthcoming political negotiations would take. The process would begin with "strand one," discussions between the Northern Ireland parties aimed at achieving **devolved** government for Northern Ireland. "Strand two" focused on relations between Northern Ireland and the Republic, while "strand three" would deal with the relationship between the **Republic of Ireland** and the United Kingdom. The negotiations in each strand were considered to be interlinked, leading participants to comment later that "nothing is agreed until everything is agreed." From one perspective Brooke's statement on the three strands approach was merely a recognition of the political geography of the British Isles in the period after Ireland was partitioned. However, it also clarified how these relationships should be approached in future negotiations, and the same three strands structure was followed in the all-party talks that led to the **Good Friday Agreement** (GFA).

**TRIMBLE, DAVID (1944– ). Ulster Unionist Party** (UUP) leader and first minister, David Trimble was born in Bangor, Co. Down, on 15 October 1944. He was educated at Bangor Grammar School and Queen's University, **Belfast** (QUB). Between 1968 and 1990, he was a lecturer in the Faculty of Law at QUB. He was called to the Bar of Northern Ireland in 1969. Among his colleagues in the Faculty of Law at QUB were **Mary McAleese** and the UUP Assembly member Edgar Graham, who was murdered by the **Irish Republican Army** (IRA) at QUB in December 1983.

In the early 1970s, Trimble was a member of the **Vanguard Unionist Progressive Party** (VUPP) and a supporter of **William Craig**. During this period he expressed support for an independent Northern Ireland in preference to a united Ireland if Northern Ireland was forced to accept the settlement outlined in the government's 1973 White Paper on Northern Ireland. He stood in the 1973 **Northern Ireland Assembly elections** in North Down but was not elected. During the **Ulster Workers' Council (UWC) strike**, he played an organizational role in support of the UWC strike committee, and in the 1975 **Constitutional Convention** elections, he was returned in the South Belfast constituency. When VUPP split over the issue of forming a voluntary coalition with the **Social Democratic and Labour Party** (SDLP), Trimble supported those in favor of a coalition and became deputy leader of VUPP. After VUPP ceased contesting elections in 1978, he joined the UUP.

In 1990 Trimble was the UUP candidate in the **Westminster** by-election in the Upper Bann constituency and comfortably won the seat. In 1991 and 1992, he was a member of the UUP team that participated in the **Brooke–Mayhew Talks** but received more attention for his role in the **Drumcree** standoff that took place within his constituency in July 1995. With **Ian Paisley** he attempted to negotiate a compromise between **Orange Order** marchers and the police on conditions for a march to proceed but initially failed. Later, however, Trimble, Paisley, and 500 Orangemen were permitted to march the route without accompanying bands. His role in the event raised his standing with **unionists** but raised hostility toward him from **nationalists**. The Drumcree factor also played a role in Trimble's unexpected election to the leadership of the UUP in 1995 following the retirement of **James Molyneaux**.

In 1996 Trimble was returned to the **Northern Ireland Forum** in Upper Bann and led his party in the subsequent political negotiations. Crucially, for the future of the **peace process**, he kept the UUP in the talks process after July 1997, when the **Democratic Unionist Party** (DUP) and United Kingdom Unionist Party (UKUP) withdrew. In April 1998 he signed the **Good Friday Agreement** (GFA) on behalf of his party, even though he had some concerns on issues such as the **decommissioning** of **paramilitary** weapons. He campaigned in favor of a *yes* vote for the referendum on the GFA and was subsequently returned to the Northern Ireland Assembly for Upper Bann.

In October 1998 Trimble and **John Hume** were awarded the Nobel Peace Prize for their work toward finding a peaceful solution to **the Troubles**. Opposition to the GFA was already increasing within the UUP and broader unionist community, however, and the debate surrounding the decommissioning of IRA weapons delayed the **devolution** of power to the Northern Ireland executive until December 1999. As first minister the protracted debate over IRA weapons along with paramilitary prisoner releases, **parades** disputes, and police reforms worked to undermine his support. He continued to push ahead with a narrowing degree of support within the party. A temporary resignation as first minister in July 2001 and again in October 2002 over the weapons debate failed to resolve the issue.

The Assembly election of November 2003 showed a swing in unionist political opinion, with the UUP being reduced to the third largest party after the DUP and **Sinn Fein** (SF), despite having a slight increase in its percentage share of the vote. Trimble's difficulties were compounded by the subsequent defection of **Jeffrey Donaldson** and two other Assembly members to the DUP. He survived a challenge to his leadership at the UUP conference in March 2004 but lost his Westminster seat to the DUP in the May 2005 general election. After the poor UUP performances in the general election and **district council** election, Trimble resigned as party leader and was succeeded by Sir **Reg Empey**.

In May 2006 Trimble wrote to the commissioner of the Metropolitan Police, demanding he take action against a website run by the Thirty-two County Sovereignty Movement, which he claimed was inciting his murder. In June 2006 he was awarded a life peerage and took the title of Lord Trimble of Lisnagarvey. In December 2006 he announced that he would not be standing in the March 2007 Northern Ireland Assembly election. In April 2007 he left the UUP and joined the **Conservative Party**.

**THE TROUBLES.** The term used to describe the violent conflict in Northern Ireland from the late 1960s until the late 1990s between members of the Protestant **unionist** community and Catholic **nationalist** community. The same term is also used to refer to the period of conflict between nationalists and unionists in the early 1920s at the time of partition.

There is some dispute as to the precise date when the recent Troubles began. Some commentators choose the **Ulster Volunteer Force** (UVF) Malvern Street killings of 1966. However, the generally accepted starting point for the Troubles is the **Derry** civil rights march of 5 October 1968. There were several points at which the conflict escalated in ferocity, most notably in August 1969 and again in August 1971 following the introduction of **internment**. The most sustained period of violence was from August 1971 through the following years until a decline began in the late 1970s. Thereafter there were intermittent peaks in violence, often surrounding periods of crisis, such as the 1981 **hunger strikes**, but these were never as persistent as the core period of the early 1970s.

There is also some debate as to when the Troubles came to an end. The declaration of **paramilitary** ceasefires in 1994 led to a significant reduction in the level of violence, while the **Good Friday Agreement** (GFA) of 1998 can also been seen as providing the political and security framework within which the Troubles could be said to have ended. Nevertheless the terrorist incident in which most people died in Northern Ireland, the **Omagh bomb**, occurred after the signing of the GFA. By 2007 paramilitary organizations, one of the key factors in the persistence of the Troubles, still remained active to some degree. Despite this, many would consider the signing of the GFA as marking the end of the Troubles.

The nature of the Troubles has also been the source of enormous public, political, and academic discussion on the question of whether they were the result of national, religious, political, social, and economic differences or imperialist aspirations. Most, though far from all, commentators see the Troubles as a conflict between communities with different national identities and aspirations, with nominal affiliation to a particular religious community (Protestant or Catholic) as the main source of identification.

**THE TRUCE.** In December 1974 discussions between Protestant churchmen and members of the Provisional **Irish Republican Army** (PIRA) Army Council took place in Feakle, Co. Clare, leading to a temporary IRA ceasefire. The PIRA leaders also produced a set of proposals for the British government that they believed could bring about a permanent IRA ceasefire.

In December 1974 and January 1975, government officials conducted talks with Provisional **Sinn Fein** (PSF) and the IRA leading to a more permanent truce. The IRA leadership believed, incorrectly, that the **Ulster Workers' Council (UWC) strike** had brought a fundamental change in British government policy and that a truce would be the first step in a British withdrawal from Northern Ireland. As a result they announced an indefinite ceasefire on 9 February 1975.

On 11 February 1975, "incident centers" manned by PSF were set up to monitor the ceasefire in liaison with British officials. The PIRA later outlined 12 points to which they claimed the government had agreed as part of the Truce, which included a scaling-down of security activity, immunity from arrest for certain individuals, and further talks between IRA leaders and senior British officials. The British government denied the authenticity of this view.

Negotiations between government officials and the IRA aroused the fears of a wide range of groups within Northern Ireland, from the **Social Democratic and Labour Party** (SDLP) to **loyalist paramilitary** groups. The Truce slowly began to break down, partly because the IRA had misread the British government's intentions, partly because of the ongoing activity of loyalist paramilitaries, and partly because of the activities of IRA units at the grassroots level. The PIRA was also involved in an ongoing feud with the **Official Irish Republican Army** (OIRA) that continued during the Truce.

On 22 September 1975, the PIRA detonated bombs in towns across Northern Ireland, effectively exposing the Truce as a façade. On 10 November 1975, the PIRA in **Derry**, which opposed the ceasefire, blew up the building in which the local incident center was located. Two days later Secretary of State **Merlyn Rees** announced the closure of the remaining incident centers.

**THE TWELFTH.** The Twelfth of July, or more colloquially, "The Twelfth," is the main day of celebration for the **Orange Order**. The celebration, which commemorates the victory of William of Orange over James II at the Battle of the Boyne in 1690, is marked by Orange marches in centers across Northern Ireland, with the largest taking place in **Belfast**.

From the early 19th century, Twelfth **parades** have been associated with controversy and intermittent sectarian clashes. Under the **Ulster Unionist Party** (UUP) government from the 1920s until 1972, the Twelfth was one of the major events associated with the state, with 12 July being a public holiday. After **direct rule** was introduced, **nationalists** increasingly campaigned for controversial Orange marches, including some of those held on the Twelfth, to be rerouted or banned. The increased level of violence or expectation of violence associated with the Twelfth marches, particularly after the **Drumcree** standoff of 1995, results in many people leaving the country on holiday over the Twelfth.

In recent years the Orange Order has promoted the Twelfth as an important celebration of Protestant culture within Northern Ireland. Official sources also give backing and financial support to the Twelfth as part of an "Orangefest." In 2006 the Grand Orange Lodge of Ireland also highlighted the tourism potential for Northern Ireland, noting that

80,000 people had attended their flagship Twelfth festival in Bangor, Co. Down, with 50,000 people each at Belfast and Coleraine, Co. Londonderry, and many others in smaller turnouts elsewhere.

**TYRIE, ANDREW (ANDY) (1940– ). Paramilitary** leader and community worker, Andy Tyrie was born in **Belfast** in 1940. He was initially a member of the **Ulster Volunteer Force** (UVF) but joined the **Ulster Defence Association** (UDA) after it was formed in 1971. He became chairman of the UDA's inner council in 1973 when he was seen as a compromise candidate between competing factions but quickly established his authority in the organization. In May 1974 his decision to throw the weight of the UDA behind the **Ulster Workers' Council (UWC) strike** was a major factor in the strike's success, though he faced criticism from within the UDA for supporting the decision to end the strike on 29 May 1974.

In 1976 he withdrew the UDA from the Ulster Loyalist Central Co-ordinating Committee (ULCCC) umbrella organization on the grounds that members of the group had been discussing the prospect of an independent Northern Ireland with **republicans**. He put the support of the UDA behind the **loyalist** strike of 1977, though this ended without success, and was reluctant to pursue a similar strategy in the wake of the **Anglo–Irish Agreement** (AIA). In 1979 he backed the launch of the New Ulster Political Research Group (NUPRG), a think tank associated with the UDA, and supported its proposal for negotiated **independence** for Northern Ireland.

In the 1980s Tyrie had to reconcile the conflicting demands of the UDA's paramilitary campaign with the organization's attempts to develop a political strategy. By late 1987 he was facing increasing opposition within the UDA, and his support base was further undermined by the **Irish Republican Army** (IRA) murder of his deputy, John McMichael, in December 1987. In March 1988 Tyrie resigned as UDA chairman soon after a bomb was found under his car. Shortly after this he severed his links with the organization. He has subsequently pursued a role as a community worker in East Belfast.

– U –

**ULSTER.** With Leinster, Munster, and Connacht, one of the four historic **provinces** of Ireland. In the political context, the term is more commonly used by **unionists** and **loyalists** to refer to the **six counties** of Northern Ireland. Where **paramilitary** groups are concerned, only loyalist organizations have adopted the word *Ulster* as part of their name.

**ULSTER CLUBS.** In the autumn of 1985, **unionists** began forming Ulster Clubs to oppose the rerouting of **loyalist parades**. With the signing of the **Anglo–Irish Agreement** (AIA) in November of that year, however, opposition to the AIA became the primary focus of the Ulster Clubs. The Ulster Clubs' objectives included ensuring the right of the people of Northern Ireland to political self-determination, maintaining the union with Great Britain while it was in the interests of Northern Ireland, opposing the encroachment of Irish nationalism, and creating greater unity within unionism.

In January 1986 the organization claimed to have 8,000 members. In the same month, it announced a campaign of civil disobedience, and a number of its members were later fined for public order offenses. In October 1988 Ulster Clubs leader Alan Wright was jailed for failing to pay fines for car tax offenses that he committed as a protest against the AIA. Politically, Ulster Clubs increasingly favored an **integrationist** approach to the governance of Northern Ireland. As the crisis surrounding the AIA settled into political stalemate, the Ulster Clubs became largely inactive.

**ULSTER DEFENCE ASSOCIATION (UDA).** The **loyalist paramilitary** organization formed in 1971 by a group of local loyalist vigilante groups. The organization was composed of local "brigades," with the "brigadiers" forming an Inner Council. The structure of the organization made it susceptible to splits and internal feuds over the years. The UDA was initially led by Charles Harding Smith, but he was ousted in 1973, and **Andy Tyrie**, as chairman of the Inner Council, became effective head of the UDA. Initially the UDA promoted itself as the defender of Protestant working-class areas against **republican** attacks, but it also organized shows of strength, with thousands of uniformed UDA members taking part in **parades** through **Belfast** and other towns. In 1972 it was estimated to have approximately 40,000 members, but by the late 1970s, this had dropped to approximately 10,000. This reduction was partly due to an improving security situation but also due to the increasing awareness of criminality within the UDA.

In July 1972 the UDA established **no-go areas** in Belfast and Portadown in response to the failure of **William Whitelaw** to take action against republican no-go areas, leading to a confrontation with the **British Army** at Ainsworth Avenue in Belfast where the UDA's numbers forced the government to make significant concessions on allowing a no-go area.

The organization worked closely with the **Vanguard Unionist Progressive Party** (VUPP) and had a largely overlapping membership with the **Loyalist Association of Workers** (LAW). In general it has supported the idea of negotiated **independence** for Northern Ireland, although there was little support for the idea outside the UDA and VUPP, even at times of greatest **unionist** disillusionment with the British government policies. It backed **Ulster Vanguard**'s strike against **direct rule** in March 1972 and organized a disastrous strike against the **internment** of UDA members in February 1973, which was characterized by widespread violence and damaged the organization's reputation among unionists.

In 1973 the name of the **Ulster Freedom Fighters** (UFF) emerged in connection with sectarian killing, and it soon became recognized as a cover name for, or an element within, the UDA. Although the UFF was declared an illegal organization almost immediately, the UDA itself remained legal until 1992.

The UDA played a major role in the **Ulster Workers' Council (UWC) strike** of May 1974, with UDA and VUPP member **Glen Barr** acting as strike committee chairman and with the UDA enforcing the strike on the streets with roadblocks and pickets. The organization also supported the unsuccessful **United Unionist Action Council (UUAC) strike** of 1977 and backed unionist protests against the **Anglo–Irish Agreement** (AIA) after 1985.

In January 1987 the UDA's political think tank, the New Ulster Political Research Group (NUPRG), published a document titled *Common Sense*, calling for a written constitution for Northern Ireland and a **devolved** government based on consensus and shared responsibility, which was widely praised as a positive attempt to break the political stalemate. In December of the same year, UDA deputy chairman John McMichael was killed by the **Irish Republican Army** (IRA) at his home in Lisburn, Co. Antrim. In March 1988 Tyrie lost a vote of confidence in the Inner Council and resigned as chairman. Following

Tyrie's departure the UDA became involved in high-profile stories surrounding the acquisition of illegal weapons and **collusion** with members of the security forces as revealed by the **Stevens Inquiry**, both leading to the arrest of a number of leading UDA members.

In the 1990s a change in the leadership of the organization coincided with an upsurge on attacks on **nationalists** and often Catholics in general. In October 1994 it supported the ceasefire announced by the **Combined Loyalist Military Command** (CLMC), and in 1996 the political party associated with the UDA, the **Ulster Democratic Party** (UDP), was represented in the **Northern Ireland Forum**. The UDA initially backed the **Good Friday Agreement** (GFA) in 1998 but, like unionists at large, increasingly came to view the implementation of the GFA as being biased in favor of nationalists. UDA opposition increased after the early release of paramilitary prisoners was completed in 2000.

During the course of **the Troubles**, the UDA had frequently been involved in feuds with the **Ulster Volunteer Force** (UVF), and in 2000 another feud between the UDA's West Belfast "C" Company, led by Johnny Adair, and the UVF broke out in the Shankill area of Belfast. In addition to this, UDA attacks on Catholics also continued in parts of Northern Ireland, leading the government to end its recognition of the UDA ceasefire in October 2001. In November 2001 the UDP was unilaterally disbanded by the UDA, partly on the basis that the UDP's support for the GFA was not in line with the views of UDA members. The UDA's political views were subsequently presented by the Ulster Political Research Group.

In the autumn of 2002 and early 2003, another feud broke out between Adair's "C" Company and other elements of the UDA, leading to Adair's reimprisonment in January 2003. Adair's supporters were subsequently forced out of the Shankill area by other UDA members. In February 2003 the organization declared another ceasefire, which was recognized by the government in November 2004. In March 2005 East Belfast UDA leader Jim Gray was forced from his position and was shot dead in October 2005. In June 2006 the UDA expelled leading members of the North Belfast Brigade, raising fears of another internal feud within the UDA, but in August the supporters of the ousted North Belfast leadership were also forced to leave Northern Ireland.

In October 2006 the Southeast Antrim Brigade of the UDA offered to wind up operations and become a postconflict organization but also asked for financial support from the government for loyalist areas. Several individuals from the Southeast Antrim Brigade who failed to support the Inner Council decision to expel the North Belfast leaders were themselves expelled by the UDA in March 2007.

In December 2006 the UDA announced that it did not support the **St. Andrews Agreement** because it undermined Northern Ireland's position in the United Kingdom. At the same time the Ulster Political Research Group stated that the UDA had been successful in purging those involved in criminal activity from its senior ranks. In March 2007 the government announced it was giving the Ulster Political Research Group £1.2 million over three years to fund a project aimed at steering loyalist communities away from violence and criminality. The decision was criticized by nationalists.

During the course of the Troubles, the UDA and UFF were responsible for 431 **deaths**, and 96 UDA and UFF members were killed.

**ULSTER DEFENCE REGIMENT (UDR).** The regiment of the **British Army** that was created in 1970 to replace the **Ulster Special Constabulary** (USC). The role of the UDR was to guard installations and carry out patrols that included road blocks and searches. Initially the UDR had 6,000 members in 7 battalions, 1 based in each county of Northern Ireland with the exception of **Belfast**, which had a separate battalion. During the first two years of its existence, the UDR was expanded to 11 battalions before being reduced to 9 in 1984 and 7 in 1991. In 1992, as part of a general reduction in military forces following the end of the cold war, it was amalgamated with the Royal Irish Rangers to form the **Royal Irish Regiment** (RIR).

Initially the UDR consisted entirely of part-time members, but full-time members were added in 1976. In the first years of its existence, nearly 20.0 percent of the regiment's soldiers were Catholic. However, attacks by both **republicans** and **loyalists** saw this figure decline rapidly until 1991 when only 3.0 percent of its members were Catholic. The part-time nature of the organization left its members particularly vulnerable to attacks by **paramilitary** organizations with 197 members and 47 former members being killed between

April 1970 and July 1992. Ninety-five percent of those murdered were killed by republican paramilitaries.

The most controversial, and contested, aspect of the regiment's history was the connection between some UDR members and illegal loyalist paramilitary groups. In one high-profile incident, two UDR members who were also UVF members were convicted of murder in connection with the killing of three members of the Miami Showband group in 1975. In 1989, 28 UDR soldiers were arrested as a result of the **Stevens Inquiry**.

By the early 1990s, the UDR consisted of approximately 3,000 part-time and 3,000 full-time members. When the amalgamation of the UDR and Royal Irish Rangers was announced, one general service and six resident, or home service, battalions were proposed for the RIR. Following the **Irish Republican Army** (IRA) statement in July 2005 that it was ending its campaign, the government announced that the home service battalions were to be disbanded in 2007. In October 2006 a disbandment **parade** was held, at which the Queen presented the regiment with the Conspicuous Gallantry Cross.

**ULSTER DEMOCRATIC PARTY (UDP).** In June 1981 the **Ulster Defence Association** (UDA) established the Ulster Loyalist Democratic Party (ULDP) in succession to its political think tank, the New Ulster Political Research Group (NUPRG). In December 1989 the name of the party was changed to the UDP.

With its links with the UDA, senior members of the organization were often targeted by **republicans**. In 1987 ULDP chairman John McMichael was murdered at his home in Lisburn, Co. Antrim. In 1991 UDP chairman Cecil McKnight was also killed at his home, and in July 1994 party spokesman Ray Smallwoods was murdered by the **Irish Republican Army** (IRA).

Although the UDP had little **electoral** success, it provided an important conduit to the thinking of the UDA for both the British and Irish governments. Although the party was supportive of the **peace process**, it was often constrained by the actions of the UDA. In January 1998 it withdrew from talks in advance of a formal expulsion from the talks as a result of a **Ulster Freedom Fighters** (UFF) killing. The party reentered talks at the end of the following month.

The UDP supported the **Good Friday Agreement** (GFA) and was critical of those **unionist** parties that opposed the GFA.

In the 1998 **Northern Ireland Assembly** elections, the UDP received only 8,651 first-preference votes (1.1 percent) and failed to win a seat. Party leader Gary McMichael, son of John McMichael, was subsequently appointed to the **Civic Forum**. As the implementation of the GFA continued, the leadership of the UDP, which supported the GFA, increasingly found itself at odds with many sections of the UDA. Continuing UDA criminality and a feud with the **Ulster Volunteer Force** (UVF) also worked to undermine the UDP's prospects of broadening support within the unionist community. In 2001 the UDP failed to register as a political party as was required under new U.K. legislation, leading to only three UDP members being returned as independent councillors in the **district council** elections of that year. In November 2001 the UDP was disbanded by the UDA and replaced by the political think tank, the Ulster Political Research Group.

**ULSTER DEMOCRATIC UNIONIST PARTY.** *See* DEMOCRATIC UNIONIST PARTY (DUP).

**ULSTER FREEDOM FIGHTERS (UFF).** The overtly military wing of the **Ulster Defence Association** (UDA), it emerged in June 1973 when it claimed responsibility for a number of murders, including that of **Gerry Fitt**'s election agent, Paddy Wilson. Although the UFF was an integral part of each UDA battalion, unlike the UDA it was declared an illegal organization almost immediately.

During the course of its existence, the organization has conducted a number of high-profile attacks. In March 1984 UFF members attacked and wounded **Sinn Fein** (SF) president **Gerry Adams** and three others while they were driving back from a court appearance in **Belfast** city center. In February 1992 the UFF killed five Catholics, including a 16-year-old boy, and wounded seven others in a gun attack on a bookmaker's shop on Ormeau Road in Belfast. In October 1993 the **Shankill bomb** was reported to have been planted by the **Irish Republican Army** (IRA) because they believed a UFF meeting was taking place in the building. Later that same month, UFF members killed 7 people and wounded 13 others in an attack on a bar in

Greysteel, Co. Londonderry. In April 1991, as part of the **Combined Loyalist Military Command** (CLMC), it declared a ceasefire to coincide with political talks and also joined in the CLMC ceasefire announced in October 1994. Despite this, in January 1998 the UFF was responsible for a number of sectarian murders before declaring that it had reinstated its ceasefire.

The UFF initially supported the **Good Friday Agreement** (GFA) but increasingly became convinced that the implementation of the GFA favored **republicans**. In July 2001 it announced that it was withdrawing its support for the GFA. It continued to be involved in attacks on Catholics and disputes with other **loyalist** groups, and in October 2001 Secretary of State **John Reid** declared their ceasefire, along with those of the UDA and LVF, to be invalid.

**ULSTER SPECIAL CONSTABULARY (USC).** The auxiliary police force formed in 1920 to defend Northern Ireland from attacks by the **Irish Republican Army** (IRA). The force consisted of full-time, part-time, and reserve sections, known respectively as A, B, and C sections. In 1925 the A and C sections were disbanded, leaving only B specials as a largely part-time reserve force to the **Royal Ulster Constabulary** (RUC). With an entirely Protestant membership, it was widely admired by **unionists** but equally distrusted by **nationalists**. In 1969 there were approximately 10,000 USC members, though only 5.0 percent of these were full time. In October 1969 the publication of the **Hunt Report**, which recommended the abolition of the USC, sparked rioting in the **loyalist** Shankill area of **Belfast**. It was during these riots that the first RUC man was killed in **the Troubles** by the **Ulster Volunteer Force** (UVF). The USC was disbanded on 30 April 1970.

**ULSTER UNIONIST PARTY (UUP).** The major **unionist** political party throughout the 20th century. The UUP was established in 1905 and, after the creation of Northern Ireland, was the party of government until **direct rule** was introduced in 1972. The party had come about as a coalition of bodies opposing home rule for Ireland, and these organizations, which included the **Orange Order**, were represented on the party's ruling body, the Ulster Unionist Council (UUC).

At times of crisis for the party, the representative nature of the UUC tended to highlight divisions within the party.

Under **Terence O'Neill** the **Northern Ireland government** undertook a modernizing and moderately reformist series of policies. However, this encouraged opposition from those within the party who believed this undermined Northern Ireland's position within the United Kingdom. At the same time, there was increasing pressure from outside the party by those demanding reforms, such as the **Northern Ireland Civil Rights Association** (NICRA) and later the British government, and opposition from individuals, such as Rev. **Ian Paisley**, and the **loyalist paramilitary** group the **Ulster Volunteer Force** (UVF).

Even after the abolition of the **Northern Ireland Parliament**, O'Neill's successors faced the same difficulty when approaching new political initiatives, that of introducing change without splitting the party. In March 1973 **William Craig** created the **Vanguard Unionist Progressive Party** (VUPP) when the UUC decided not to reject **power sharing** out of hand, but by the 1980s many VUPP supporters had rejoined the UUP. In January 1974 following the **Sunningdale** Conference, **Brian Faulkner** was defeated in the UUC on the issue of a Council of Ireland, essentially ending the Sunningdale package as an effective political initiative. The February 1974 **Westminster** general **election** was also significant in that it saw the end of the historic link between the UUP and the British **Conservative Party**. Under **Harry West** the party remained part of the **United Ulster Unionist Council** (UUUC) until the **United Unionist Action Council** (**UUAC**) **strike** of 1977. The fragmentation of the unionist parties at this time was such that the UUP was frequently referred to as the Official Unionist Party.

Although the UUP faced competition for the unionist vote from the **Democratic Unionist Party** (DUP), on only one occasion (outside the more personalized European Parliament elections) during the 20th century did the DUP outpoll the UUP, and this was in the 1981 **district council** elections held amid the heated atmosphere of the **hunger strike**.

Under the leadership of **James Molyneaux**, partly due to the influence of **Enoch Powell**, the party appeared less than committed to **devolution** and withdrew on several occasions from the 1982–86

**Northern Ireland Assembly**. The **Anglo–Irish Agreement** (AIA) helped reestablish a degree of unionist unity, although, as had been the case with the **Ulster Workers' Council (UWC) strike** in 1974, UUP supporters were concerned about the impact loyalist violence would have on their campaign against the AIA.

As the fears and expectations surrounding the AIA declined, the party participated in the **Brooke–Mayhew Talks** along with the DUP. The two parties split once again over the **Downing Street Declaration** in December 1993, with the UUP making a generally positive response to the declaration. As the **peace process** developed, the UUP participated in talks with local parties and with the British and Irish governments. The pro-**nationalist** tenor of the **Frameworks Documents** of February 1995 led the party to reject the proposals and arguably helped hurry the departure of Molyneaux as leader and the subsequent unexpected election of **David Trimble** as leader in September.

In July 1997, in a crucial moment for the peace process, the UUP chose not to withdraw from talks when **Sinn Fein** (SF) was admitted. In 1998 the party signed the **Good Friday Agreement** (GFA), although senior party member **Jeffrey Donaldson** withdrew from the negotiations late in the process. On 18 April 1998, the UUP endorsed the GFA, with 72.0 percent voting in favor. A worrying sign for the party came in the Northern Ireland Assembly election, when the UUP received fewer votes than the **Social Democratic and Labour Party** (SDLP), although vote transfers helped make it the largest party in the Assembly.

In September 1998 David Trimble met **Gerry Adams** in the first meeting between SF and UUP leaders in 75 years. Despite such symbolic gestures, lack of movement on paramilitary **decommissioning** and issues, such as police reform and the rerouting of Orange **parades**, began to undermine support for the UUP. In December 1999 the UUP entered government with SF in advance of **Irish Republican Army** (IRA) weapons being decommissioned, and the protracted process of decommissioning proved unpopular with unionist voters. Partly as a consequence of this, in September 2000, the party lost a by-election to the DUP in the previously safe UUP seat of South Antrim. In the Northern Ireland executive, the party held the first minister's post, as well as the three ministries of enterprise, trade, and investment; environment and culture; and arts and leisure.

The UUP regained the South Antrim seat in the 2001 Westminster general election but lost four seats overall, retaining only six. The unpopularity of the way in which the GFA had been implemented among unionist voters, along with continuing disputes within the UUP, was reflected in subsequent election results. In the 2003 Northern Ireland Assembly elections, the UUP received 22.7 percent of first-preference votes and won 27 seats. Their position was further weakened by the defection of Donaldson and two others to the DUP. March 2005 witnessed the ending of the formal link between the UUP and the Orange Order, when the Orange Order voted to break the connection. In the May 2005 district council elections, the UUP received 18.0 percent of votes and 115 counselors. In the Westminster general election, held on the same day, the party received 17.7 percent of the vote but was reduced to having only one Member of Parliament (MP), leading to the resignation of Trimble and the election of Sir **Reg Empey** as party leader.

In one of Empey's first significant moves as party leader, he attempted to form an alliance with **David Ervine** of the **Progressive Unionist Party** (PUP) in the Assembly; however, in September 2006 the speaker of the Northern Ireland Assembly ruled against this coalition. In October 2006 senior UUP member David Burnside suggested that the party should go into opposition if an executive was formed within the terms of the **St. Andrews Agreement**.

In the March 2007 Northern Ireland Assembly election, there was another significant decline in the UUP vote. The party received 14.9 percent of first-preference votes and won 18 seats. At the UUP annual conference in March 2007, the party voted to conduct a major reform of its structures. In April 2007 the party selected the two departments of health (Michael McGimpsey) and employment and learning (Sir Reg Empey) for their ministers in the Northern Ireland executive, which assumed power in May 2007.

**ULSTER VANGUARD.** With the prospect of **direct rule** becoming increasingly more likely, on 9 February 1972, **William Craig** announced the formation of Ulster Vanguard as an umbrella organization to coordinate opposition. Although Ulster Vanguard was led by **elected unionist** representatives, it received strong support from **loyalist paramilitary** groups and even had its own paramilitary group in the Vanguard Service Corps. It organized a number of rallies, including a show of strength at Parliament buildings at **Stormont** on 28 March 1972, when it protested the introduction of direct rule. Vanguard's advocacy of a policy of negotiated **independence** for Northern Ireland cost it the support of many traditional unionists, but it remained close to the **Ulster Defence Association** (UDA) and **Loyalist Association of Workers** (LAW). In 1973 it developed into the **Vanguard Unionist Progressive Party** (VUPP) but reemerged in February 1978 after the political party was wound up. After Craig lost his East **Belfast** seat at **Westminster** to **Peter Robinson** in 1979, however, Ulster Vanguard played no further significant role.

**ULSTER VOLUNTEER FORCE (UVF).** The **loyalist paramilitary** organization formed in 1966 in response to a perceived threat to the existence of Northern Ireland from Irish **nationalism**. The UVF adopted the name of the organization formed by **unionist** leader Sir Edward Carson to oppose home rule for Ireland in the early 20th century but, despite the claims of the modern organization, has no significant organic connection with the earlier organization.

In June 1966, 18-year-old Catholic barman Peter Ward was shot dead by the UVF in **Belfast** in what was probably the organization's third killing of the year. The UVF was subsequently declared an illegal organization, and UVF member **Gusty Spence** was later convicted of Ward's murder.

The UVF opposed the reformist policies of **Terence O'Neill** and, in March and April 1969, detonated bombs, which were initially attributed to the **Irish Republican Army** (IRA), at water and electricity facilities in an attempt to undermine O'Neill. After the outbreak of **the Troubles**, it expanded in numbers to approximately 1,500 in 1972. During the early and mid-1970s, it was involved in a number of high-profile attacks including the **McGurk's Bar bombing** in 1971, the **Dublin and Monaghan bombs** of May 1974 (though the latter attacks were not claimed at the time), and the activities of the **Shankill Butchers**. In 1975 the UVF also killed three members of the Miami Showband group.

Although during the course of the Troubles it was occasionally in conflict with its chief rival, the **Ulster Defence Association** (UDA), at times of perceived crisis for loyalists, it was also prepared to cooperate with the UDA, for example, during the course of the **Ulster Workers' Council (UWC) strike** in May 1974. In April 1974 the UVF was deproscribed in an attempt to draw the organization into politics, and the UVF formed the Volunteer Political Party. However, the continuing paramilitary activity of the UVF led to it being banned again in October 1975.

In the late 1970s and early 1980s, the organization was disrupted as a result of mass arrests and **Supergrass trials**. The UVF continued its campaign throughout the 1980s but in 1991, as part of the **Combined Loyalist Military Command** (CLMC), declared a temporary ceasefire to coincide with the **Brooke–Mayhew Talks**.

Despite the gathering pace of the **peace process**, it continued to attack **republicans** and Catholic civilians. This included an attack on a bar in Loughinisland, Co. Down, when UVF gunmen murdered six men and wounded five others who were watching a televised soccer match. In October 1994 the CLMC announcement of a loyalist paramilitary ceasefire was read by Spence. Tensions within the organization over the ceasefire were exacerbated in 1995 by the **Drumcree** crisis, leading to a split in the organization's ranks and the formation of the **Loyalist Volunteer Force** (LVF) under **Billy Wright**. The ongoing, intermittent feud between the UVF and LVF threatened to undermine the faith of unionists and others in the peace process in subsequent years.

The UVF's political wing, the **Progressive Unionist Party** (PUP), strongly supported the peace process and the **Good Friday Agreement** (GFA) and appeared close to a significant electoral breakthrough after the signing of the GFA and subsequent **Northern Ireland Assembly** elections, but a renewed feud with the UDA in 2000 centered around the Shankill area of **Belfast** damaged both the UVF's and PUP's credibility among the wider unionist community. Another feud with the LVF, in which four people were killed, ended in October 2005, with the LVF announcing that it was disbanding. In September 2005 rioting in loyalist areas of Belfast led the **Northern Ireland Office** (NIO) to declare that it no longer recognized the UVF ceasefire.

In August 2006 the UVF claimed that they had planted a bomb at **Sinn Fein**'s (SF) 1981 ard fheis at the Mansion House in Dublin but that the device had failed to explode. They suggested the bomb might still be in the building but a search revealed nothing. At the same time, the organization also rejected rumors that it was about to announce a military stand-down. Despite this, on 3 May 2007, the UVF announced that it assumed a "nonmilitary, civilianised role" from midnight. It also said that UVF weapons were now "beyond reach," however, this received some criticism as not meeting the full requirements for the **decommissioning** of weapons.

The UVF and the associated paramilitary group the Red Hand Commando were responsible for approximately 569 **deaths**, while 65 members of the organizations were killed during the Troubles.

**ULSTER WORKERS' COUNCIL (UWC) STRIKE.** The Ulster Workers' Council (UWC) was a group composed of **loyalist** trade unionists, formed around November 1973, which instigated the UWC strike of May 1974. As an organization the UWC had only a few hundred members, but it established links with power station workers, petroleum refinery workers, and workers in other Protestant-dominated areas of heavy industry in the wake of the **Sunningdale** Conference of December 1973. UWC chairman, shipyard trade unionist Harry Murray, and his colleagues believed that political developments, such as the Council of Ireland, would inevitably lead to a united Ireland, and they began organizing support for an all-out open ended "constitutional stoppage" in opposition.

The landslide victory of anti-Sunningdale **unionists** in the **Westminster** general **election** of February 1974 added a democratic veneer to the actions of the UWC and, on 14 May 1974, Murray announced an all out strike across Northern Ireland in favor of fresh elections to the **Northern Ireland Assembly**.

In the first days of the strike, its success hung in the balance. While most unionists were opposed to Sunningdale, there appeared to be little appetite for strike action as a form of protest. On 15 May 1974, the **Ulster Defence Association** (UDA) and other loyalist **paramilitary** groups announced their support for the strike, and they began a campaign of intimidation to ensure that the strike became more effective. In the ensuing days, unionist politicians also began to throw their weight behind the strike, with **William Craig** of the **Vanguard Unionist Progressive Party** (VUPP) being the most fervent supporter of the strike among the politicians.

The creation of a Strike Committee, headed by **Glen Barr**, and the use of power station workers sympathetic to their objectives saw the strike become more effective in stopping power supplies to industry and in organizing the distribution of some basic food supplies. By the end of the strike's first week, the UWC had the initiative and the Northern Ireland executive and **Northern Ireland Office** (NIO) appeared incapable of providing an effective plan to counter the impact of the strike. **British Army** engineers lacked the skills to run Northern Ireland's power stations without local support, while Secretary of State **Merlyn Rees** believed that a more confrontational approach toward the strikers would lead to bloodshed.

The final propaganda success for the strikers came on 25 May 1974, when Prime Minister **Harold Wilson** made a televised speech in which he appeared to accuse unionists of being "spongers" and succeeded in uniting almost the entire unionist community against him. On 28 May 1974, with Northern Ireland's electricity grid apparently on the brink of collapse, Chief Executive **Brian Faulkner** appealed to Rees to negotiate with the UWC strike committee. When Rees refused, Faulkner and the other unionist members of the Northern Ireland executive resigned, effectively ending the executive and Sunningdale package as a whole.

With the collapse of the executive, there were disputes within the strike committee as to whether the strike itself could be continued. Murray, Barr, and others realized that the unionist community at large believed that there was no reason to continue the strike and had already begun returning to work. The strike itself was called off on 29 May 1974 without having achieved its stated objective of fresh Assembly elections.

In the following months, control of the UWC became a source of competition between the rival unionist **political parties**, which led Murray and several others who had been prominent in the UWC's development to resign. Although the UWC was increasingly influenced by individuals sympathetic to the **Democratic Unionist Party** (DUP) and it played a nominal role in the loyalist strike of 1977, it had no significant impact after 1974.

**UNIONIST.** An individual or group that supports the maintenance of the union between Great Britain and Northern Ireland. In Northern

Ireland almost all unionists are members of the Protestant community, though not necessarily practicing members of the various Protestant churches. The term can also be used to refer to the mainstream group of those who support the union but who would not generally be prepared to use violence in support of their political objectives, as opposed to those referred to as **loyalists**. The name **unionist** is also often used to refer to the **Ulster Unionist Party** (UUP) and its supporters because it was the predominant unionist political party in the 20th century.

**UNIONIST PARTY OF NORTHERN IRELAND (UPNI).** A moderate **unionist** party launched by **Brian Faulkner** in September 1974. The UPNI reflected what had been the pro-**Sunningdale** wing of the **Ulster Unionist Party** (UUP). In the **election** to the Northern Ireland **Constitutional Convention**, the party continued to support **power sharing** but not the Council of Ireland. It received nearly 51,000 first-preference votes, 7.7 percent of the total, and won 5 seats. Although this was a respectable performance, it was clear that the party was competing with the **Alliance Party of Northern Ireland** (APNI) for a similar vote and was likely to remain a minor party.

In August 1976 UPNI suffered another blow when Faulkner, its leader and most prominent figure, announced his retirement from active politics. In September 1976 he was succeeded by Anne Dickson, the first woman to lead a political party in Ireland. In the May 1977 **district council** election, the party received only 2.4 percent of first-preference votes and won only 6 of the 526 council seats available.

In 1979 the UPNI ran three candidates in the **Westminster** general election, but they received just over 8,000 votes, 1.2 percent of the total. The party also polled poorly in the 1979 European Parliament election and again in the 1981 district council election, after which the organization disbanded.

**UNITED STATES OF AMERICA.** The United States was undoubtedly the most significant political actor in relation to **the Troubles** and **peace process** outside Europe. American interest in Northern Ireland was stimulated by the historic impact of Ulster–Scots and particularly Irish immigration to the U.S. in the 18th and 19th centuries as well as by the "special relationship" with Great Britain.

The relationship between the United States and Northern Ireland was asymmetrical in that the interest of a comparatively small group in the United States could have a great impact in Northern Ireland. In geographical terms, interest in Northern Ireland tended to be greatest in areas that retained a sense of a historical connection with Ireland, in particular the northeastern states. The overwhelming preponderance of those groups with an interest in Northern Ireland affairs took a viewpoint that was generally sympathetic to the **nationalist** or **republican** position.

Throughout the Troubles consecutive American administrations remained largely supportive of the British government's position on Northern Ireland. Under President Jimmy Carter, the United States increased its interest in Northern Ireland and took a slightly more critical view. It banned the sale of American weapons to the **Royal Ulster Constabulary** (RUC) but encouraged the **Atkins Talks**. The Reagan administration was less influenced by the Irish American lobby but largely maintained the Carter administration position. Criticism of Britain after the **hunger strike** of 1981 was limited by continuing Anglo–Irish dialogue and the fear of international terrorism, while Reagan also opposed greater U.S. involvement.

In the 1970s the Irish Northern Aid Committee (NORAID) was a significant source of support for the Provisional **Irish Republican Army** (PIRA); however, the PIRA's left-wing views were not usually well received in United States and were therefore downplayed for U.S. audiences.

In 1974 the emergence of the Irish National Caucus (INC), led by Fr. Sean McManus and others, took a pronationalist, pro–civil rights and antiviolence stance. The INC played an important role in the production of the unofficial MacBride Principles on **fair employment** in 1984. The principles were widely supported in the United States but not by constitutional nationalism, which believed the principles could lead to disinvestment and a loss of jobs. Despite this, the debate was influential in leading to the Fair Employment Act of 1989.

In 1981 Friends of Ireland, involving Irish American politicians and notably "The Four Horsemen"—Edward Kennedy, Tip O'Neill, Hugh Carey, and Patrick Moynihan—was established. It took a position that supported constitutional nationalism and especially **John Hume**. It was also later influential in helping to establish the **International Fund for Ireland** (IFI). By the 1980s Irish Americans were more middle class and less linked to the Democratic Party than had previously been the case, and this led to some "bidding" for votes from politicians on Irish issues. President **Bill Clinton** had maintained an interest in Irish affairs since the 1970s but also had a debt to the Irish American lobby, which had helped elect him in 1992. The end of the cold war also provided an opportunity for new U.S. foreign policy objectives. Under Clinton the U.S. administration played an increasing role in Northern Ireland affairs, using its influence to support the peace process and leading to a number of personal visits by the president.

Under George W. Bush, the U.S. administration has been involved less directly. This might be attributed to a change in American foreign policy priorities in the wake of the attacks on 11 September 2001 but also to a perception of the conflict in Northern Ireland as having been resolved by the signing and endorsement of the **Good Friday Agreement** (GFA). In April 2003 Bush and Prime Minister **Tony Blair** met in Hillsborough, Co. Down, in a so-called war and peace summit to discuss the situation in Iraq and in Northern Ireland.

**UNITED ULSTER UNIONIST COUNCIL (UUUC).** On 6 December 1973, the opening day of the **Sunningdale** Conference, 600 delegates from **Ulster Unionist Party** (UUP) constituency associations, the **Vanguard Unionist Progressive Party** (VUPP), the **Democratic Unionist Party** (DUP), and the **Orange Order**, held a rally in the Ulster Hall in **Belfast** and voted to form the UUUC (sometimes also referred to as the United Ulster Unionist Coalition) to oppose **power sharing**. This objection later expanded to include the entire remit of the Sunningdale Agreement.

In the February 1974 U.K. general **election**, the UUUC put forward a single candidate in each of the Northern Ireland constituencies, winning 11 of the 12 seats and subsequently producing a program calling for the end of power sharing and fresh elections to the **Northern Ireland Assembly**. Although initially hesitant the UUUC eventually gave its support to the **Ulster Workers' Council (UWC) strike** of May 1974, and this helped give the stoppage a more broadly based **unionist** mandate.

In the October 1974 general election, the UUUC lost a seat to a compromise **nationalist** candidate in Fermanagh-South Tyrone but retained significant political influence at **Westminster**, where the

**Labour** government had only a narrow majority and in 1976 became a minority government. In this political environment, the UUUC was able to exert its influence to win a review of Northern Ireland representation at Westminster. This eventually led to a decision to increase Northern Ireland representation in the House of Commons from 12 to between 16 and 18 seats.

The UUUC won an overall majority of seats in the Northern Ireland **Constitutional Convention** election of May 1975, but the traditionally unionist report of the Convention, opposing power sharing and an **Irish dimension**, was rejected by the government and by nationalists. With the apparent threat to Northern Ireland's constitutional position, receding divisions within the organization began to increase, with VUPP splitting over the issue of a voluntary coalition with the **Social Democratic and Labour Party** (SDLP). The final blow for the UUUC came in 1977 with the **United Unionist Action Council (UUAC) strike**, which was supported by the DUP and **loyalist paramilitary** groups but was opposed by the UUP. The UUAC strike was effectively the end of the UUUC.

**UNITED ULSTER UNIONIST PARTY (UUUP).** When the **Vanguard Unionist Progressive Party** (VUPP) split in the Northern Ireland **Constitutional Convention**, those who opposed **William Craig**'s proposal for a voluntary coalition government formed the United Ulster Unionist Movement (UUUM). The UUUM, led by Ernest Baird with **Reg Empey** as his deputy, subsequently became the UUUP.

In 1977 the UUUP contested the **district council elections**, receiving 3.2 percent of first-preference votes and winning 12 seats. In the 1979 **Westminster** general election, sitting Member of Parliament (MP) John Dunlop, who had been elected as a VUPP member, retained his seat in Mid-Ulster, but Ernest Baird failed to be elected in Fermanagh-South Tyrone. The UUUP again contested district council elections in 1981 and won five seats; however, it was increasingly competing against the **Democratic Unionist Party** (DUP) for a similar electoral constituency. In 1982 the UUUP put forward 12 candidates in the **Northern Ireland Assembly** election, and the party received 1.8 percent of first-preference votes, but none of its candidates were elected. The UUUP then effectively ceased to exist with many of its members either joining the **Ulster Unionist Party** (UUP) or withdrawing from active politics.

**UNITED UNIONIST ACTION COUNCIL (UUAC) STRIKE.** On 25 April 1977, a **unionist** and **loyalist** coalition, led by **Ian Paisley** of the **Democratic Unionist Party** (DUP) and Ernest Baird of the **United Ulster Unionist Party** (UUUP) and supported by the **Ulster Defence Association** (UDA), announced it would call a strike in May in protest of the government's security policy and in favor of a return to a majority-rule government in Northern Ireland. Under the name UUAC the group launched a strike on 3 May 1977, and despite road-blocks and threats of intimidation, the strike failed to gain momentum and was eventually called off on 13 May 1977.

Although the government's response to the UUAC strike was better coordinated than it had been during the **Ulster Workers' Council (UWC) strike** in 1974, the key difference between the two strikes was that the loyalist strike of 1974 took place against a background of great uncertainty of Northern Ireland's future, while by 1977 the political and security situation had stabilized somewhat. In 1977, therefore, the majority of unionists were not prepared to support the tenuous objectives outlined by the strike leaders. In the lead-up to the UUAC strike, Paisley threatened to retire from politics if the strike failed, and although most observers took the view that the strike had failed, this position was not supported by Paisley.

– V –

**VANGUARD UNIONIST PROGRESSIVE PARTY (VUPP).** On 27 March 1973, the **Ulster Unionist Party** (UUP) voted not to reject the government's *Northern Ireland Constitutional Proposals*, leading **William Craig** and his supporters to leave the party and form the VUPP. VUPP rejected the government proposals for a compulsory **power-sharing** administration and an **Irish dimension**, and Craig and some of his supporters instead toyed with the idea of pursuing **independence** for Northern Ireland in preference to the proposals outlined by the government. Like its predecessor, the **Ulster Vanguard** ginger group, it drew its support from the more radical wing of

**unionism** and from those disillusioned with the direction being followed by the UUP, the **Ulster Defence Association** (UDA) and the **Loyalist Association of Workers** (LAW).

In the 1973 **Northern Ireland Assembly election**, VUPP took 10.5 percent of first-preference votes and won seven seats. It was the party most associated with the **Ulster Workers' Council (UWC) strike** and capitalized on this, resulting in 12.7 percent of votes in the election to the Northern Ireland **Constitutional Convention** and 14 seats. In the convention Craig's support for the idea of a voluntary cross-community coalition led to a major split in the party, with Craig being supported by **David Trimble** and **Glen Barr** among others but being opposed by his deputy Ernest Baird and **Reg Empey**. Baird subsequently led the United Ulster Unionist Movement (UUUM). In February 1978 VUPP was finished as a political party and returned to being a pressure group. Many of the leading VUPP members, including Craig and Trimble, subsequently returned to the UUP.

**VICTIMS.** In October 1997 a Victims Commission was established under the chairmanship of Sir **Kenneth Bloomfield** with the task of reporting on how those killed and injured in **the Troubles** should be remembered. In April 1998 a report titled *We Will Remember Them* suggested that up to December 1997, 3,585 people had been killed as a result of the conflict; 91.0 percent of those killed were male; 37.0 percent of those killed were under 24, 53.0 percent under 29, and 74.0 percent under 39. Fifty-three percent of those who died were civilians with no connection to the security forces or **paramilitary** organizations, while another 28.8 percent were serving members of the security forces. Twelve and a half percent of those killed were **republican** paramilitaries, and just over 3.0 percent were **loyalist** paramilitaries. In proportion to the makeup of the population, more Catholics were killed than Protestants. Eighty-seven percent were killed by paramilitary groups (59.0 percent by republicans and 28.0 percent by loyalists) and approximately 11.0 percent by the security forces.

The report also emphasized the fact that many others suffered continuing physical or financial damage as a result of the Troubles. The report noted that each **death** also had an effect on those who survived. The report recommended greater resources be allocated to the need of victims and that an official ombudsman be appointed to deal with the demands of victims. In the 2002 report *Reshape, Rebuild, Achieve*, the office of the first minister and deputy first minister of the Northern Ireland executive government defined victims as the "surviving physically and psychologically injured of violent, conflict-related incidents and those close relatives or partners who care for them, along with those close relatives or partners who mourn their dead."

In March 2005 the government announced that a victims and survivors' commissioner was to be appointed and responsible for setting up a forum for victims of the Troubles. In 2005 Bertha Mc-Dougall, a former primary school teacher and widow of a **Royal Ulster Constabulary** (RUC) reservist killed by the **Irish National Liberation Army** (INLA), was appointed victims' commissioner. Her role included establishing the forum and assessing a service provision for victims' families and survivors. Some **nationalists** criticized her selection as being based on a nomination by the **Democratic Unionist Party** (DUP). In June 2006 her first report was critical of the degree of financial support provided for victims. In November 2006 the **Belfast** High Court permitted a judicial review of Mrs. McDougall's appointment by the **Northern Ireland Office** (NIO). There has continued to be a debate over who should be defined as a victim of the Troubles, particularly in relation to those who were combatants in the conflict.

– W –

**WARRENPOINT.** On 27 August 1979, 18 **British Army** soldiers were killed by an **Irish Republican Army** (IRA) bomb blast at Narrow Water near Warrenpoint in Co. Down. A 500-lb bomb planted in a lorry loaded with hay was detonated by the IRA as an army convoy drove past, killing six members of the parachute regiment. A second IRA explosion in the same area damaged a helicopter carrying members of a "quick reaction force" from the Queen's Own Highlanders, killing 12 soldiers, including the commanding officer. A subsequent gun battle between soldiers and IRA men firing across the border from the **Republic of Ireland** led to the shooting of a civilian on the Republic's side of the border.

The Warrenpoint attack was the largest number of British casualties in Northern Ireland on a single day. The attack came on the same day as the assassination of Earl Mountbatten, also by the IRA, in Co. Sligo in the Republic. The killings were followed by an upsurge in **loyalist paramilitary** attacks on Catholic civilians.

**WEST, HAROLD (HARRY) (1917–2004).** Ulster Unionist Party (UUP) leader, Harry West was born in Enniskillen, Co. Fermanagh, on 27 March 1917. He was educated at Portora Royal School, Enniskillen, before becoming a farmer. In 1954 he was **elected** to the **Northern Ireland Parliament** as a UUP Member of Parliament (MP) for the constituency of Enniskillen and held the seat until the abolition of the **Stormont** Parliament in 1972. During this period he served as minister of agriculture between 1960 and 1967 and again from 1971 to 1972. In 1967 he was fired by **Terence O'Neill** following allegations that there were conflicts of interest between his business interests and his ministerial responsibilities. Out of office he was a strong critic of O'Neill's policies and also of his successor, **James Chichester-Clark**, fearing that their reforms would split the **unionist** political bloc.

On the right wing of the UUP, West returned to government in 1971 under **Brian Faulkner**, as he believed Faulkner would pursue a strong security line against **republicans**. In June 1973 he was elected to the **Northern Ireland Assembly** in the constituency of Fermanagh-South Tyrone. However, he refused to support Faulkner's moves toward **power sharing** and in January 1974 succeeded Faulkner as UUP leader. In the February 1974 **Westminster** general election, a split in the **nationalist** vote helped him win the Fermanagh-South Tyrone seat, but he lost the seat in the November 1974 election when he faced a single nationalist candidate. He supported the **Ulster Workers' Council (UWC) strike** in May 1974, but there was mutual suspicion between West and **loyalist paramilitary** leaders as to what their objectives should be once the Northern Ireland executive had been brought down. In 1977 he refused to support the **United Unionist Action Council (UUAC) strike**, leading to a split with Rev. **Ian Paisley**.

In May 1975 he topped the poll in the Fermanagh-South Tyrone constituency in the election to the Northern Ireland **Constitutional**

**Convention.** Although he was on the **devolutionist** wing of the party, he again opposed any proposal for a power-sharing executive, which may have led to the return of a Northern Ireland–based administration. In June 1979 he stood as one of the two UUP candidates in the European Parliament election but was not elected and subsequently resigned as UUP leader. In April 1981 he stood against **hunger strike** leader **Bobby Sands** in the Fermanagh-South Tyrone by-election to **Westminster** but lost narrowly on a high turnout. West died on 5 February 2004.

**WESTMINSTER.** The London location of the Parliament of the United Kingdom of Great Britain and Northern Ireland. Parliament consists of the Upper House (the House of Lords) and the Lower House (the House of Commons). The House of Lords consists of lords spiritual (senior clergy of the Anglican Church in the United Kingdom) and lords temporal. The House of Lords has hereditary peers and appointed life peers, the latter often former members of the House of Commons. Members of the Commons (known as members of Parliament, MPs) are **elected** by popular vote from single-member constituencies throughout the United Kingdom.

During the period in which the **Northern Ireland Parliament** operated (1921–72), Northern Ireland was underrepresented at Westminster in relation to its population as a proportion of the United Kingdom as a whole. This was viewed as a tradeoff for the Northern Ireland Parliament having control of **devolved** matters. Even after the abolition of the Northern Ireland Parliament in 1972, Northern Ireland continued to return 12 MPs to Westminster, as the suspension of the Northern Ireland administration was initially viewed as a temporary measure.

By the late 1970s, it was clear that returning a devolved administration to Northern Ireland was likely to be a lengthy process. Partly because of this and partly as a matter of political expediency on the part of the **Labour** government to retain **Ulster Unionist Party** (UUP) support for their minority government, Prime Minister **James Callaghan** agreed to increase the number of Northern Ireland seats in April 1978. The revised constituency boundaries came into effect at the 1983 Westminster general election, when Northern Ireland returned 17 MPs. Further boundary changes led to one additional seat being added in time for the 1997 general election. An all-party Northern Ireland Affairs Committee made up of MPs and established in 1997 also has the power to examine issues relating to Northern Ireland and publishes reports based on their investigations. In December 2006 the U.K. Parliament's Northern Ireland Grand Committee, consisting of 38 MPs from Northern Ireland parties, the **Conservative Party**, Labour Party, and **Liberal Democrats** met in **Belfast**, the first time the Grand Committee had met in Northern Ireland.

**WESTON PARK TALKS.** In the wake of **David Trimble**'s resignation as first minister over the issue of the **decommissioning** of **Irish Republican Army** (IRA) weapons in July 2001, the governments of the United Kingdom and **Republic of Ireland** and Northern Ireland political representatives met at Weston Park, a secluded hotel in Shropshire, England, to agree on a package that would resolve the problem. On 14 July 2001, after six days of negotiations, the talks stalled, leading the British and Irish governments to release a "final package" of proposals for the parties to consider. The proposals included the normalization of security and inquiries into a number of murder cases (including Pat Finucane and **Billy Wright**) where there was alleged **collusion** of security forces. Although the parties did not accept the British–Irish package as a basis for resolving the weapons issue, many of its proposals were later implemented.

**WHITELAW, WILLIAM (1918–99). Conservative Party** politician and secretary of state for Northern Ireland, William Whitelaw was born in Edinburgh on 28 June 1918. He was born into a long-time Conservative Party family; both his great-grandfather and grandfather had been Conservative Members of Parliament (MP). His father had served in World War I but died of pneumonia before Whitelaw was one year old. He was educated at Winchester College and Trinity College, Cambridge, where he received a degree in history and law (although he was said to be more interested in golf than formal education). At the outbreak of World War II, he joined the Scots Guards. He won the Military Cross in France in July 1944 and served in Palestine after the war, where he was mentioned in dispatches.

After he resigned from the **British Army**, Whitelaw became increasingly involved in public life. On the paternalistic wing of the

Conservative Party, he was also a supportive of the consensus politics that dominated British politics in the postwar decades. In 1950 and 1951, he failed to win a seat in the strong **Labour** constituency of East Dunbartonshire but in 1955 was **elected** for the safe Conservative seat of Penrith and the Border in England, with a record majority.

In Parliament Whitelaw served in a number of junior positions but built a reputation as a likable and efficient party administrator, eventually becoming the party's chief whip (1964–70). Under Alec Douglas-Home and **Edward Heath**, he was seen as an approachable channel of communication to the party leader. He played a key role in the Conservatives' unexpected win in the 1970 general election and was subsequently appointed lord president of the council and leader of the House of Commons.

In March 1972, after the suspension of the **Stormont** Parliament, the **Northern Ireland Office** (NIO) was established, with Whitelaw becoming Northern Ireland's first secretary of state. Whitelaw arrived amid a heady atmosphere of Catholic grievance and Protestant resentment at the abolition of the **Northern Ireland government**. His sympathetic overtones to Catholics soon earned him the nickname "Willie Whitewash" from **unionists** but failed to win much support from **nationalists**. One of Whitelaw's major objectives was the restoration of a locally elected provincial administration in Northern Ireland. Difficult as Whitelaw knew the task would be, he still underestimated the problem. A number of his decisions were to have long-term repercussions. In July 1972 a secret meeting with Provisional **Irish Republican Army** (PIRA) leaders encouraged them in the belief that the continuation of violence would lead the British government to negotiate with them. He also conceded **special category status** to **paramilitary** prisoners, sowing the seeds of the **hunger strike** protests of the 1980s.

In the wake of **Bloody Friday** in July 1972, he ordered **Operation Motorman**, ending **no-go areas**. Whitelaw also oversaw the introduction of nonjury **Diplock Courts** in the face of the intimidation of juries by paramilitaries. In October 1973 he met **Ulster Unionist Party** (UUP), **Social Democratic and Labour Party** (SDLP), and **Alliance Party of Northern Ireland** (APNI) leaders for talks at Stormont Castle, which, it was hoped, would lead to the restoration of **devolution**. To the surprise of many observers, agreement was reached, although the details of relations between Northern Ireland and the **Republic of Ireland** had still to be decided.

Whitelaw left Northern Ireland in November 1973 to become secretary of state for employment with his reputation enhanced, but before the **Sunningdale** Conference, he undermined unionist support for the political deal. He argued against calling a general election in February 1974 over the coalminers' dispute in Britain, partly because of the negative impact it was likely to have on the Sunningdale Agreement in Northern Ireland. The outcome of the election led to the return of a Labour government in March.

In 1975 he challenged for the Conservative Party leadership but lost to **Margaret Thatcher**. Despite obvious differences of personality and political attitudes, he developed a close working relationship with Thatcher and served as home secretary (1979–83) and, after receiving a life peerage in 1983 (becoming Viscount Whitelaw of Penrith), leader of the House of Lords (1983–87). From 1979 until 1987, he was also deputy prime minister. He resigned from the government after suffering a mild stroke in December 1987, but his health slowly deteriorated thereafter. Whitelaw died on 1 July 1999.

**WILLIAMS, ELIZABETH (BETTY) (1943– ).** Peace campaigner, Betty Williams was born in **Belfast** on 22 May 1943 and educated at St. Dominic's Grammar School in the city. In 1961 she married Ralph Williams. In August 1976 she witnessed the **deaths** of the three Maguire children when they were struck by a gunman's getaway car. In the wake of the event, she approached neighbors in the staunchly **republican** Andersonstown area in an attempt to win support for a campaign to end violence. One of the first people to join Williams was the Maguire children's aunt, **Mairead Corrigan**. They were later joined by the third leading figure of the **Peace People**, Ciaran McKeown.

On 14 August 1976, 10,000 people from both Protestant and Catholic areas marched through Belfast as part of a campaign for peace. The spontaneous movement led to further, and larger, rallies in Belfast and across Northern Ireland. The peace movement received particular support in West Germany, Norway, and the **United States**. With Corrigan, Williams was subsequently awarded the Nobel Peace Prize for 1976. In 1978 she resigned from the executive committee o the Peace People, and in 1980 she ended her association with the Peace People following disagreements within the organization. In 1982 she married American businessman Jim Perkins and moved to the United States. She went on to work on children's rights issues within the United States.

**WILSON, GORDON (1927–95).** Peace campaigner, Gordon Wilson was born in Manorhamilton, Co. Leitrim, in the **Republic of Ireland** on 25 September 1927. The oldest of four children, he was educated at Wesley College in Dublin. In 1946 the family moved to Enniskillen, Co. Fermanagh, in Northern Ireland, where Wilson worked in his father's drapery business. On 8 November 1987, he and his younger daughter Marie, a trainee nurse, attended the Remembrance Sunday service in the center of **Enniskillen**. The **Irish Republican Army** (IRA) bomb that exploded shortly after injured Wilson and fatally wounded his daughter and 10 other people. The emotional, but forgiving, response of Wilson to the death of his daughter won him the respect of many people around the world. Almost by accident he acquired a reputation as a peace campaigner.

In February 1993 he was appointed to the Irish Senate as an independent member on the nomination of Taoiseach **Albert Reynolds**, and two months later he met IRA representatives in Northern Ireland to persuade the organization to end its armed campaign. However, he subsequently stated that his attitude had been somewhat naïve and that the meeting had not brought peace any closer. Despite this, he was part of a group that had talks with members of **loyalist paramilitary** organizations later in the same year. In February 1994 he attended **Sinn Fein**'s (SF) peace commission and asked **republicans** to end the use of violence. In late 1994 he suffered another personal tragedy when his son was killed in a car accident. Wilson died of a heart attack on 27 June 1995.

**WILSON, HAROLD (1916–95). Labour Party** politician and prime minister, Harold Wilson was born in Huddersfield, Yorkshire, on 11 March 1916. His father was a factory chemist and his mother a school teacher. Wilson was educated at Royds Hall School, Huddersfield, and Wirral Grammar School in Bebington, Cheshire. Later he won a scholarship at Jesus College, Oxford, where he graduated with a first-class honors degree in politics, philosophy, and economics and subsequently became a lecturer in economics at the college.

During World War II, he worked in the civil service. His bureaucratic endeavors during this period led to his being awarded an Order of the British Empire (OBE) in 1945. In 1940 he married Mary Baldwin, daughter of a congregational minister and a minor poet in her own right. In the 1945 general **election**, he was voted as a Labour Member of Parliament (MP) for Ormskirk in Lancashire but in 1950 won the new constituency of Huyton, which he retained until his retirement from the House of Commons in 1983. He became a junior minister in the newly elected Labour government at the age of 29, and his appointment to the cabinet in September 1947 as president of the board of trade made him the youngest cabinet member since Sir Robert Peel.

As a result of a dispute over government policy on the issues of rearmament and the cost of welfare services, Wilson resigned as president of the board of trade in 1951. Labour subsequently lost to the **Conservative Party** in the general election of the same year. During Labour's period in opposition, Wilson held a number of party positions. He challenged, and lost to, Hugh Gaitskell for the party leadership in 1960 before becoming party leader in 1963 in the wake of Gaitskell's premature death.

During his first term in office, Wilson had only a narrow overall majority in the Commons, but in the March 1966 general election, this increased to a 97 majority. By late 1967, however, Wilson's fortunes were already in decline in the wake of industrial disputes, public expenditure cuts, and the devaluation of sterling. The defeat of the government's proposals for the reform of industrial relations in the first half of 1969 caused further damage to Wilson and Labour's reputation.

Throughout this period Northern Ireland had remained a minor but growing issue. With the return to power of the Labour government in 1964, **nationalists** had sought to interest Labour MPs in complaints of **discrimination** by the **Stormont** regime. This process would eventually lead to the creation of the **Campaign for Democracy in Ulster** (CDU)—a group largely made up of Labour MPs with an interest in the situation in Northern Ireland. Although this group exerted pressure on Wilson to take a more active role in Northern Ire land's affairs, Wilson's approach was initially cautious, mainly aimed at encouraging **Terence O'Neill** to introduce a program of reforms within Northern Ireland.

By late 1968, however, Wilson and home secretary **James Callaghan** were facing a situation of growing civil unrest in Northern Ireland. In August 1969 the outbreak of severe rioting and the deployment of **British Army** troops on the streets of **Belfast** and **Derry** inevitably entailed a greater degree of time and effort from the British government on Northern Ireland affairs. The result of the June 1970 **Westminster** general election, with an unexpected win by the Conservative Party, sent Wilson into opposition for the next four years.

In November 1971 he outlined a 15-point plan for a solution to the Irish problem based on achieving **unionist** support for a united Ireland over the next 15 years; however, he failed to explain how this consent was to be achieved. He supported the decision to introduce **direct rule** and in July 1972 also met members of the Provisional **Irish Republican Army** (PIRA) for talks.

In February 1974 a minority Labour government was returned on the back of electoral disillusionment with industrial unrest and spiraling oil prices. In Northern Ireland the Labour government was faced with maintaining a policy based on the **Sunningdale** Agreement, which was strongly opposed by unionists. The situation came to a head in May 1974 when the **Ulster Workers' Council (UWC) strike** opposing Sunningdale brought much of Northern Ireland to a standstill. On 25 May 1974, Wilson, who had never been particularly sympathetic to unionist concerns, made a television address attacking the strikers and spoke of those who were "sponging on Westminster and British democracy." The speech served only to rally further unionist support to the side of the strikers, and the unionist members of the executive resigned three days later. In 1975 he traveled to Belfast to announce elections to the Northern Ireland **Constitutional Convention**; however, this failed to make significant progress and was dissolved by the time Wilson resigned as prime minister on 5 April 1976.

In the following four years, he wrote three books and recorded a television series on former British prime ministers. In 1980, however, his health began to decline, and he played little active part in the Commons thereafter. In 1983 he became a life peer, taking the title of Baron Wilson of Rievaulx. Wilson died on 23 May 1995.

**WOMEN, POLITICAL REPRESENTATION.** The number of women elected to representative bodies in Northern Ireland has traditionally been very low. The degree to which women did not feel comfortable running for office in an inherently conservative society or alternately were discouraged by a male-dominated party political ethos is a matter of debate. Of the women who might be considered to have played a major role in the course of **the Troubles**—**Bernadette Devlin, Mairead Corrigan** and **Betty Williams, Mary Robinson, Mary McAleese,** and most significantly **Margaret Thatcher**—none was the leader of a major political party within Northern Ireland. During the course of the Troubles, the energies of many women were channeled into the voluntary and community sector, and it was from this area that the **Northern Ireland Women's Coalition** (NIWC) emerged in the 1990s.

In the 1998 Northern Ireland Assembly **election**, 14 women were elected to the 108-member **Northern Ireland Assembly** (13.0 percent). Two female ministers were appointed in 1999, one each by the **Social Democratic and Labour Party** (SDLP) and **Sinn Fein** (SF), with the SDLP appointing another female minister in 2001. In 2003, 18 women were elected (16.7 percent), although the NIWC lost both its seats. Although **political parties** are legally permitted to have all-women shortlists for candidates, no party in Northern Ireland has used this option.

In the 2001 **district council** elections, 108 women were elected (19.0 percent), and in 2005, 125 (21.5 percent). In March 2007, 47 of the 248 candidates in the Northern Ireland Assembly election were women (19.0 percent). As in 2003, 18 women were again elected to the Northern Ireland Assembly in 2007.

In the 2005 general election, 3 of the 18 Northern Ireland Members of Parliament (MP) returned to **Westminster** were women. A minor point of interest in this campaign was that the two leading candidates in the Fermanagh and South Tyrone constituency, Michelle Gildernew of SF and Arlene Foster of the **Democratic Unionist Party** (DUP), were both women. This was arguably the first time that two women were the leading candidates in a major election since Bernadette Devlin won the Mid-Ulster by-election in April 1969.

In November 2006, in an effort to address the issue of female underrepresentation, Secretary of State **Peter Hain** announced a gende equality strategy that would include the objective of active and equal participation of men and women at all levels of public and political life.

**WORKERS' PARTY (WP).** The origins of the WP can be traced to the split in the **republican** movement that occurred in January 1970 when the more left-wing section became Official **Sinn Fein** (OSF) and the **Official Irish Republican Army** (OIRA). In 1977 OSF became SF: The Workers' Party and won representation in the **Dail** in 1981, increasing to seven Dail seats in 1989. In the 1989 European Parliament election, party president Proinsias DeRossa was elected in the Dublin constituency.

In Northern Ireland the party campaigned under the name Republican Clubs, becoming the Workers' Party: Republican Clubs in 1981 and the WP in 1982.

In 1992 the WP split over the issue of continuing OIRA activity, with six of the party's seven teachta dalas (TD) in the Republic forming a new party, Democratic Left. The remaining WP TD lost his seat in the following election. The WP participated in the coalition government of December 1994 to June 1997 with **Fine Gael** (FG) and the **Irish Labour Party** before merging with the Labour Party in January 1999.

In 1973 Republican Clubs won seven **district council** seats, but by 1992 the WP retained only four. When the party split, two councilors supported Democratic Left, one became an independent, and one remained with the WP. In the 1997 Northern Ireland district council, it won 0.4 percent of first-preference votes to the Democratic Left's 0.1 percent but lost its last council seat. In the 2001 district council elections, the WP received 0.2 percent of first-preference votes and won no seats. In 2005 it received 0.1 percent of first-preference votes and failed to win any seats.

In 2004 a British Broadcasting Corporation (BBC) documentary alleged that the party's president, Sean Garland, was involved in the distribution of counterfeit U.S. dollars. In 2005 Garland was arrested by the **Police Service of Northern Ireland** (PSNI) during the party's annual conference in **Belfast**. He subsequently skipped bail and returned to the **Republic of Ireland**.

In the March 2007 Northern Ireland Assembly election, the WP received 0.1 percent of first-preference votes and won no seats.

**WRIGHT, WILLIAM (BILLY) (1960–97).** Loyalist paramilitary leader, Billy Wright was born in Wolverhampton, England, on 7 July 1960 but raised in Co. Armagh. In 1976 he joined the **Ulster Volunteer Force** (UVF), in part as a response to the Kingsmill massacre. In 1977 he was sentenced to six years imprisonment for hijacking and firearms offenses. On his release he briefly moved to Scotland but soon returned to Portadown and resumed his connections with the UVF. During the 1980s he was repeatedly arrested in connection with terrorist offenses but not convicted. He was a particular target of **republican** paramilitaries and was nicknamed "King Rat" by the press.

As commander of a UVF brigade around Portadown, Wright is believed to have organized nearly 20 sectarian murders. In 1996 he broke away from the UVF when the organization failed to take action in support of Orange marchers at **Drumcree**. The murder of two Catholics in the area by Wright's unit without UVF approval led to his expulsion from the organization and death threats against him. In response Wright formed the **Loyalist Volunteer Force** (LVF), which drew support from former UVF members in the area and others opposed to the **peace process**.

Despite continuing LVF activity, Wright was not imprisoned until March 1997, when he was jailed for threatening to kill a woman. In April 1997 he was sent to Maghaberry prison, and LVF prisoners were kept in the same H block as **Irish National Liberation Army** (INLA) prisoners, though in separate wings. In December 1997 he was shot dead inside **Maze Prison** by three INLA prisoners.

In November 2004, in the wake of a report by Judge Peter Cory, Secretary of State **Paul Murphy** announced an inquiry into possible **collusion** in the events surrounding the killing of Wright. In November 2005 it was announced that the inquiry would be converted so that it would be held under the terms of the Inquiries Act of 2005. The inquiry began in **Belfast** in October 2006.

# Bibliography

## INTRODUCTION

Given the comparatively small scale of the Northern Ireland conflict and peace process, an enormous amount of material has been produced on the subject over a relatively short period of time. The Northern Ireland Political Collection of the Linen Hall Library (an essential point of research for any serious student of the Troubles) alone holds a collection that includes 15,000 books, pamphlets, and off-prints; 1,600 files containing newspaper cuttings; 6,000 videos; and 2,500 periodical titles relating to the Troubles and peace process. The following titles, therefore, represent only some of the most significant works on the various aspects of the conflict and are by no means exhaustive.

For those seeking a single in-depth reference work on the Troubles, a good recommendation would be Elliott and Flackes's *Northern Ireland: A Political Directory*. A more detailed chronology of the course of events can be found in *Northern Ireland: A Chronology of the Troubles* by Paul Bew and Gordon Gillespie. An extremely useful, though harrowing, source for deaths associated with the Troubles is *Lost Lives* by David McKittrick, Seamus Kelters, Brian Feeney, and Chris Thornton. Two essential works with a more theoretical approach to the conflict are John Whyte's *Interpreting Northern Ireland* and *The Politics of Antagonism: Understanding Northern Ireland* by Brendan O'Leary and John McGarry.

The Internet has become an increasingly important source for information. Relating the conflict in this regard, the CAIN Web service, the Northern Ireland Elections website, and the Northern Ireland Devolution Monitoring Reports (on events after 1998) are essential sources of reference.

## CONTENTS

## THE HISTORICAL BACKGROUND

Bardon, Jonathan. *A History of Ulster*. Belfast: Blackstaff Press, 1992.
Barton, Brian. *A Pocket History of Ulster*. Dublin: O'Brien Press, 1996.
Beckett, J. C. *The Making of Modern Ireland 1603–1923*. London: Faber and Faber, 1981.

Bew, Paul. *Ireland: The Politics of Enmity 1789–2006*. Oxford: Oxford University Press, 2007.

Boal, Frederick W., and Stephen A. Royle. *Enduring City: Belfast in the Twentieth Century*. Belfast: Blackstaff Press, 2006.

Buckland, Patrick. *A History of Northern Ireland*. Dublin: Gill and Macmillan, 1981.

Farrell, Michael. *Northern Ireland: The Orange State*. London: Pluto Press, 1980.

Fraser, T. G. *Ireland in Conflict 1922–1998*. London: Routledge, 2000.

Hennessey, Thomas. *A History of Northern Ireland 1920–1996*. Dublin: Gill and Macmillan, 1997.

Kee, Robert. *Ireland: A History*. London: Sphere Books, 1982.

Patterson, Henry. *Ireland since 1939: The Persistence of Conflict*. Dublin: Penguin Ireland, 2006.

Stewart, A. T. Q. *The Narrow Ground: The Roots of the Conflict in Ulster*. London: Faber, 1989.

———. *The Ulster Crisis*. London: Faber, 1967.

Wichert, Sabine. *Northern Ireland since 1945*. London: Longman, 1991.

Wilson, Thomas. *Ulster: Conflict and Consent*. Oxford: Basil Blackwell, 1989.

## GENERAL WORKS OF REFERENCE

Bew, Paul, and Gordon Gillespie. *Northern Ireland: A Chronology of the Troubles 1968–1999*. Dublin: Gill and Macmillan, 1999.

Deutsch, Richard, and Vivien Magowan. *Northern Ireland 1968–1973: A Chronology of Events: Vol. 1: 1968–1971*. Belfast: Blackstaff Press, 1973.

———. *Northern Ireland 1968–1973: A Chronology of Events: Vol. 2: 1972–1973*. Belfast: Blackstaff Press, 1974.

———. *Northern Ireland 1968–1974: A Chronology of Events: Vol. 3: 1974*. Belfast: Blackstaff Press, 1975.

Elliott, Sydney, and W. D. Flackes. *Northern Ireland: A Political Directory 1968–1999*. Belfast: Blackstaff Press, 1999.

Lalor, Brian, ed. *The Encyclopaedia of Ireland*. Dublin: Gill and Macmillan, 2003.

Law, Gary. *The Cultural Traditions Dictionary*. Belfast: Blackstaff Press, 1998.

McRedmond, Louis, ed. *Modern Irish Lives: Dictionary of 20th-Century Biography*. Dublin: Gill and Macmillan, 1998.

Ramsden, John, ed. *The Oxford Companion to Twentieth-Century British Politics*. Oxford: Oxford University Press, 2002.

## GENERAL HISTORIES OF THE TROUBLES

Bell, J. Bowyer. *The Irish Troubles: A Generation of Violence, 1967–1992.* Dublin: Gill and Macmillan, 1993.

Coogan, Tim Pat. *The Troubles: Ireland's Ordeal 1966–1996 and the Search for Peace.* London: Hutchinson, 1995.

Dixon, Paul. *Northern Ireland: The Politics of War and Peace.* Basingstoke: Palgrave, 2001.

Holland, Jack. *Hope against History: The Ulster Conflict.* London: Coronet Lir Books, 1999.

McKittrick, David. *Making Sense of the Troubles.* Belfast: Blackstaff Press, 2000.


## NORTHERN IRELAND POLITICS

Arthur, Paul. *Special Relationships: Britain, Ireland and the Northern Ireland Problem.* Belfast: Blackstaff, 2000.

Arthur, Paul, and Keith Jeffery. *Northern Ireland since 1968.* 2nd ed. Oxford: Basil Blackwell, 1996.

Aughey, Arthur, and Duncan Morrow, eds. *Northern Ireland Politics.* Harlow: Longman, 1996.

Bew, Paul, Peter Gibbon, and Henry Patterson. *Northern Ireland 1921–2001: Political Forces and Social Classes.* London: Serif, 2001.

Bew, Paul, and Henry Patterson. *The British State and the Ulster Crisis: From Wilson to Thatcher.* London: Verso, 1985.

Bew, Paul, Henry Patterson, and Paul Teague. *Between War and Peace: The Political Future of Northern Ireland.* London: Lawrence and Wishart, 1997.

Connolly, Michael. *Politics and Policy Making in Northern Ireland.* London: Philip Allan, 1990.

Cunningham, Michael J. *British Government Policy in Northern Ireland, 1969–2000.* Manchester: Manchester University Press, 2001.

Hadfield, Brigid. *Northern Ireland: Politics and the Constitution.* Buckingham: Open University Press, 1992.

Mitchell, Paul, and Rick Wilford, eds. *Politics in Northern Ireland.* Boulder CO: Westview Press, 1999.

Moxon-Browne, Edward. *Nation, Class and Creed in Northern Ireland.* Aldershot, UK: Gower, 1983.

O'Dowd, Liam, Bill Rolston, and Mike Tomlinson. *Northern Ireland: Between Civil Rights and Civil War.* London: CSE Books, 1980.

O'Leary, Brendan, Tom Lyne, Jim Marshall, and Bob Rowthorn. *Northern Ireland: Sharing Authority.* London: Institute for Public Policy Research, 1993.

O'Leary, Brendan, and John McGarry, eds. *The Future of Northern Ireland.* Oxford: Clarendon, 1990.

O'Leary, Cornelius Sydney Elliott, and R. A. Wilford. *The Northern Ireland Assembly 1982–1986: A Constitutional Experiment.* London: Hurst, 1988.

Rose, Richard. *Governing without Consensus: An Irish Perspective.* London: Faber and Faber, 1971.

Tonge, Jonathan. *Northern Ireland.* Cambridge: Polity Press, 2006.

———. *Northern Ireland: Conflict and Change.* 2nd ed. Harlow: Longman, 2002.

Wilford, Rick, Robin Wilson, and Kathleen Claussen. *Power to the People?: Assessing Democracy in Northern Ireland.* Dublin: Tasc, 2007.

Wilson, Robin, ed. *A Guide to the Northern Ireland Assembly: Agreeing to Disagree.* Norwich, UK: The Stationery Office, 2001.

## WORKS ON THE REPUBLIC OF IRELAND RELEVANT TO THE CONFLICT

Arnold, Bruce. *Haughey: His Life and Unlucky Deeds.* London: HarperCollins, 1994.

Collins, Stephen. *The Haughey File: The Unprecedented Career and Last Years of the Boss.* Dublin: O'Brien Press, 1992.

———. *The Power Game: Fianna Fail since Lemass.* Dublin: O'Brien, 2000.

Downey, James. *Lenihan: His Life and Loyalties.* Dublin: New Island Books, 1998.

Downing, John. *Most Skilful, Most Devious, Most Cunning: A Political Biography of Bertie Ahern.* Dublin: Blackwater Press, 2004.

Dwyer, T. Ryle. *Nice Fellow: A Biography of Jack Lynch.* Dublin: Mercier Press, 2001.

Fitzgerald, Garret. *All in a Life: An Autobiography.* Dublin: Gill and Macmillan, 1991.

Kearney, Richard. *Post-nationalist Ireland.* London: Routledge, 1997.

Maye, Brian. *Fine Gael 1923–1987: A General History with Biographical Sketches of Leading Members.* Dublin: Blackwater, 1993.

O'Brien, Justin. *The Arms Trial.* Dublin: Gill and Macmillan, 2000.

Rafter, Kevin. *Martin Mansergh: A Biography.* Dublin: New Island Books, 2002.

Ryan, Tim. *Albert Reynolds: The Longford Leader.* Dublin: Blackwater Press, 1994.

Whelan, Ken, and Eugene Masterson. *Bertie Ahern—Taoiseach and Peacemaker.* Dublin: Blackwater Press, 1998.

## BIOGRAPHIES AND MEMOIRS

Adams, Gerry. *Before the Dawn: An Autobiography*. London: Heinemann, 1996.
———. *Selected Writings*. Dingle: Brandon Books, 1994.
Bloomfield, Kenneth. *Stormont in Crisis: A Memoir*. Belfast: Blackstaff Press, 1994.
Callaghan, James. *A House Divided: The Dilemma of Northern Ireland*. London: Collins, 1973.
———. *Time and Chance*. London: Collins, 1987.
Campbell, John. *Edward Heath: A Biography*. London: Jonathan Cape, 1993.
Clarke, Liam, and Kathryn Johnston. *Martin McGuinness: From Guns to Government*. Edinburgh: Mainstream, 2003.
Currie, Austin. *All Hell Will Break Loose*. Dublin: O'Brien, 2004.
Devlin, Bernadette. *The Price of My Soul*. London: Pan Books, 1969.
Devlin, Paddy. *Straight Left: An Autobiography*. Belfast: Blackstaff, 1993.
Donoughue, Bernard. *Prime Minister: The Conduct of Policy under Harold Wilson and James Callaghan*. London: Cape, 1987.
Fitzgerald, Garrett. *All in a Life*. Dublin: Gill and Macmillan, 1991.
Heath, Edward. *The Course of My Life: The Autobiography of Edward Heath*. London: Coronet, 1998.
Hume, John. *Personal Views, Peace, Politics and Reconciliation in Ireland*. Dublin: Town House, 1996.
Langdon, Julia. *Mo Mowlam*. London: Little, Brown, 1999.
Major, John. *John Major: The Autobiography*. London: HarperCollins, 1999.
Mason, Roy. *Paying the Price*. London: John Hale, 1999.
McCann, Eamonn. *War and an Irish Town*. 3rd rev. ed. London: Pluto, 1993.
McCreary, Alf. *Nobody's Fool: The Life of Archbishop Robin Eames*. London: Hodder and Stoughton, 2004.
McDonald, Henry. *David Trimble*. London: Bloomsbury, 2000.
Mitchell, George. *Making Peace*. London: Heinemann, 1999.
Moloney, Ed, and Andy Pollak. *Paisley*. Dublin: Poolbeg, 1986.
Morgan, Kenneth. *Callaghan: A Life*. Oxford: Oxford University Press, 1997.
Mowlam, Mo. *Momentum: The Struggle for Peace, Politics, and the People*. London: Hodder and Stoughton, 2002.
Murphy, Michael A. *Gerry Fitt: A Political Chameleon*. Cork: Mercier Press 2007.
Needham, Richard. *Battling for Peace*. Belfast: Blackstaff Press, 1998.
O'Brien, Conor Cruise. *Memoir: My Life and Themes*. Dublin: Poolbeg, 1998.
Prior, James. *A Balance of Power*. London: Hamilton, 1986.
Purdy, Ann. *Molyneaux: The Long View*. Antrim, Northern Ireland: Greystone 1989.

Pym, Francis. *The Politics of Consent.* London: Hamish Hamilton, 1984.

Rentoul, John. *Tony Blair: Prime Minister.* London: Little, Brown, 2002.

Restorick, Rita. *Death of a Soldier: A Mother's Search for Peace.* Belfast: Blackstaff Press, 2000.

Routledge, Paul. *John Hume: A Biography.* London: HarperCollins, 1997.

Ryder, Chris. *Fighting Fitt: The Gerry Fitt Story.* Belfast: Brehon Press, 2006.

Sands, Bobby. *Bobby Sands: Writings from Prison.* Boulder, CO: Roberts Rinehart, 1997.

Scoular, Clive William. *James Chichester-Clark: Prime Minister of Northern Ireland.* Belfast: Clive Scoular, 2000.

Sharrock, David, and Mark Devenport. *Man of War, Man of Peace?: The Unauthorised Biography of Gerry Adams.* London: Macmillan, 1997.

Sopel, Jon. *Tony Blair: The Moderniser.* London: Bantam, 1995.

White, Barry. *John Hume: Statesman of the Troubles.* Belfast: Blackstaff Press, 1984.

White, Robert W. *Ruairi O Bradaigh: The Life and Politics of an Irish Revolutionary.* Bloomington: Indiana University Press, 2006.

Wilson, Gordon, and Alf McCreary. *Marie: A Story from Enniskillen.* London: Collins, 1990.

## NATIONALISM AND REPUBLICANISM

Boyce, D. G. *Nationalism in Ireland.* 2nd ed. London: Routledge, 1991.

English, Richard. *Irish Freedom: A History of Nationalism in Ireland.* London: Macmillan, 2006.

Feeney, Brian. *Sinn Fein: A Hundred Turbulent Years.* Dublin: O'Brien Press, 2002.

Fitzgerald, Garret. *Towards a New Ireland.* London: C. Knight, 1972.

Lynn, Brendan. *Holding the Ground: The Nationalist Party in Northern Ireland, 1945–1972.* Aldershot, UK: Ashgate, 1997.

Maillot, Agnes. *New Sinn Fein: Irish Republicanism in the Twenty-first Century.* Abingdon, UK: Routledge, 2005.

McAllister, Ian. *The Northern Ireland Social Democratic and Labour Party: Political Opposition in a Divided Society.* London: Macmillan, 1977.

Murray, Gerard. *John Hume and the SDLP: Impact and Survival in Northern Ireland.* Dublin: Irish Academic Press, 1998.

Murray, Gerard, and Jonathan Tonge. *Sinn Fein and the SDLP: From Alienation to Participation.* Dublin: O'Brien Press, 2005.

O'Brien, Conor Cruise. *Ancestral Voices: Religion and Nationalism in Ireland.* Dublin: Poolbeg Press, 1994.

————. *States of Ireland*. London: Hutchinson, 1972.

O'Connor, Fionnuala. *In Search of a State: Catholics in Northern Ireland.* Belfast: Blackstaff Press, 1993.

O'Doherty, Malachi. *The Trouble with Guns: Republican Strategy and the Provisional IRA.* Belfast: Blackstaff Press, 1998.

O'Halloran, Clare. *Partition and the Limits of Irish Nationalism: An Ideology under Stress.* Dublin: Gill and Macmillan, 1987.

Porter, Norman, ed. *The Republican Ideal: Current Perspectives.* Belfast: Blackstaff Press, 1998.

Rafter, Kevin. *Sinn Fein: A Centenary History.* Dublin: Gill and Macmillan, 2005.

## UNIONISM AND LOYALISM

Aughey, Arthur. *Under Siege: Ulster Unionism and the Anglo–Irish Agreement.* Belfast: Blackstaff Press, 1989.

Bruce, Steve. *The Edge of the Union: The Ulster Loyalist Political Vision.* Oxford: Oxford University Press, 1994.

————. *God Save Ulster: The Religion and Politics of Paisleyism.* Oxford: Clarendon, 1986.

————. *Paisley: Religion and Politics in Northern Ireland.* Oxford: Oxford University Press, 2007.

Cochrane, Feargal. *Unionist Politics and the Politics of Unionism since the Anglo–Irish Agreement.* Cork, Ireland: Cork University Press, 2001.

English, Richard, and Graham Walker, eds. *Unionism in Modern Ireland: New Perspectives on Politics and Culture.* Dublin: Gill and Macmillan, 1996.

Garland, Roy. *Gusty Spence.* Belfast: Blackstaff Press, 2001.

Godson, Dean. *Himself Alone: David Trimble and the Ordeal of Unionism.* London: HarperCollins, 2004.

Harbinson, John Fitzsimons. *The Ulster Unionist Party, 1882–1973: Its Development and Organisation.* Belfast: Blackstaff Press, 1973.

Hennessey, Thomas. *The Northern Ireland Peace Process: Ending the Troubles?* Dublin: Gill and Macmillan, 2000.

Houston, John, ed. *Brian Faulkner: Memoirs of a Statesman.* London: Weidenfield and Nicolson, 1978.

Miller, David W. *Queen's Rebels: Ulster Loyalism in Historical Perspective.* Dublin: Gill and Macmillan, 1978.

Mulholland, Marc. *Northern Ireland at the Crossroads: Ulster Unionism in the O'Neill Years 1960–69.* Basingstoke, UK: Macmillan, 2000.

Nelson, Sarah. *Ulster's Uncertain Defenders: Protestant Political, Paramilitary, and Community Groups and the Northern Ireland Conflict.* Belfast: Appletree Press, 1984.

Patterson, Henry, and Eric P. Kaufmann. *Unionism and Orangeism in Northern Ireland since 1945: the Decline of the Loyal Family.* Manchester: Manchester University Press, 2007.

Porter, Norman. *Rethinking Unionism: An Alternative Vision for Northern Ireland.* Belfast: Blackstaff Press, 1996.

Shirlow, Peter, and Mark McGovern. *Who Are "The People"? Unionism, Protestantism and Loyalism in Northern Ireland.* London: Pluto Press, 1997.

Sinnerton, Henry. *David Ervine.* Dublin: Brandon, 2002.

Walker, Graham. *A History of the Ulster Unionist Party: Protest, Pragmatism and Pessimism.* Manchester: Manchester University Press, 2004.

## PARAMILITARY ORGANIZATIONS

Anderson, Chris. *The Billy Boy: The Life and Death of LVF Leader Billy Wright.* Edinburgh: Mainstream, 2002.

Bell, J. Bowyer. *IRA: Tactics and Targets.* Dublin: Poolbeg, 1990.

———. *The IRA 1968–2000: Analysis of a Secret Army.* London: Frank Cass, 2000.

———. *The Secret Army: The IRA 1916–1979.* Dublin: Academy Press, 1979.

Bishop, Patrick, and Eamonn Mallie. *The Provisional IRA.* London: Heinemann, 1987.

Bolton, David. *The UVF 1966–73: An Anatomy of Loyalist Rebellion.* Dublin: Gill and Macmillan, 1973.

Bruce, Steve. *The Red Hand: Protestant Paramilitaries in Northern Ireland.* Oxford: Oxford University Press, 1992.

Collins, Eamonn. *Killing Rage.* London: Jonathan Cape, 1996.

Coogan, Tim Pat. *The IRA.* London: HarperCollins, 1987.

Cusack, Jim, and Henry McDonald. *The UVF.* Dublin: Poolbeg, 1997.

Dillon, Martin. *The Dirty War.* London: Arrow Books, 1991.

———. *God and the Gun: The Church and Irish Terrorism.* London: Orion, 1998.

———. *The Shankill Butchers: A Case Study for Mass Murder.* London: Hutchinson, 1989.

———. *Stone Cold.* London: Arrow, 1993.

———. *Twenty-Five Years of Terror: The IRA's War against the British.* London: Bantam, 1996.

English, Richard. *Armed Struggle: A History of the IRA*. London: Macmillan, 2003.

Harnden, Toby. *"Bandit Country": The IRA and South Armagh*. London: Hodder and Stoughton, 1999.

Holland, Jack, and Henry McDonald. *INLA: Deadly Divisions*. Dublin: Torc, 1994.

Lister, David, and Hugh Jordan. *Mad Dog: The Rise and Fall of Johnny Adair and "C Company."* Edinburgh: Mainstream, 2003.

McGladdery, Gary. *The Provisional IRA in England: The Bombing Campaign 1973–1997*. Dublin: Irish Academic Press, 2006.

Moloney, Ed. *A Secret History of the IRA*. London: Penguin Books, 2002.

O'Brien, Brendan. *The Long War: The IRA and Sinn Fein*. 2nd ed. Syracuse, NY: Syracuse University Press, 1999.

———. *Pocket History of the IRA: From 1916 Onwards*. Dublin: O'Brien, 2000.

O'Callaghan, Sean. *The Informer*. London: Corgi Books, 1999.

O'Day, Alan, ed. *Terrorism's Laboratory: The Case of Northern Ireland*. Aldershot, UK: Dartmouth, 1995.

Patterson, Henry. *The Politics of Illusion: A Political History of the IRA*. Rev. ed. London: Serif, 1997.

Smith. M. L. R. *Fighting for Ireland?: The Military Strategy of the Irish Republican Movement*. London: Routledge, 1995.

Taylor, Peter. *Loyalists*. London: Bloomsbury, 1999.

———. *Provos: The IRA and Sinn Fein*. London: Bloomsbury, 1997.

Toolis, Kevin. *Rebel Hearts: Journeys within the IRA's Soul*. London: Picador, 1995.

Wood, Ian S. *Crimes of Loyalty: A History of the UDA*. Edinburgh: Edinburgh University Press, 2006.

## SECURITY FORCES

Cargo, David. *Battles beyond the Boyne: Orangemen in the Ranks 1798–2000*. Belfast: Grand Orange Lodge of Ireland, 2005.

Dewar, Michael. *The British Army in Northern Ireland*. London: Arms and Armour, 1997.

Doherty, Richard. *The Thin Green Line: A History of the Royal Ulster Constabulary GC*. Barnsley: Pen and Sword Military, 2004.

Foot, Paul. *Who Framed Colin Wallace?* London: Macmillan, 1989.

Hamill, Desmond. *Pig in the Middle: The Army in Northern Ireland 1969–1985*. London: Methuen, 1985.

Hermon, John. *Holding the Line: An Autobiography.* Dublin: Gill and Macmillan, 1997.

Holland, Jack. *Phoenix: Policing the Shadows, The Secret War against Terrorism in Northern Ireland.* London: Hodder and Stoughton, 1997.

Murray, Raymond. *The SAS in Ireland 1969–1989.* Cork, Ireland: Mercier Press, 1990.

——. *State Violence: Northern Ireland 1969–1997.* Dublin: Mercier Press, 1998.

Ní Aoláin, Fionnuala. *The Politics of Force: Conflict Management and State Violence in Northern Ireland.* Belfast: Blackstaff Press, 2000.

Rolston, Bill. *Unfinished Business: State Killings and the Quest for Truth.* Belfast: Beyond the Pale, 2000.

Ryder, Chris. *Inside the Maze: The Untold Story of the Northern Ireland Prison Service.* London: Methuen, 2001.

——. *The RUC 1922–2000: A Force under Fire.* London: Arrow, 2000.

——. *The Ulster Defence Regiment: An Instrument of Peace?* London: Methuen, 2001.

Stalker, John. *Stalker.* London: Harrap, 1988.

Taylor, Peter. *Brits: The War against the IRA.* London: Bloomsbury, 2001.

Urban, Mark. *Big Boys' Rules: The Secret Struggle against the IRA.* London: Faber and Faber, 1992.

## EVENTS

Anderson, Don. *14 May Days: The Inside Story of the Loyalist Strike of 1974.* Dublin: Gill and Macmillan, 1994.

Arthur, Paul. *The People's Democracy 1968–1973.* Belfast: Blackstaff Press, 1974.

Bell, J. Bowyer. *In Dubious Battle: The Dublin and Monaghan Bombings 1972–1974.* Dublin: Poolbeg Press, 1996.

Beresford, David. *Ten Men Dead: The Story of the 1981 Irish Hunger Strike.* London: Grafton, 1987.

Bloomfield, David. *Political Dialogue in Northern Ireland: The Brooke Initiative 1989–92.* London: Macmillan Press, 1998.

Boyd, Andrew. *Holy War in Belfast.* Dublin: Anvil Books, 1969.

Campbell, Brian, Laurence McKeown, and Felim O'Hagan, eds. *Nor Meekly Serve My Time: The H-Block Struggle of 1976–1981.* Belfast: Beyond the Pale, 1994.

Fisk, Robert. *The Point of No Return: The Strike Which Broke the British in Ulster.* London: Times Books/Deutsch, 1975.

Hayes, Patrick, and Jim Campbell. *Bloody Sunday: Trauma, Pain and Politics.* London: Pluto Press, 2005.

Hennessey, Thomas. *Northern Ireland: The Origins of the Troubles.* Dublin: Gill and Macmillan, 2005.

Kelly, James. *The Thimble Riggers: The Dublin Arms Trials of 1970.* Dublin: Author, 1999.

McCann, Eamonn, and Maureen Shiels, eds. *Bloody Sunday in Derry: What Really Happened.* Dingle, Ireland: Brandon Books, 1992.

McDaniel, Denzil. *Enniskillen: The Remembrance Day Bombing.* Dublin: Wolfhound, 1997.

Mullan, Don. *Eyewitness Bloody Sunday: The Truth.* Dublin: Wolfhound, 1997.

Mullin, Chris. *Error of Judgement: The Truth about the Birmingham Pub Bombings.* Dublin: Poolbeg Press, 1980.

O Dochartaigh, Naill. *From Civil Rights to Armalites: Derry and the Birth of the Irish Troubles.* 2nd ed. Basingstoke, UK: Palgrave Macmillan, 2004.

O'Doherty, Malachi. *The Telling Year: Belfast 1972.* Dublin: Gill and Macmillan, 2007.

Pringle, Peter, and Philip Jacobson. *Those Are Real Bullets, Aren't They? Bloody Sunday, Derry, 30 January 1972.* London: Fourth Estate, 2000.

Purdie, Bob. *Politics in the Streets: The Origins of the Civil Rights Movement in Northern Ireland.* Belfast: Blackstaff Press, 1990.

Spencer, Graham. *Omagh: Voices of Loss.* Belfast: Appletree Press, 2005.

## ISSUES

Bryan, Dominic. *Orange Parades: The Politics of Ritual, Tradition and Control.* London: Pluto Press, 2000.

Cairns, Ed. *Caught in the Crossfire: Children and the Northern Ireland Conflict.* Belfast: Appletree Press, 1987.

Conway, Mary, and Johnny Byrne. *Interface Issues: An Annotated Bibliography.* Belfast: Institute for Conflict Research, 2005.

Dickson, Brice, and Martin O'Brien, eds. *Civil Liberties in Northern Ireland: CAJ Handbook.* 4th ed. Belfast: Committee on the Administration of Justice, 2003

Ellison, Graham, and Jim Smyth. *The Crowned Harp: Policing Northern Ireland.* London: Pluto Press, 2000.

Greer, Steven. *Supergrasses: A Study in Anti-terrorist Law Enforcement in Northern Ireland.* Oxford: Clarendon Press, 1995.

Hamber, Brandon, ed. *Past Imperfect: Dealing with the Past in Northern Ireland and Societies in Transition.* Derry, Northern Ireland: INCORE University of Ulster, 1998.

Jarman, Neil, and Dominic Bryan. *From Riots to Rights: Nationalist Parades in the North of Ireland*. Coleraine, Northern Ireland: Centre for the Study of Conflict, University of Ulster, 1998.

———. *Parade and Protest: A Discussion of Parading, Disputes in Northern Ireland*. Coleraine, Northern Ireland: Centre for the Study of Conflict, University of Ulster, 1996.

McGarry, John, and Brendan O'Leary. *Policing Northern Ireland: Proposals for a New Start*. Belfast: Blackstaff, 1999.

McKeown, Ciaran. *The Passion of Peace*. Belfast: Blackstaff Press, 1984.

Miller, David. *Don't Mention the War: Northern Ireland, Propaganda and the Media*. London: Pluto Press, 1994.

O'Malley, Padraig. *Biting at the Grave: the Irish Hunger Strikes and the Politics of Despair*. Belfast: Blackstaff, 1990.

Osborne, Bob, and Ian Shuttleworth. *Fair Employment in Northern Ireland a Generation On*. Belfast: Blackstaff, 2004.

Rolston, Bill, and David Miller. *War and Words: The Northern Ireland Media Reader*. Belfast: Beyond the Pale, 1996.

Rowthorn, Bob, and Naomi Wayne. *Northern Ireland: The Political Economy of Conflict*. Cambridge: Polity Press 1988.

Wilson, Desmond. *Democracy Denied*. Cork, Ireland: Mercier Press, 1997.

## THE PEACE PROCESS

Adams, Gerry. *Free Ireland: Towards a Lasting Peace*. Dingle, Ireland: Brandon Books, 1995. (Previous edition published as *Politics of Irish Freedom*.)

Bew, Paul, and Gordon Gillespie. *The Northern Ireland Peace Process 1993–1996: A Chronology*. London: Serif, 1996.

Bloomfield, David. *Peacemaking Strategies in Northern Ireland: Building Complementarity in Conflict Management Theory*. Basingstoke, UK: Macmillan, 1997.

Cox, Michael, Adrian Guelke, and Fiona Stephen, eds. *A Farewell to Arms?: From "Long War" to Long Peace in Northern Ireland*. 2nd ed. Manchester: Manchester University Press, 2005.

Darby, John, and Roger MacGinty, eds. *The Management of Peace Processes*. London: Macmillan Press, 2000.

Elliott, Marianne, ed. *The Long Road to Peace in Northern Ireland: Lectures from the Institute of Irish Studies at Liverpool University*. Liverpool, UK: Liverpool University Press, 2001.

Mallie, Eamonn, and David McKittrick. *The Fight for Peace: The Secret Story behind the Irish Peace Process*. London: Heinemann, 1996.

McKittrick, David. *Endgame—The Search for Peace in Northern Ireland.* Belfast: Blackstaff Press, 1994

Mitchell, George. *Making Peace.* London: William Heinemann, 1999.

Rowan, Brian. *Behind the Lines: The Story of the IRA and Loyalist Ceasefires.* Belfast: Blackstaff Press, 1995.

Todd, Jennifer, and Joseph Ruane. *After the Good Friday Agreement: Analysing Political Change in Northern Ireland.* Dublin: UCD Press, 1999.

Tonge, Jonathan. *The New Northern Irish Politics?* Basingstoke, UK: Palgrave Macmillan, 2005.

Wilford, Rick, ed. *Aspects of the Belfast Agreement.* Oxford: Oxford University Press, 2001.

## UNDERSTANDING THE CONFLICT

Barritt, Denis. *Northern Ireland: A Problem to Every Solution.* London: Quaker Peace and Service, 1982.

Barritt, Denis, and Charles Carter. *The Northern Ireland Problem.* Oxford: Oxford University Press, 1962.

Barton, Brian, and Patrick Roche, eds. *The Northern Ireland Question: Perspectives and Policies.* Aldershot, UK: Avebury, 1994.

Boyce, D. G., and Alan O'Day, eds. *The Making of Modern Irish History: Revisionism and the Revisionist Controversy.* London: Routledge, 1996.

Boyle, Kevin, and Tom Hadden. *Ireland: A Positive Proposal.* Harmondsworth, UK: Penguin, 1985.

———. *Northern Ireland: The Choice.* London: Penguin Books, 1994.

Brady, Ciaran, ed. *Interpreting Irish History: The Debate on Historical Revisionism.* Dublin: Irish Academic Press, 1994.

Darby, John. *Conflict in Northern Ireland: The Development of a Polarised Community.* Dublin: Gill and Macmillan, 1976.

———. *Intimidation and the Control of Conflict in Northern Ireland.* Dublin: Gill and Macmillan, 1986.

———. *Scorpions in a Bottle: Conflicting Cultures in Northern Ireland.* London: Minority Rights, 1997.

Dunn, Seamus, ed. *Facets of the Conflict in Northern Ireland.* London: Macmillan Press, 1995.

Farrell, Michael. *Northern Ireland: The Orange State.* 2nd ed. London: Pluto, 1980.

Heslinga, M. W. *The Irish Border as a Cultural Divide: A Contribution to the Study of Regionalism in the British Isles.* Assen, Netherlands: Van Gorcum, 1979.

Hutton, Sean, and Paul Stewart, eds. *Ireland's Histories: An Aspect of State, Society and Ideology.* London: Routledge, 1991.